ALSO BY GIL MARKS

*The World
of Jewish Cooking*

*The World
of Jewish Entertaining*

More than
400 Delectable Recipes
from Jewish Communities
from Alsace to India

SIMON & SCHUSTER
New York   London   Toronto   Sydney   Singapore

The World of Jewish Desserts

GIL MARKS

SIMON & SCHUSTER
ROCKEFELLER CENTER
1230 AVENUE OF THE AMERICAS
NEW YORK, NY 10020

BOOK DESIGN BY DEBORAH KERNER

ILLUSTRATIONS BY RICHARD WAXBERG

Manufactured in the United States of America
10 9 8 7 6 5 4 3 2 1

Library of Congress Cataloging-in-Publication Data

Marks, Gil.
The world of Jewish desserts: more than 400 delectable recipes
from Jewish communities from Alsace to India / Gil Marks.
        p. cm.
Includes index.
1. Cookery, Jewish.   2. Desserts.   I. Title.
TX724.M31952 2000
641.8'6—dc21   00-041270

ISBN 0-684-87003-7

To my sisters

and brothers

and their spouses—

Rabbi William and Sharon Altshul,

Rabbi Jeffrey and Shari Marks,

Rabbi Arthur and Aviva Marks,

and Rabbi Labby and Carol Vegh

Acknowledgments

This book owes an enormous debt to many people, both in America and abroad. Among those who shared their recipes, ideas, and time with me are Adam and Annie Anik, Dalia Carmel and Herbert Goldstein, Michelle Comet, Lillian Cooper, Rae Dayan, Poopa Dweck, Allen and Ellen Federman, Diane Feldman, Liselotte Gorlin, Levana Levy Kirschenbaum, Phyllis Koegel, Emile de Vidas Levy, Adina Mishkoff, Faye Reichwald, Jackie Rivkin Rubin, Stanley Allan Sherman, Nach Waxman, Eva Weiss, and various relatives and friends.

I want to express my gratitude to all the people involved in the production of this book. Most especially I want to thank my editor, Sydny Miner, for her encouragement and advice, and editorial assistant Andrea Mullins.

Very special thanks go to my parents—Beverly and Harold Marks—and my nieces and nephews—Efrat Zipporah and Elli Schorr, Asher Yaakov Altshul, Ora Rivka and Naftali Derovan, Esther Chana Altshul, Aryeh Dov Altshul, Eliana Bracha Altshul, Shlomo Yosef Marks, Miriam Malka Marks, Efrayim Marks, Tehila Marks, Ashira Marks, Rivka Marks, Moshe Marks, Leah Marks, Shmuel Marks, Ahron Marks, Yeshai Marks, Yakov Marks, Daniel Marks, Devora Marks, Chana Tzipora Vegh, Shifra Miriam Vegh, Avrohom Boruch Vegh, Elisheva Vegh, Yisroel Vegh, Adina Rivka Vegh, Moshe Yakov Vegh, Moshe Raphael Schorr, and Adira Tova Schorr—who bore the brunt of my culinary development and experimentation.

Contents

The World of
Jewish Desserts

Introduction

Honey and sweet foods enlighten the eyes of man.
—TALMUD YOMA 83B

The word *dessert* derives from the French, "to clear the table," reflecting something served following the meal. Yet for most of us dessert is more than simply an afterthought; it is not only the finale to a repast but often also the highlight of the entire day. A slice of cake or a luscious confection transforms even normally staid adults into little children. Just look at the faces of diners as a dessert cart rolls by, or watch pedestrians passing a bakery window. Sweets can conjure memories of childhood as well as set the tone for a sophisticated gathering. Some of my most treasured recollections involve sugar-laden treats: the finales to various holiday feasts and life-cycle celebrations, homemade birthday cakes, my grandmother's cookie jar, seasonal pies (rhubarb in the spring, berry in the summer, pumpkin and sweet potato in the fall), and the trio of cookies my mother serves on all special occasions—*rugelach*, *kupferlin* (nut crescents), and florentines.

Dessert—whether plain or fancy, old-fashioned or cutting edge—should be a matter of pleasure. (It should be noted that the word *sweet* derives from the Latin *suavis*, "to make pleasing.") When I am asked, "What's a good low-fat dessert?" my reply is "Fresh fruit." Why waste time and, for that matter, calories on some dry and taste-challenged concoction simply to save a few grams of fat? It is a shame that so many people miss out on what can only be described as some of life's genuine pleasures: biting into a satisfying hunk of a freshly baked sweet bread, savoring a melt-in-your-mouth flaky pie crust, or enjoying an incredibly tender cake that does not need to be hidden under layers of frosting to exhibit some character. Better to splurge on a smaller piece of a delicious nosh (and maybe run or walk a few extra miles the next day) or stay with something naturally good. After all, according to the Talmud, one of the questions that the heavenly court asks each person is "Did you enjoy My world?" And if we are honest, few, if any, low-cal items can be labeled enjoyable.

Unfortunately, commercially produced items, no matter how well intentioned or ornate (and many are neither), simply cannot compare to homemade baked goods. I am not merely referring to freshness or quality and flavor, which, of course, vary according to the skills of the baker. Desserts do not even have to be fancy to be special; comfort foods that evoke our early years can supply a greater degree of gratification than more refined or trendy treats. Beyond any sensory pleasures, there exist metaphysical benefits in transforming and enhancing an occasion through dishes that we prepare. When you serve a cake made by your own hands, even if it turns out less than perfect, it is more gratifying than a store-bought item.

The acts of serving and consuming food can be an expression of who we are, as well as a genuine spiritual experience. And few foods have the power to please and uplift us as desserts do. Each Passover I prepare all sorts of fancy desserts for my family and friends, often experimenting with adaptations of sophisticated modern fare. Yet every year I repeat one particular dish, *chremslach* (bite-size matza meal pancakes in honey). The recipe I use is scribbled in my grandmother's handwriting on a yellowed, wine-splattered index card. I scrupulously follow the directions, making certain that the pancakes are the size of a quarter and not too brown. Inevitably my father sneaks a sample of the nearly finished product with the excuse of "quality control," remarking on how they take him back to his childhood

and the ones his mother used to make. The sampling of a piece of pancake transcends time, linking generations.

A sweet tooth is endemic to the human condition; after all, it was a fruit (albeit a forbidden one) that tempted Eve. Evidence of man's love of sweets is found throughout the ancient world. Cave paintings in Valencia, Spain, dating to around 8000 BCE depict human raids on beehives. Some six thousand years later the domesticated beehive was simultaneously developed in both India and Egypt, providing a more constant supply of this first sweetener. The Egyptians devised a multitude of sweets and baked goods, leaving rather explicit directions for making confections in some of their pyramids. A cuneiform tablet dating to the thirty-fifth year of the Babylonian king Hammurabi (c. 1757 BCE) describes a sort of sweet roll made from flour, dates, apples, figs, cheese, butter, and wine. The patriarch Abraham, born into a noble Sumerian family around this time, probably grew up enjoying similar treats.

An early Jewish affinity for sweets can be seen by the description of the Manna as tasting like honey, as well as numerous other biblical and Talmudic references to fruits and sweet foods. The wealthy in monarchical Israel ate well: "Solomon's provisions for one day was thirty measures of fine flour and sixty measures of meal; ten fat oxen, and twenty oxen from pasture, and a hundred sheep, beside harts, gazelles, roebucks, and fatted fowl" (I Kings 5:2-3). The masses, on the other hand, subsisted on grains, legumes, a sparse number of vegetables, and a few fruits (apples, dates, figs, grapes, olives, pomegranates, and watermelons). Savory dishes were enlivened with indigenous herbs and spices. Honey, primarily in the form of fruit syrups made from dates and grapes, served as the principal sweetener.

Over the centuries, traders and invaders introduced new ingredients to the Holy Land. From the Far East came rice, citrus fruit, cinnamon, cloves, ginger, nutmeg, and pepper. The Persians added apricots, cherries, mulberries, plums, quinces, and roses. Europeans brought basil, oregano, and rosemary. Each of these foreign influences also shared its culinary specialties, enriching the Jewish table. The most considerable changes, however, occurred when the Jews found themselves in the Diaspora.

As Jews scattered to various parts of the globe, they adopted and adapted local fare, further expanding the Jewish culinary repertoire. The two largest Jewish cultural communities developed, then spread out from the Rhine River valley (the Ashkenazim) and from the Iberian Peninsula (the Sephardim). To further complicate matters, Ashkenazic and

Sephardic food developed differently in the new homelands of the refugees from Franco-Germany (including Alsace, Austria, Bohemia, Germany, Hungary, Romania, Slovakia, Ukraine, Poland, and the Baltic states) and Iberia (including Turkey, the Maghreb, the Levant, Egypt, Greece, Iraq, Syria, and western Europe). In addition, a mosaic of Jewish cultural communities of varying sizes and antiquity grew up across the globe—including in Armenia, Azerbaijan, Ethiopia, Georgia, Kurdistan, India (Bombay, Cochin, and Calcutta), Iran (Persia), Italy, Kazakhstan, Uzbekistan, and Yemen—each possessing its own unique history, customs, and cuisine. Nonetheless, since occasional interaction between various Jewish communities led to a sharing of dishes, the food was sometimes similar.

After 2,000 years of Jews living in the Diaspora, the scope of Jewish desserts literally encompasses anything from the *petites madeleines* so cherished by Marcel Proust (his mother was a member of a prominent Alsatian Jewish family) to the beloved *wyskrobek* (jam turnovers made from scraps of challah dough) of Isaac Bashevis Singer's Polish childhood. They include Teutonic butter cakes as well as Middle Eastern syrup-soaked semolina bars; *kheer* (a creamy coconut-accented rice pudding of India) and eastern European cheese blintzes.

So what is a Jewish dessert? To quote from my first book, *The World of Jewish Cooking*, "It is food that evokes the spirit of a Jewish community as it celebrates its festivals and life-cycle events. It is a dish that conjures up the joy of millions of Sabbath dinners or resounds with the memory of the *mellahs* (Jewish quarters in Moslem countries), ghettos, and *shtetlach*, in which for millennia Jews struggled to eke out a living. It is tradition."

The World of Jewish Desserts explores the products of kitchens from the various Jewish communities across the globe. Cakes and pastries include the Teutonic *kuchen*, Austrian *rugelach*, Hungarian *kakosh* (chocolate roll), Alsatian charlotte, Polish babka, Italian tortes, and Middle Eastern *tishpishti* (nut cake in sugar syrup). Relevant historical, religious, and sociological information, as well as anecdotes and helpful cooking tips, complement the recipes, so that this book offers not only a unique collection of dishes but an invaluable record of Jewish cultural heritage.

A NOTE ON RECIPE TITLES

If a recipe is common to both Sephardic and Ashkenazic cuisines, two names are given in the recipe title—the first in Ladino (a dialect of Castilian Spanish written in Hebrew) and the second in Yiddish (a form of Middle High German written in Hebrew). In these instances, no geographic identification is given in the translation found in the accompanying parentheses. However, if a dish is exclusive to a specific cultural community or area, then a singular ethnic or regional term is employed in the title and the applicable geographic identification follows in the accompanying translation.

The
Baker's Assistant

And bread that sustains man's heart.

—PSALMS 104:15

BAKING IS FUNDAMENTAL TO JEWISH CULTURE. FOR MILLENNIA, BREAD CONSTITUTED THE BULK OF THE JEWISH DIET. INDEED, THE HEBREW WORD FOR "BREAD" (*LECHEM*) SERVES AS A GENERIC TERM FOR FOOD, AND A DERIVATIVE, REFLECTING ITS IMPORTANCE, means "war" (*milchamah*). (Contrast this to the comparable Arabic *lahum*, which possesses the specific denotation of "meat.") All Sabbath, festival, and celebration meals commence with bread and generally end with some pastry or cake.

Until relatively recently, Ashkenazic baking remained rather medieval, characterized by very heavy honey cakes. Sephardim, on the other hand, early on began developing a sophisticated cuisine encompassing various *bolas* (Ladino for "balls," spheres of yeast dough), *pan dulce* (sweet breads), *biscochos* (cookies), and egg-foam cakes. The Spanish Expulsion in 1492 spread Iberian culinary refinements to many parts of the Middle East and Europe, including to some Ashkenazim. The Ottoman Empire, during its occupation of Hungary (1526–1687) and the Balkans, introduced phyllo dough and other Middle Eastern innovations to central and eastern Europe. Around the same time that the Turks were being driven from Europe, sugar and white flour became increasingly accessible and inexpensive. Capitalizing on these developments, central European bakers of the seventeenth and eighteenth centuries created a vast array of refined *kuchen* and pastries, many of which became standard Ashkenazic desserts.

The result of these culinary developments is displayed in a heritage of Jewish baking. Among Ashkenazim it consists of *lekach* (honey cake) and *teiglach* during Rosh Hashanah, strudel and *fluden* for Sukkot, doughnuts and *rugelach* during Hanukkah, *hamantaschen* and gingerbread men on Purim, sponge cake and nut tortes during Passover, cheesecakes and coffee cakes for Shavuot, and *eier kichlach* (egg cookies), *mandelbrot*, marble cake, and *babka* on the Sabbath. Sephardim might serve *tishpishti* and baklava for Rosh Hashanah, filled phyllo pastries for Sukkot, *ma'amoul* (nut-filled cookies) and *zangula/zelabiya* (funnel cakes) for Hanukkah, baklava, *kadayif* (shredded wheat pastries), and *travados* (pastry horns) for Purim, sponge cake and nut tortes during Passover, *biscochos Har Sinai* (mounded cookies representing Mount Sinai) for Shavuot, and *biscochos de huevo* (cookie rings), *biscochos dulces* (cookie fingers), *biscochos de rake* (anise cookies), and *borekitas* (almond pastries) on the Sabbath.

If You Can't Take the Heat

Baking is a process of heating, raising, setting, and drying a batter or dough. If the temperature is too low, the structure will not set sufficiently, resulting in poor volume or collapse. If it is too high, the structure will set before it has risen sufficiently. The density of the food, its size, and its moisture content all play a role in determining the baking temperature and time.

In conventional ovens, the heat source, usually at the bottom of the appliance, warms the air closest to it, causing the air to rise and displace the cooler molecules above. As the hot air moves away from the heat source and touches the cooler oven walls and food, it begins to cool and fall. Then, as the cooling air nears the heat source, the process is repeated as the molecules warm and rise again. In the enclosed space of the oven, the circulating air molecules create convection currents that transfer some of their heat to the food and bake it. Due to the flow of air, the most accurate location in conventional ovens is in the center. Since most home ovens are generally off, often by 50 degrees or more, it is advisable to check the temperature with an oven thermometer.

Convection, or forced air, ovens contain a built-in fan that moves the hot air in a fast, uniform flow. This creates the same temperature in every part of the oven, making more efficient use of the heat. Convection ovens are particularly beneficial for breads, cakes, and pastries, providing a more uniformly brown color as well as quicker baking. If using a convection oven, set the temperature at 25 to 50 degrees lower than for conventional ovens.

Although most of the heat in an oven is produced by convection, there are simultaneously other forms of energy at work. In a process called radiation heat, electromagnetic waves transmitted by oven surfaces are transferred to the food; that is why baked goods placed near the top of the oven may overbrown on top and those on a lower shelf overbrown on the bottom or sides. Ovens vary greatly in the amount of radiant heat emitted.

In addition, baking pans and oven shelves absorb heat from the air currents and, in a process called conduction, transfer it to the food. The speed of conduction varies among different materials. Silver and copper are the best conductors; aluminum is relatively quick; cast iron and carbon steel are moderate; stainless steel is rather slow; and glass, earthenware, and wood are poor conductors.

Dull or darkened metals—such as cast iron and carbon steel—absorb radiant heat coming from the oven surfaces, while shiny metals—such as stainless steel—reflect it. Quick-cooking baked goods such as cookies benefit from a shiny baking sheet that protects their bottoms from burning. In most baked goods, however, the reflection of radiant heat by shiny surfaces increases the baking time and therefore the probability of the top burning or the bottom being undercooked. Stains on shiny pans act like darkened metals, producing more heat at those spots and, as a result, irregularly colored food. Therefore, it is important to keep shiny utensils free of discolorations. Although glass is a poor conductor, it is transparent, which means that radiation heat passes directly through it and into the food. If using glass utensils, reduce the oven temperature by 25 degrees.

About Baking Ingredients

Baking is fundamentally about chemical reactions; no matter how inspired the baker, the laws of science apply just as strictly to the kitchen as to the laboratory. Success, therefore, depends on using the proper ingredients and accurately following directions. Faulty measuring, mixing, chilling, or baking results in poorly textured or collapsed baked goods. Fresh, high-quality ingredients produce superior results. Skimp at the sacrifice of flavor and texture. To avoid finding some vital component missing, assemble all of the listed ingredients and utensils before starting the preparation.

FLOUR

Man could live without spices, but not without wheat.

—MIDRASH PSALMS 2:16

Wheat spread from its home in the Fertile Crescent to serve as the "staff of life," providing the energy that fueled Middle Eastern and Western civilization. Two species of wheat were found in ancient Israel—*aestivum*, used for bread and pastries, and durum, used to make semolina. Early on, aristocrats developed a preference for flour made solely from the endosperm (the central part of the kernel) and free of the bran and germ. Refined flour produces more tender baked goods and higher-rising breads, allows for more variety, and stays fresh longer. For most of history, however, white flour remained primarily the province of the upper class, proving much too expensive for the masses to enjoy except on rare occasions. Indeed, until recently, the primary form of flour in Europe was made from maslin, a natural mixture of wheat and rye grains. Only in the wake of the improved technology and milling methods of the Industrial Revolution did white flour became accessible and the most widely used kind.

There are three basic types of wheat used to make flour: soft (winter), hard (spring), and durum. The basic difference among them is the amount of protein, ranging from 6 to nearly 14 grams per cup of flour, and the amount of starch. Soft wheat has a low-protein, high-starch content and a fine, starch-like texture. Hard wheat has a high-protein, low-starch content and a coarse, granular texture. Durum, a different species, possesses a very high gluten content (13 to 14 grams).

The endosperm of wheat contains about equal amounts of two types of protein—glutenin and gliadin. When these proteins come in contact with water, they combine to form strands of a viscid substance called gluten. It is gluten that gives flour the elasticity to rise and to keep its structure when subjected to heat. Few grains possess any gluten, and none, except wheat, have enough to produce the light texture that we associate with breads and cakes. When gluten encounters friction, it becomes flexible. The more it is worked, the more elastic it becomes. This is a desirable quality in breads but makes for tough pastries. Resting and chilling dough help to relax the gluten. However, if the gluten strands are built up too much, as in kneading or overmixing, no amount of relaxation will completely weaken them.

Most of flour consists of starch, which helps create the baked good's structure. The higher the amount of starch, the more water the flour is capable of absorbing. Mixing $1/2$ cup of water with 1 cup of high-protein flour yields a firm dough, while soft wheat flour will require about 25 percent more moisture, a major difference in recipes in which a precise amount of liquid is given.

Flour is bleached—either naturally (by oxygen in the air) or chemically—to improve baking and storage properties as well as to produce a uniform white color. Without some bleaching, the gluten would be too weak to work properly, resulting in flat breads and tough cakes. Chemical bleaching, however, modifies the proteins, weakening their ability to form gluten. The higher the amount of protein, the quicker baked goods brown.

All flour contains some acid. Chemically treating it changes the pH level, and therefore the amount of acid varies among types of flour. Even the chemicals in water may upset the pH balance. An increase in acid relaxes the gluten and lowers the temperature at which it congeals, resulting in a fine texture and flavor. In addition, the more acid, the more slowly baked goods brown. A small amount of acid—such as lemon juice, vinegar, cream of tartar, or a crushed vitamin C tablet—is commonly added to pastry dough to facilitate rolling, to yeast doughs to help gluten development, and to cake batters for a finer texture. On the other hand, alkalis (such as baking soda) impede the coagulation of protein and, if not counterbalanced, result in a coarse texture, off flavor, and dark color.

Hard wheat flour, available in health food and specialty food stores, is chemically untreated high-gluten spring flour. Professional bakers use it to make breads, phyllo dough, and cream puffs.

All-purpose flour is a blend of soft and hard wheat, the proportions varying slightly among companies and even regions. Southern brands of all-purpose flour contain less protein (9 grams) than national labels (around 11 grams), producing superior pastries, quick breads, and pancakes. Canadian flour tends to be even higher in protein than American. Unbleached all-purpose flour, usually aged with potassium bromate, is higher in gluten (12 to 13 grams) than bleached all-purpose flour.

Cake flour, made from soft wheat, contains a high amount of starch and only sufficient gluten (8 grams) to support the structure created by the leavening, but not enough to make a cake tough. Cake flour is treated with chlorine gas and benzoyl peroxide, which act as maturing agents and whiteners. This process affects the starch in the flour so that it gelatinizes at a lower temperature, sustaining a larger amount of sugar and fat and resulting in a lighter cake. The chlorine enhances the gluten's ability to bond with sugar, helping to raise the cake and set its structure. The chlorine adds acid, affecting the pH balance, producing a fine texture as well as slowing the browning. Cake flour is primarily beneficial in batters leavened with baking powder.

Pastry flour is a low-gluten (about 9.2 grams) soft wheat flour used for pie and tart shells, quick breads, biscuits, and pancakes. Unlike cake flour, it is not chlorinated.

Semolina, the endosperm of durum wheat, is available in Middle Eastern, Italian, and health food stores in three forms: fine grind, sometimes labeled #1 quality, a slightly granular meal; coarse grind; and flour, a powdery product used to make pasta and bread. Semolina adds crunch, a pale yellow color, and a distinctive nutty flavor to pastries, cakes, and puddings. Farina can be substituted for fine semolina in many recipes; however, semolina cooked in water and baked becomes hard, while farina remains soft.

LEAVENINGS

Without one of the three types of leavening—air, steam, or gas—cakes and breads would turn out flat and tough.

Air: Air is incorporated into a batter or dough through creaming (beating fat with sugar) and foaming (beating eggs, sometimes with sugar). Gluten and eggs are the primary proteins that form the stretchable network used to trap leavenings. In the presence of heat, the trapped air expands, further raising and lightening the baked goods. This is particularly true of batters containing eggs, which possess a singular ability to incorporate impressive amounts of air. In some baked goods—notably sponge cakes and meringues—air serves as the sole leavening. In others, such as butter cakes, it works in combination with a chemical leavening agent.

Steam: When the heat of the oven hits the moisture and fat in baked goods, it produces steam, which then enters and expands the air spaces. Steam works alone in some recipes, producing the tender flakiness of puff pastry and pie crusts or stretching the elastic walls of *pâte à choux* (cream puff pastry) and popovers. In other baked goods, such as biscuits, steam works in concord with a chemical agent.

Gas: Carbon dioxide is produced in baked goods in one of two ways: the action of yeast or the reaction of an alkali. When baking soda (sodium bicarbonate) is exposed to heat, it breaks down into carbon dioxide and sodium carbonate, the latter producing a soapy flavor. If there is an acid present, however, it reacts with the alkali, neutralizing any bad taste. After doing its work during the initial stages of baking, the gas dissipates. Baking soda is generally preferable for quick-cooking baked goods such as pancakes and cookies, which need to produce sufficient gas in a short period, and batters containing acidic ingredients such as buttermilk and molasses.

Baking powder is a combination of alkali (sodium bicarbonate) with the proper amount of acid salts (phosphate or sulfate) to neutralize the soda. Some starch is added to act as a buffer and absorb moisture. Calcium dihydrogen phosphate works in contact with a liquid, while sodium aluminum sulfate (alum) reacts in the presence of heat. Single-acting baking powder contains only calcium dihydrogen phosphate and therefore is inappropriate for long-cooking items such as cakes and quick breads because too much gas escapes before the heat of the oven sets the baked good and traps the carbon dioxide. Double-acting baking powders contain both types of acidic compounds and react twice: initially when the baking powder is mixed with a liquid to create numerous small cells and again when subjected to heat to expand those cells. There is also an all-phosphate double-acting baking powder containing calcium acid phosphate, which is preferable in pastries and some cakes in which aluminum sulfate–based powders would impart a bitter aftertaste. The two types of baking powder should not be used interchangeably. Use one-fourth less double-acting than single-acting: if a recipe calls for 3/4 teaspoon double-acting baking powder, use 1 teaspoon single-acting; for 1 teaspoon double-acting baking powder, use 1 1/4 teaspoons single-acting. Too much baking powder produces bubbles that are too large and pop, resulting in a collapsed product.

Yeast is a microscopic single-cell plant responsible for turning juice into wine, barley into beer, milk into cheese, and flour into leavened bread. With the proper combination of moisture, air, and warmth, yeast feeds on carbohydrates, breaking them down into carbon dioxide and alcohol in a chemical reaction called fermentation. The heat of the oven burns off the alcohol and kills the yeast during baking, leaving only the raised bread as a reminder of its work.

Around 1876, Charles Louis Fleishmann, a Hungarian-Jewish immigrant distressed by the poor quality of American bread, started selling compressed fresh yeast. Today it is commercially available in 0.6-ounce (18-gram), 1-ounce (35-gram), and 2-ounce (70-gram) cakes and, at baking supply stores, in 1-pound blocks. Highly perishable, fresh yeast keeps in the refrigerator for only one to two weeks and sometimes dies in the grocery. When too old, it turns dry and brown and no longer crumbles easily. To use fresh yeast, bring it to room temperature, then dissolve, without stirring, in a little lukewarm water (85 to 95 degrees) until foamy or mix it directly into the dough. One 0.6-ounce cake of compressed fresh yeast equals a $1/4$-ounce package of active dry yeast; 2 ounces of compressed yeast equals 3 packages of dry yeast.

In the 1930s, Fleishmann's introduced active dry yeast, a dehydrated strain that becomes reactivated when combined with moisture. The longer shelf life and handiness of the newcomer quickly made it the type used in most homes. Dry yeast requires a higher heat (105 to 115 degrees) and more moisture than compressed yeast to activate. One $1/4$-ounce package of active dry yeast, containing about $2^{1/4}$ teaspoons, will raise about 4 cups of all-purpose flour. Dry yeast is available in bulk packages—with a much lower price tag. It keeps for more than a year in a cool, dry place.

A new dry yeast variety was recently developed. Rapid-rising yeast saves time, but sometimes at the expense of the bread's flavor, since it ferments before complex flavors can be formed. Rapid-rising yeast is also more temperamental, requiring a higher temperature for the liquid (about 120 degrees) and the rising (80 to 90 degrees). Have all the ingredients, including the yeast, at room temperature. Rapid-rising yeast is more porous and granular than the active dry type and is not dissolved in liquid but mixed directly into the flour. When substituting rapid-rising yeast for the older types, reduce the amount by 25 percent.

FATS

Fat contributes richness, tenderness, moistness, and in the case of butter, flavor. When solid fat melts, it releases steam, leavening the batter. In some baked goods, fat serves as the crucial creaming agent, used to hold the incorporated air. In the process of mixing, fat does not actually dissolve but rather is broken into minute particles that are distributed throughout the mixture. The fat surrounds and coats the gluten in a process called shortening, inhibiting the gluten's ability to absorb liquid, stretch, and form a network. The result is a very tender baked good with a soft texture. If the dough is worked too much, however, the gluten begins to absorb liquid despite the fat.

Butter is the most popular fat for baking because of its superior flavor, texture, and creaming ability. Butterfat melts in the mouth, creating a very pleasing sensation. Most other fats, with the primary exception of cocoa butter, end up coating the mouth, a feeling many people find unpleasant.

Sweet cream butter is churned from heavy cream. Salt is sometimes added as a preservative and to bring out the flavor; if salted, butter is labeled simply as butter. A stick ($^1/2$ cup) of salted butter generally contains about $^1/2$ teaspoon salt. In order to control the amount of salt, sweet (unsalted) butter is recommended for baking.

By law, butter must contain at least 80 percent butterfat; the remainder is made up primarily of water and milk solids. American butters generally contain more moisture than European brands, and salted sticks tend to have a larger amount of water than sweet butters. Because of the liquid it contains, butter has less "shortening" ability (on gluten) than vegetable shortening, which is 100 percent fat. Butters with more water produce tough pastries.

Margarine is made from a bland oil, primarily soy or cottonseed, that is artificially saturated. Similar to butter, it is usually composed of 80 percent fat and 20 percent water. Do not use diet margarine, which contains a large amount of water, in baking. Some brands of margarine are dairy free, while others contain skim milk or buttermilk.

When a recipe calls for softened butter or margarine, bring it to room temperature, but do not leave it out to the point that it becomes oily. To test if butter is properly softened, press a finger into it—there should be an impression but the butter should still be firm. Melted butter and softened butter react differently in baked goods. In melting, the fat and water separate, and when the water comes in contact with the flour, it leads to the formation of gluten, resulting in a chewy texture.

Vegetable shortening is lighter than animal fat, can be stored at room temperature for extended periods, does not absorb odors and flavors from fried foods, and does not smoke when heated. Its texture is perfect for creating flaky pie crusts and fluffy biscuits. In addition, dough made from shortening is easier to handle. Shortening has one major drawback—lack of flavor. As a result, some bakers use a combination of shortening and butter.

SWEETENERS

Sugar plays numerous roles in baking beyond imparting sweetness. It partially dissolves gluten, producing a more tender product. It provides food for yeast; adding too much sugar, however, impairs the dough's ability to rise. Sugar also produces a smoother batter, resulting in more volume. It plays a special role in the leavening process, serving as the creaming agent with fats and the foaming agent with eggs. As sugar crystals are beaten with a solid fat, the jagged edges create air cells in the fat. Superfine sugar, called caster sugar in England, is preferable for cakes and cookies because it dissolves more easily and creates more uniform air pockets in the fat, resulting in more volume.

Sugar is hygroscopic, meaning it attracts moisture. In baked goods containing only a small amount of liquid (most notably cookies), sugar competes with the flour to absorb the liquid, thereby inhibiting the gluten's ability to form and tenderizing the baked good. Sugar also contains its own moistness, which contributes to the baked good's freshness. After baking, high-sugar items such as cookies absorb moisture from the environment.

When acid is added to sucrose and subjected to heat, it produces an invert sugar, which resists crystallization. (This is why lemon juice and cream of tartar are frequently added to sugar syrups.) In addition, invert sugars absorb and hold moisture better than other types of sweeteners, a trait that makes baked goods softer and keeps them moist for a longer time. Honey is an invert sugar.

Dark (or "sulfured") molasses, a by-product of sugar making, is a thick, dark liquid. Unsulphured (light) molasses, made from pure sugar juices, is sweeter and milder. Brown sugar is superfine sugar mixed with a little molasses (3.5 percent for light brown and 6.5 percent for dark brown).

Confectioners' (powdered) sugar is made by finely grinding sugar crystals and mixing them with a starch, usually 3 percent cornstarch. The starch prevents the absorption of moisture and clumping. The finer the sugar has been ground, the higher the number (4X, 6X, and 10X). In most icings 10X is preferred (for its smoothness), while 4X is recommended when a thicker icing is required (as in flowers).

EGGS

Eggs contribute richness, flavor, moisture, color, texture, and nutrition to baked goods. Their protein serves to incorporate and hold leavenings and coagulate to form the structure. In addition, eggs contain bicarbonate, a natural leavening that, when subjected to heat, breaks down into carbon dioxide and steam. Egg yolks contain lecithin, an emulsifier, which serves to shorten the gluten by surrounding the strands and inhibiting the absorption of water. The yolk's emulsifying ability helps to produce a smooth batter and thereby better volume and texture, as well as keeping breads from staling. The presence of eggs makes a baked good chewy unless it is balanced by large amounts of sugar and fat.

The recipes in this book call for large eggs, weighing (in shell) 2 ounces (56.7 grams) and containing about 2 tablespoons egg white and 1 tablespoon plus 1/2 teaspoon egg yolk.

THE GENTLE ART OF BEATING EGG WHITES

 Egg whites are made up of about 10 percent albumen, a protein that coagulates and toughens baked goods, and 90 percent water. Beating egg whites produces a foam of air trapped in the liquid and protein. The more the whites are beaten, the firmer the walls of the protein become. This multitude of bubbles adds lightness to a mousse or expands during baking for airy baked goods.

Fat hinders the formation of air cells. Since the yolk is one-third fat, even a speck of yolk in the whites will reduce the volume. Make sure the beaters and bowl are clean of grease.

Chilled proteins expand too slowly to reach maximum volume, so the egg whites need to be at room temperature. Remove the eggs from the refrigerator at least a half hour before using. You can speed up the warming process by soaking them in warm water for at least 10 minutes.

Unstable egg whites tend to become watery and lose their gloss. Cream of tartar chemically alters the protein in egg whites (use 1/4 teaspoon cream of tartar for 4 large whites). The denatured protein remains moist and pliant, thereby increasing volume and reducing the possibility of dry whites. In addition, a protein in egg whites binds with ions in copper, producing molecules that are more stable. Therefore, beating the whites in a copper bowl produces bubbles that are smaller and denser, are more difficult to overbeat, and deflate slower. Do not use cream of tartar with copper, or the egg whites will take on a greenish tint.

After carefully separating the egg white from the yolk, place it and chalaza (the twisted white projection that anchors the yolk) in a large round-bottomed bowl. For best results, use a metal bowl (stainless steel or copper), since whites slip down the slick surface of glass or ceramic, hampering the beating process. Avoid plastic bowls, which retain fat, and aluminum, which can discolor the whites. To prevent the bowl from moving, place it on a damp towel or dishcloth.

To beat, use a large thin-wired (balloon) whisk or electric mixer; a handheld mixer produces greater volume than a stand-mounted one. Once you begin beating, do not stop until you reach your goal, or the egg whites may become grainy. Beat at low speed—too high a speed at first creates large, unstable bubbles—until foamy, about 30 seconds. At this stage, small bubbles form on the top, but the whites are still liquidy and transparent. Cream of tartar and salt delay foaming; thus, if they are added at the beginning, the whites will not reach full volume. If added at the end of beating, they will not be incorporated. Therefore, add them at the foamy stage.

Gradually increase the speed to high while moving the whisk or mixer around the bowl to evenly beat all of the whites. At the soft-peak stage, they form shiny peaks that curl over when the beaters are lifted. When making meringues, begin to gradually add the sugar at this point. At the stiff-peak stage, the whites are glossy and stand straight up when the beaters are lifted. Properly beaten egg whites will increase to six to eight times their original volume and remain moist and pliant. Insufficient beating produces too few air bubbles or large bubbles (which are unstable), resulting in stunted volume or collapse. Too much beating produces dull, dry whites, which are too firm for folding and break up during baking, allowing the air to escape.

Fold—do not stir—the whites into the base. First add about one-fourth of the whites to lighten the base, then fold in the remainder. To fold, use a rubber spatula or your hand to reach down the middle of the mixture, then scrape along the bottom and move up the sides. Rotate the bowl slightly and repeat. Keep folding gently until all of the whites have been incorporated. Do not overwork, or you will deflate them.

NUTS

Nut refers to any dry fruit or seed surrounded by a hard shell. Most nuts are very rich in oil and go rancid relatively quickly. To prevent spoiling, store them in the refrigerator or freezer. It is advisable to taste one nut before using to make sure they are fresh.

Toasting brings out the nut's flavor. Pan-toasting provides the most intense flavor in walnuts. To pan-toast, put the shelled nuts in a dry heavy skillet, preferably cast-iron, place over medium heat, and toast, stirring frequently, until they begin to sizzle, about 5 minutes. To oven-toast, spread the shelled nuts on a baking sheet and place in a 350-degree oven, shaking the sheet occasionally, for about 10 minutes.

To blanch almonds, place in boiling water until the skins begin to wrinkle, 3 to 5 minutes. Drain and rub off the skins. Spread over a paper towel in a single layer and let dry.

To blanch hazelnuts, for each cup of nuts, bring 3 cups of water to a boil. Add 1/4 cup baking soda, then the nuts. Boil for about 4 minutes. (The water will turn black.) Drain, rinse under cold water, and rub off the skins.

To skin pistachios, roast on a baking sheet in a 400-degree oven for 4 minutes or, alternatively, blanch in boiling water. Cool slightly and rub off the skins.

Because of their high oil content, nuts turn into a paste (like peanut butter) when overground. To avoid this, Europeans traditionally use a hand-powered nut grinder. When grinding nuts in a food processor, add a little of the sugar called for in the recipe to prevent sticking. It is advisable not to grind more than 2 cups at a time. Push the pulse button a few times, then check the consistency.

Measuring Ingredients

Measure liquid ingredients in standard glass measuring cups with a pouring spout. Place the cup on a level surface and fill to the appropriate line. Bend down to examine it rather than lifting the cup to inspect the accuracy. For small amounts, use measuring spoons.

Measure dry ingredients using standard gradated cups or spoons with exactly the capacity desired. If the recipe calls for "sifted flour," sift before measuring; if it calls for "flour, sifted" or simply "flour," sift it after measuring. The method of measuring affects the amount in the cup (1 cup of unsifted all-purpose flour measured by the dip-and-sweep method equals about 5 ounces/140 grams, while 1 cup measured by the spoon-and-sweep method yields about 4¼ ounces/121 grams). Unless otherwise indicated, measure flour using the dip-and-sweep method: dip a gradated measuring cup into the flour, filling it above the rim—do not tap—then level the top with a flat instrument such as the back of a knife.

Since cake flour clumps up more than other types, it is generally sifted before measuring. Use the spoon-and-sweep method to measure cake flour: sift the flour, spoon into a gradated measuring cup above the rim—do not tap—then level the top with the back of a knife.

To measure brown sugar, pack it firmly into a measuring cup.

To measure shortening, pack it into a gradated measuring cup and run the back of a knife over the top. For easy removal, first line the cup with plastic wrap. If adding both shortening and a liquid sweetener such as honey to a recipe, measure the sweetener in the same cup after the shortening and it will slide out easily.

STALING

 During baking, gluten coagulates and exudes some of its moisture, while the starch softens and absorbs water. As soon as the baked good starts to cool, the starch begins to harden and gradually discharges its water. As it stands, more and more of the moisture makes its way to the surface, where it gradually evaporates. Thus, starting from the center outward, baked goods begin to harden as they stand. Wrapping them in plastic wrap or foil retards evaporation (although this promotes mold in yeast breads), and freezing slows it even longer. Eventually, however, evaporation occurs, resulting in staleness. Reheating gelatinizes the starch, temporarily softening the texture.

High-Altitude Baking

Most recipes are designed for altitudes up to 3,000 feet above sea level. Because atmospheric pressure decreases the higher one goes from sea level, the thinner air at higher elevations exerts less pressure during baking. As a result, the carbon dioxide produced by baking powder and yeast meets less resistance from the air. In addition, flour tends to dry out quicker at higher elevations. Most cookies are not adversely affected by altitude, but if they spread too much, reduce the amount of sugar. However, pastries puff up higher with less air pressure, and the amount of leavening needed to raise the same amount of batter is less than at lower elevations. Beaten eggs require less air at higher elevations, so beat eggs and sugar only until a ribbon just starts to form. When both beaten eggs and carbon dioxide play major roles in raising the batter as in chiffon cakes, the amount of baking powder should be reduced even more than stated below.

Cakes and quick breads are most affected by altitude. When cakes rise too quickly, as they do at higher elevations, they do not have time to incorporate all of the liquid in the batter. The result is a dry, fallen cake. To help set cell structure at altitudes over 3,500 feet, increase the oven temperature by 25 degrees. Since cakes baked at a higher elevation tend to have a coarser texture, use cake flour, which is softer and finer. Despite these precautions, you may have to experiment with the ingredients and oven temperature to achieve the proper results.

For cakes and quick breads from 3,000 to 5,000 feet:
- reduce the baking powder or baking soda by 1/8 teaspoon per teaspoon
- reduce the sugar by 1 tablespoon per cup
- increase the liquid by 1 to 2 tablespoons per cup
- increase the flour by 1 tablespoon per cup

For cakes and quick breads from 5,000 to 7,000 feet:
- reduce the baking powder or baking soda by 1/8 to 1/4 teaspoon per teaspoon
- reduce the sugar by 1 to 2 tablespoons per cup
- increase the liquid by 2 to 4 tablespoons per cup
- increase the flour by 1 to 2 tablespoons per cup

For cakes and quick breads above 7,000 feet:
- reduce the baking powder or baking soda by 1/4 teaspoon per teaspoon
- reduce the sugar by 2 to 3 tablespoons per cup
- increase the liquid by 3 to 4 tablespoons per cup
- increase the flour by 2 to 3 tablespoons per cup

Yeast Cakes
and Pastries

And Abraham hurried into the tent to Sarah and said:
Make quickly out of three measures of fine flour,
knead it, and make cakes.

—GENESIS 18:6

THE FIRST BREADS CONSISTED OF GRUEL COOKED ON CAMPFIRES AND HOT ROCKS. AT SOME POINT, WILD YEAST FOUND ITS WAY INTO A WHEAT BATTER, GIVING BIRTH TO LEAVENED BREAD. AFTER COOKS LEARNED HOW TO PRESERVE THESE UNICELLULAR FUNGI IN starter doughs, bread emerged as the major component of the diet in many parts of the world. Eventually bakers, probably in Egypt, began to enrich the dough by adding honey and oil, creating cakes. Bas-reliefs in the tomb of Ramses II depict the royal bakery with its vast and sophisticated stock of breads and cakes. At the same time, residents of Mesopotamia prepared hundreds of types of breads, mostly variations of round flat loaves.

Bread in ancient Israel was made from the "five species": bread wheat, durum wheat, spelt (a relative of wheat), and two species of barley. Bread was still cooked over a fire, but loaves were also baked on a griddle and later on the sides of a heated clay oven. By the time of King Herod, wheat supplanted barley as the primary bread grain in Judea, and professional bakeries supplied the needs of many of the residents of the larger cities. Foreign influences, including Persian, Greek, and Roman, increasingly impacted on the Jewish table as bakers began to use dough to make more than flat breads. The Mishnah (Challah 1:4) mentioned a quartet of yeast dough cakes: *soufganin* (cakes made from a spongy dough), *duvshaneen* (honey cakes), *eskarayteen* (dumplings), and *challat hamashrait* (pancakes). Other popular Talmudic-era baked goods included *ashishim* (honey lentil cakes; Nedarim 40a), *kenoovkeoat* (crumb cake; Challah 1:5), and *syrikeen* ("Syrian cakes," fancy yeast cakes containing oil, honey, and sometimes milk and usually shaped like figures; Pesachim 37a). As Jews moved into the Diaspora, each community acquired its own repertoire of yeast cakes and pastries.

Baking Sweet Breads

Preheat the oven about 20 minutes before you plan to bake. If the oven is too hot (375 degrees or higher), the exterior of a sweet yeast loaf will burn before the inside is entirely cooked. If baked at too low a temperature (325 degrees or lower), the loaf will rise too much, lose its shape, and develop a thick crust. Therefore a moderate oven temperature (350 degrees) is recommended for sweet doughs, except for some small breads.

Because of the large amount of sugar and milk, sweet yeast breads brown faster than lean ones, especially on the bottom. It is therefore advisable to use double-stacked baking sheets. Be careful not to panic and remove the loaves before they are actually done, or the inner part might still be raw. If the loaves look as if they are starting to burn, cover them loosely with foil, dull side down, during the latter part of baking.

The best way to test for doneness is to insert an instant-read thermometer into the center of the loaf; it should register about 185 degrees. A more practical method for most home cooks is to tap the loaf on the bottom; it should be hollow sounding. The exterior should have a rich brown color, be symmetrically balanced, and have a smooth, evenly rounded top without any bumps or crevices. The interior should be uniformly colored, the texture soft and fluffy, and the grain (the shape of the air holes) uniformly tiny.

Pandericas/Heifeteig ❧ *(Sweet Yeast Dough)*

ABOUT 2¼ POUNDS DOUGH; ENOUGH FOR 1 LARGE OR 2 MEDIUM CAKES

Sweet yeast dough serves as the basis for a number of Sephardic and Ashkenazic cakes and pastries. Dough pieces of 2½ ounces or less become rolls and buns called *panisico dulces* by Sephardim and *bobkes* or *pultabulkas* by Ashkenazim.

This recipe offers three variations of sweet yeast dough, each one richer than the previous. The texture of loaves made from Basic Sweet Yeast Dough is light and moist, yet firm enough to slice when fresh. The amount of fat yields a loaf that is rich without being too unctuous or heavy. Sephardim commonly use oil; Ashkenazim, butter or oil. Using only water as the liquid produces a leaner texture; milk gives the loaf a softer, deeper-colored crust, a soft texture, and a light grain, and because it acts as a preservative, the bread stays soft for a longer period of time. The quantity of sugar flavors the bread without competing with any filling. Rich Sweet Yeast Dough produces a firmer and more flavorful loaf. Extra-Rich Sweet Yeast Dough is stickier than the others and produces a brioche-like consistency and lushness; it can be baked on its own as a dessert, without any filling or topping.

Sweet yeast dough is minimally kneaded until springy (not elastic), about 5 minutes. In contrast to lean yeast doughs, too much gluten is unwanted, as the dough will not relax sufficiently, resulting in a tough texture. The large amount of sweetener and fat slows down the yeast's growth, thereby increasing the rising time. Using milk will also increase the rising time.

Basic Sweet Yeast Dough:

1 (¼-ounce) package (2¼ teaspoons) active dry yeast, or 1 (0.6-ounce) cake fresh yeast

1 cup warm water (105 to 115 degrees for dry yeast; 80 to 85 degrees for fresh yeast), or ¼ cup warm water and ¾ cup warm milk, or 1 cup warm water mixed with ¼ cup nonfat dry milk

⅓ cup sugar

⅓ cup vegetable oil, peanut oil, or softened butter

2 large eggs

1 teaspoon table salt, or 2 teaspoons kosher salt

About 4 cups high-gluten flour or unbleached all-purpose flour

Rich Sweet Yeast Dough:

1 (*1/4-ounce*) package (2*1/4* teaspoons)
   active dry yeast, or 1 (0.6-ounce)
   cake fresh yeast

3/4 cup warm water (105 to 115 degrees
   for dry yeast; 80 to 85 degrees for
   fresh yeast), or *1/4* cup warm water
   and *1/2* cup warm milk, or *3/4* cup
   water mixed with *1/4* cup nonfat dry
   milk

1/2 cup sugar

1/2 cup vegetable oil, peanut oil, or
   softened butter

3 large eggs

1 teaspoon table salt, or 2 teaspoons
   kosher salt

About 4 cups high-gluten flour or
   unbleached all-purpose flour

Extra-Rich Sweet Yeast Dough:

2 (*1/4-ounce*) packages (4*1/2* teaspoons)
   active dry yeast, or 2 (0.6-ounce)
   cakes fresh yeast

1/2 cup warm water (105 to 115 degrees
   for dry yeast; 80 to 85 degrees for
   fresh yeast), or *1/4* cup warm water
   and *1/4* cup warm milk, or *1/2* cup
   water mixed with *1/4* cup nonfat dry
   milk

1/2 cup sugar

1 cup unsalted butter or margarine,
   softened

4 large eggs

1*1/2* teaspoons table salt, or
   2*1/2* teaspoons kosher salt

About 4*1/4* cups high-gluten flour or
   unbleached all-purpose flour

1. Dissolve the yeast in *1/4* cup water. Stir in 1 teaspoon sugar and let stand until foamy, 5 to 10 minutes.

2. Add the remaining water, sugar, oil or butter, eggs, and salt. Blend in 1*1/2* cups flour. Add enough of the remaining flour, *1/2* cup at a time, to make a workable dough. To mix in a food processor: Combine the flour, remaining sugar, and salt in the work bowl of a food processor fitted with a dough or metal blade. With the machine on, add the dissolved yeast mixture, then the eggs and oil or butter. With the machine on, gradually add enough of the remaining warm water to form a ball of dough that cleans the sides of the bowl. Process around the bowl about 25 times. Let the dough stand for 2 minutes to allow the flour to absorb the liquid. If necessary, add enough additional liquid to make the dough soft and smooth and process around the bowl about 15 times. Do not over-process—the heat of the engine can kill some of the yeast. The food processor method kneads the dough, but I like to knead it a little by hand, as the human touch seems to produce a better bread.

3. On a lightly floured surface or in a mixer with a dough hook, knead the dough, adding more flour as needed to prevent sticking, until smooth and springy, about 5 minutes (this is not necessary if you used a food processor in Step 2). Place in an oiled bowl, turning to coat. Cover and let rise in a warm, draft-free place until nearly double in bulk, $1^1/2$ to 2 hours, or cover with plastic wrap and refrigerate overnight. (To test if the dough is sufficiently risen, press two fingers 1 inch deep into the center; if the indentations remain, the dough is ready.)

4. Punch down the dough. Fold over and press together several times (this redistributes the yeast and its food). Let stand for 10 minutes.

5. Form the dough into the desired shape. Place on a baking sheet lined with parchment paper or lightly greased. Cover and let rise until nearly double in bulk, about $1^1/4$ hours (if the dough was just removed from the refrigerator, about $2^1/2$ hours).

6. Preheat the oven to 350 degrees.

7. Bake until golden brown and hollow sounding when tapped on the bottom, about 35 minutes. Transfer to a rack and let cool.

HINT: ☙ Use leftover sweet yeast bread to make bread pudding, toast, French toast, or rum balls, or drizzle with a sugar syrup to moisten.

VARIATIONS

Anise Sweet Yeast Dough: Add 2 to 3 teaspoons anise seeds or 1 to 2 teaspoons anise liqueur.

Cardamom Sweet Yeast Dough: Add 1 teaspoon ground cardamom.

Fruit and Nut Sweet Yeast Dough: Add 1 cup raisins, $1/2$ to 1 cup chopped candied fruit, and $1/3$ to $2/3$ cup slivered almonds or coarsely chopped walnuts or pecans.

Orange Sweet Yeast Dough: Add 2 to 3 teaspoons grated orange zest.

Pan Dulce ❧ *(Sephardic Sweet Yeast Loaf)*

2 MEDIUM LOAVES

This bread, in loaf form or rolls, is served for Sabbath *desayuno* (breakfast) and before and after the fast of Yom Kippur.

---

1 recipe (2¹/₄ pounds) Basic Sweet Yeast Dough, Orange Sweet Yeast Dough, or Anise Sweet Yeast Dough (pages 35 and 37)

Egg wash (1 large egg beaten with 1 teaspoon water)
About ¹/₄ cup sesame seeds or sugar for sprinkling

---

1. Prepare the dough through Step 4.
2. Divide the dough in half. On a lightly oiled surface, roll each piece into a 12- by-8-inch rectangle. Starting from a narrow side, roll up jelly roll style and pinch the seams to seal. Place seam side down in 2 greased 8-by-4-inch loaf pans or a greased 11-by-5¹/₂-inch pan. Cover and let rise until nearly double in bulk, about 1 hour.
3. Preheat the oven to 350 degrees.
4. Brush with the egg wash, then lightly sprinkle with the sesame seeds. Bake until golden brown and hollow sounding when tapped on the bottom, about 30 minutes. Transfer to a rack and let cool.

VARIATIONS

Bolas (Sephardic Sweet Rounds): Shape the dough into rounds and place on a greased baking sheet. These are also called *mounas* in the Maghreb.

Panisicos Dulces (Sephardic Sweet Buns): These are called *petits pains* and *mounettes* in the Maghreb, where they are frequently shaped into the initials of family and guests. Divide the dough into 12 to 15 equal pieces, form into balls, let rise on a baking sheet, brush with egg wash, sprinkle with sesame seeds, and bake for 15 to 20 minutes.

Roscas ❧ *(Sephardic Sweet Yeast Bread Rings)*

3 MEDIUM LOAVES

This bread, also called *tsoureki* in Greece, is sometimes braided. In Salonika, *roscas* was served with feta and kasseri cheeses, olives, and coffee for *desayuno* (breakfast) on the Sabbath and Shavuot.

---

1 recipe (2¹/₄ pounds) Anise Sweet
Yeast Dough (page 37) or Rich
Sweet Yeast Dough (page 36)
Egg wash (1 large egg beaten with
1 teaspoon water)

About ¹/₄ cup sesame seeds for
sprinkling

---

1. Prepare the dough through Step 4.
2. Divide the dough into 3 equal pieces and form into balls. Poke a hole in the center of each ball and form into 2-inch-thick doughnuts. Place 4 inches apart on a baking sheet lined with parchment paper or lightly greased. Cover and let rise until nearly double in bulk, about 1 hour.
3. Preheat the oven to 350 degrees.
4. Brush with the egg wash, then lightly sprinkle with the sesame seeds. Bake until golden brown and hollow sounding when tapped on the bottom, about 30 minutes. Transfer to a rack and let cool.

VARIATION

Roscas Rolls: Follow the directions for *roscas*, but divide the dough into 12 to 15 equal pieces and shape into small doughnuts. Bake at 375 degrees until golden brown, about 20 minutes.

SALONIKA

 In no other location was the presence of Iberian refugees so profoundly felt as in Salonika, today Thessalonika, Greece. Following the Expulsion from Spain in 1492 until the nineteenth century, this metropolis in the Ottoman Empire boasted the world's largest Jewish community, with Jews comprising the majority of the city's population and dominating every aspect of its commercial life. Salonika was no ordinary city, since it served as the transfer point between Eastern and Western trade. Nevertheless, the bustling port, as well as most of the city's shops, closed on the Sabbath and Jewish festivals because Jewish porters and merchants would not work. There was a synagogue on nearly every block.

Following the Balkan Wars (1913) and the annexation of Salonika by Greece, its role in international trade ended. The Greek government's policy of Hellenization and a fire that incinerated much of the town produced a flood of emigration, primarily to the United States, Italy, France, and Israel. The biggest blow to the Greek Jewish community came in the form of the Nazis, who invaded the country on April 6, 1941. At the start of World War II, about 77,000 Jews lived in Greece, and most of them were deported to death camps in Poland. At the war's end, much of the remnant of this "mother city in Israel" opted to emigrate. Today only about 6,000 Jews remain in all of Greece, and Salonika's rich Jewish legacy is relegated to history.

The cuisine of Salonika, a synthesis of Turkish and Spanish, generally remained an uncomplicated fare featuring bread, cheese, beans, and olives. Favorite desserts included baklava, *kadaif, sutlach* (rice flour pudding), *dulce blanco* (fondant), and assorted preserves.

Nazuki ❧ *(Georgian Sweet Yeast Breads)*

2 MEDIUM LOAVES

I spent the summer of my junior year in college doing social work in the Israeli town of Upper Nazareth, working with new immigrants living in the local absorption center, as well as residents of the surrounding neighborhood, a number of whom were Georgian Jews. I was impressed by their affection, hospitality, and joie de vivre. Many had managed to maintain their religious beliefs even in the Soviet Union. We were frequently invited into their homes, as well as to personal events such as weddings and bar mitzvahs, all of which featured plenty of Israeli and Georgian foods. Since then, I have had a special fondness for Georgian cuisine, which just happens to be the best from the former Soviet Union.

Georgians have a pronounced love of bread and, over the course of history, adopted and adapted the doughs of other cultures into their culinary repertoire. Originally this bread was baked on the inner wall of a *tone* (a clay oven similar to the Indian *tandoor* and the Talmudic *tanur*). A metal baking sheet is used in modern kitchens.

---

1 recipe (2¼ pounds) Basic Sweet Yeast Dough (page 35)

Egg wash (1 large egg beaten with 1 teaspoon cream, milk, or water)

---

1. Prepare the dough through Step 4.
2. Divide the dough in half and shape into rounds. Place on a baking sheet lined with parchment paper or greased. Flatten slightly, cover, and let rise until nearly double in bulk, about 1 hour.
3. Preheat the oven to 350 degrees.
4. Brush the rounds with the egg wash. Bake until golden brown, 30 to 40 minutes. Serve warm or at room temperature.

Il Bollo ❧ *(Italian Sweet Yeast Bread)*

2 MEDIUM OVAL LOAVES

Modern bread baking has all but eliminated one step—the sponge. A sponge is a light dough composed of yeast mixed with at least half and up to all of the liquid and part of the flour in a recipe. A little sweetener is usually used to facilitate the fermentation. Salt, which would inhibit the yeast, is never added at this point. The sponge mixture is left to rise in a warm place for anywhere from one to eight hours, during which time the yeast ferments, giving the dough a head start before the bulk of the ingredients is added. As carbon dioxide is produced, the sponge begins to bubble and increase in size. Although a sponge may at first appear a waste of time, the long fermentation period produces a more flavorful and lighter-textured loaf. And a sponge actually offers more flexibility than standard yeast mixtures because it can be kept in the refrigerator for several days until needed.

This very rich and flavorful bread, an adaptation of the Sephardic *bola,* is customarily served by Italians on Sukkot and to break the fast of Yom Kippur.

Sponge:

1 (1/4-ounce) package (2 1/4 teaspoons) active dry yeast, or 1 (0.6-ounce) cake fresh yeast

1 cup warm water (105 to 110 degrees for dry yeast; 80 to 85 degrees for fresh yeast)

1 teaspoon sugar

2 cups high-gluten flour or unbleached all-purpose flour

Dough:

3/4 cup sugar

1/3 cup extra virgin olive oil or vegetable oil

2 to 3 large eggs

1 to 2 tablespoons anise seeds

1 teaspoon vanilla extract

1 teaspoon grated lemon zest

1/2 teaspoon grated orange zest (optional)

1 teaspoon table salt, or 2 teaspoons kosher salt

About 2 cups high-gluten flour or unbleached all-purpose flour

2/3 cup raisins (optional)

Egg wash (1 large egg beaten with 1 teaspoon water)

1. To make the sponge: In a large nonmetalic bowl, dissolve the yeast in the water. Add the sugar and let stand until foamy, 5 to 10 minutes. Using a wooden spoon, stir in the flour until smooth. Cover with plastic wrap and let stand at room temperature until more than double in bulk, at least 1 and up to 8 hours. The sponge can be stored in the refrigerator for up to 3 days.

2. To make the dough: Combine the sugar, oil, eggs, anise, vanilla, zest, and salt. Beat in the sponge. Add the flour, $1/2$ cup at a time, to form a soft, slightly sticky dough. On a lightly floured surface or in a mixer with a dough hook, knead the dough until smooth and springy, about 5 minutes. If desired, add the raisins. Place on a flat surface, cover with a large bowl or pot, and let rise until double in bulk, about $1^1/2$ hours.

3. Punch down the dough. Fold over and press together several times. Let stand for 10 minutes. Divide in half and shape each half into an oval. Place on a baking sheet lined with parchment paper or lightly greased. Cover and let rise until nearly double in bulk, about 1 hour.

4. Preheat the oven to 350 degrees.

5. Brush the top and sides of the ovals with the egg wash. Bake until golden brown and hollow sounding when tapped on the bottom, 30 to 40 minutes. Transfer to a rack and let cool.

VARIATION

Buccellato (Tuscan Coffee Cake Ring): The name of this Italian cake means "bracelet." Roll each dough half into a log about 22 inches long, place on 2 prepared baking sheets, bring the ends together to form rings, and pinch the ends to seal.

Kugelhopf ❧ *(Alsatian Yeast Cake)*

This delicate and porous egg bread, claimed by both Vienna and Alsace as its place of origin, is similar to the Italian panettone and French brioche. It is traditionally baked in a tall fluted mold. *Kugelhopf* is commonly served as a breakfast bread and Sabbath dessert. Moisten stale or even fresh *kugelhopf* with kirsch or rum syrup.

1/2 cup golden raisins	*4 large eggs, lightly beaten*
1/2 cup dark raisins	*2 teaspoons vanilla extract*
1/4 cup kirsch or light rum	*1 teaspoon table salt, or 2 teaspoons*
2 (1/4-ounce) packages (41/2 teaspoons)	*kosher salt*
active dry yeast, or 2 (0.6-ounce)	*1 teaspoon grated lemon zest (optional)*
cakes fresh yeast	*1 cup (2 sticks) unsalted butter or*
1 cup warm water (105 to 110 degrees	*margarine, divided into 1-tablespoon*
for dry yeast; 80 to 85 degrees for	*pieces and softened*
fresh yeast)	*14 to 16 whole blanched almonds*
3/4 cup sugar	*(optional)*
4 cups unbleached all-purpose flour	*Confectioners' sugar for sprinkling*

1. Soak the raisins in the kirsch until softened, at least 30 minutes.

2. Dissolve the yeast in 1/4 cup water. Add 1 teaspoon sugar and let stand until foamy, 5 to 10 minutes.

3. Place the flour in a large bowl and make a crater in the center. Add the yeast mixture, remaining water and sugar, eggs, vanilla, salt, zest if using, and any excess kirsch from the raisins (but not the raisins) and mix thoroughly. Beat with an electric mixer or a wooden spoon until the dough clears the sides of the bowl, about 5 minutes using a mixer. Do not use a food processor.

4. Lift the dough out of the bowl, then return. With the mixer on low speed, gradually beat in the butter, about 2 minutes. Add the raisins. Cover and let rise in a warm, draft-free place until nearly double in bulk, about 1 1/2 hours.

5. Grease a 12-cup *kugelhopf* pan or 10-inch Bundt pan and, if desired, arrange the almonds in the crevices of the pan. Stir down the dough and pour into the prepared pan (the dough should reach halfway up the sides). Cover and let rise in a warm, draft-free place until nearly double in bulk, about 1 hour.

6. Preheat the oven to 350 degrees.

7. Bake until golden brown and a knife inserted in the center comes out clean, 50 to 60 minutes. (If the *kugelhopf* browns too quickly, cover loosely with aluminum foil.) Let cool in the pan for 10 minutes, then unmold while still warm and transfer to a rack. Just before serving, sprinkle with the confectioners' sugar.

AN ALSATIAN ACCENT

The French province of Alsace, the site of the original Ashkenaz, lies between the Rhine River and the Vosges Mountains. Separated historically and geographically from France and Germany, it has long been claimed and influenced by both countries. After its acquisition by France in 1648, Alsace remained semiautonomous until the French Revolution. Following the absorption of Provence into France in 1481 and the subsequent expulsion of its Jews, Alsace remained the only part of modern France in which Jews resided until the beginning of the eighteenth century. A government report published in 1784 listed the Jewish population in the province at almost 20,000. The number increased to 50,000 by 1970, before a large influx of North African Jews in the 1960s altered the size and makeup of the community. The newcomers tended to be very religious, while many of the old-timers had been assimilated.

Alsatian cuisine reflects a strong German influence. Few spices besides cinnamon are used. Cabbage is the predominant vegetable. Noodles and dumplings enjoy greater popularity here than in the rest of France. Foods are cooked in fat, particularly goose fat, not butter.

Jewish cooking became an integral part of general Alsatian cuisine, and many dishes include the term *à la Juive* ("in the Jewish style"). Sabbath dessert generally consists of *kuchen, kugelhopf, tarte Alsacienne,* or chocolate mousse. Traditional Purim treats include doughnuts, which both the Alsatians and the Dutch claim to have invented, and gingerbread men. The plums, raspberries, cherries, pears, apples, and apricots of the region are used as fresh fruit for pastry, as well as in world-renowned liqueurs.

Apfelkuchen ❧ *(German Apple Coffee Cake)*

9 TO 12 SERVINGS

Among my mother's most cherished possessions is a small, noticeably worn metal file box purchased at the beginning of her marriage. It is crammed with index cards containing her favorite recipes collected over more than fifty years. Some of these dishes, such as this apple coffee cake, were added well before I was born.

Kuchen, literally "baked good" in German, refers to an assortment of coffee cakes that originated in the central European kitchen. The original treat was made from a rich yeast dough, although today there are also chemically leavened versions. A *kuchen* can be a plain cake or topped with streusel, cheese, custard, fruit, or any combination. Fruit kuchen, making use of seasonal produce, are commonly served on the Sabbath, Rosh Hashanah, and Sukkot, while cheese versions are traditional for Shavuot, Hanukkah, and the meal following Yom Kippur.

---

1 recipe (2¹/4 pounds) Basic Sweet Yeast Dough (page 35) or Rich Sweet Yeast Dough (page 36)

5 to 7 medium cooking apples, such as Golden Delicious, Granny Smith, Gravenstein, Greening, Jonathan, Macoun, Pippin, Starr, Winesap, Yellow Transparent, or any combination, peeled, cored, and sliced

¹/4 cup (¹/2 stick) unsalted butter or margarine, melted

¹/2 cup sugar

1¹/2 to 2 teaspoons ground cinnamon (optional)

¹/3 cup raisins, chopped dried apricots, or chopped walnuts (optional)

---

1. Prepare the dough through Step 4.
2. Press the dough into a greased 14-by-10-inch baking pan, 13-by-9-inch pan, or two 9-inch round pans. Or form the dough into a 12-inch round and transfer to a baking sheet lined with parchment paper or greased.
3. Arrange the apples over the top and brush with the butter. Combine the sugar and cinnamon if using, and sprinkle over the apples. If desired, scatter the raisins over the top. Let stand until nearly double in bulk, about 50 minutes.
4. Preheat the oven to 375 degrees (350 degrees if using a glass pan).
5. Bake until golden brown, about 30 minutes. Let cool in the pan for 10 minutes, then transfer to a rack. The cake can be frozen for up to 2 weeks and reheated, unthawed, in a 350-degree oven for about 20 minutes.

VARIATIONS

Aprikoshkuchen (German Apricot Coffee Cake): Substitute 2 pounds halved or quartered and pitted fresh or well-drained canned apricots for the apples.

Zwetschenkuchen (German Plum Coffee Cake): Substitute 2 pounds halved or quartered and pitted Italian plums for the apples.

Kaesekuchen (German Cheese Coffee Cake): Puree 1 1/2 cups ricotta or drained cottage cheese, 2 large eggs, 6 tablespoons sugar, 2 tablespoons cornstarch, 1 tablespoon lemon juice, 1/2 teaspoon vanilla extract, and a pinch of salt until smooth and spread over the dough. If desired, omit the fruit.

Beesting Kuchen (German Almond Coffee Cake): Omit the apples. Melt 6 tablespoons butter in a small saucepan. Add 1/3 cup sugar, 3/4 cup sliced almonds, 2 tablespoons milk, 1/2 teaspoon ground cinnamon, and 1/4 teaspoon salt and stir until the sugar dissolves. Simmer for 1 minute. Let cool slightly. Using your fingers, lightly poke indentations in the dough, then spread the almond mixture over the top.

GERMAN GASTRONOMY

In the wake of Charlemagne's rule, Franco-Germany emerged as a major center of Jewish learning and life. Subsequently, the Jews of the area suffered a series of anti-Semitic attacks, including the Crusades, the Rindfleisch massacres (1298–99), the Armleder massacres (1336–37), and the Black Death massacres (1348–50). Most surviving Ashkenazim relocated to more favorable conditions in the east. A small number, however, remained in Germany, which disintegrated into a collection of small feudal states. When life grew intolerable in one of these states, the oppressed Jews sought haven in another, usually living in small towns. Facing prohibitions from pursuing most occupations, the Jews struggled to earn a living in such fields as money lending and petty trade. Only in the eighteenth century were German Jews able to use their business experience to take advantage of the growing opportunities emerging in the face of industrialization. Some, most notably the Rothschilds, managed to amass incredible fortunes. A new wave of anti-Semitism in the nineteenth century induced many German Jews to emigrate to America, where quite a few—including families with such famous names as Guggenheim, Strauss, Belmont, Lehman, Warburg, Fleischmann, and Schiff—found phenomenal success.

By force of their numbers and affluence, German Jews dominated the American Jewish community until the early twentieth century. They were then overwhelmed by a massive wave of eastern European immigrants; it was eastern European culture and cooking rather than German that most impacted the American Jewish community. The newcomers, however, did acknowledge the more sophisticated German baked goods by adopting a wide range of German breads, *kuchen,* and tortes.

Kuchen-Buchen ❧ *(Central European Cocoa-Dipped Bubble Ring)*

1 LARGE CAKE

The name of this variation of *kuchen* is typical of Yiddish rhyming. The dough is shaped into small balls, coated with cocoa sugar, and stacked in a deep pan to bake. Diners pull individual balls of dough from the loaf or cut the cake into wedges.

1 recipe (2¹/4 pounds) Basic Sweet Yeast Dough (page 35) or Rich Sweet Yeast Dough (page 36)	*¹/4 cup unsweetened cocoa powder, preferably alkalized (Dutch processed)*
³/4 cup sugar	*About ¹/2 cup (1 stick) unsalted butter or margarine, melted*

1. Prepare the dough through Step 4.
2. Combine the sugar and cocoa powder. Shape the dough into 1-inch balls. Dip each ball into the butter, then roll in the cocoa sugar to coat. Arrange in layers in a greased 10-inch tube pan. Cover and let rise in a warm place until nearly double in bulk, about 45 minutes.
3. Position a rack in the lower third of the oven. Preheat the oven to 375 degrees.
4. Bake until golden brown, 40 to 50 minutes. Loosen the sides of the loaf and invert onto a serving platter. Serve slightly warm or at room temperature.

HINT: ❧ In place of a tube pan, place a custard cup or foil-lined 1¹/2-inch tube in the center of a round, deep baking pan or casserole.

VARIATIONS

Double the cocoa sugar and press a teaspoon of it into the center of each dough ball. Press the edges together and reshape into balls.

Arany Galuska (Hungarian "Golden Dumpling" Coffee Cake): Substitute 1 cup sugar mixed with 1¹/2 teaspoons ground cinnamon for the cocoa sugar. If desired, add ¹/2 to 1 cup (2 to 4 ounces) finely chopped walnuts or pecans to the cinnamon sugar.

Makosh ❧ *(Central European Poppy Seed Roll)*

2 MEDIUM CAKES

One of my roommates during my freshman year at college came from a Hungarian Brooklyn family. He always spent the Sabbath at home and every Sunday returned to the dormitory loaded with loaves of his mother's *makosh* and *kakosh* (chocolate roll) well protected in aluminum foil. They were inevitably gone within a few days, if not sooner. To this day, my mouth starts watering when I reflect on those thin layers of yeast dough and filling.

Originally these cake rolls were filled with *mohn* (German for "poppy seeds"); thus *mohn kuchen* (poppy seed cake) became *makosh* or *makoshbeigli* and, in Poland, *makowiec.* Enterprising cooks experimented with a variety of other fillings to produce a host of new tastes, including cinnamon, almond paste, apricot, raspberry, and walnut. When cocoa powder (*kahkahaw* in Yiddish) was introduced from America, it soon became the most popular filling, and appropriately this form of the pastry acquired the name *kakosh.*

Makosh is generally made in a large batch using 3 to 5 pounds of flour, as these loaves tend to disappear very quickly. Many Hungarians serve *makosh, kakosh,* or one of the other variations on the Sabbath and at various life-cycle events.

Poppy Seed Filling:

3 cups (about 1 pound) poppy seeds

1½ cups water

1½ cups sugar or honey, or 1 cup honey and ⅓ cup light corn syrup

2½ tablespoons fresh lemon juice

½ teaspoon grated lemon zest

Pinch of salt

1 recipe (2¼ pounds) Rich Sweet Yeast Dough (page 36) or Extra-Rich Sweet Yeast Dough (page 36)

Egg wash (1 large egg beaten with 1 teaspoon water)

---

1. To make the filling: In a nut grinder, coffee grinder, food processor, or blender, grind the poppy seeds. Or seal the poppy seeds in a plastic bag and crush using a rolling pin. Combine all the ingredients in a small saucepan and simmer over medium-low heat, stirring frequently, until the mixture thickens, about 12 minutes. Let cool. Store in the refrigerator for up to 1 week.

2. Prepare the dough through Step 4.

3. Preheat the oven to 350 degrees. Line a large baking sheet with parchment paper or grease.

4. Divide the dough in half. On a lightly floured surface, roll out each piece into a very thin rectangle. (The thinner the dough, the thinner the cake layers.) Spread with the filling, leaving a 1/2-inch border along the edges. Starting from a long edge, roll up jelly roll style. Place on the prepared sheet. (Baking without letting the cake rise produces thin alternating layers of pastry and filling. For slightly thicker cake layers, cover and let rise for about 40 minutes.) Brush with the egg wash.

5. Bake until golden brown, 35 to 45 minutes. Let cool on the baking sheet for 5 minutes, then transfer to a rack and let cool completely. Wrap and store at room temperature for up to 3 days or in the freezer for up to 2 months.

VARIATION

Poppy Seed Buns: Cut the rolls into 1-inch-thick slices, place cut side down on a greased baking sheet, flatten slightly, and bake at 350 degrees until golden brown, about 20 minutes.

MAKOSH VARIATIONS ❧

Kakosh *(Hungarian Chocolate Roll)*

2/3 *cup sugar*

1/3 *cup unsweetened cocoa powder*

1/2 *teaspoon ground cinnamon or vanilla sugar (optional)*

Vegetable oil or melted margarine for brushing

Combine the sugar, cocoa powder, and cinnamon if using. Brush the rolled dough with the oil before sprinkling with the cocoa mixture. Use in place of the poppy seed filling.

Zimtkuchen *(Hungarian Cinnamon Roll)*

1/2 cup light brown or granulated sugar	*1 teaspoon ground cinnamon*
1/4 cup (1/2 stick) unsalted butter or margarine, softened	*1 cup raisins (optional)*

Combine all the ingredients. Use in place of the poppy seed filling.

Mandel Kuchen *(Central European Almond Roll)*

2 cups (8 ounces) ground almonds	*2 large egg whites*
3/4 cup sugar	*3 tablespoons rum or almond liqueur*

In a food processor, combine all the ingredients until smooth. Use in place of the poppy seed filling.

Dios Kuchen/Dios Szelet *(Hungarian Walnut Roll)*

2 cups (8 ounces) finely chopped walnuts	*1/4 cup apricot jam or honey*
1/2 cup sugar	*2 to 3 tablespoons rum or fresh lemon juice*

In a food processor, combine all of the ingredients until smooth. Use in place of the poppy seed filling.

POLAND AND THE BALTIC STATES

 In need of population growth and economic development, the leaders of twelfth- and thirteenth-century Poland and Lithuania invited the persecuted Jews of Franco-Germany to settle in their domains. In return, Jews were allowed to compete in every form of commerce and were even granted autonomy in regulating their own communities. Waves of immigration from the west soon made eastern Europe a branch of Ashkenazic Jewry. By the fourteenth century, Poland hosted the world's largest Jewish population, a position maintained for 600 years, until World War II. Gradually eastern European Jewry developed its own distinctive form of Ashkenazic culture.

The initial period of prosperity and security came to an end in 1648, when Bogdan Chmielnicki and his Cossack hordes devastated Polish Jewry, destroying hundreds of Jewish settlements and taking more than 100,000 Jewish lives. Most Poles, both Jews and gentiles, subsequently eked by on a subsistence level. In the eighteenth century, Poland was partitioned by its neighbors, so that many Polish Jews found themselves residents of Lithuania, Germany, Belorussia, Hungary (Galicia), and the Ukraine. Following the assassination of Czar Alexander II in 1881, the Russian government sponsored a series of pogroms, inducing more than two million eastern European Jews (at least a third of the total) to immigrate to the United States. The newcomers overwhelmed the smaller extant Sephardic and German communities, and as a result, the eastern European form of Ashkenazic cooking became that which most Americans associate with Jewish food.

The fare of northern Poland and the Baltic states was strongly affected by that of Russia and Scandinavia, while the southern part of the country reflects the influences of Germany, the Ukraine, and Hungary. Polish and Baltic cooking is distinguished from that of western and central European Ashkenazim by the scarcity of herbs and spices and the addition of regional ingredients such as kasha (buckwheat) and rhubarb, as well as Slavic dishes, including knishes (baked dumplings), *pirogen,* and *kissel* (berry pudding). Poland has long boasted an advanced dairy industry; sour cream, butter, and fresh cheeses became staples of the diet and common additions to dishes. Apples and plums are the primary fruits. Northern Polish desserts tend to be rather simple such as fruit compote, *varenikes* (fruit *kreplach*), *babka,* honey cake, *mandelbrot,* and *kichlach* (egg cookies). On the other hand, southern treats, including strudels and tortes, are generally more elaborate and refined. Black tea—freshly made in samovars, served in glass cups, and accompanied with sugar cubes—was the eastern European drink of choice and a common accompaniment to desserts.

Babka ❧ *(Polish Cinnamon Sweet Bread)*

There are actually two styles of *babka* (literally "grandmother's loaf"). The Polish version is similar in texture and shape to a *kugelhopf,* with raisins and nuts mixed into a butter-rich soft dough. The Jewish style, made from a firm yeast dough, is spread with a filling, then rolled up jelly roll style. Cinnamon is the most traditional flavor, but almond, apricot, cheese, chocolate, poppy seed, and walnut are also popular. *Shikkera babka* (literally "drunken *babka*"), sometimes served on Purim, is an unfilled cake drizzled with a rum-, whiskey-, or brandy-laced syrup.

1 recipe (2¹/₄ pounds) Rich Sweet Yeast Dough (page 36) or Extra-Rich Sweet Yeast Dough (page 36)

Cinnamon Filling:
1 cup granulated or brown sugar, or ¹/₂ cup each
2 to 3 teaspoons ground cinnamon
¹/₄ cup (¹/₂ stick) unsalted butter or margarine, melted
2 tablespoons corn syrup or honey
¹/₂ to 1 cup raisins, dried currants, or chopped walnuts (optional)

Streusel Topping (optional):
¹/₂ cup brown sugar, or ¹/₄ cup brown sugar and ¹/₄ cup granulated sugar
¹/₂ cup all-purpose flour
Pinch of salt
³/₄ teaspoon ground cinnamon (optional)
¹/₄ cup (¹/₂ stick) unsalted butter or margarine, chilled

Egg wash (1 large egg beaten with 1 teaspoon water)

1. Prepare the dough through Step 4.
2. To make the filling: Combine the sugar and cinnamon. Stir in the butter and corn syrup to make a smooth paste.
3. Divide the dough in half. Roll each piece into a 12-by-8-inch rectangle about ¹/₂ inch thick. Spread with the cinnamon filling, leaving a 1-inch border on all sides. If desired, sprinkle with the raisins. Starting from a narrow end, roll up jelly roll style, pinching the seams to seal.
4. Place each *babka*, seam side down, in a greased 9-by-5-inch loaf pan, 9-inch tube pan, or 10-inch round cake pan. Cover and let rise until nearly double in bulk, about 1¹/₂ hours at room temperature or overnight in the refrigerator.

5. Preheat the oven to 350 degrees (325 degrees if using glass pans).
6. To make the streusel if using: Combine the sugar, flour, salt, and cinnamon, if desired. Cut in the butter to resemble coarse crumbs.
7. Brush each *babka* with the egg wash and, if desired, sprinkle with the streusel topping. Bake until golden brown and hollow sounding when tapped on the bottom, about 35 minutes. Transfer to a rack and let cool. Wrap and store at room temperature for up to 2 days or in the freezer for up to 2 months.

BABKA VARIATIONS

Kahkahaw Babka *(Polish Chocolate Sweet Bread)*

8 ounces semisweet or bittersweet
   chocolate, finely ground
1/2 cup sugar
1/4 cup unsweetened cocoa powder
3 tablespoons unsalted butter or
   margarine, melted

1 teaspoon vanilla extract
1/2 teaspoon ground cinnamon
   (optional)

Combine all the ingredients. Use as the filling in Step 3.

Nuss Babka *(Polish Nut Sweet Bread)*

3 cups (about 12 ounces) ground
   blanched almonds or walnuts
2 cups brown or granulated sugar, or
   1 cup each

3/4 cup (1 1/2 sticks) unsalted butter or
   margarine, softened
1 tablespoon ground cinnamon, or
   2 teaspoons vanilla extract

In a food processor, combine all the ingredients until smooth. Use as the filling in Step 3.

Fluden ❧ *(Ashkenazic Layered Yeast Cake)*

9 TO 12 SERVINGS

The practice of stacking a filling between thin layers of dough dates back at least 2,000 years. Both the Jerusalem Talmud (Hallah I 57d) and Babylonian Talmud (Berachot 37b) mention *tracta*, a dough rolled out to make layered pastries. On a symbolic level, the dough represented the double portion of Manna collected for the Sabbath, as well as the lower and upper layers of dew that protected the Manna.

This culinary practice survived among Franco-German Jews in various forms, most notably *pashtida* (meat-filled pies) and *fluden,* from the Old French *plata* ("flat"), a cheese-filled pastry that for many centuries served as the favorite dessert of Ashkenazim. The earliest recorded mention of *fluden* occurred in the writings of Rabbi Gershom ben Yehuda of Mainz (a city on the Rhine River) around the year 1000 CE in which he discussed an argument between his teacher, Rabbi Yehuda Hacohain ben Meir Leontin (from Lyon, France), and Rabbi Eleazar ben Gilo over whether it was permitted "to eat bread with meat even if it was baked in an oven with a cheese dish called *fluden.*" Since this disagreement persisted for centuries, similar references appear in rabbinic writings on a frequent basis throughout the period.

Sometimes *fluden* was made with several thick layers so that each one could be separately removed and served at different times while the remaining layers of filling stayed fresh. As the dish evolved, the hard, thick pastry was replaced with thinner layers of soft-wheat pastry or rich yeast dough and was served by cutting into sections. For Purim, some people cut it into triangles. Cooks developed several other fillings. The original cheese version became a traditional Rosh Hashanah dish. (Franco-German Jews waited only one hour between eating meat and dairy, so a cheese *fluden* could be served as dessert soon after a meat meal.) Apples or raisins, sometimes combined with cheese, were common on Sukkot and Simchat Torah. Jam, nut, and poppy seed fillings were used on other festivals. All of these variations were commonplace on the Sabbath.

With the destruction of the Franco-German Jewish communities, the popularity of *fluden* declined. Nonetheless, descendants of this pastry are still served by some Ashkenazim. Alsatians prepare a similar dish called *schalet à la Juive,* consisting of an apple filling rolled up in a yeast dough or, as described by *Larousse Gastronomique,* a sort of deep-dish apple pie made with layers of flaky pastry. Hungarians often use a different filling for each layer in what they call *flodni* or *zserbo/jerbeau;* Romanians call it *flandi.* For a pastry version of *fluden,* see pages 174–75.

Dough:

1 (¹/4-ounce) package (2¹/4 teaspoons)
   active dry yeast, or 1 (0.6-ounce)
   cake fresh yeast

¹/4 cup warm water (105 to 110 degrees
   for dry yeast; 80 to 85 degrees for
   fresh yeast)

2 tablespoons sugar

1³/4 cups (3¹/2 sticks) unsalted butter or
   margarine, softened

¹/2 cup water, at room temperature

3 large egg yolks

1 large egg

1 teaspoon table salt, or 2 teaspoons
   kosher salt

About 4 cups unbleached all-purpose
   flour

Filling:

10 to 12 medium apples or pears,
   peeled, cored, and thinly sliced

1¹/2 to 2 cups (6 to 8 ounces) chopped
   blanched almonds, hazelnuts, or
   walnuts, or 1 cup fine bread crumbs

1¹/4 to 1¹/2 cups sugar, or 1 cup sugar
   and ¹/2 cup (6 ounces) apricot or
   strawberry preserves

1 teaspoon ground cinnamon

¹/2 teaspoon grated nutmeg (optional)

³/4 cup raisins, chopped dried apricots,
   or chopped dates (optional)

Egg wash (1 large egg beaten with
   1 tablespoon water)

Additional sugar for sprinkling

1. Preheat the oven to 350 degrees (325 degrees if using a glass pan). Grease a 13-by-9-inch baking pan.

2. To make the dough: Dissolve the yeast in ¹/4 cup warm water. Add 1 teaspoon sugar and let stand until foamy, 5 to 10 minutes. Meanwhile, beat the butter and remaining sugar until light and fluffy, about 5 minutes. Mix in the yeast mixture, ¹/2 cup water, egg yolks, egg, and salt. Gradually add enough of the flour to make a soft, manageable dough. Place on a lightly floured surface and knead until blended.

3. To make the filling: Combine all the filling ingredients.

4. Divide the dough into 3 equal pieces. On a lightly floured surface, roll the dough pieces into 13-by-9-inch rectangles. Fit a rectangle into the prepared pan and spread with half of the filling. Repeat layering with the remaining dough and filling, ending with a layer of dough. Brush the top with the egg wash and lightly sprinkle with the additional sugar.

5. Bake until golden brown, about 40 minutes. Let cool. *Fluden* is best if not refrigerated.

FLUDEN VARIATIONS ❧

Apfelschalet *(Western European Apple Roll)*

Making *fluden* into a roll is very popular in Alsace and the adjacent parts of southwestern Germany, where it is called *apfelbuwele* ("apple boy") and served on the Sabbath. Cut the amount of apple filling in half. In Step 4, roll the dough into a 24-by-18-inch rectangle about 1/8 inch thick. Spread with the filling, leaving a 1-inch border on all sides. Starting from a long edge, roll up jelly roll style, pinching the edges to seal. Place on a greased baking sheet or bend into a circle and place in a greased 10-inch round pan. Bake as directed in Step 5.

Kaese Fluden *(Ashkenazic Layered Cheese Pastry)*

On Shavuot, this version, sometimes called Mount Sinai cake, is traditionally garnished with white flowers as a symbol of purity.

4 cups (2 pounds) pot, farmer's, or ricotta cheese, or 1 pound small curd cottage cheese or pot cheese and 1 pound cream cheese	*1/4 cup all-purpose flour, or 1/2 cup fine semolina or farina*
4 large eggs	*2 teaspoons vanilla extract, or 1 tablespoon grated lemon zest*
About 1 cup sugar	*Pinch of salt*
	1/2 to 1 cup (3 to 5 ounces) golden raisins (optional)

Combine all the ingredients. Use as the filling in Step 4.

Feigen Fluden *(Ashkenazic Layered Fig Pastry)*

My sister and brother-in-law returned from a trip to Paris, bringing me a gift of a bottle of the most delicious Moroccan fig liqueur. Several years later I was surprised and delighted to discover this liqueur in a New York City liquor store.

4 quarts water	*12 cups (about 3 pounds) dried figs, stemmed*
8 tea bags	
1 cup lemon juice	*1 1/3 cups sugar*
About 1 tablespoon grated lemon zest	*1/2 cup fig liqueur, kirsch, or other fruit liqueur*
6 to 8 (3-inch) sticks cinnamon	

1. Bring the water to a boil in a large saucepan. Reduce the heat to low, add the tea bags, lemon juice, zest, and cinnamon sticks, and simmer for 2 minutes. Remove the tea bags. Add the figs and simmer until tender, about 5 minutes. Using a slotted spoon, remove the figs.
2. In a food processor or blender, process the figs, sugar, and liqueur until well blended but not smooth. If necessary, add a little of the cooking liquid to make a jamlike consistency.
3. Use as the filling in Step 4.

Zserbo/Jerbeau *(Hungarian Walnut* Fluden*)*

6 cups (1½ pounds) finely chopped walnuts	1 cup (12 ounces) apricot jam or apple jelly
1½ cups sugar	

Omit the apple filling. In Step 4, divide the dough into 4 equal pieces; roll each into a thin 13-by-9-inch rectangle. Combine the nuts and sugar. Over each dough layer (except the top one), spread about ⅓ cup jam and sprinkle with about 2½ cups of the nut mixture.

Variation

Zserbo is sometimes topped with a chocolate glaze. Invert the baked cake onto a rack or cookie sheet and let cool. To make the glaze: Melt 10 ounces semisweet or bittersweet chocolate with ½ cup (1 stick) butter or margarine and ½ cup water, stirring until smooth. Or dissolve 6 tablespoons unsweetened cocoa powder in 6 tablespoons boiling water; stir in 6 tablespoons vegetable oil, then 12 ounces (about 3 cups plus 2 tablespoons) confectioners' sugar. Pour either glaze over the inverted *fluden* and let stand until set.

Flodni *(Hungarian Nut-and-Apple* Fluden*)*

2 cups (about 8 ounces) ground walnuts	About 1 cup Prune Lekvar (page 75),
½ to 1 cup sugar	Apricot Lekvar (page 75), or
1 tablespoon ground cinnamon	Ashkenazic Poppy Seed Filling
1 teaspoon grated lemon zest	(page 73)
3 tablespoons fresh lemon juice	
6 large apples, peeled, cored, and sliced or coarsely grated	

Omit the apple filling on page 57. In Step 4, divide the dough into 4 equal pieces and roll each into a thin 13-by-9-inch rectangle. Combine the nuts, sugar, cinnamon, zest, and lemon juice. Remove about ²/3 cup of the nut mixture and mix with the grated apples. Spread the remaining nut mixture over the bottom layer of dough. Spread the apple mixture over the next layer. Spread the lekvar over the third layer.

ROMANIA

 The first Romanian state, Walachia, emerged on the Balkan peninsula in the early fourteenth century, followed by Moldavia in 1349. Both states shortly fell to the surging Ottoman Empire and would remain under its control until the nineteenth century. The de facto union of the states was formalized in 1859, at which time the new country adopted its current name.

According to a local legend, the first Jews arrived in the Balkans during the reign of King Xerxes of Persia. The small Jewish community was enhanced by a progression of refugees: Jews from the oppressive Byzantine Empire; Hungarians relocating after their expulsion in 1367; Sephardim taking up the Turkish sultan's invitation to settle in his realm; Polish Jews fleeing the Chmielnicki massacres; and Russians moving southward after the czarist expulsions. Harsh repression beginning in the 1880s led to a mass immigration to Israel and America. Of the more than 600,000 Jews living in Greater Romania at the onset of World War II, nearly half were murdered. About one-third of the survivors took the opportunity to immigrate, primarily to Israel, and more followed through the 1960s. Today only about 14,000 Jews remain.

Romania's cuisine is a composite of its more powerful neighbors, and its baking evinces strong Hungarian and Turkish influences, including strudel, *palacsinta* (crepes), and baklava. *Fladni* (multilayered pastry) and honey cake are traditional on Rosh Hashanah, and *chremslach* on Passover, reflecting an Ashkenazic heritage. A Sabbath breakfast might feature sweet cheese turnovers and *kipplach* (poppy seed horns). *Kindli* (wrapped pastries) are popular Purim treats. Pastry is generally served with Turkish coffee.

Pogácha ❧ *(Hungarian Sour Cream Yeast Cookies)*

ABOUT 20 LARGE COOKIES

In many Hungarian households, no Sabbath would be complete without at least one type of cookie for family and guests to nosh. Among the most popular is *pogácha*, also spelled *pogácsa* and *pogacheles*. These subtle treats evolved from a *schmaltz*-yeast biscuit, which in turn derived from a simple Turkish bread called *bogaca*. Cooks also developed a more modern baking powder version (see page 156).

---

1 ($1/4$-ounce) package ($2^{1}/4$ teaspoons)
   active dry yeast, or 1 (0.6-ounce)
   cake fresh yeast
3 tablespoons warm milk
1 cup (2 sticks) butter, softened
$3^{1}/2$ cups unbleached all-purpose flour
1 teaspoon table salt, or 2 teaspoons
   kosher salt

6 tablespoons sugar
$1/2$ cup sour cream
2 large egg yolks
Egg wash (1 large egg beaten with
   1 teaspoon water)

---

1. Dissolve the yeast in the milk. Beat the butter until smooth. Blend in the flour and salt, about 2 minutes. Beat in the sugar, about 2 minutes. Add the yeast mixture, sour cream, and egg yolks and beat until the mixture is smooth and forms a ball, about 2 minutes.
2. On a lightly floured surface, roll the dough into a 13-by-9-inch rectangle about $1/2$ inch thick. Fold over the top one-third of the dough, then fold over the bottom one-third. Cover and refrigerate for 20 minutes. Roll out, fold as above, and refrigerate for another 20 minutes. Roll into a $1/4$-inch-thick square. Bring the right and left sides together to meet in the center, then fold the top and bottom to meet in the center. Wrap in plastic wrap and refrigerate overnight.
3. On a lightly floured surface, roll the dough into a 10-by-8-inch rectangle about $3/4$ inch thick. Using a floured 2-inch biscuit cutter, cut out rounds. Reroll and cut out the scraps. Place on a baking sheet lined with parchment paper or greased. Cover and let rise for about 40 minutes.
4. Preheat the oven to 350 degrees.
5. Brush the tops of the cookies with the egg wash. Bake until golden brown, about 15 minutes. Transfer to a rack and let cool. Wrap and store at room temperature for up to 2 days or in the freezer for up to 2 months.

Kindli ⌁ *(Ashkenazic Filled Yeast Pastries)*

ABOUT 18 PASTRIES

This pastry, also called *baigli* and akin to *rugelach*, resembles a baby wrapped in a blanket—thus the whimsical name *kindli* ("little children"). Germans and Austrians prefer a poppy seed filling, while Hungarians favor a walnut mixture. Romanians like all types. *Kindli* are popular Purim fare; the poppy seed filling and wine added to the dough are appropriate for the tone of the day. A sour cream dough (see *kipfel*, pages 64–65) is used to make this pastry for Shavuot and other celebrations for which a dairy meal is traditional. For a cookie dough version of *kindli*, see pages 172–73.

Dough:

1 (¹/₄-ounce) package (2¹/₄ teaspoons) active dry yeast, or 1 (0.6-ounce) cake fresh yeast

¹/₄ cup warm water (105 to 110 degrees for dry yeast; 80 to 85 degrees for fresh yeast)

¹/₂ cup confectioners' sugar

¹/₂ cup sweet red wine or water

³/₄ cup (1¹/₂ sticks) vegetable shortening, unsalted butter, or margarine, softened

2 large egg yolks

¹/₂ teaspoon table salt, or 1 teaspoon kosher salt

1 teaspoon grated lemon zest (optional)

About 4 cups unbleached all-purpose flour

Nut Filling:

1¹/₂ cups (6 ounces) ground walnuts

³/₄ to 1 cup sugar or honey

1 teaspoon grated lemon zest or ground cinnamon

¹/₄ cup raisins (optional)

Egg wash (1 large egg beaten with 1 teaspoon water)

---

1. To make the dough: Dissolve the yeast in the warm water. Stir in 1 teaspoon confectioners' sugar and let stand until foamy, 5 to 10 minutes. Add the wine, remaining sugar, shortening, egg yolks, salt, and zest if using. Blend in 1¹/₂ cups flour. Gradually add enough of the remaining flour to make a soft, workable dough.

2. On a lightly floured surface, knead the dough until smooth and springy, about 5 minutes. Place in an oiled bowl, turning to coat. Cover and let rise in a warm place until double in bulk, about 1¹/₂ hours, or in the refrigerator overnight.

3. To make the filling: Combine all the filling ingredients.

4. Punch down the dough. Fold over and press together several times. Divide into 1-inch balls, cover, and let stand for 10 minutes. On a lightly floured surface, roll out each ball into a thin round about 3 inches in diameter. Spoon a heaping tablespoon of the filling into the center of each round. Bring the top and bottom edges together over the filling, then bring the other 2 sides together, tucking them in the center like a baby's blanket.

5. Place on a baking sheet lined with parchment paper or lightly greased. Cover loosely with plastic wrap or a towel and let rise until puffy, about 20 minutes.

6. Preheat the oven to 375 degrees.

7. Brush the *kindli* with the egg wash. Bake until golden brown, about 20 minutes. Transfer to a rack and let cool. Wrap and store at room temperature for up to 2 days or in the freezer for up to 2 months.

VARIATIONS

In place of the nut filling, use about 1 1/2 cups Ashkenazic Poppy Seed Filling (page 73).

Large Kindli: Divide the dough into fourths, roll out each piece into a 6- to 7-inch round, spread with 1/3 cup filling, and fold the edges together as above.

Pressburger Kipplach (Slovakian Yeast Crescents): Spread the filling along 1 edge of the dough rounds, roll up from the filling side, and bend the ends to produce a crescent.

NOTE: ❧ This yeast pastry is named after Pressburg, the German name for Bratislava, one of the oldest and most important European Jewish communities and commonly considered the dividing line between eastern and western Ashkenazim. Today Bratislava is the capital of Slovakia. To complicate matters further, this pastry is also called *Pozsonyi kifli* after the Hungarian name for Pressburg/Bratislava.

Kipfel ❧ *(Austrian Filled Yeast Crescents)*

In 1683, the Turks began a lengthy siege of Vienna, Austria, a city already weakened by an outbreak of the bubonic plague four years earlier that had wiped out a third of the population. The frustrated Turks undertook to secretly dig tunnels under the barricades in the darkness of night. The city's bakers, at work in the wee hours of the morning, heard the noise of the construction, alerted the authorities, and foiled the underground attack. With the military help of the Poles, Bavarians, and others, the Austrians soon repelled the Turks. The bakers were acknowledged for their part in the victory and, to celebrate the occasion, created various special pastries in the shape of a crescent (*kipferlin* in German), the symbol found on the Ottoman flag. Three centuries later, many of these pastries and their descendants—including croissants, *nusskipferlin* (nut crescents), and *rugelach*—remain popular throughout much of the world. This dough is similar to *kugelhopf* but uses sour cream as the liquid.

Dough:

2 cups unbleached all-purpose flour

1 (¼-ounce) package (2¼ teaspoons) active dry yeast, or 1 (0.6-ounce) cake fresh yeast

½ cup sour cream

2 large egg yolks

½ teaspoon table salt, or 1 teaspoon kosher salt

½ cup (1 stick) unsalted butter, divided into 1-tablespoon pieces and softened

Filling:

1 cup ground blanched almonds, hazelnuts, pecans, or walnuts

½ cup granulated or brown sugar, or ¼ cup each

½ teaspoon vanilla extract, or 1 tablespoon fresh lemon juice

1 tablespoon grated orange zest, or 1 teaspoon ground cinnamon (optional)

2 large egg whites

Coating:

½ cup confectioners' sugar

¼ cup granulated sugar

1. To make the dough: Put the flour into a large bowl and make a crater in the center. Place the yeast, sour cream, egg yolks, and salt in the crater and beat with an electric mixer or wooden spoon until the dough clears the sides of the bowl, about 5 minutes.
2. Lift the dough out of the bowl, then return. With the mixer on low speed, gradually beat in the butter, about 2 minutes. (The dough will be very soft.) Divide into 3 equal pieces, form into balls, flatten, wrap, and refrigerate for at least 4 hours or up to 1 day.
3. Preheat the oven to 325 degrees. Line a large baking sheet with parchment paper or lightly grease.
4. To make the filling: Combine the nuts, sugar, vanilla, and zest if using. Beat the egg whites on low until foamy, about 30 seconds. Increase the speed to high and beat until stiff but not dry. Fold into the nut mixture.
5. To make the coating: Combine the sugars and lightly sprinkle about 1/4 cup for each piece of dough onto a flat surface.
6. Place each piece of dough on the sugar and roll out into a 1/8-inch-thick round about 10 to 12 inches in diameter. Cut into equal wedges—8 for large pastries, 12 for medium pastries, or 16 for small pastries.
7. Place 1 tablespoon of the filling on the wide end of each large wedge (2 teaspoons on each medium wedge; 1 teaspoon on each small wedge). Roll up from the wide end to the point. Place on the prepared baking sheet, seam side down, and curve the ends to form a crescent shape.
8. Bake (without rising) until golden brown, about 20 minutes. Transfer to a rack and let cool. Wrap and store at room temperature for up to 2 days or in the freezer for up to 2 months.

VARIATIONS

Omit the egg whites from the filling. Brush the dough rounds with 1/4 cup (1/2 stick) melted butter and sprinkle with the nut mixture, leaving a 1/2-inch border at the outer rim.

Kipfel Kuchen (Austrian Crescent Coffee Cake): Arrange the crescents in a greased 8-inch square baking pan, cover, and let rise until nearly doubled, about 45 minutes. Or double the recipe and place in a 13-by-9-inch pan. Bake in a 350-degree oven until golden brown, 20 to 30 minutes.

Kynuté Knedlíky ❧ *(Czech Yeast Dumplings)*

It is a rare Czech meal that fails to include some sort of dumpling, either in the soup, as a side dish, or for dessert. Dumplings may be made from bread, flour, semolina, potatoes, matza, cheese, or even liver. This one is a poached sweet bread dough. The fruit-filled variation, called *pflaumen en schlaffrok* ("plums in nightgowns") in Germany, is a popular Czech Sukkot and Simchat Torah treat that makes use of seasonal produce. At other times, cooks substitute a spoonful of *povidla* (plum preserves) or other fruit preserves for the fresh fruit. By tradition, no Czech will use a knife to cut a dumpling, as it is said to spoil the flavor.

---

1 (1/4-ounce) package (2 1/4 teaspoons) active dry yeast, or 1 (0.6-ounce) cake fresh yeast

1/2 cup warm water (105 to 110 degrees for dry yeast; 80 to 85 degrees for fresh yeast), or 1/4 cup warm water and 1/4 cup milk

2 to 4 tablespoons sugar

3 large egg yolks, or 2 large eggs

1/2 teaspoon table salt, or 1 teaspoon kosher salt

1/2 teaspoon vanilla extract (optional)

1/4 teaspoon grated lemon zest (optional)

About 2 cups unbleached all-purpose flour

1/2 cup (1 stick) butter or margarine, melted

Sugar, cinnamon sugar, or poppy seeds for sprinkling (optional)

---

1. Dissolve the yeast in 1/4 cup warm water. Stir in 1 teaspoon sugar and let stand until foamy, 5 to 10 minutes.
2. Add the remaining water, remaining sugar, eggs, salt, and vanilla and/or zest if using. Stir in the flour, 1/2 cup at a time, to make a soft dough. On a lightly floured surface, knead until smooth and springy, about 5 minutes. Place in an oiled bowl, turning to coat. Cover and let rise until double in bulk, about 1 hour.
3. Punch down the dough. Fold over and press together several times. Divide into 12 equal pieces, form into balls, cover, and let rise until nearly doubled, about 30 minutes.
4. Bring about 3 quarts of lightly salted water to a boil in a 4-quart saucepan. In batches, carefully lower the dumplings into the water, cover, and boil until dry and spongy on the inside, about 15 minutes. Remove with a slotted spoon. Repeat with the remaining

dumplings. Drizzle the *knedlíky* with the melted butter and sprinkle with the sugar. Serve warm.

Variation

Kynuté Ovocné Knedlíky (Czech Fruit-Filled Yeast Dumplings): Roll the dough into a 16-by-12-inch rectangle about 1/2 inch thick and cut into 4-inch squares. Place a pitted Italian plum or apricot (if the fruit is big, use a half for each dumpling) in the center of each square. If desired, insert a sugar cube or 1 teaspoon cinnamon sugar into the cavity of the fruit. The sugar melts during cooking, producing a sugar sauce. Press the edges of the dough together to enclose the fruit, form into balls, cover, and let stand until puffy, about 15 minutes.

RAISINS

Sustain me with raisin cakes (according to Rashi),
spread out apples before me . . .
—SONG OF SONGS 2:5

 From its home somewhere north of the Fertile Crescent, not far from Mount Ararat, the grape spread across the ancient world. Grape seeds have been found in the earliest archeological excavations. Paintings on the walls of Egyptian tombs depict viticulture. Vines were among the plants included in the hanging gardens of Babylon. Grapes so influenced life in ancient Israel that the Bible mentioned eighteen different words for the branches. Soon after grapes were discovered, man learned to make wine from them and to create new varieties.

Raisins are dried sweet grapes, the best sun-dried on paper-lined trays. All grapes, whatever their natural color, become dark raisins as the result of a natural enzymatic action. However, adding sulfur dioxide to grapes before drying preserves the natural color. The two most popular raisins in most of the world are Muscat (a large, sweet, smoky-flavored black raisin) and Sultana/Sultanieh (a small, amber-colored, rich, pearish-flavored raisin native to Turkey). Most American raisins, both dark and golden, are made from Thompson seedless grapes, a form of Sultana. Golden Thompsons are paler, plumper, and less sweet than Sultanas.

Currants are small raisins made from Black Corinth grapes, named after an isthmus and city in ancient Greece. They are also called Zante currants after the Greek island of the same name. Do not confuse them with fresh currants, which are European berries.

Schnecken ✎ *(German Sweet Rolls)*

I spent many years living in the Washington Heights section of New York City, home to a large and active German Jewish community. On numerous occasions, I shared Sabbath and holiday meals at various households, where I was introduced to the German form of Ashkenazic customs and cooking. Of particular interest to me were the baked goods, such as *vasser challah* (water challah), a lean oval loaf that, in texture, resembles French and Italian bread. Among the treats offered on Shavuot was a delightful cinnamon roll called *schnecken* (German for "snails"), referring to its coiled shape.

Sour cream contains fat, acid, and milk sugars and creates a richer, moister, denser cake than basic sweet yeast dough, traits desired in some smaller pastries and coffee cakes. For nondairy occasions, substitute Rich Sweet Yeast Dough (page 36).

Dough:

1 ($\frac{1}{4}$-ounce) package ($2\frac{1}{4}$ teaspoons) active dry yeast, or 1 (0.6-ounce) cake fresh yeast

$\frac{1}{4}$ cup warm water (105 to 110 degrees for dry yeast; 80 to 85 degrees for fresh yeast)

$\frac{1}{4}$ cup sugar

1 cup (2 sticks) unsalted butter, softened

2 large eggs

1 cup sour cream

$\frac{1}{4}$ cup milk

$\frac{1}{2}$ teaspoon vanilla extract

$\frac{1}{2}$ teaspoon table salt, or 1 teaspoon kosher salt

4 cups unbleached all-purpose flour

Filling:

1 cup granulated or brown sugar, or $\frac{1}{2}$ cup each

$1\frac{1}{2}$ teaspoons ground cinnamon

$\frac{1}{2}$ cup (1 stick) unsalted butter or margarine, melted

1 cup dried currants or chopped raisins

1 cup chopped pecans or walnuts (optional)

---

1. To make the dough: Dissolve the yeast in the warm water. Stir in 1 teaspoon sugar and let stand until foamy, 5 to 10 minutes. Meanwhile, beat the butter until light and fluffy. Gradually beat in the remaining sugar. Beat in the eggs, one at a time. Blend in the yeast mixture, sour cream, milk, vanilla, salt, and $1\frac{1}{2}$ cups flour. Gradually add enough of the remaining flour to make a smooth, very soft dough. Place in an oiled bowl, turning to coat. Cover and refrigerate overnight or up to 3 days.

2. Punch down the dough. Fold over and press together several times. Divide in half and let stand for 10 minutes.
3. To make the filling: Combine the sugar and cinnamon. Roll each dough piece into a $^1/_4$-inch-thick rectangle about 9 by 5 inches. Brush with the melted butter and sprinkle with the cinnamon sugar, currants or raisins, and nuts if using. (A rolling pin helps to spread the filling evenly as well as embed it in the dough.) Starting from a long side, roll up jelly roll style. Using a sharp knife or dental floss, cut into $^1/_2$-inch-thick slices.
4. Place the slices, cut side down, on a baking sheet lined with parchment paper or lightly greased. Cover and let rise until nearly double in bulk, about 1 hour.
5. Preheat the oven to 375 degrees.
6. Bake until golden brown, about 20 minutes. Transfer to a wire rack. Serve warm or at room temperature.

VARIATIONS

Substitute 1 cup light cream for the sour cream and milk.

Caramel-Topped Schnecken: Combine 1 cup brown sugar, $^1/_3$ cup melted butter, and 2 tablespoons corn syrup. Place 1 teaspoon of the mixture in each of 36 greased muffin cups. If desired, place a pecan half in each cup. Place the *schnecken* in the muffin tins. After baking, immediately invert onto a sheet of aluminum foil.

Mishmash Delki ❧ *(Hungarian Cheese Buns)*

This Hungarian form of cheese Danish, also called *decklach* (*delkel* or *deckel* in the singular), is based on techniques that originated in Austria. The butter is enmeshed between layers of dough, as well as incorporated inside, producing a flakier pastry. An Austrian baker brought this technique to Denmark, where his counterparts soon imitated it, and Americans mistakenly started calling these baked goods Danish pastry. Although *delki* takes a little work, the result is a flaky, flavorful pastry.

I mentioned this dish in my first book, *The World of Jewish Cooking,* and subsequently received a letter from a woman in New Jersey relating that her mother used to make it and asking if I could furnish the recipe. I happily complied. Several years later, I received another letter from the woman explaining that her family enjoyed the *delki* and it had become a Shavuot tradition, but apologizing that someone had accidentally thrown out the recipe and asking if I could send it again. Considering such a compliment and the stamped envelope, I could hardly refuse. In case of another mishap, she can now look it up here to uphold her family tradition.

$^1/_2$ *recipe (18 ounces) Basic Sweet Yeast Dough (page 35)*

6 tablespoons ($^3/_4$ stick) unsalted butter, softened

Filling:

$^3/_4$ *cup (6 ounces) pot or drained small-curd cottage cheese*

2 to 3 tablespoons sugar or Prune Lekvar (page 75)

$^1/_2$ *teaspoon vanilla extract*

Pinch of salt

Egg wash (1 large egg beaten with 1 teaspoon cream, milk, or water)

---

1. Prepare the dough through Step 4.
2. On a lightly oiled or floured surface, roll the dough into a 20-by-10-inch rectangle about $^1/_4$ inch thick. Spread with the butter. Bring the right and left sides of the dough together to meet in the center, then bring the top and bottom together to meet in the center. Let stand in the refrigerator for 20 minutes, then roll out and fold twice more, allowing the dough to rest in the refrigerator 20 minutes between each rolling.

3. Preheat the oven to 425 degrees. Line a large baking sheet with parchment paper or grease.

4. To make the filling: Combine all the filling ingredients.

5. Roll the dough into a 25-by-10-inch rectangle and cut into ten 5-inch squares. Spread a heaping tablespoon of the filling on each dough square, leaving a $1/2$-inch border on all sides. Pinch the edges together over the filling.

6. Place seam side down on the prepared baking sheet and brush with the egg wash. Bake until golden brown, about 7 minutes. Transfer to a rack and let cool. Wrap and store at room temperature for up to 1 day or in the freezer for up to 2 months.

Hamantaschen ❧ *(Ashkenazic Triangular Yeast Pastries)*

One of the most popular medieval Teutonic pastries was a triangular-shaped yeast dough treat called *mohntasch* ("poppy seed pocket"). The similarity of the German word for "poppy seed" (*mohn*) to the villain of the Purim story, Haman (pronounced "Ha-mohn" in Hebrew), led to renaming this cookie *hamantasch* ("Haman's pocket"). The first mention of this pastry appears in *Machzor Vitry*, an eleventh-century prayer book compiled by Simcha ben Samuel (died c. 1105) of Vitry, a small town in Marne, France. (*Machzor Vitry* is based upon the rulings and practices of Simcha's teacher, the great commentator Rashi.) Since then, various symbolic meanings have been ascribed to *hamantaschen*. The triangular shape came to represent either Haman's pockets, alluding to the bribes the prime minister took; his ear, which was purported to resemble a donkey's, but also alluding to the medieval custom of cutting off a condemned man's ear before his execution; or his tri-cornered hat, alluding to his hanging (although Persians never wore tri-cornered hats; such headwear became popular in Europe around 1690). Making cookies shaped like various parts of the body was in line with a widespread custom of symbolically eating some part of Haman and thereby erasing his name. According to the mystics, the three corners symbolize the three patriarchs—Abraham, Isaac, and Jacob—whose merit saved their descendants from Haman's plot.

When Ashkenazim moved eastward, they brought the *hamantasch* with them, and it quickly became the preeminent eastern European Purim pastry. On the other hand, these triangular pastries never gained such popularity in western Europe, where gingerbread men became the predominant Purim pastry. In any case, this ancient Purim treat can now be found on the shelves of many modern non-Jewish American bakeries, filled with fruits, nuts (nut-filled versions are also called *pireshkes*), and even chocolate. The most common flavor, however, remains the original poppy seed.

For a cookie dough version of *hamantaschen*, see page 169.

---

1 recipe (2¹/₄ pounds) Rich Sweet Yeast Dough (page 36) or Extra-Rich Sweet Yeast Dough (page 36)

1 recipe (about 2¹/₂ cups) hamantaschen filling (recipes follow), Prune Lekvar (page 75), or Apricot Lekvar (page 75)

Egg wash (1 large egg beaten with 1 tablespoon water)

---

1. Prepare the dough through Step 4.
2. Line several large baking sheets with parchment paper or lightly grease.
3. On a lightly floured surface, roll out the dough ¼ inch thick. Cut out 3- to 4-inch rounds. Place about 1 tablespoon filling in the center of each round. Pinch the edge of the dough to form a point, then pinch two more points together to form a triangle, folding the sides of the dough over the filling, but leaving a little of the filling visible in the center. Place on the prepared baking sheets, cover, and let rise until nearly double, about 45 minutes.
4. Preheat the oven to 350 degrees.
5. Brush the top of the dough with the egg wash. Bake until golden brown, 25 to 30 minutes. Transfer to a rack and let cool. (Wrap and store at room temperature for up to 2 days or in the freezer for up to 2 months.)

HAMANTASCHEN FILLINGS ❧

Mohnfullung (Ashkenazic Poppy Seed Filling)

ABOUT 2½ CUPS

2 cups (about 10 ounces) poppy seeds

1 cup water

1 cup sugar or honey, or ⅔ cup honey
  and ¼ cup light corn syrup

1 to 2 tablespoons fresh lemon juice, or
  ½ teaspoon vanilla extract

Pinch of salt

1 teaspoon grated lemon zest (optional)

½ cup golden raisins (optional)

In a nut grinder, coffee grinder, food processor, or blender, grind the poppy seeds. Or seal the poppy seeds in a plastic bag and crush using a rolling pin. Combine the poppy seeds, water, sugar, lemon juice, salt, and zest if using in a small saucepan and simmer over medium-low heat, stirring frequently, until the mixture thickens, about 10 minutes. Remove from the heat and add the raisins if using. Let cool. Store in the refrigerator for up to 1 week.

Cheese Filling

ABOUT 1¾ CUPS

8 ounces farmer's, pot, or drained cottage cheese	⅓ cup sugar
3 ounces cream cheese, softened	2 tablespoons all-purpose flour
2 large eggs, lightly beaten	1 teaspoon vanilla extract

Beat together the cheeses. Add the remaining ingredients.

Chocolate Filling

ABOUT 2 CUPS

Okay, this is not a traditional *hamantaschen* filling. However, I have found that those Westerners who lack a taste for poppy and prune enjoy this chocolate filling that I developed.

³/₄ cup unsweetened cocoa powder	2 tablespoons vegetable shortening, melted
³/₄ cup sugar	1 cup raisins or chopped nuts (optional)
Pinch of salt	
¹/₄ cup milk, nondairy creamer, or brewed coffee	

Combine all the ingredients.

Prune Lekvar ❧ *(Ashkenazic Prune Preserves)*

ABOUT 2½ CUPS

Ashkenazim use plums and prunes in many dishes, from meat *tzimmes* to numerous desserts. Their role as a traditional *hamantaschen* filling started in 1731 when a Bohemian merchant named David Brandeis was accused of selling poisoned *povidl* (plum jam). After the charge was proved false, he was freed from prison four days before Purim. The Jews of his town celebrated Brandeis's release, and from that day forward, his family marked that occasion as a holiday, the Povidl Purim. Today prune rivals poppy seed in popularity as a *hamantaschen* filling.

---

1 pound (about 4 cups) pitted prunes

2 cups water

About ¹/₃ cup sugar or honey

Pinch of salt

1 tablespoon fresh lemon juice
    (optional)

1 teaspoon grated lemon zest, or
    ¹/₂ teaspoon ground cinnamon
    (optional)

---

1. Combine the prunes and water in a large saucepan and let stand for 2 hours. Bring to a boil, cover, reduce the heat to low, and simmer until very tender, about 30 minutes.
2. Add the sugar, salt, and, if desired, the lemon juice and zest or cinnamon. Mash or puree in a food processor until almost smooth.
3. Return to the saucepan and simmer, stirring constantly, until thickened, about 10 minutes. Let cool. Store in an airtight container in the refrigerator for up to 1 month.

VARIATION

Apricot Lekvar (Apricot Preserves): Substitute 1 pound (about 3 cups) dried apricots for the prunes and increase the sugar to about 1 cup.

PURIM KATAN

 Whenever a community or individual was saved from imminent peril, whether natural or man-made, the anniversary of that deliverance was commemorated with a special Purim Katan (literally "small Purim"). The first known community-wide Purim Katan was instituted in 1039 by Shumuel Hanagid, vizier and military commander of Granada. It was held in commemoration of his escape from an assassination attempt, as well as his victory in a war. More than a hundred community Purim Katans were subsequently instituted across the globe. In some instances, they were commemorated only once or for a few years; in other cases, for centuries.

Many of these near disasters are reminiscent of the original Purim story. Cairo, Egypt, celebrated the day in 1524 on which the recently appointed governor planned to massacre the Jews of his realm but instead was assassinated by forces loyal to Sultan Suleiman. Frankfurt, Germany, memorialized the day in 1614 on which the emperor executed a virulent anti-Semite who was preparing to lead a mob against the Jewish quarters. A double Purim was celebrated on Rhodes on the fourteenth of Adar in 1840, when the sultan removed a governor who had instigated a blood libel against the Jews. Some communities established multiple Purim Katans, such as the town of Ancona, Italy, which memorialized four such acts of deliverance during a hundred-year period.

The day preceding a Purim Katan is customarily observed with a fast. The day itself is commemorated with the recitation of special prayers, gifts of charity to the poor, a festive meal, and in some instances, a public reading of a special *megillah* (story scroll) and the giving of *shalach manot* (food gifts) to friends.

Parmak ❧ *(Sephardic Sweet Bread Sticks)*

ABOUT SIXTY 3-INCH BREAD STICKS

These breakfast treats are also called *biscochatha.*

---

1 recipe biscochos dulces *dough (page 83)*
Egg wash (1 large egg beaten with
  1 teaspoon water)

About ¹/₂ cup sesame seeds for
  sprinkling

---

1. Prepare the dough through Step 3.
2. Roll the dough into 1-inch-thick ropes and cut into 3-inch-long strips. Arrange the pieces, touching each other, on a greased baking sheet or in a greased baking pan. Brush with the egg wash, then sprinkle with the sesame seeds. Let stand for 30 minutes.
3. Preheat the oven to 350 degrees.
4. Bake until golden brown, about 20 minutes. While still warm, separate into 3-inch squares (groups of 3 sticks) or individual sticks. Transfer to a rack and let cool.
5. Lower the oven to 225 degrees.
6. Place the *parmak* on a baking sheet and toast until very crisp, about 2 hours. Transfer to a rack and let cool. Store in an airtight container at room temperature for several weeks.

DESAYUNO

Following Sabbath and festival morning synagogue services, Sephardim return home to a *desayuno* (Ladino for "breakfast"). It is a casual meal consisting primarily of finger foods, including *biscochos,* cheese pastries, *huevos haminados* (brown eggs), cheeses, olives, rice pudding, fresh fruit, jams, yogurt, and an anise-flavored liqueur called *ouzo* in Greek, *raki* in Turkish, and *arak* in Arabic.

Fackasch ❧ *(Moroccan Sweet Yeast Buns)*

My friend Levana Levy Kirschenbaum is a native of Casablanca, Morocco. At seventeen, she moved to France, eventually earning a master's degree in psychology at the Sorbonne as well as becoming proficient in French cooking. In 1972, she relocated to New York City and, at the urging of admirers, began sharing her culinary secrets in cooking classes. Today Levana owns (along with her husband, Maurice Kirschenbaum, and his brothers, Avram and Sol) the Upper West Side kosher restaurant that bears her name. For all her culinary diversity, Levana's main love remains her native Moroccan cuisine, which I am privileged to sample whenever I am a guest at her table. Among my favorites of her dishes are the characteristic Moroccan breads, generally flavored with anise.

1 ($1/4$-ounce) package ($2^{1}/4$ teaspoons) active dry yeast, or 1 (0.6-ounce) cake fresh yeast	1 teaspoon poppy seeds
	$1/2$ teaspoon caraway seeds (optional)
1 cup warm water (105 to 110 degrees for dry yeast; 80 to 85 degrees for fresh yeast)	1 teaspoon table salt, or 2 teaspoons kosher salt
	About 4 cups unbleached all-purpose flour
$1/4$ to $1/2$ cup sugar	Egg wash (1 large egg beaten with 1 teaspoon water)
2 large eggs	
2 tablespoons anise seeds	

1. Dissolve the yeast in $1/4$ cup warm water. Stir in 1 teaspoon sugar and let stand until foamy, 5 to 10 minutes.
2. Add the remaining water, remaining sugar, eggs, seeds, and salt. Blend in $1^{1}/2$ cups flour. Add enough of the remaining flour, $1/2$ cup at a time, to make a workable dough.
3. On a lightly floured surface or in a mixer with a dough hook, knead the dough, adding more flour as necessary, until smooth and springy, about 5 minutes. Place on a flat surface, cover with a large bowl or pot, and let rise in a warm place until nearly double in bulk, about $1^{1}/2$ hours, or in the refrigerator overnight.
4. Punch down the dough. Fold over and press together several times. Let stand for 10 minutes. Divide into 8 equal pieces and form into balls. Place on a baking sheet lined with parchment paper or greased. Flatten slightly, cover, and let rise until nearly double in bulk, about 1 hour.

5. Preheat the oven to 375 degrees.

6. Brush the dough balls with the egg wash. Bake until golden brown and hollow sounding when tapped on the bottom, 30 to 35 minutes. Transfer to a rack and let cool. Wrap and store at room temperature for up to 2 days or in the freezer for up to 2 months.

ANISE

 Anise or aniseed, a native of the Near East, is one of the most ancient spices. It once grew wild throughout Israel and Egypt, where it was greatly valued as a medicine and seasoning. Today anise remains one of the most popular flavoring agents in the Middle East, as well as in parts of Europe.

Anise contains anethol, an essential oil with a licorice-like flavor. The yellowish brown seeds resemble the yellowish green seeds of fennel, but anise seeds are smaller, slightly sweeter, and have a more intense licorice flavor. Fennel is generally used in savory dishes such as sausage, while anise is used in sweeter dishes. Star anise (Chinese anise), which possesses a similar flavor, is a different spice.

Anise, both whole and ground, is used in confections, pasta sauces, sugar cookies, breads, puddings, and peach and plum desserts. Strong anise-flavored liquors abound in the Mediterranean, including Middle Eastern *arak,* Greek *ouzo,* Turkish *raki,* and French *pastis,* as well as the milder liqueur, anisette.

Klaitcha ✎ *(Persian Filled Yeast Pastries)*

Yeast dough pastries are prominent in Syrian, Lebanese, Iraqi, and Iranian communities. Although most of these pastries contain a savory filling, a few are intended for dessert. Unlike European yeast pastries, the dough is neither sweetened nor very rich. Therefore, much of the flavor derives from the filling. These little date- or nut-filled pies are called *kasmay* in Kurdistan, *baba bi tamar* or *kileicha* in Iraq, and *sambusak* in Calcutta. Triangles are called *fatayar*. Whatever the name, they are a favorite for special occasions, served with Turkish coffee or tea.

1 (1/4-ounce) package (2 1/4 teaspoons) active dry yeast, or 1 (0.6-ounce) cake fresh yeast

1 1/4 cups warm water (105 to 110 degrees for dry yeast; 80 to 85 degrees for fresh yeast), or 1/4 cup warm water and 1 cup milk

1 teaspoon sugar

1/2 cup (1 stick) unsalted butter or margarine, melted

1/2 teaspoon table salt, or 1 teaspoon kosher salt

4 cups unbleached all-purpose flour

2 cups nut or date filling (recipes follow)

Egg wash (1 large egg beaten with 1 teaspoon water)

1/4 cup sesame seeds for sprinkling (optional)

1. Dissolve the yeast in 1/4 cup warm water. Stir in the sugar and let stand until foamy, 5 to 10 minutes.
2. Add the remaining water, butter, salt, and 2 cups flour. Add enough of the remaining flour, 1/2 cup at a time, to make a workable dough. On a lightly floured surface or in a mixer with a dough hook, knead the dough until smooth and springy, about 5 minutes. Place on a flat surface, cover with a large bowl or pot, and let rise in a warm place until double in bulk, about 1 1/2 hours.
3. Preheat the oven to 375 degrees. Line several large baking sheets with parchment paper or lightly grease.
4. Punch down the dough. Fold over and press together several times. Let rest for 10 minutes. Divide the dough into 1-inch balls and roll each ball into a thin round about 3 inches in diameter. Or roll out the dough 1/8 inch thick and cut out 3-inch rounds,

rerolling the scraps. Spoon 1 teaspoon of the filling in the center of each round, fold over an edge to form a half moon, and press the edges to seal.

5. Place 2 inches apart on the prepared baking sheets. Brush the tops with the egg wash and prick several times with the tines of a fork. If desired, lightly sprinkle with the sesame seeds. Bake until golden brown, about 15 minutes. Transfer to a rack and let cool. Wrap and store at room temperature for up to 2 days or in the freezer for up to 2 months.

VARIATION

Fatayar (Middle Eastern Triangular Yeast Pastries): In Step 4, after adding the filling, fold an edge of dough over the filling, but not to the other edge, pressing down firmly to seal. Pinch together at the corners, then fold two more sides over the filling to form a triangle, pinching the edges to seal.

KLAITCHA Fillings

Nut Filling

ABOUT 2 CUPS

8 ounces (2 cups) almonds, pistachios, or walnuts, finely chopped

1/2 to 1 cup sugar

1 tablespoon rose water, orange blossom water, or plain water

1 tablespoon vegetable oil or lightly beaten egg

1/2 teaspoon ground cinnamon (optional)

In a food processor, process all the ingredients until smooth.

VARIATION

Badam Sambusak (Calcutta Almond Filling): Add 6 crushed cardamom pods or 1/4 to 1/2 teaspoon ground cardamom.

Date Filling

ABOUT 2 CUPS

*1 pound (about 3 cups) dates, pitted
  and finely chopped*
1/2 cup water

*2 to 3 tablespoons unsalted butter or
  margarine*

Cook the dates in the water in a large saucepan over low heat, stirring frequently, for 10 minutes. Add the butter and cook until the mixture forms an almost uniform mass, about 5 minutes. Let cool.

VARIATIONS

Instead of cooking the dates, soak in cold water for several hours, then drain and puree in a food processor.

Date-Nut Filling: Reduce the dates to 12 ounces and, after pureeing, stir in 1 cup chopped almonds or walnuts and 1 teaspoon ground cinnamon.

Biscochos Dulces ❧ *(Sephardic Sweet Bread Rings)*

ABOUT 48 PASTRIES

Among the most ancient of pastries are bread rings variously known as *kaak* (Talmud Berachot 38a), *biscochos dulces,* and *roskitas* ("little screws" in Ladino). Large dough-nut-shaped breads are called *roscas.* Sephardim usually flavor them with anise. Many serve these refreshing rings or the pretzel-shaped *reshicas* at the meal following Yom Kippur, for Sabbath *desayuno* (breakfast), and on other special occasions. They are generally prepared in a large batch so that plenty will be available for unexpected company.

Dough:

1 ($1/4$-ounce) package ($2^1/4$ teaspoons) active dry yeast, or 1 (0.6-ounce) cake fresh yeast

$1^1/4$ cups warm water (105 to 110 degrees for dry yeast; 80 to 85 degrees for fresh yeast)

$1/4$ to $1/2$ cup sugar

$1/4$ cup vegetable oil, untoasted sesame oil, or melted vegetable shortening

1 tablespoon anise liqueur, or 1 to 2 teaspoons ground anise

1 teaspoon table salt, or 2 teaspoons kosher salt

About 4 cups unbleached all-purpose flour

Egg wash (2 large eggs beaten with 2 teaspoons water)

About $1/2$ cup sesame seeds for coating

---

1. Dissolve the yeast in $1/4$ cup warm water. Stir in 1 teaspoon sugar and let stand until foamy, 5 to 10 minutes.
2. Add the remaining water, remaining sugar, oil, anise, salt, and 2 cups flour. Gradually add enough of the remaining flour until the mixture holds together. On a lightly floured surface or in a mixer with a dough hook, knead the dough until smooth and springy, about 5 minutes. Place on a flat surface, cover with a large bowl or pot, and let rise at room temperature until double in bulk, about $1^1/2$ hours.
3. Punch down the dough. Fold over and press together several times. Cover and let stand for 10 minutes.
4. Preheat the oven to 400 degrees. Line several large baking sheets with parchment paper or lightly grease.

continued

5. Divide the dough into 4 pieces and roll into $^1/_2$-inch-thick ropes. Cut into 4-inch-long strips. Bring the ends together to form a ring and pinch to seal. Dip the top of the rings into the egg wash, then into the sesame seeds.

6. Place sesame side up on the prepared baking sheets, leaving about 1 inch between the rings. Bake until lightly colored, about 10 minutes.

7. After all the rings are lightly colored, reduce the heat to 250 degrees, return the rings to the oven, and bake until golden brown and crisp, about 20 minutes. Transfer to a rack and let cool completely. Store in an airtight container at room temperature for several weeks or in the freezer for several months.

VARIATION

Reshicas (Sephardic Sweet Pretzels): Loop the ends of the dough ropes over the middle to produce a pretzel shape.

Foulares ✿ *(Turkish "Haman's Egg" Pastries)*

This treat, called *folarikos* in Greece, is traditionally served on Purim and the Sabbath before the holiday (when the Torah portion mentions Haman's ancestor, Amalek). The shape of the pastry is meant to symbolize either Haman's prison bars or parts of his anatomy, while the name of the eggs sounds similar to that of the evil prime minister. *Huevos haminados* (**beid hamin** in Arabic) are eggs cooked with onion skins over low heat for a long time, producing a rich brown color and flavor. Sephardim customarily serve them on the Sabbath, holidays, and at the Passover Seder.

---

*1/2 recipe (about 1¼ pounds) Basic
    Sweet Yeast Dough (page 35)*
*12 haminados (Sephardic brown eggs)
    or hard-boiled eggs in their shells*

*Egg wash (1 large egg beaten with
    1 teaspoon water)*

---

1. Prepare the dough through Step 4.
2. On a lightly floured surface, roll out the dough ¼ inch thick. Cut out 3-inch rounds. Cut the remaining dough into thin strips. Place an egg, large end down, on each round and bring up the edges of the base to form a cup. Use several dough strips to secure the eggs to the bases. Place on a baking sheet lined with parchment paper or greased. Cover and let rise until double in bulk, about 1 hour.
3. Preheat the oven to 350 degrees.
4. Brush the dough with the egg wash. Bake until golden brown, about 35 minutes. Transfer to a rack and let cool.

VARIATION

Cut the pastry into ear or foot shapes (these are flat) and secure the eggs to the bases with the dough strips.

Boyicos de Azucar y Pimienta ❧
(Turkish Sugar and Pepper Rolls)

The addition of pepper to the dough creates an intriguing flavor and enhances yeast activity.

1 (¹/₄-ounce) package (2¹/₄ teaspoons) active dry yeast, or 1 (0.6-ounce) cake fresh yeast	1 teaspoon table salt, or 2 teaspoons kosher salt
¹/₂ cup warm water (105 to 110 degrees for dry yeast; 80 to 85 degrees for fresh yeast)	¹/₂ teaspoon freshly ground black pepper
¹/₄ to ¹/₂ cup sugar	About 4 cups unbleached all-purpose flour
1 cup vegetable oil	Egg wash (1 large egg beaten with 1 teaspoon water)

1. Dissolve the yeast in ¹/₄ cup warm water. Stir in 1 teaspoon sugar and let stand until foamy, 5 to 10 minutes.
2. Add the remaining water, remaining sugar, oil, salt, and pepper. Blend in 1¹/₂ cups flour. Gradually add enough of the remaining flour to make a workable dough.
3. On a lightly floured surface or in a mixer with a dough hook, knead the dough until smooth and springy, about 5 minutes. Place on a flat surface, cover with a large bowl or pot, and let rise at room temperature until nearly double in bulk, 1¹/₂ to 2 hours.
4. Punch down the dough. Fold over and press together several times. Let stand for 10 minutes. On a lightly floured surface, roll out the dough ¹/₂ inch thick. Cut into 2¹/₂-inch triangles. Place on a baking sheet lined with parchment paper or lightly greased. Cover and let rise until nearly double in bulk, about 1 hour.
5. Preheat the oven to 375 degrees.
6. Brush with the egg wash. Bake until golden brown, about 40 minutes. Transfer to a rack and let cool. Wrap and store at room temperature for up to 2 days or in the freezer for up to 2 months.

TURKEY

Over the course of history, many groups invaded Asia Minor, including the one whose name the area now bears, the Turks. These nomadic people originated in Mongolia and, in the tenth century, began advancing into western Asia, eventually supplanting the Byzantine Empire. The Ottoman Empire reached its height under Suleiman the Magnificent (1494–1566), whose domain stretched to Hungary, westward to Algeria, northeast to Georgia, and eastward to the Euphrates River.

Ottoman rule was marked by tolerance toward non-Muslims, a policy that greatly contributed to its success. Although Jews lived in Anatolia for millennia, their numbers swelled in 1492 as Bayazid II eagerly welcomed Spanish-Portuguese exiles into his realm. The sultan even thanked the Spanish monarchs, Ferdinand and Isabella, for enriching his kingdom while impoverishing their own. Two areas of expertise for which the Ottomans were particularly grateful were the exiles' knowledge of gunpowder and firearms and printing.

Following the Peace Treaty of Lausanne on July 24, 1923, Turkey officially became a secular state. At the time, around 80,000 Jews lived in the country, about half of them in Istanbul. Turkish Jews were generally spared the harsh abuse endured by other Middle Eastern Jews in the twentieth century, so Turkey never experienced the mass exodus of its Jewish community. Still, emigration to Israel reduced the number of Turkish Jews by half. Today about 26,000 Jews remain in Turkey.

The influx of Spanish-Portuguese Jews into the lands of the sultan overwhelmed the native Jewish communities, called Romaniots, and in many cases the customs of the Sephardim supplanted theirs. The Iberian Jews, although maintaining many of their traditional dishes, gradually adopted and synthesized local fare. The Turks developed an array of cookies, pastries, cakes, and multilayered phyllo pastries, many soaked in a syrup. These rich treats are usually served with Turkish coffee.

Cakes

*And he [King David] gave to every one of Israel,
both man and woman, to every one a loaf of bread,
and a cake made in a pan, and a sweet cake.*

—II SAMUEL 6:19

A CAKE, IN ITS SIMPLEST MEANING, IS A SHAPED MASS OR, MORE EXPLICITLY AS IT PERTAINS TO DESSERTS, A SWEETENED MASS. YET CAKES HOLD A MUCH MORE EXALTED POSITION IN OUR LIVES AND MEMORIES THAN MERE DEFINITION SUGGESTS. THEY SERVE AS A comfort food, conjuring up warm moments of childhood, and they are used to mark special occasions, such as birthdays, weddings, anniversaries, and holidays. Cakes are the embodiment of celebration.

The earliest cakes consisted of fried patties of mashed legumes or grain flavored with honey. After yeast breads developed, bakers added honey and other enriching ingredients to create lighter, more versatile cakes. Middle Eastern baking became further refined with the popularization of sugar, first grown in the region in the fourth century CE and having largely replaced honey by the seventh century. Soon bakers began to beat eggs with sugar, creating lighter treats such as sponge cake, and utilized a host of spices and nuts.

The situation in Europe was vastly different, marked by relatively primitive cooking techniques, coarse flour, and the absence of sugar. The early Ashkenazic dessert repertoire included *fluden* (layered pastry), *obliet* (a waffle cookie), *boonyish* (doughnuts), various honey cakes, a cake made from the skins of fermented grapes, bird-shaped pastries, and baked apples. Medieval leavenings, such as wood ash, left a disagreeable taste, requiring the addition of copious amounts of spices and resulting in heavy cakes such as *lebkuchen* (gingerbread) and *lekhach* (honey cake).

Middle Eastern baking advances, along with sugar, first reached Europe through the major ports of Italy in the twelfth century, during the Crusades. Italian chefs adapted these new baking techniques to create light, airy cakes called *torta* (Latin for "a round bread"). Sponge cake was transformed into *genoise*, named after the city of Genoa. By the thirteenth century, *torten* reached western and central European Jews, as first mentioned in the *Tashbetz*, a work by Samson Ben Zadok, a student of Meir of Rothenberg. The first record of these desserts in non-Jewish German sources, however, is dated some two centuries later, in 1418. Subsequently, Sephardic exiles brought their cakes and techniques to the areas in which they found refuge throughout the Mediterranean, as well as western Europe and even America.

In the seventeenth century, the popularization of sugar in Europe due to cheap sources from the Caribbean resulted in a new era of cake making. Flavors became more refined, and baking techniques more sophisticated. The English invented a cake lightened by beating butter with sugar, which evolved into the still-popular pound cake. When someone baked a pound cake batter in a thin layer and then spread it with jelly and rolled it up or stacked it, they produced the classic jelly roll and the first layer cake.

The advent of baking powder in 1856, around the same time that the cast-iron oven replaced the brick hearth, marks the beginning of modern cake making. Soon a large variety of elaborate layer cakes appeared. In the 1930s, the first cake mix, for gingerbread, was created. With the advent of World War II, mixes gained unprecedented popularity, partially because they were not included in rationing. For many households, cakes from scratch became a memory of the past. Still, nothing compares to the taste of a homemade cake.

Cake Baking

The myriad cakes we enjoy today fall into two basic categories—butter and egg foam. Butter cakes rely on air incorporated into the fat and (usually) chemical leavenings to raise them. Egg-foam cakes depend primarily on beaten air for leavening. Tortes are egg-foam cakes that contain little or no flour. As a rule of thumb, butter cakes enjoy more popularity in America than in other parts of the world, while Europeans fancy lighter and more versatile egg-foam cakes. Whichever category you prefer, all cakes should be tender, uniformly textured, and pleasantly flavored.

For maximum lightness, all cake ingredients should be at room temperature (70 degrees). If the ingredients are too cold, the fat will solidify and the air bubbles will burst too soon during baking. If the ingredients are too warm, the fat will melt and be unable to hold the air. In either case, the result will be damage to the air bubbles and a cake that does not rise properly and has a coarse texture.

Conductive pans that absorb and transmit heat quickly produce superior results in cake baking; those made from dull metals such as dull aluminum and iron are best. Heat reflectors such as stainless steel or bright aluminum are not recommended, as they result in underbrowning. On the other hand, heat absorbers such as black metal tend to produce an overbrowned crust. If using glass or dark pans, reduce the oven temperature by 25 degrees.

Using the correct size pan for the amount of batter is crucial. If the pan is too big, the cake will bake too slowly; if too small, it will rise too high and sink. Pans for butter cakes are generally 1¹/₂ to 2 inches deep; for egg-foam cakes, about 4 inches deep.

Baking pans are generally greased—preferably with vegetable shortening or margarine—to produce a more evenly risen cake and prevent sticking to the pan. The greasy surface, however, prevents the cake from clinging to the sides and rising to its fullest potential. To help the cake rise higher after greasing, the pan is usually dusted with flour or cocoa powder. To dust, add a little flour and shake around the sides and bottom, then invert the pan and tap out any excess flour.

The preferable temperature for baking fat-rich cakes is 350 degrees. Higher temperatures will overbrown the top and cause fruits and nuts to slip to the bottom; lower temperatures will produce a coarse texture. At elevations above 3,500 feet, increase the oven temperature by 25 degrees.

There are several visible signs of doneness, a golden color being the most obvious. When a cake reaches the proper state of doneness, the air bubbles inside burst and the cake begins to sink slightly and come away from the sides of the pan. If cakes are left in the oven after this point, they begin drying out. To test for doneness, insert a tester in the center. If it comes out with no crumbs clinging to it, it is done. Or lightly touch the top of the cake. If it springs back, leaving no impression, it is ready.

After baking, remove the pan from the oven, place on a wire rack, and let the cake cool in the pan for 10 to 15 minutes. Run a thin knife around the edges, pushing against the pan and not the cake. Place a wire rack on top of the pan and, holding the pan and rack together, invert. Remove the pan and paper liner, if one was used, then reinvert onto another rack and let cool completely.

Since the fat in butter cakes will harden when chilled, toughening the cake, butter cakes generally should not be refrigerated. After cooling, wrap unfrosted butter cakes in plastic, then foil, and store at room temperature or in the freezer.

Pan de Espagna/Tawrt ❧ *(Sponge Cake)*

Innovative Middle Eastern bakers discovered that beating eggs with sugar trapped numerous air bubbles in the protein, making possible the leavening of batters without yeast. During baking, the bubbles, which are loosely connected to each other, swell and thereby raise the batter. The result is a light, airy texture. If the egg whites are overbeaten, however, the protein loses its elasticity and the bubbles cannot expand.

Sponge cake—called *pan de Espagna* ("bread of Spain") or *pan esponjado* (sponge cake) by Sephardim, *pane di Spagna* by Italians, and *tawrt* by Ashkenazim—contains no shortening. The high amount of sugar and relatively small amount of flour (there is actually twice as much sugar than flour in weight) keep the cake moist. Because of the large amount of sugar, covering a sponge cake with frosting is a bit like gilding the lily. It is usually topped with only a sprinkling of confectioners' sugar or served with fresh fruit.

---

6 large eggs, separated

1 cup superfine or granulated sugar

1/4 cup fresh lemon or orange juice

1/2 teaspoon vanilla extract

1 1/2 teaspoons grated lemon zest, or
    1 tablespoon grated orange zest
    (optional)

1 1/3 cups sifted cake flour, or 1 cup plus
    2 tablespoons all-purpose flour, sifted

Scant 1/8 teaspoon salt, or 3/4 teaspoon
    cream of tartar

Confectioners' sugar for dusting
    (optional)

---

1. Preheat the oven to 350 degrees. Set aside an ungreased 9-inch two-piece tube pan.
2. Beat the egg yolks on medium-high speed until light, about 5 minutes. Gradually add the sugar and continue beating until thick and creamy, about 8 minutes total. Stir in the juice, vanilla, and zest if using. Sift the flour over the egg mixture, then whisk in.
3. Using clean beaters, beat the egg whites on low speed until foamy, about 30 seconds. Add the salt, increase the speed to high, and beat until stiff but not dry. Fold one-fourth of the egg whites into the yolk mixture to lighten, then gently fold in the remaining whites.
4. Pour into the prepared pan, leveling the surface. Tap the pan to release any large air bubbles. Bake until the cake is golden brown and springs back when lightly touched, about 45 minutes.

5. Invert the pan over the neck of a bottle and let cool completely. Wrap in plastic wrap and store at room temperature for up to 2 days, in the refrigerator for up to 5 days, or in the freezer for up to 2 months. If desired, sprinkle with confectioners' sugar.

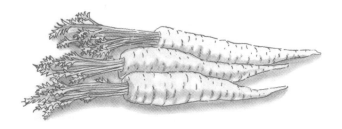

VARIATIONS

Carrot Sponge Cake: Stir in 1 cup grated carrots and, if desired, $1/2$ cup raisins or chopped nuts before folding in the egg whites.

Chocolate Chip Sponge Cake: Stir in 2 ounces coarsely grated semisweet or bittersweet chocolate before folding in the egg whites.

Date-Nut Sponge Cake: Stir in 2 cups (12 ounces) finely chopped dates and $1/2$ cup chopped almonds, hazelnuts, pecans, or walnuts before folding in the egg whites.

8-Egg Sponge Cake

8 large eggs, separated	*2 cups sifted cake flour, or $1^1/2$ cups*
$1^1/4$ cups superfine or granulated sugar	*all-purpose flour, sifted*
$1/3$ cup fresh lemon or orange juice	*$1/8$ teaspoon salt, or $3/4$ teaspoon cream*
1 teaspoon vanilla extract	*of tartar*
2 teaspoons grated lemon zest, or	*Confectioners' sugar for dusting*
4 teaspoons orange zest (optional)	*(optional)*

Proceed as above, but bake in a 10-inch two-piece tube pan.

Torta de las Reyes ❧ *(Sephardic Orange-Almond Cake)*

ONE 9-INCH ROUND CAKE; 8 TO 10 SERVINGS

K ing's, the name of this vintage Sephardic cake, refers to its being fit to serve to royalty. Beating a whole egg produces an emulsification of the lecithin in the yolk, which surrounds the air bubbles instead of the protein strands in the whites. As a result, whole-egg batters are more fragile than those made from separated eggs, but also moister. This cake, a characteristically Sephardic combination of almonds and oranges, has a macaroon-like texture. The matza meal version is a popular Passover dessert. Sephardim make an orange custard by using the same ingredients and adding orange juice, a variation perhaps created when some cook made a mistake in adding ingredients.

2 cups (10 ounces) almonds	*1 teaspoon ground cinnamon (optional)*
1 1/2 cups sugar	*5 large eggs*
1/4 cup bread crumbs or matza meal	*About 1 tablespoon orange blossom*
1 tablespoon grated orange zest	*water, or 2 tablespoons fresh orange*
1/8 teaspoon salt	*juice*

1. Preheat the oven to 375 degrees. Grease the bottom (but not the sides) of a 9-inch springform pan, line with parchment or waxed paper, and grease the bottom again.

2. In a food processor fitted with a metal blade, process the almonds and 1/4 cup sugar until finely ground. (If using a nut grinder, process the almonds only and add the 1/4 cup sugar with the crumbs.) Add the crumbs, zest, salt, and cinnamon if using.

3. Beat the eggs and remaining 1 1/4 cups sugar until thick and creamy, 10 to 15 minutes. Stir in the nut mixture and orange blossom water.

4. Pour into the prepared pan. Bake until a tester inserted into the center comes out clean, about 1 hour. Place on a rack and let cool. Wrap in plastic wrap and store at room temperature for up to 2 days, in the refrigerator for up to 5 days, or in the freezer for up to 2 months.

VARIATION

Sephardic Orange-Almond Flan: Increase the eggs to 14 and add 2 1/2 cups fresh orange juice and, if desired, 1/4 cup orange liqueur. Beat the eggs and sugar together only to blend. Divide the custard between two 1 1/2-quart baking dishes, place in a large baking pan, add hot water to reach halfway up the sides of the dishes, cover loosely with aluminum foil, and bake in a 350-degree oven until set, about 1¹/₄ hours. Refrigerate until chilled. Each dish serves 6 to 8 people.

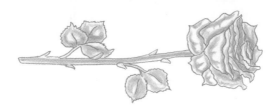

DISTILLED WATERS RUN DEEP

In 800 CE the Arab scholar Jabir ibn Hayyan invented an improved still, allowing not only the production of alcohol but also the distillation of *mai ward* (rose water) and *mai zahr/mai qedda* (orange blossom water, also called orange flower water). The distillation process has changed little over the centuries, and some families continue to make their own waters in basements and garages throughout the Middle East. Kilos of petals are placed in a large copper still and covered with plain water. The Damask variety of rose—with leaves that are glossy on the top and hairy on the bottom and small pink and white flowers—is preferred for distilling into rose water as well as making preserves. After the lid is secured, the still is placed over a fire and left to boil. The vapor passes through a tube, where it condenses at the other end and drips into bottles.

Most commercial distilled waters come diluted, the strength varying depending on the amount of dilution. Adjust the amount used in cooking according to the individual product and your personal preference. Too much rose water in baked goods and puddings results in a soapy taste. For reasons of *kashruth,* avoid distilled waters containing glycerine.

Middle Easterners use these aromatic distilled waters to add flavor and perfume to baked goods, confections, puddings, and fruit dishes, and some even use them to wash. Add several drops of orange blossom water to cups of hot water to create *cahve blanco* (white coffee). Rose water is a traditional flavoring on Shavuot among Sephardim, who call the holiday the Feast of Roses.

Smeteneh Kuchen ❧ *(Ashkenazic Sour Cream Coffee Cake)*

ONE 9-INCH SQUARE OR BUNDT CAKE; 6 TO 9 SERVINGS

Coffee cakes rank among the most popular of comfort foods, welcomed at breakfast, lunch, afternoon tea, dinner, and as the name indicates, coffee breaks. A coffee cake batter is generally more liquid than a quick bread one and contains a bit more sugar, and as a result, the final product is lighter and moister. On the other hand, coffee cakes tend to be less sweet than butter cakes. There are many versions of *kuchen,* this streusel-topped sour cream type being a very popular one. It is commonly served at the meal following Yom Kippur, on Shavuot, and on Sabbath afternoons or the *melaveh malcha* ("accompanying the queen") party following the Sabbath. For the latter occasion, spices are added to the batter and topping, reflecting those used during the *havdallah* ceremony signaling the end of the Sabbath.

Streusel Topping:

¹/₂ cup granulated or brown sugar, or
  ¹/₄ cup each

¹/₂ cup all-purpose flour

³/₄ teaspoon ground cinnamon

¹/₈ teaspoon salt

¹/₄ to ¹/₂ teaspoon ground nutmeg or
  cloves (optional)

¹/₄ cup (¹/₂ stick) unsalted butter or
  margarine, softened

¹/₂ cup coarsely chopped walnuts or
  pecans, grated coconut, golden
  raisins, or chocolate chips, or 1 cup
  any combination (optional)

Batter:

2 cups all-purpose flour

1 teaspoon double-acting baking powder

1 teaspoon baking soda

¹/₂ teaspoon salt

¹/₂ cup (1 stick) unsalted butter or
  margarine, softened

1 cup granulated or brown sugar or
  ¹/₂ cup each

4 large egg yolks, or 3 large eggs

1 cup (8 ounces) sour cream or plain
  yogurt

1¹/₂ teaspoons vanilla extract

1 teaspoon finely grated lemon zest
  (optional)

Glaze (optional):

1 cup confectioners' sugar

¹/₂ teaspoon vanilla or almond extract

1 to 2 tablespoons milk or water

1. Preheat the oven to 350 degrees (325 degrees if using a glass pan). Grease one 9-inch square pan, 9-inch Bundt or tube pan, or 9-inch springform pan. Line with parchment or waxed paper, grease again, and dust with flour.
2. To make the streusel: Combine the sugar, flour, cinnamon, salt, and nutmeg if using. Cut in the butter to resemble coarse crumbs. If desired, stir in the nuts.
3. To make the batter: Sift together the flour, baking powder, baking soda, and salt. In a large bowl, beat the butter until smooth, about 1 minute. Gradually add the sugar and beat until light and fluffy, about 4 minutes. Beat in the egg yolks, one at a time. Blend in the sour cream, vanilla, and zest if using. Stir in the flour mixture.
4. Spread half of the batter in the prepared pan. Sprinkle with half of the streusel. Carefully cover with the remaining batter and sprinkle with the remaining streusel.
5. Bake until the cake is golden and pulls away from the sides of the pan, about 50 minutes. Set on a rack and let cool in the pan for at least 15 minutes. Serve warm or at room temperature. Wrap the *kuchen* in plastic and store at room temperature for up to 2 days or in the freezer for up to 3 months.
6. To make the glaze if using: Combine all the glaze ingredients, stirring until smooth and of pouring consistency. Drizzle over the cake and let stand until set.

HINT: ❧ When baking and storing a cake containing an acidic ingredient such as sour cream in an aluminum pan, line the bottom with parchment paper to prevent the juices from reacting with the aluminum and creating a metallic flavor.

VARIATIONS

Single-Layer Coffee Cake: Spread all the batter in a 13-by-9-inch pan, sprinkle with all of the topping, and bake for 30 to 35 minutes.

Fruit-Filled Coffee Cake: After adding the middle layer of streusel, top with 1 cup peeled, cored, and thinly sliced cooking apples, 1 cup peeled, pitted, and sliced peaches, or 1 cup pitted cherries, blueberries, blackberries, or raspberries.

Cheese Coffee Cake: Combine 8 ounces softened cream cheese, 1/4 cup sugar, 1 large egg, and 1 teaspoon vanilla extract. Spread over the top of the batter, leaving a 1-inch border on all sides. If desired, spread 1/2 cup melted blueberry, cherry, raspberry, or strawberry preserves or pie filling over the cheese mixture. Sprinkle with the streusel.

SOUR CREAM

 Early in history, people learned to extend the life of highly perishable dairy products by allowing them to become fermented by acid-producing bacteria. Sour cream became the primary cultured milk product in Slavic regions. Along with various other sours, such as pickles, it played the important role of enlivening an otherwise bland diet consisting primarily of starches. In addition, sour cream had a crucial role in providing balanced nutrition, containing the major vitamins (A and D) lacking in the staple of the eastern European diet, potatoes.

In 1882, Lithuanian immigrants Isaac and Joseph Breakstone opened a small shop on Manhattan's Lower East Side to sell traditional eastern European dairy products, most notably sour cream. In those days before prepackaged foods, the products were spooned out of large barrels into various receptacles. When innovation led to sour cream being sold in small plastic containers, this Old World necessity became a standard of the American kitchen as well.

Originally, sour cream consisted of heavy cream left at room temperature until slightly soured. Today it is made by adding a bacterial culture to cream and heating to about 72 degrees to achieve the desired level of lactic acid. Various additives are used to prevent separation and extend the shelf life. Yogurt can be substituted for sour cream in most recipes, but the flavor of the finished product will be a little tangier.

Versunkener Apfelkuchen ❧ *(German Apple Cake)*

ONE 10-INCH BUNDT CAKE; 8 TO 10 SERVINGS

This is one of the many types of apple cake popular throughout central Europe. I have seen apple cakes, a traditional Rosh Hashanah dessert, served on Sabbath and holiday tables from Israel to Australia.

3 cups all-purpose flour

1 tablespoon double-acting baking powder

1/2 teaspoon salt

1 cup (2 sticks) unsalted butter or margarine, softened

1 3/4 cups sugar

3 large eggs, separated

1/2 cup milk

8 medium (about 3 pounds) cooking apples, such as Golden Delicious, Granny Smith, Gravenstein, Greening, Jonathan, Macoun, Pippin, Starr, Winesap, Yellow Transparent, or any combination, cored and diced (peeling is optional)

Glaze (optional):

1 cup confectioners' sugar, or 1/2 cup confectioners' sugar and 1/2 cup light brown sugar

1/2 teaspoon vanilla or almond extract

1 to 2 tablespoons milk or water

1. Preheat the oven to 350 degrees. Grease a *kugelhopf* or 10-inch Bundt pan.
2. Sift together the flour, baking powder, and salt. Beat the butter until smooth, about 1 minute. Gradually add the sugar and beat until light and fluffy, about 4 minutes. Beat in the egg yolks, one at a time. Stir in the flour mixture and milk.
3. Beat the egg whites on low speed until foamy, about 30 seconds. Increase the speed to high and beat until stiff but not dry. Fold one-fourth of the whites into the batter, then gently fold in the remaining whites.
4. Pour half of the batter into the prepared pan. Spread with half of the apples. Top with the remaining batter, then the remaining apples.
5. Bake until golden brown, 50 to 60 minutes. Let cool in the pan for 20 minutes, then transfer to a rack and let cool completely.
6. To make the glaze if using: Combine all the glaze ingredients, stirring until smooth and of pouring consistency. Drizzle over the cake and let stand until set.

Appelkaka ❧ *(Danish Apple Cake)*

There are many versions of this flourless cake consisting of applesauce layered with bread crumbs. Some are rather simple, while others, like this one, require a few more steps. One variation uses rye bread for an intriguing flavor.

Applesauce:

10 medium (about 3 1/2 pounds) cooking
  apples, such as Golden Delicious,
  Granny Smith, Gravenstein,
  Greening, Jonathan, Macoun, Pippin,
  Starr, Winesap, or any combination,
  peeled, cored, and diced

5 tablespoons unsalted butter or
  margarine

Pinch of salt

About 1/2 cup sugar

4 large eggs, separated

1 cup raisins (optional)

Crumbs:

1 cup bread crumbs, unsalted cracker
  crumbs, or matza meal

3 tablespoons sugar

1/2 teaspoon ground cinnamon

Glaze:

3/4 cup confectioners' sugar

About 1 tablespoon fresh lemon juice

1. To make the applesauce: Cook the apples in a large saucepan over medium heat, stirring frequently, until very soft. Be careful not to let them burn. Mash the apples. Remove from the heat and add the butter, salt, and sugar to taste. Let cool slightly, then stir in the egg yolks and raisins if using.

2. Preheat the oven to 350 degrees. Grease a 9-inch springform pan.

3. To make the crumbs: Combine the crumbs, sugar, and cinnamon. Reserve 3 tablespoons of the crumb mixture to sprinkle over the top.

4. With the mixer on low speed, beat the egg whites until foamy, about 30 seconds. Add the salt, increase the speed to high, and beat until stiff but not dry. Fold one-fourth of the whites into the apple mixture, then gently fold in the remaining whites.

5. Sprinkle half of the crumb mixture over the bottom of the prepared pan. Top with half of the apple mixture. Sprinkle with the crumb mixture, then top with the remaining apple mixture. Sprinkle with the reserved 3 tablespoons crumbs.

6. Bake until golden and firm, about 50 minutes. Let cool.

7. To make the glaze: Combine the confectioners' sugar and enough lemon juice to produce a pouring consistency. Drizzle over the cake and let stand until set. Or omit the glaze and serve with whipped cream.

VARIATIONS

Substitute 5 cups store-bought sweetened applesauce for the apples and the $1/2$ cup sugar.

Omit the eggs. Increase the bread crumbs to 3 cups and the cinnamon to 1 teaspoon. Stir the crumbs into $3/4$ cup ($1 1/2$ sticks) melted butter and sauté in a large skillet over medium heat for 5 minutes.

Fruchtkuchen ❧ *(Ashkenazic Fruit Coffee Cake)*

ONE 8-INCH SQUARE OR 9-INCH ROUND CAKE; 6 TO 8 SERVINGS

This version of *kuchen* contains no liquid besides eggs and has a large proportion of butter. The fruit sinks into the thick batter during baking. Double the recipe and bake in a 13-by-9-inch pan.

Batter:

1 cup all-purpose flour

1 teaspoon double-acting baking powder

$1/4$ teaspoon salt

$1/2$ cup (1 stick) unsalted butter or
   margarine, softened

$1/2$ cup sugar

2 large eggs

$1/2$ teaspoon vanilla extract, or
   1 teaspoon grated lemon zest

Topping:

About 2 cups peeled, cored, and sliced
   fruit

$1/3$ cup sugar

2 teaspoons ground cinnamon

3 tablespoons chopped walnuts or
   pecans (optional)

2 tablespoons unsalted butter or
   margarine

---

1. Preheat the oven to 350 degrees (325 degrees if using a glass pan). Grease and dust with flour an 8-inch square baking pan, 9-inch springform pan, 11-inch tart pan, or 9-inch pie plate.
2. To make the batter: Sift together the flour, baking powder, and salt. In a large bowl, beat the butter until smooth, about 1 minute. Gradually add the sugar and beat until light and fluffy, about 4 minutes. Beat in the eggs, one at a time. Add the vanilla. Stir in the flour mixture. Spread in the prepared pan.
3. To make the topping: Arrange the fruit over the batter. Combine the sugar, cinnamon, and nuts if using, and sprinkle over the top. Dot with the butter.
4. Bake until golden brown, about 45 minutes. Set on a rack and let cool in the pan for at least 15 minutes. Serve warm or at room temperature. The *kuchen* can be cooled, frozen, thawed, and reheated in a 300-degree oven.

VARIATIONS

Apfelkuchen (Ashkenazic Apple Coffee Cake): Use 3 peeled, cored, and sliced apples tossed with 1 tablespoon lemon juice.

Birnekuchen (Ashkenazic Pear Coffee Cake): Use 3 peeled, cored, and sliced ripe pears tossed with 1 tablespoon lemon juice

Pflaumenkuchen (Ashkenazic Plum Coffee Cake): Use 1 pound (about 14) halved and pitted Italian or other plums. This is a popular Rosh Hashanah dessert making use of Italian plums that come to season in late August and early September. Italian plums, also called Lombard, are a small, oval, low-juice variety with a dark blue skin and yellow flesh and are commonly used in baking.

Pfirsichkuchen (Ashkenazic Peach Coffee Cake): Use 1¹/₂ pounds (4 large) peeled, pitted, and sliced peaches.

HINT: ↝ To peel peaches, cut an X at the bottom of the peaches, drop into a pot of boiling water for 20 to 30 seconds, then immediately place in a bowl of ice water to stop the cooking. The skins will slip off easily.

Lepeny ❧ *(Hungarian Coffee Cake with Fruit)*

ONE 10-INCH BUNDT CAKE; 8 TO 10 SERVINGS

This cake—basically an old-fashioned pound cake containing equal amounts by weight of butter, sugar, flour, and eggs—is leavened by beaten egg whites.

3/4 cup (1 1/2 sticks) unsalted butter or margarine, softened

3/4 cup plus 2 tablespoons sugar

3 large eggs, separated

1/2 teaspoon vanilla extract, or 1 teaspoon grated lemon zest

1/4 teaspoon salt

1 cup plus 2 tablespoons all-purpose flour

2 to 3 cups (12 to 16 ounces) blackberries, blueberries, raspberries, or pitted cherries

Glaze:

1 cup confectioners' sugar

1/2 teaspoon vanilla or almond extract

1 to 2 tablespoons milk or water

1. Preheat the oven to 350 degrees. Grease and dust with flour a 10-by-4-inch Bundt or tube pan or an 8-inch springform pan.

2. Beat the butter until smooth, about 1 minute. Gradually add 1/2 cup sugar and beat until light and fluffy, about 4 minutes. Beat in the egg yolks, one at a time. Add the vanilla and salt. Stir in the flour.

3. Beat the egg whites on low until foamy. Increase the speed to medium-high and beat until soft peaks form, 1 to 2 minutes. Gradually add the remaining 6 tablespoons sugar and beat until stiff and glossy, 5 to 8 minutes. Fold one-fourth of the whites into the batter, then gently fold in the remaining whites.

4. Pour into the prepared pan and spoon the fruit over the top. (It will sink into the batter during baking.) Bake until golden brown and a wooden tester inserted in the center comes out clean, about 40 minutes. Set on a rack and let cool in the pan for at least 15 minutes. Invert onto a rack. Serve warm or at room temperature. Wrap tightly in plastic, then foil. Store at room temperature for up to 2 days or in the freezer for up to 2 months.

5. To make the glaze: Combine all the glaze ingredients, stirring until smooth and of pouring consistency. Drizzle over the cake.

Variation

ONE 9-INCH ROUND COFFEE CAKE; 6 TO 8 SERVINGS

*1¹/₄ cups plus 1 tablespoon (2¹/₂ sticks
   plus 1 tablespoon) unsalted butter or
   margarine, softened*
1¹/₂ cups sugar
6 large eggs, separated
*1 teaspoon vanilla extract or grated
   lemon zest*

¹/₄ teaspoon salt
*2 cups plus 2 tablespoons all-purpose
   flour*
*3 cups (about 1 pound) blackberries,
   blueberries, raspberries, or pitted
   cherries*

Prepare as above, but bake in a greased 9-inch springform pan for about 1 hour. Use the same amount of glaze as above.

Kaesekuchen ❧ *(Ashkenazic Creamy Cheesecake)*

ONE 9-INCH CAKE; 10 TO 12 SERVINGS

The ancient Greeks made a variety of cakes from fresh curd cheese and honey. This dessert was refined over the centuries with the addition of cream, sugar, eggs, lemon, and vanilla, as well as a bottom crust. Cheesecakes became a particular favorite of central and eastern European Jews, who made use of local curd cheeses and sour cream. In New York State in 1872, a fresh cow's milk cheese called cream cheese, based on France's Neufchâtel, first appeared. In 1920, the Breakstone Company began mass-marketing cream cheese, which quickly became popular among New York's Jews, who began shmearing it on bagels and substituting it for curd cheese in their cakes. Today there are two primary types of cheesecake: the smoother cream cheese (sometimes called New York or Jewish cheesecake) and the firmer ricotta/cottage cheese type (sometimes called Italian cheesecake).

The basis of a classic creamy cheesecake is cream cheese. In this case, more expensive is not best. Fresh cream cheese lacks the stabilizers of commercial brands and tends to break up during baking, which gives the cake a grainy texture. Let the cream cheese, sour cream, and eggs stand at room temperature for at least 30 minutes before using.

Cheesecake is a traditional dessert during Shavuot and Hanukkah. Since cheesecake freezes well, it can be prepared far in advance, relieving any last-minute holiday hassles. Do not freeze the topping, but add it shortly before serving. To thaw cheesecakes, place in the refrigerator overnight.

Crust:	Filling:
1 cup all-purpose flour	*2 pounds cream cheese, softened*
1/4 cup sugar	*1 1/2 cups sugar*
1/4 teaspoon salt	*1/4 cup sour cream*
1/2 cup (1 stick) unsalted butter or	*1/4 cup heavy cream*
vegetable shortening, softened	*1 tablespoon fresh lemon juice*
1 large egg yolk	*2 teaspoons vanilla extract*
1/2 teaspoon vanilla extract	*1/4 teaspoon salt*
	4 large eggs

Strawberry Glaze (optional):
1 cup crushed strawberries
1 cup water
¹/₂ to ³/₄ cup sugar
Pinch of salt

2 tablespoons cornstarch dissolved in
1 tablespoon water
Several drops red food coloring
(optional)
2 cups fresh strawberries, halved
(optional)

1. To make the crust: Combine the flour, sugar, and salt. Combine the butter, egg yolk, and vanilla. Add the flour mixture and knead until the dough holds together. Form into a disc, wrap, and refrigerate for about 30 minutes.
2. Preheat the oven to 375 degrees.
3. On a piece of waxed paper or plastic wrap, roll the dough into a ¹/₈-inch-thick round. Press onto the bottom and partway up the sides of a 9-inch springform pan. Bake until golden, about 10 minutes. Let cool.
4. Lower the oven to 350 degrees. Double-wrap the outside of the springform pan with heavy-duty foil.
5. To make the filling: Beat the cream cheese until smooth. Gradually beat in the sugar. Blend in the sour cream, heavy cream, lemon juice, vanilla, and salt. Beat in the eggs. Pour into the prepared pan.
6. Place the springform pan in a larger pan (it should not touch the sides of the larger pan), place on the oven rack, and add boiling water to reach halfway up the sides. Bake until lightly browned and firm around the edges (2 inches in the center will jiggle slightly but will firm during cooling), about 1¹/₄ hours. Do not test with a knife, which cracks the cake.
7. Turn off the oven, open the door, and let the cake cool in the oven for 30 minutes. Place the springform pan on a rack and let cool completely. Cover with plastic wrap or an inverted large bowl and refrigerate overnight or up to 4 days or freeze for up to 2 months. Let stand at room temperature for at least 30 minutes before serving.
8. To make the glaze if using: In a medium saucepan, bring the crushed strawberries and water to a boil. Press through a sieve. Add the sugar and salt and return to a boil. Stir in the cornstarch mixture and cook, stirring, until bubbly and thickened, about 5 minutes. If desired, stir in the red food coloring. Let cool to room temperature. Spread the glaze over the top of the cake or, if desired, first arrange the strawberry halves over the cake, then brush the glaze on top.

VARIATION

Passover Cheesecake Crust: Substitute 1 cup matza cake meal for the flour.

Torta di Ricotta ❦ (*Italian Ricotta Cheesecake*)

10 TO 12 SERVINGS

This is lighter but not as smooth as a cream cheese cake. Refrigeration alters the texture of this cake; it will keep for 8 hours at room temperature.

5 tablespoons brandy or marsala	*4 large eggs*
1/2 cup golden raisins	*3/4 cup heavy cream*
1 cup sugar	*1 1/2 teaspoons vanilla extract*
5 tablespoons all-purpose flour	*Pinch of salt*
2 pounds (4 cups) ricotta cheese, drained	*1/2 cup pine nuts or coarsely chopped almonds, lightly toasted*

1. Pour the brandy over the raisins and let soak until plump, about 30 minutes.
2. Preheat the oven to 350 degrees. Grease a 9-inch springform pan.
3. Combine the sugar and flour. Beat the cheese or process in a food processor until smooth. Blend in the sugar mixture, eggs, cream, vanilla, and salt. Fold in the raisins (including the soaking liquid) and nuts.
4. Pour into the prepared pan. Bake until firm around the edges and lightly browned, about 1 1/4 hours. Turn off the oven, open the door, and let cool in the oven for 30 minutes. Remove and serve warm or at room temperature. If the cake is refrigerated, you can warm it in a 350-degree oven for about 20 minutes.

VARIATION

Chocolate Italian Cheesecake: Add 1/2 cup unsweetened cocoa powder and 1 ounce finely grated unsweetened chocolate.

Kayka Tamir <small>(Iraqi Date-Nut Cake)</small>

ABOUT 36 SMALL SERVINGS

This is a synthesis of Western and Middle Eastern styles, resulting in a sweet, moist cake.

1 cup all-purpose flour	1 cup sugar
1½ teaspoons double-acting baking powder	3 large eggs
1 teaspoon ground cinnamon	1½ teaspoons vanilla extract
½ teaspoon salt	1½ cups (about 10 ounces) finely chopped dates
¾ cup (1½ sticks) unsalted butter or margarine, softened	¾ cup chopped blanched almonds
	¾ cup chopped walnuts

1. Preheat the oven to 350 degrees (325 degrees if using a glass pan). Grease a 12-by-8-inch baking pan.

2. Sift together the flour, baking powder, cinnamon, and salt. Beat the butter until smooth, about 1 minute. Gradually add the sugar and beat until light and fluffy, about 4 minutes. Beat in the eggs, one at a time. Add the vanilla. Stir in the flour mixture. Add the dates and nuts.

3. Pour into the prepared pan. Bake until golden brown, about 30 minutes. Cut into diamonds or squares and let cool.

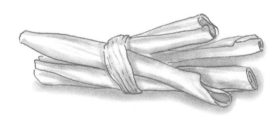

Lekach ❧ *(Ashkenazic Honey Cake)*

ONE 9-INCH LOAF; 9 TO 12 SERVINGS

Honey cakes, along with gingerbread, became the primary festive treat of early Ashkenazim. These desserts are found in Ashkenazic texts dating several centuries before the first record in non-Jewish Franco-German sources, perhaps because the Jews learned of them first from Italian coreligionists. *Lekach* (from the German word *lecke*, "lick") was mentioned in the *Machzor Vitry*, an eleventh-century prayer book compiled by Simcha ben Samuel, as well as most subsequent Ashkenazic works. For more than a thousand years, honey cake has remained a common sight at various Ashkenazic rituals, such as a *kiddush*, a brit, and a wedding. Honey cakes were once given to new students on their first day of school, reflecting how sweet learning could be. Generations of holiday meals ended with *lekach*—Purim, Hanukkah, the meal following Yom Kippur, and even flourless versions for Passover. Honey cakes shaped like a ladder were prepared for Shavuot (honey being compared to the Torah, which was given to the Jewish people on this day). Most notably the honey cake serves as a traditional Ashkenazic Rosh Hashanah dessert, starting the New Year off on a sweet note. This cake has a lighter texture than many other variations.

2 cups all-purpose flour

3/4 teaspoon double-acting baking powder

3/4 teaspoon baking soda

1 1/2 teaspoons ground cinnamon, or 1 teaspoon ground cinnamon, 1/2 teaspoon ground cloves or ginger, and 1/4 teaspoon ground nutmeg

1/2 teaspoon salt

3 large eggs

3/4 cup brown sugar

3 tablespoons vegetable oil or melted unsalted margarine

3/4 cup (9 ounces) honey

2 teaspoons grated orange zest (optional)

3/4 cup strong brewed coffee or tea

1/2 to 1 cup raisins, chopped pitted dates, or chopped candied citron (optional)

1. Preheat the oven to 350 degrees. Grease and flour a 9-by-5-inch loaf pan.
2. Sift together the flour, baking powder, baking soda, cinnamon, and salt. Lightly beat together the eggs and sugar. Stir in the oil, honey, and zest if using. Blend in half of the flour mixture. Gradually stir in the coffee, then blend in the remaining flour mixture. If desired, add the raisins.

3. Pour into the prepared pan. Bake until the top springs back when lightly touched and the cake begins to shrink slightly, about 1¹/₄ hours. Let cool in the pan for 10 minutes, then remove to a rack and let cool completely. Wrap tightly in plastic, then foil, and store at room temperature for up to 1 week or in the freezer for up to 2 months. Using a serrated knife, cut into slices.

VARIATIONS

Large Honey Cake: Double the recipe and bake in a 13-by-9-inch baking pan for about 1 hour.

Mini Honey Cakes: This makes about 60 bite-size cakes. Pour 1 tablespoon batter into greased and floured miniature muffin tins and bake for about 15 minutes.

Marmorgugelhupf ❧ *(Ashkenazic Marble Cake)*

ONE 9-BY-5-INCH LOAF; 8 TO 10 SERVINGS

The original marble cake consisted of a sponge cake with a dark portion colored with molasses, cinnamon, and cloves. As chocolate gained more prominence in Europe, it replaced molasses in this classic treat. Eventually the marbleizing process was applied to various butter cakes, including this rich, moist loaf. In any case, *marmorgugelhupf* became a popular Ashkenazic Sabbath cake.

---

1 cup (2 sticks) unsalted butter or margarine, softened

1⅓ cups sugar

5 large eggs, or 3 large eggs and 3 large egg yolks, lightly beaten

2 teaspoons vanilla extract

½ teaspoon salt

2 cups sifted cake flour, or 1¾ cups all-purpose flour, sifted

2 ounces bittersweet or unsweetened chocolate, melted and cooled, or 2 tablespoons unsweetened cocoa powder

2 teaspoons instant coffee powder (optional)

---

1. Preheat the oven to 350 degrees. Grease a 9-by-5-inch loaf pan or 9-inch springform pan. Line the bottom and sides with parchment paper (to prevent burning during the long baking time of the thick batter in a deep pan), grease again, and dust with flour.
2. Beat the butter until smooth, about 1 minute. Gradually add the sugar and beat until light and fluffy, about 4 minutes. Gradually add the eggs, beating well after each addition. The total time for beating in the eggs is about 4 minutes. Add the vanilla and salt. In 3 additions, fold in the flour.
3. Remove one-fourth of the batter (about 1½ cups) to a small bowl and stir in the chocolate and, if desired, the coffee powder.
4. Spoon half of the plain batter into the prepared pan and drop half of the chocolate batter by spoonfuls over the top. Repeat with the remaining plain and chocolate batter. Swirl with a knife. Do not overmix.
5. Bake until a tester inserted in the center comes out clean, about 1 hour 10 minutes for a loaf pan; 50 minutes for a springform pan. Let cool in the pan for 10 minutes, then remove to a wire rack and let cool completely. Wrap tightly in plastic, then foil, and store at room temperature for up to 5 days or in the freezer for up to 2 months. Using a serrated knife, cut into slices.

VARIATIONS

Reduce the eggs to 4 and add 1 teaspoon double-acting baking powder and 3 tablespoons milk or 1^1/$_2$ tablespoons bourbon, brandy, or Scotch.

Large Marble Cake: Double the recipe and bake in a 10-by-4-inch Bundt or tube pan.

Marble-Orange Cake: After separating the chocolate batter, add 1^1/$_2$ tablespoons grated orange zest to the plain batter.

Marble-Spice Cake: Stir ^{3}/$_4$ teaspoon ground cinnamon and a pinch of ground cloves into the chocolate.

Mohn Kuchen (Ashkenazic Poppy Seed Cake): Omit the chocolate and coffee and add ^{1}/$_4$ cup poppy seeds. For Lemon Poppy Seed Cake: Add ^{1}/$_4$ cup lemon extract (or 1 tablespoon fresh lemon juice and 1 tablespoon grated lemon zest).

COCOA POWDER

 After cocoa beans are roasted and the cocoa butter extracted, a dry cake remains that is then ground into a powder. Untreated cocoa powder (called natural processed or nonalkalized) contains a moderate degree of natural acidity, with a pH value ranging from 5.2 to 5.6 (similar to that of coffee). Adding a little alkali, usually potassium carbonate, raises the pH to around 7.5 (7 is neutral), thereby neutralizing the acidity in the cocoa powder. Alkalized cocoa (also called Dutch processed in reference to the nationality of its creator, Coenraad Van Houten) has a milder flavor and darker color, and is more soluble than nonalkalized cocoa. Most American brands are nonalkalized, while European imports tend to be alkalized.

The type of cocoa powder used in baking sometimes has an effect on the finished product, and the two should generally not be interchanged. If there is little or no baking soda in the recipe, alkalized cocoa is the preferable type. If baking soda is the only or primary leavening agent, it is preferable to use nonalkalized cocoa so that its acid can neutralize the alkali in the baking soda.

Dobostorte ❧ *(Hungarian Seven-Layer Cake)*

8 TO 10 SERVINGS

Hungary is justly renowned for its baked goods, and *dobostorte,* probably inspired by Turkish layered pastries such as baklava, is one of its best and arguably the favorite. This famous seven-layer cake is purportedly named after a nineteenth-century Budapest pastry master, but the idea of thin cake layers sandwiched with creamy frosting dates much further back. This version uses thin sponge cake layers complemented with a rich buttercream. To create a batter with the proper consistency, it is preferable to weigh the flour and sugar. Since most home ovens heat unevenly, it is advisable not to bake too many layers at the same time.

Chocolate Buttercream:

1 1/2 cups sugar

3/4 cup water

6 large egg yolks

2 cups (4 sticks) unsalted butter or
 margarine, softened

1/2 cup vegetable shortening

10 ounces bittersweet or semisweet
 chocolate, melted and cooled, or
 2/3 cup unsweetened cocoa powder

2 teaspoons vanilla extract

Pinch of salt

2 to 3 tablespoons rum or kirsch
 (optional)

Batter:

6 large eggs

1 1/4 cups plus 1 tablespoon (9 ounces)
 sugar

1 teaspoon vanilla extract

1/4 teaspoon salt

1 1/2 cups (7 1/2 ounces) all-purpose
 flour, measured by dip-and-sweep
 method

Caramel (optional):

1 1/2 cups sugar

3/4 cup water

1/2 teaspoon cream of tartar

1. To make the buttercream: Stir the sugar and water in a small saucepan over low heat until the sugar dissolves, about 5 minutes. Increase the heat to medium and boil, without stirring, until the syrup reaches the soft-ball stage, or 250 degrees on a candy thermometer, about 10 minutes.
2. Meanwhile, beat the egg yolks until pale and thick, about 4 minutes. In a slow, steady stream, pour the hot syrup into the eggs, beating continuously as you pour. (Do not let the syrup touch the beaters or it will spin into threads.) Continue beating until the mixture thickens and cools to room temperature, about 10 minutes.

3. Beat in the butter and shortening, 2 tablespoons at a time, until absorbed. Gradually beat in the chocolate. Blend in the vanilla, salt, and rum if using. Do not add the flavoring too quickly or the buttercream might curdle. Chill until of spreading consistency, at least 2 hours or up to 1 week. If the buttercream firms too much, return to room temperature before using, about 1 hour.

4. Preheat the oven to 350 degrees. Grease the bottoms of several 9-inch round cake pans and dust with flour, tapping out the excess. Or grease and flour several large baking sheets and, using a 9-inch saucepan lid or springform pan, mark 9-inch circles on the sheets.

5. To make the batter: Beat the eggs and sugar until thick and creamy, 5 to 10 minutes. Add the vanilla and salt. Sift the flour over the top and carefully fold it in.

6. Spread about $1/4$ cup of the batter evenly over the bottom of the prepared pans or over each circle on the baking sheets.

7. Bake until the edges begin to color, 5 to 7 minutes. Loosen with a spatula, invert onto a rack, and let cool. Wipe the pans, regrease, dust with flour, and repeat until there are 7 or 8 matching layers.

8. To make the caramel if using: Stir all the caramel ingredients in a small saucepan over low heat until the sugar dissolves, about 5 minutes. Stop stirring, increase the heat to medium, and cook, swirling the pan occasionally, until the syrup turns a deep amber color. Do not burn.

9. Using a lightly oiled metal spatula, spread all of the caramel evenly over one of the cake layers. Let set slightly (but do not let it harden), then use an oiled knife to cut just the caramel into 8 to 10 wedges (indicating where the cake will be sliced).

10. To assemble: Place a cake layer on a serving plate, spread with a $1/8$-inch-thick layer of buttercream, then place a second layer on top. Repeat layering the buttercream and cake layers. Cover the top of the cake with buttercream. If using the caramel layer, place on top of the cake. Cover the sides of the cake with buttercream. Chill. Store in the refrigerator for up to 1 day or in the freezer. Let stand at room temperature for at least 30 minutes before serving.

VARIATION

Oblong Layer Cake: Divide the batter between two $15^{1}/2$-by-$10^{1}/2$-inch jelly roll pans and bake. After cooling the cakes, cut each lengthwise into 3 equal pieces to make a 6-layer cake.

Torta di Zucca ❧ *(Italian Pumpkin Cake)*

The presence of pumpkin in many Italian desserts generally marks them of Sephardic origin. This relative of squash has been widely cultivated throughout the Americas since ancient times and was among the first New World foods introduced to Europeans. Although the flesh of the bright orange jack-o'-lantern pumpkin can be used, it tends to be very stringy. A better choice is the cheese pumpkin, a smaller, paler, less stringy, and sweeter variety.

Pure-pack canned pumpkin is 100 percent cooked pumpkin. An undamaged can will keep for up to two years. Once opened, store in the refrigerator for no more than two weeks. Do not substitute pumpkin pie mix.

---

3 cups all-purpose flour	2 cups cooked and pureed pumpkin, or
2 teaspoons double-acting baking	16 ounces pure-pack pumpkin
powder	2 cups sugar, or 1 cup granulated sugar
2 teaspoons baking soda	and 1 cup brown sugar
1 teaspoon salt	1¼ cups vegetable oil
2 teaspoons ground cinnamon	4 large eggs
½ teaspoon ground ginger or cardamom	1 cup raisins or chopped pitted dates
½ teaspoon ground cloves	1 cup chopped candied citron or coarsely
¼ teaspoon ground allspice or nutmeg	chopped walnuts or pecans

---

1. Preheat the oven to 350 degrees. Grease and dust with flour one 10-inch (12-cup) Bundt pan, one 13-by-9-inch baking pan, or two 9-inch round baking pans.
2. Sift together the flour, baking powder, baking soda, salt, and spices. Blend together the pumpkin, sugar, and oil. Beat in the eggs, one at a time. Stir in the flour mixture. Add the raisins and citron.
3. Pour into the prepared pan, smoothing the surface. Bake until a tester inserted into the center comes out clean, about 1 hour 10 minutes for the Bundt pan; 45 minutes for the 13-by-9-inch baking pan; or 35 minutes for the 9-inch round pans. Let cool in the pan for 15 minutes, then remove to a rack and let cool completely.

Basboosah Yaourt ❧ *(Middle Eastern Semolina Yogurt Cake)*

8 TO 10 SERVINGS

This version of semolina cake is lighter than the previous one, thanks to the presence of yogurt and flour. Yogurt, originally created when milk was accidentally fermented, has been a part of the Middle Eastern diet for more than 6,000 years. In the Middle East, yogurt is also made from sheep's milk, which produces a thicker, tarter product.

Syrup:
3 cups sugar
1 1/2 cups water
1/4 cup lemon juice
1 tablespoon orange blossom water
   (optional)

Cake:
1 cup coarse semolina or farina
1 cup all-purpose flour

1 teaspoon baking soda
1/4 teaspoon salt
4 large eggs
1 cup sugar
1 cup plain yogurt
1/2 cup vegetable oil
1/4 cup fresh orange juice or water
1 teaspoon grated lemon zest
1 teaspoon grated orange zest

1. To make the syrup: Stir the sugar, water, and lemon juice in a medium saucepan over low heat until the sugar dissolves, about 5 minutes. Stop stirring, increase the heat to medium, and boil until the syrup begins to thicken, about 5 minutes (it will register 225 degrees on a candy thermometer). Remove from the heat, stir in the orange blossom water if using, and let cool.

2. Preheat the oven to 350 degrees (325 degrees if using a glass pan). Grease a 13-by-9-inch baking pan.

3. To make the cake: Combine the semolina, flour, baking soda, and salt. Beat the eggs and sugar until light and fluffy, about 5 minutes. Beat in the yogurt, oil, orange juice, and zest. Blend in the semolina mixture.

4. Spoon into the prepared pan, leveling the top. Bake until golden brown, about 35 minutes.

5. Gradually drizzle the cooled syrup over the hot cake. Cover and let stand until the syrup is absorbed. Store at room temperature for up to 3 days.

Basboosah ❧ *(Middle Eastern Semolina Cake)*

ABOUT 24 SMALL PIECES

The semolina found in various Middle Eastern cakes and pastries imparts an intriguing crunch and nutty flavor. Because this version does not contain flour, it has a rather dense texture.

Syrup:	*$1/4$ teaspoon salt*
3 cups sugar	*1 cup (2 sticks) unsalted butter or*
$1^1/2$ cups water	*margarine, softened*
2 to 4 tablespoons lemon juice	*$3/4$ cup sugar*
About 1 tablespoon rose water or orange	*6 large eggs, or 2 large eggs and 1 cup*
blossom water (optional)	*milk*
	$1/2$ cup coarsely chopped blanched
Cake:	*almonds, or $1/4$ cup grated fresh or*
2 cups fine semolina or farina	*unsweetened desiccated coconut*
1 teaspoon ground cinnamon, grated	*(optional)*
lemon zest, or vanilla extract	*About 24 whole blanched almonds*
1 teaspoon double-acting baking powder	*(optional)*

1. To make the syrup: Stir the sugar, water, and lemon juice in a medium saucepan over low heat until the sugar dissolves, about 5 minutes. Stop stirring, increase the heat to medium-high, and boil until the syrup begins to thicken, about 5 minutes (it will register 225 degrees on a candy thermometer). Remove from the heat, stir in the rose water if using, and let cool.

2. Preheat the oven to 350 degrees (325 degrees if using a glass pan). For a thin cake, grease a 13-by-9-inch baking pan; for a thicker cake, use a 9-inch square pan.

3. To make the cake: Combine the semolina, cinnamon, baking powder, and salt. Beat the butter until smooth, about 1 minute. Gradually add the sugar and beat until light and creamy, about 4 minutes. Beat in the eggs, one at a time. Blend in the semolina mixture and, if desired, the chopped almonds. (The almonds can also be sprinkled on top of the cake, or add half of the batter to the pan, sprinkle with the almonds, then cover with the remaining batter.)

4. Spoon into the prepared pan, leveling the top. Cut into diamond shapes and, if desired, press a whole almond onto the top of each piece. Bake until golden brown, 30 minutes for the 13-by-9-inch pan; 45 minutes for the 9-inch square pan.

5. Gradually drizzle the cooled syrup over the hot cake. Cover and let stand until the syrup is absorbed. Store at room temperature for up to 3 days.

VARIATIONS

Cochini Semolina Cake: This southern Indian adaptation of the Middle Eastern treat is served at all special occasions. Omit the sugar syrup. Increase the sugar in the batter to $1^1/3$ cups. Add 2 cups finely chopped raisins, 2 cups finely chopped cashews, $1/4$ cup rum or brandy, 1 teaspoon ground cardamom, $1/2$ teaspoon ground cloves, and $1/2$ teaspoon grated nutmeg.

Chamali (Turkish Semolina and Almond Cake): Omit the sugar syrup. Reduce the eggs to 2, increase the sugar to $1^1/2$ cups, and add 1 cup (5 ounces) finely ground blanched almonds and 1 cup water.

Torta de Portokal  *(Syrian Orange Cake)*

8 TO 10 SERVINGS

Variations of this cake, also called *gâteau à l'orange* in the Maghreb, are found in most Sephardic communities. Iraqis like to add ¹/₂ cup grated unsweetened desiccated coconut.

2 cups all-purpose flour	2 cups sugar
1 tablespoon double-acting baking	1 cup orange juice
powder	1 tablespoon grated orange zest
¹/₈ teaspoon salt	1 teaspoon vanilla extract
6 large eggs	Confectioners' sugar for dusting

1. Preheat the oven to 325 degrees. Grease a 3-quart Bundt or tube pan.
2. Sift together the flour, baking powder, and salt. Beat the eggs and sugar until thick and creamy. Beat in the orange juice, zest, and vanilla. Blend in the flour mixture.
3. Pour into the prepared pan. Bake until golden brown, about 35 minutes. Let stand in the pan for 15 minutes, then transfer to a rack and let cool completely. Sprinkle with confectioners' sugar.

ORANGES

 Oranges, which probably originated in India, were cultivated in China as early as 4,400 years ago. This colorful fruit eventually spread to the Middle East, where it was referred to as golden apples (*tapuach zehav* in Hebrew); many scholars believe that the golden apples of Hercules were actually oranges. The Talmudic references (Shabbat 109b) to sweet citron probably refer to oranges. Although citrus fruit vanished from medieval Europe, the Arabs reintroduced them to Iberia, where these fruits thrived. Both the Ladino name for oranges, *portokal,* and the Arabic *bortugal* reflect the Iberian sojourn. So enthralled were Mediterranean Jews with citrus fruits that the presence of oranges in baked goods is frequently a sign of Sephardic influence.

Today there are more than 2,000 orange varieties, from sugary sweet to bitter, of which about 100 are cultivated on a major scale. Sweet oranges (*Citrus sinensis*) are divided into three types: common (or juice), navel, and blood. In a separate category are bitter or sour oranges (*Citrus aurantium*). Valencias, America's primary juice orange, originated on the Iberian Peninsula. The navel, the primary American eating variety, is a round, medium-sized orange that, as its name indicates, is recognizable by a secondary fetal orange on its apex end. Another common orange, the Shamouti, which originated in the Mediterranean, gave rise to the famous Jaffa orange of Israel. Blood oranges, or pigmented oranges, are small, generally seedless oranges that have a deeper flavor and redder color than other sweet oranges.

Cookies *and* Bars

And the house of Israel called its name Manna;
and it resembled coriander seed, white; and its taste
was like wafers made with honey.

—EXODUS 16:31

Of the vast assortment of baked goods, none projects a more comforting feeling than cookies—conjuring up smiles, memories of childhood, and a sense of abundance. Modern cookie making dates to seventh-century Persia and its cultivation of sugar cane. Those early treats, similar to contemporary ones found throughout the Middle East, were commonly mixed or filled with two local favorites, dates and nuts. Sephardim were soon making a variety of tender *biscochos*. On the other hand, it was another seven centuries before most European cookies evolved beyond heavy medieval honey-and-spice bars and fried wafers, primarily made from rye flour or maslin, a natural mixture of wheat and rye grains. Early Ashkenazic rabbinic literature contains numerous mentions of the term *oublie* (also called *oblaten* or *obleit*), referring to a variety of Franco-German wafers. Some *oblaten* stood on their own as cookies, while others were used as a base for various bars, such as *lebkuchen*. The most popular type was a waffle-like pastry similar to the surviving *zimtwaffen*, made on an iron heated over a flame.

Today almost every country includes at least one cookie (the word is derived from the Dutch *koekje,* "little cake") in its list of favorite foods. In this book, the term *cookie* (or *biscuit* in England) designates small, flat cakes made from doughs containing a high proportion of fat and sugar. Varying the proportions of flour, fat, and sugar, as well as adding a few other ingredients, produces interesting differences in texture, flavor, and richness. Bring all the ingredients to room temperature before blending.

Chilling the dough in the refrigerator allows the flavors to meld and the gluten to rest and makes the dough easier to handle. In addition, when the chilled dough is exposed to heat, it produces more expansion, resulting in a lighter, softer cookie. Doughs made with baking soda or without leavening can be refrigerated for up to 1 week. Most cookie doughs freeze well for up to 6 months, and dough takes up less room in the freezer than baked cookies. Thaw frozen dough in the refrigerator overnight or use it frozen, but increase the baking time by a few minutes. Most cookies taste best when eaten within a day of baking.

Flour: Too much gluten produces a tough cookie; too little yields an overly crumbly one. Many professional bakers prefer unbleached pastry flour. Bleached all-purpose flour contains less protein than unbleached and absorbs less liquid, resulting in crisper, thinner, lighter-colored, more tender cookies. Unbleached all-purpose flour produces a chewier, darker cookie with a raw flour undertone. Do not use cake flour, as the chlorine in it produces tough cookies and the acid sets the eggs faster. Use the dip-and-sweep method to measure flour for cookies: Dip a gradated measuring cup into the flour canister, filling it above the rim. Do not tap. Level the top with the back of a knife.

Fat: High-fat cookies are very tender and crumbly because the fat coats the protein, reducing the gluten's ability to absorb liquid and form a network. Butter, which can contain 18 percent water, as well as a little protein, produces a crisper cookie, which spreads and browns more than those made with vegetable shortening. A combination of one part shortening to three parts butter allows for both of these fats' attributes. Do not use diet margarine, which contains a large amount of water and produces a tough cookie. Butter and margarine should be softened until malleable yet still firm, a state that better traps air bubbles and produces a better texture.

Sweeteners: Sugar competes with the flour to absorb the small amount of liquid in a cookie, inhibiting the gluten's ability to form and producing a tender texture. Sugar also contains its own moistness, which contributes to the cookie's freshness. Sweeteners containing fructose (such as honey and molasses) are more hygroscopic than sucrose, producing soft cookies that soften further as they stand. In addition, the acid in molasses and honey reacts with any egg in the dough, setting it faster and restricting spreading. Brown sugar, which contains a little molasses, will produce a slightly softer, moister cookie than granulated sugar. Superfine sugar produces a lighter, finer-textured cookie than granulated sugar. Confectioners' sugar, which contains cornstarch, generates a more tender and delicate cookie.

Eggs: The lecithin in egg yolks coats the gluten, inhibiting its development and producing a more tender, crisper cookie. The albumen in egg whites, on the other hand, coagulates and toughens the cookie. The more whole eggs, the more the cookie puffs and the less it spreads.

Liquid: Cookie doughs call for little or no liquid besides that in the eggs and fat, as liquid increases gluten development, producing a tougher product. Some cookies contain a little milk, cream, or water to counteract the drying effect of the egg whites.

Leavening: Without leavening, cookies tend to be hard and compact. Too much leavening, however, leads to cookies that spread too much and have an off flavor. Since baking soda increases the pH of the dough, cookies containing it and no or little acid brown more quickly and deeply. Baking powder does not affect browning.

Miscellaneous Ingredients: Salt serves as a flavor enhancer. The higher the amount of sugar in the dough, the more salt that is required for balance. Cocoa powder gives a more intense flavor than chocolate in cookies and blends better with the other ingredients. Raisins and other dried fruits should be soft or they will extract moisture from the cookies, drying them. If the fruits are too dry, soak them in liquid for about 30 minutes to replenish the moisture.

Baking Cookies

Most cookies are baked in a moderate oven between 350 and 375 degrees. Use clean, heavy, flat, unwarped baking sheets with low or, preferably, no sides. Do not use pans with sides higher than $1/2$ inch, which restrict the airflow. Shiny baking sheets are preferable for cookies, as dark sheets tend to brown the bottoms. Thin sheets tend to warp and produce burned bottoms. If you have only dark baking sheets or you are baking a high-fat dough, stack a second sheet underneath. In order to allow proper air circulation, the cookie sheet should be at least 2 inches shorter in width and length than the oven.

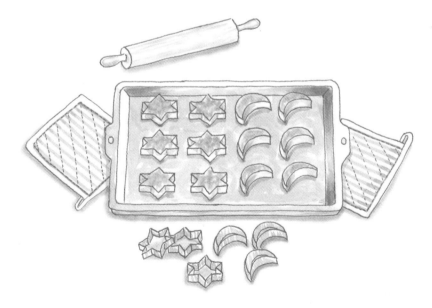

Line the sheets with parchment paper to make removal and cleanup easy and to help eliminate burned bottoms. If not using parchment paper, grease the baking sheets only if the recipe calls for it, as high-fat doughs do not require greasing. When greasing the baking sheets, use shortening or margarine and do it lightly and evenly.

To ensure uniform, evenly browned cookies, spoon or pipe out of a pastry bag equal amounts of dough and space evenly on the baking sheets, allowing room for spreading. A $1/2$-ounce (for $2^1/2$- to 3-inch cookies) to 1-ounce ice cream scoop is one of the best utensils for ensuring equal amounts. A 17-by-15-inch baking sheet holds 12 to 16 medium cookies. Since high-fat doughs spread more than low-fat ones, leave 1 to 2 inches between these types of cookies and at least 1 inch from the edges of the baking sheet. Heat is attracted to the part of the baking sheet containing the cookies, so partially filled sheets generally result in burned bottoms. To compensate, place an inverted baking pan on the unoccupied part of the sheet. Dough placed on warm baking sheets spreads more, producing flatter, crisper cookies. Cooling the baking sheets between batches will produce softer cookies. To cool cookie sheets quickly, spray with cold water, then wipe dry.

If using more than one sheet at a time, shift them halfway through baking to ensure even browning. If the cookies are browning unevenly, rotate the baking sheet. Due to the cookies' short baking time and high temperatures, be constantly on the alert for signs of doneness. Since cookies continue to bake after being removed from the oven, it's better if they are slightly underdone. If the cookies cool too much and stick to the baking sheet, return the sheet to the oven until it is warm, about 45 seconds.

High altitudes do not adversely affect most cookies. If they spread too much, reduce the amount of sugar. At elevations of 3,500 to 6,500 feet, increase the baking time by 3 to 6 minutes.

Storing Cookies

Always cool cookies completely before storing. Layer sticky or decorated cookies between sheets of waxed paper. For short-term storage, place soft cookies in an airtight container at room temperature for up to a week. To keep them soft, place a slice of apple or bread in the container, discarding them after a day or two. The cookies absorb moisture from these items and remain soft. Place crisp cookies in a loosely covered container at room temperature for up to 3 days. To keep them crisp, place a sugar cube in the container to absorb any moisture. Do not decorate with icing too far in advance, as it softens crisp cookies. Do not store soft and crisp cookies together, or the crisp cookies will soften. For long-term storage, freeze, never refrigerate, cookies in an airtight container for up to six months. Frozen cookies thaw in about 30 minutes at room temperature.

Zimtkuchen ❧ *(Alsatian Cinnamon Cookies)*

ABOUT 24 TO 30 COOKIES

I received this recipe from Lislotte Gorlin, a native of Strasbourg and member of a family that traces its roots in the area to at least 1700. When her husband, Boris, was sent to the United States in 1939 to buy machine tools, they remained in New York City. She notes that the Alsatian Jewish community has changed since her childhood as a result of the influx of eastern Europeans and North Africans. Gorlin still likes to keep alive the ancient dishes of her homeland.

1 cup plus 2 tablespoons (2^1/$_4$ sticks) unsalted butter or margarine, softened	*1 teaspoon vanilla extract*
	^{1}/$_8$ teaspoon salt
	4^1/$_2$ cups all-purpose flour, sifted
1 cup plus 2 tablespoons sugar	*^{1}/$_2$ cup sugar mixed with 2 teaspoons*
1 large egg	*ground cinnamon*

1. Preheat the oven to 350 degrees. Line 2 large baking sheets with parchment paper or lightly grease.
2. Beat the butter until creamy, about 1 minute. Gradually add the sugar and beat until light and fluffy, about 4 minutes. Beat in the egg. Add the vanilla and salt. Stir in the flour.
3. Spread the dough about ^{1}/$_4$ inch thick over the prepared baking sheets. Sprinkle with the cinnamon sugar.
4. Bake until lightly browned, 15 to 20 minutes. Let cool slightly, then cut into diamonds. Store in an airtight container at room temperature for up to 1 week or in the freezer for up to 6 months.

SPICING UP LIFE

*Spikenard and saffron, calamus and cinnamon, myrrh and aloes,
with all the chief spices.*
—SONG OF SONGS 4:14

 Before the first settlement, people discovered that parts of some plants make food taste and smell better. Archeological digs point to either cumin or poppy seeds as the first spice. Since spices store well and are relatively light, they were easily transported. Nonetheless, scarcity and shipping meant that most spices were expensive and fought over: spice trading was one of the primary movers of history.

In the sixth century, the Arabs gained a monopoly over the Eastern spice trade. Indian and Malaysian ships brought their wares to Arabia, at which point caravans carried them to Mediterranean ports, where Jewish merchants arranged for their sale in Europe. In 973 CE, Ibrahim ibn Yaacub, a Moorish merchant visiting Mainz (a city along the Rhine River and a center of early Ashkenazic life), noted the presence of cinnamon, cloves, ginger, and pepper in the marketplace. The traveler explained that these spices were all supplied by Jewish merchants called Radanites, who maintained international trade routes between the Christian and Islamic worlds. Jewish merchants filled this role until the Byzantine Empire granted Venice a trade monopoly in 992, thereafter demoting the Jews to middlemen. These four spices remained common flavorings in Ashkenazic cooking for the next thousand years.

The desire to break the Venetian monopoly on the Mediterranean spice trade led Vasco de Gama to sail around southern Africa and Columbus to venture westward to find an all-water route to the Spice Islands. Spice trading then shifted from Venice to Lisbon. The Portuguese monopoly was short-lived, for in the sixteenth century, the Dutch, noted for their sailing and business acuity, achieved control of the spice trade. In turn, the British gained dominance over India in the late seventeenth century and subsumed control of the spice trade. Eventually political intrigue led to a dispersal of spices. For example, the French smuggled cloves from their home in the Moluccas and successfully planted them on the islands of Mauritius and Réunion. Soon more cloves were being grown outside than in their native East Indies. This widening availability of spices caused a decrease in prices and a corresponding increase in general use.

Lebkuchen Hamohns ❧ *(Alsatian Gingerbread Men)*

ABOUT THIRTY 3-INCH ROUND COOKIES OR TWELVE 8-INCH GINGERBREAD MEN

Gingerbread was one of the earliest and most popular of Ashkenazic baked goods. This cookie is tender yet firm enough to hold its shape. The whimsical form makes it a popular western European Purim pastry, the figures representing the dastardly Prime Minister Haman. To make a gingerbread Zeresh (Haman's wife), squeeze a little dough through a garlic press and arrange the strands on the head of the figures to resemble hair. For Rosh Hashanah entertaining, cut the dough into *shofars* (ram's horns) and *magen Davids* (Jewish stars); for Sukkot, make leaf or fruit shapes; and for Hanukkah, dreidels (tops) and menorahs. The cookies can be decorated with an icing (see *lebkuchen,* pages 130–31).

2³/₄ *cups all-purpose flour*	¹/₂ *cup (1 stick) vegetable shortening or*
1 *teaspoon baking soda*	*margarine, softened*
¹/₂ *teaspoon salt*	¹/₂ *cup brown or granulated sugar*
1¹/₂ *teaspoons ground ginger*	1 *large egg*
1 *teaspoon ground cinnamon*	¹/₂ *cup molasses*
¹/₂ *teaspoon ground cloves*	1 *teaspoon vanilla extract*
¹/₄ *teaspoon ground allspice or nutmeg*	

1. Sift together the flour, baking soda, salt, and spices. Beat the shortening and sugar until light and fluffy, about 5 minutes. Beat in the egg, then the molasses and vanilla. Stir in the flour mixture to make a firm dough. (If the dough is too moist, add a little more flour.) Wrap in plastic wrap and refrigerate overnight. Let stand at room temperature until malleable, about 40 minutes.

2. Preheat the oven to 350 degrees. Line 2 large baking sheets with parchment paper or lightly grease.

3. Sprinkle a flat surface lightly with flour or confectioners' sugar and roll out the dough ¹/₄ inch thick. Cut into 4- to 8-inch gingerbread men or 3-inch rounds. Using a metal spatula, transfer the cookies to the prepared baking sheets.

4. Bake until lightly browned around the edges, 8 to 12 minutes. Let the cookies stand until firm, about 2 minutes, then remove to a rack and let cool completely. Store in an airtight container at room temperature for up to 2 weeks or in the freezer for up to 6 months.

Lebkuchen ❧ *(Ashkenazic Honey-Spice Cookies)*

ABOUT 25 LARGE OR 42 SMALL BARS

Lebkuchen, originally made from rye flour, were among the earliest of European cookies. The addition of an egg in this recipe produces a more tender cookie than the eggless versions. *Lebkuchen* are popular on Sukkot because of the presence of fruits and nuts. These cookies become better as they stand for a day or two.

Pastry:

1 cup (12 ounces) honey, or ¹/₂ cup honey and ¹/₂ cup molasses

³/₄ cup brown sugar

3 cups all-purpose flour

¹/₂ teaspoon baking soda

¹/₄ teaspoon salt

1 teaspoon ground cinnamon

¹/₂ teaspoon ground cloves

¹/₂ teaspoon ground ginger (optional)

¹/₄ teaspoon ground nutmeg or mace

1 large egg, lightly beaten

1 tablespoon lemon juice

2 teaspoons grated lemon or orange zest (optional)

1¹/₂ cups (8 ounces) almonds or hazelnuts, or ³/₄ cup each, finely chopped but not ground

¹/₂ cup (about 3 ounces) finely diced candied citron, orange peel, pineapple, or any combination

Icing:

1¹/₄ cups confectioners' sugar

¹/₂ teaspoon vanilla extract, or 1 tablespoon lemon juice

About 2 tablespoons warm water

---

1. To make the pastry: Stir the honey and sugar in a small saucepan over low heat until the sugar dissolves, about 5 minutes. Let cool. Sift together the flour, baking soda, salt, and spices. Stir the egg, lemon juice, and zest if using into the honey mixture. Add the nuts and fruit. Stir in the flour mixture to make a stiff dough. Cover and refrigerate for at least 2 hours or overnight. Let stand at room temperature until malleable, about 40 minutes.

2. Preheat the oven to 325 degrees. Line 2 large baking sheets with parchment paper or line with foil and lightly grease.

3. On a lightly floured surface, roll the dough into a ¹/₄-inch-thick rectangle. Cut into about twenty-five 3-by-2-inch bars or forty-two 2-by-1¹/₂-inch pieces. Place on the prepared baking sheets.

4. Bake the cookies until firm and lightly colored, about 25 minutes. Transfer to a rack and let cool completely.

5. To make the icing: Stir together the sugar, vanilla, and enough water to make a spreadable icing. Spread over the cookies and let stand until firm.

6. For softer cookies, place in an airtight container at room temperature with several apple slices.

VARIATION

Lebkuchen Bars: Line a 15^1/$_2$-by-10^1/$_2$-inch jelly roll pan with parchment paper or greased foil. Press the dough into the pan. Bake as above, place the pan on a rack, and let cool. Spread the icing over the top, let stand for 10 minutes, then cut into 2-by-1^1/$_2$-inch rectangles.

Eier Kichlach ❧ *(Ashkenazic Egg Cookies)*

ABOUT 36 COOKIES

Following Sabbath and holiday morning services, Ashkenazim traditionally enjoy a buffet in the synagogue called a *kiddush,* named after the Hebrew word for the blessing over wine. A *kiddush* may be a simple affair consisting solely of wine or schnapps (liquor) and a few cookies, or it may be an elaborate sit-down spread replete with *cholent,* kugel, and assorted baked goods.

These days at the conclusion of Sabbath morning services, I frequently find myself recalling those of my childhood and how the synagogue's *gabbai* (sexton), Mr. Wallace, would loudly announce, "*Keydoush, keydoush.*" The congregation then crowded around the tables laden with various foods, waiting for the rabbi to recite the blessing over the wine before commencing. Featured prominently among the weekly fare were trays of *kichlach.* Although simple and unexciting, these cookies remain among my favorite treats. The name of this crisp, light, sugar-topped egg cookie (*kichel* in the singular), a derivative of *kuchen,* reveals its Teutonic origins. Yet its popularity thrives among eastern European Jews, who commonly serve them accompanied by traditional appetizers such as pickled herring and egg salad or at home with tea. When possible, oil was used as the fat rather than butter or *schmaltz,* so that the cookies could be used with either meat or dairy foods.

1½ cups all-purpose flour

½ teaspoon double-acting baking powder

½ teaspoon salt

3 large eggs, lightly beaten

3 tablespoons sugar

½ cup vegetable oil

About 1½ teaspoons additional vegetable oil for brushing

About ¼ cup additional sugar (if desired, mixed with 1½ teaspoons ground cinnamon) for sprinkling

---

1. Arrange the rack in the middle of the oven. Preheat the oven to 375 degrees. Line 2 large baking sheets with parchment paper or grease.
2. Sift together the flour, baking powder, and salt. Beat the eggs and sugar until light and creamy, 5 to 10 minutes. Add the oil and beat for 10 minutes. Stir in the flour mixture.

3. On a piece of waxed paper or plastic wrap or on a lightly floured surface, roll out the dough $1/4$ inch thick. Brush with the additional oil, sprinkle with the additional sugar, and gently run a rolling pin over the top to embed the crystals. Cut into 2-inch diamonds or squares. Place on the prepared baking sheets.

4. Bake 1 sheet at a time until lightly browned, 25 to 30 minutes. Transfer to a rack and let cool. Store in a paper or cloth bag at room temperature for up to 1 week or in the freezer for up to 6 months.

VARIATION

Mohn Kichlach (Ashkenazic Poppy Seed Egg Cookies): Add 3 to 4 tablespoons poppy seeds with the flour mixture.

Mohn Platzen ❧ *(Ashkenazic Poppy Seed Cookies)*

ABOUT FIFTY 2-INCH COOKIES

Numerous versions of poppy seed cookies, also called *mohn kichlach*, can be found throughout central and eastern Europe. These treats were originally made with *schmaltz*, but most modern recipes use shortening. Poppy seed cookies are traditional Purim fare, the square and triangular shapes symbolizing Haman's pockets or hat. However, don't save them just for Purim, as they make a delicious treat at any time.

3¹/₂ *cups all-purpose flour*	2 *large eggs*
2 *teaspoons double-acting baking powder*	3 *tablespoons water*
¹/₂ *teaspoon salt*	1 *teaspoon vanilla extract*
¹/₂ *cup poppy seeds*	*About 1 cup additional sugar (if desired,*
1 *cup vegetable shortening*	*mixed with 2 tablespoons ground*
1 *cup sugar*	*cinnamon) for sprinkling*

1. Preheat the oven to 350 degrees. Line large baking sheets with parchment paper or grease.
2. Sift together the flour, baking powder, and salt. Stir in the poppy seeds. Beat the shortening and sugar until light and fluffy, about 5 minutes. Beat in the eggs, one at a time. Add the water and vanilla. Stir in the flour mixture to make a soft dough.
3. Sprinkle a flat surface with confectioners' sugar or flour and roll out the dough ¹/₄ inch thick. Sprinkle with the additional sugar and gently run a rolling pin over the top to embed the crystals. Cut into 2-inch squares, diamonds, or triangles and place on the prepared sheets. Or shape the dough into 1-inch balls, place 2 inches apart on the prepared baking sheets, dip the bottom of a glass into the additional sugar, and press onto the dough balls to flatten.
4. Bake until golden brown, about 15 minutes. Let the cookies stand until firm, about 2 minutes, then remove to a rack and let cool completely. Store in an airtight container at room temperature for up to 1 week or in the freezer for up to 6 months.

GINGER

 Ginger is the knotty rhizome (tuber-like stem) of an orchid-like plant grown in tropical climates. The name comes from the Sanskrit *sringabera,* or horn-root. Ginger's exact birthplace is impossible to pinpoint, since by the beginning of recorded history, this spicy rhizome had spread throughout much of the Orient. As international trade expanded, its pungency became an integral part of cuisines and medicines throughout most of the ancient world. Traders brought ginger to the Greeks and Romans, who in turn spread it to all parts of Europe. The Talmud (Berachot 36b; Yoma 81b) recorded that it was available both fresh and dried. With the breakdown of trade during the early medieval period, ginger and other Oriental spices became scarce commodities in the West. On his return from China, Marco Polo created a renaissance for ginger in Europe, and with the resumption of trade, its availability returned. However, ginger regained its former popularity only in northern and eastern Europe. Southerners had developed a taste for more delicate flavors, and ginger failed to win back its previously prized position.

Historically, Sephardim favored cinnamon, cardamom, and cloves, while ginger, exclusively in its dried form, became the favorite spice of eastern Europeans, who used it in such classic desserts as *ingberlach* (ginger candy), *teiglach* (dough balls), *chremslach* (matza pancakes), *lekach* (honey cake), and of course, *lebkuchen* (gingerbread). Ground ginger has a different flavor from fresh, and the two do not generally serve as substitutes for each other in most dishes. Ground ginger's primary role is in baking.

Teiglach ✎ *(Ashkenazic Dough Balls in Honey)*

ABOUT 100 SMALL COOKIE PIECES

In the days before refrigeration and vacuum packaging, ingenious cooks found other ways of preserving foods. One of these ancient culinary practices, still very much in vogue today, was soaking pastries and cakes in a syrup, a way to keep them from drying out as well as to refresh them once stale. Baklava and *baba au rhum* are arguably the two most famous examples of this technique. Italians, who have been coating pastries in honey since Roman times, developed a dish of fried dough balls in honey called *strufali* (see page 253) or *ceciarchiata* (because of its resemblance to chickpeas, *ceci* in Italian). Sephardic Jews prepare a similar dish called *pinyonati/pinionati*, commonly mixed with almonds. Eastern Europeans borrowed this concept, cooking little nuggets of noodle dough in a honey syrup and calling the dish *teiglach/tayglach* (literally "little doughies").

There are several variations of this dish. The small dough pieces can be round, cylindrical, or tied into knots. Nuts or candied fruit can be added, although eastern Europeans traditionally eschew nuts on Rosh Hashanah. The dough can be cooked in the syrup or baked first and then added to the syrup. Ashkenazim commonly flavor the syrup with ground ginger.

This treat is enjoyed on many occasions. It is a long-standing Purim dish among both Sephardim and Ashkenazim. Some people serve it at the meal following Yom Kippur. There is even a Passover version made from matza meal. *Teiglach*, however, are most prominently featured on Rosh Hashanah to start the new year on a sweet note.

Pastry:	Syrup:
About 2¹/₂ cups all-purpose flour	*2 cups (1¹/₂ pounds) dark honey, or*
1 teaspoon double-acting baking	*1³/₄ cups (1 pound) honey and*
* powder*	* ³/₄ cup sugar*
¹/₄ teaspoon salt	*1 to 3 teaspoons ground ginger,*
¹/₄ to ¹/₂ teaspoon ground ginger	* 1 teaspoon grated lemon zest, or*
* (optional)*	* 1 tablespoon lemon juice*
4 large eggs, lightly beaten	*1 cup coarsely chopped blanched*
3 tablespoons vegetable oil	* almonds, hazelnuts, pecans, or*
	* walnuts (optional)*

1. Preheat the oven to 375 degrees. Grease a baking sheet.
2. To make the pastry: Sift together the flour, baking powder, salt, and ginger if using. Combine the eggs and oil. Stir in the flour mixture, adding more flour if necessary to make a soft, workable dough. On a lightly floured surface, knead until smooth, 2 to 3 minutes. If the dough is sticky, flour your hands. To make the pastry in a food processor: In a food processor fitted with a metal blade, process all the pastry ingredients until the pastry holds together. Remove and knead several strokes until smooth.
3. Divide the dough into pieces and roll into $1/2$-inch-thick ropes. Cut into $1/2$-inch pieces. Leave as oblong shapes or roll into balls.
4. To make the syrup: Stir the honey in a large pot over low heat until it melts, about 5 minutes. Increase the heat to medium and bring to a boil.
5. Add the dough pieces, a few at a time to prevent sticking and to keep the syrup boiling. When all of the pieces are in the pot, cover and cook over medium heat for 5 minutes. Stir the *teiglach*. The pieces will expand like dumplings.
6. Cover, place in the oven, and bake for 30 minutes, stirring after 15 minutes. Stir in the ginger and, if desired, the nuts and continue baking until the *teiglach* are golden brown and hollow sounding when tapped, 5 to 15 minutes.
7. Have a bowl of ice water handy. Pour the *teiglach* onto the prepared baking sheet. Dipping your hands into the ice water, shape the *teiglach* into 1 large mound or several 3-inch mounds. Or spread to a $1^1/2$-inch thickness and cut into diamonds or squares. Let cool completely. Store in a container at room temperature for up to 2 weeks.

VARIATIONS

Baked Teiglach: Arrange the raw dough balls on a greased baking sheet and bake in a 350-degree oven until lightly browned, about 20 minutes. Add to the syrup and simmer, stirring constantly, until the *teiglach* are a rich brown color, about 10 minutes. The nuggets prepared this way tend to be harder.

Place a raisin in the center of each dough piece.

Teiglach Knots: Cut the dough ropes into $2^1/2$-inch-long pieces (about 48) and tie into knots. After cooking in the syrup, separate the knots instead of placing in mounds.

Biscochadas Dulces/Mandelbrot ❧
(Crisp Almond Slices)

ABOUT FORTY 1/2-INCH-THICK SLICES

Mandelbrot (literally "almond bread"), called *kamishbroit* in the Ukraine, is a favorite Ashkenazic cookie, derived from either the Italian *biscotti* or the Sephardic *biscochadas dulces*. *Mandelbrot* and *biscochadas dulces* commonly contain fat, giving them a richer, more cookie-like texture than classic *biscotti*. All of these cookies are "twice baked," a step that gives them a crispy texture and lengthens their shelf life, making them perfect for unexpected company. Indeed, in many Ashkenazic households, no Sabbath would be complete without a batch of *mandelbrot*.

---

2 cups all-purpose flour, preferably unbleached	2 large eggs
1 1/2 teaspoons double-acting baking powder	1 teaspoon almond extract
1/2 teaspoon salt	1/2 teaspoon vanilla extract, or 1 tablespoon lemon juice
6 tablespoons (3/4 stick) unsalted butter or margarine, softened, or 1/2 cup vegetable oil	1/2 to 1 cup coarsely chopped or sliced almonds
3/4 cup sugar	2 tablespoons sugar mixed with 1 teaspoon ground cinnamon (optional)

---

1. Preheat the oven to 375 degrees. Line a large baking sheet with parchment paper or grease and dust with flour.
2. Sift together the flour, baking powder, and salt. Beat the butter until creamy, about 1 minute. Gradually add the sugar and beat until light and fluffy, about 4 minutes. Beat in the eggs, one at a time. Add the extracts. Stir in the flour mixture, then the almonds.
3. Divide the dough in half (it will be a little sticky). Arrange each half in a long log on the prepared sheet, leaving at least 3 inches between the logs. Using floured hands, shape each log until it is about 12 inches long, 2 inches wide, and 3/4 inch high. Pat to smooth the surface. If desired, sprinkle with the cinnamon sugar.
4. Bake until lightly browned, about 20 minutes. Let the loaves cool slightly, about 10 minutes.
5. Reduce the heat to 300 degrees,
6. Using a serrated knife, cut the logs diagonally into 1/2-inch-thick slices. For softer cookies, do not bake the slices. For crispy cookies, place the slices, cut side down, on the bak-

ing sheet. Bake until crisp, about 12 minutes. Transfer to a rack and let cool. Store in an airtight container at room temperature for up to 2 weeks or in the freezer for up to 6 months. If desired, serve with coffee, tea, sweet wine, *kissel* (berry pudding), or fruit compote.

HINT: ∾ Use *mandelbrot* crumbs in strudel instead of bread crumbs.

VARIATIONS

Chocolate Mandelbrot: Add 3 ounces melted semisweet or bittersweet chocolate or 3 tablespoons unsweetened alkalized (Dutch-processed) cocoa powder. If desired, add 1/2 to 3/4 cup chocolate chips.

Coconut Mandelbrot: Substitute 1/2 cup grated unsweetened desiccated coconut for the almonds.

Lemon Mandelbrot: Substitute 1 tablespoon grated lemon zest or 1 teaspoon lemon extract for the almond extract.

Marble Mandelbrot: Remove 1/2 cup dough and stir in 2 tablespoons cocoa powder or 1 ounce melted semisweet or bittersweet chocolate. Swirl the chocolate dough into the plain dough.

Orange Mandelbrot: Substitute 2 tablespoons grated orange zest or 1/2 teaspoon orange extract for the almond extract.

Poppy Seed Mandelbrot: Substitute 1/4 cup poppy seeds for the almonds and omit the almond extract. If desired, add 1 tablespoon grated lemon zest or 1/2 teaspoon lemon extract.

Chocolate-Filled Mandelbrot: Combine 1 ounce melted unsweetened chocolate, 1/4 cup confectioners' sugar, and 1 large egg white. Flatten the dough logs, spread the chocolate mixture down the center, fold the sides over the filling, and press to seal.

Jam-Filled Mandelbrot: Flatten the dough logs, spread about 1/4 cup jam or marmalade down the center of each loaf, fold the sides over the filling, and press to seal.

Biscotti ❧ *(Italian Twice-Baked Cookies)*

ABOUT FORTY 1/2-INCH-THICK COOKIES

Biscotti (Italian for "twice cooked") are, as the name reveals, baked a second time, thereby drying them and extending their shelf life. This cookie is harder and keeps longer than those containing butter or oil. Since it contains whole eggs, it is a crunchier cookie than *biscotti* containing only egg yolks. On the other hand, those containing no fat or yolks, only egg whites, are extremely hard. *Biscotti* are traditionally eaten by first dipping into **vin santo** (sweet wine) or coffee.

2 cups all-purpose flour, preferably unbleached	1/2 teaspoon salt
1/2 teaspoon double-acting baking powder	2 large eggs, lightly beaten
	3/4 cup plus 2 tablespoons sugar
1/2 teaspoon baking soda	1 teaspoon vanilla extract

1. Preheat the oven to 350 degrees. Line a large baking sheet with parchment paper or grease and flour the sheet.
2. Sift together the flour, baking powder, baking soda, and salt. Beat the eggs and sugar until light and creamy, 5 to 10 minutes. Add the vanilla. Stir in the flour mixture.
3. Divide the dough in half. Arrange each half in a long log on the prepared sheet, leaving 3 inches between the logs. Using floured hands, shape each log until it is about 12 inches long, 2 inches wide, and 3/4 inch high. Pat to smooth the surface.
4. Bake until firm and lightly browned, 30 to 40 minutes. Let the logs cool slightly on the baking sheets, about 10 minutes.
5. Reduce the heat to 300 degrees.
6. Using a serrated knife, cut the logs diagonally into 1/2-inch-thick slices. Arrange the slices, cut side down, on the baking sheet. Bake, turning once, until golden brown and dry, about 7 minutes per side. Transfer to racks and let cool completely. Store in an airtight container at room temperature for up to 1 month or in the freezer for up to 6 months.

VARIATIONS

Biscotti di Anice (Anise Biscotti): Add 1 to 2 tablespoons anise seeds and 2 tablespoons anise-flavored liqueur.

Biscotti di Limone (Lemon Biscotti): Add 1 tablespoon grated lemon zest. If desired, add 1 tablespoon anise seeds or $1/2$ cup sesame seeds.

Biscotti di Arancia (Orange Biscotti): Add 1 to 2 tablespoons grated orange zest.

Biscotti di Nocciuola (Hazelnut Biscotti): Add $2/3$ cup toasted, skinned, and coarsely chopped hazelnuts.

Chocolate Chip and Almond Biscotti: Add 12 ounces (2 cups) chocolate chips and 5 ounces (1 cup) toasted and coarsely chopped blanched almonds.

ITALY

 The first known Jews to have visited Italy were members of a delegation sent by Judah Maccabee in 161 BCE to conduct a treaty between Rome and Judea. Soon thereafter, Jewish traders made their way to the growing Mediterranean power, and Jews have lived in the country ever since. Jewish numbers substantially increased in 63 BCE, when Pompey brought captives back to Rome after capturing Jerusalem.

For nearly 1,500 years, most of Italy's Jewish population resided in the southern part of the country. In 1492, the Spanish, then in control of Sicily and Sardinia, forced the Jews from those islands. Nine years later Spain acquired the kingdom of Naples, which at the time consisted of all of southern Italy, and expelled its Jews. Thereafter, Jewish life shifted to northern and central Italy.

Conditions in Venice, the second largest Jewish community in Italy and surpassed in size only by Rome, were generally better than in other parts of the country. Still, it was the Venetians who in 1516 established the first ghetto, the Italian word for a foundry located next to the Jewish area. For nearly three centuries, until the arrival of Napoleon in 1800, Jews in every Italian city remained segregated in ghettos—some, like the one in Rome, terribly overcrowded.

The breaching of the ghetto walls introduced non-Jewish Italians to some of the most ancient Jewish dishes. As late as the mid-1880s, eggplant and fennel were still considered, in the words of the Florentine cookbook writer Pellegrino Artusi, "the vile food of the Jews." Eventually Jewish fare became an integral part of Italian cuisine, bearing such phrases as *all' Ebraica* ("from the Hebrew") and *alla Giudia* (Giudia is the name of the Roman ghetto).

Kooleecha ❧ *(Calcutta Coconut Cookies)*

ABOUT 24 COOKIES

Indians use coconut to make a number of confections. This cookie reflects a synthesis of Asian and Middle Eastern influences.

---

2 cups (6 ounces) grated fresh or
    unsweetened desiccated coconut
$^2/_3$ cup milk or nondairy creamer
1 cup (6 ounces) fine semolina (not
    semolina flour)
1 teaspoon double-acting baking powder
Pinch of salt

$^1/_2$ cup (1 stick) unsalted butter or
    margarine, softened
$^3/_4$ cup sugar, preferably superfine
Vegetable oil for brushing
About $^1/_4$ cup kala jeera/kelonji (nigella,
    a seed mistakenly called black onion
    seeds) or poppy seeds

---

1. Preheat the oven to 350 degrees. Line 2 large baking sheets with parchment paper or grease.
2. Stir the coconut into the milk and let soak for 5 minutes.
3. Combine the semolina, baking powder, and salt. Beat the butter until smooth, about 1 minute. Gradually add the sugar and beat until light and fluffy, about 4 minutes. Stir in the semolina mixture and coconut mixture.
4. Shape into 1-inch balls, place on a prepared baking sheet, and flatten slightly. Brush with the oil and sprinkle with the seeds.
5. Bake until golden brown, about 20 minutes. Let the cookies stand until firm, about 2 minutes, then remove to a rack and let cool completely. Store in an airtight container at room temperature for up to 1 week or in the freezer for up to 6 months.

Joodse Boterkocke ❧ *(Dutch Butter Cookies)*

ABOUT 36 COOKIES

The Netherlands became a haven for Sephardim and Conversos (Jews forcibly converted) from Spain and Portugal. These exiles merged their Iberian fare with the local cuisine, creating such dishes as these rich cookies, which the Dutch called Jewish butter cookies. The absence of leavening and liquid and the high proportion of fat and sugar result in a very tender cookie. This recipe calls for only egg yolks, since the whites detract from its tenderness. However, since shaped cookies are not worked as much as rolled cookies, one whole egg can be substituted for the two egg yolks without making the final product tough. Because the dough contains no leavening, the cookies hold their basic shape during baking.

---

1 cup (2 sticks) unsalted butter or
   margarine, softened, or $3/4$ cup butter
   and $1/4$ cup vegetable shortening
$2/3$ cup sugar, preferably superfine, or
   $3/4$ cup confectioners' sugar

2 large egg yolks
1 teaspoon vanilla extract
$1/4$ teaspoon salt
2 cups all-purpose flour, sifted

---

1. Beat the butter until smooth, about 1 minute. Gradually add the sugar and beat until light and fluffy, about 4 minutes. Beat in the egg yolks. Add the vanilla and salt. Stir in the flour. Wrap in plastic wrap and refrigerate for at least 1 hour or up to 5 days.
2. Preheat the oven to 375 degrees.
3. Pipe the dough through a pastry bag into 2- to 3-inch sticks (a fluted tip creates attractive ridges), spacing them 2 inches apart on large ungreased baking sheets. Or shape into 1-inch balls, place 2 inches apart on the baking sheets, and flatten slightly.
4. Bake until set but not browned, 8 to 10 minutes. Let the cookies stand until firm, about 1 minute, then remove to a rack and let cool completely. Store in an airtight container at room temperature for up to 1 week or in the freezer for up to 6 months.

VARIATION

Jodekager (Danish "Jewish Cakes"): Substitute 1 cup dark brown sugar for the granulated sugar and add 1 teaspoon grated lemon zest and a pinch of ground cardamom.

Anisplatzchen ⤜ *(German Anise Drops)*

ABOUT NINETY 1½-INCH COOKIES

These soft cookies form their own icing during baking.

1½ *cups all-purpose flour*	3 *large eggs*
½ *teaspoon double-acting baking powder*	1 *cup plus 2 tablespoons sugar*
½ *teaspoon salt*	1 *tablespoon anise seeds*

1. Grease and dust with flour 3 large baking sheets. Sift together the flour, baking powder, and salt. Beat the eggs until light and fluffy, 5 to 10 minutes. Gradually beat in the sugar, then continue beating for 20 minutes. Stir in the flour mixture and anise seeds.
2. Drop the batter by heaping teaspoonfuls onto the prepared baking sheets, leaving 2 inches between the cookies. Let stand at room temperature, uncovered, overnight.
3. Preheat the oven to 325 degrees.
4. Bake until golden on the bottoms and creamy on the tops, about 10 minutes. Transfer to a rack and let cool completely. Store at room temperature in an airtight container with a large slice of apple.

Mahltaschen ❧ *(German Meringue-Topped Cookies)*

ABOUT 48 COOKIES

German bakers prepare a large array of plain meringue kisses, as well as various meringue-based cookies. Bakers developed treats like this meringue-topped one to utilize egg whites that were not used in the dough.

Pastry:	Meringue:
2 cups all-purpose flour, sifted	6 large egg whites
3 tablespoons sugar	1 cup sugar
Pinch of salt	8 ounces ground blanched almonds
1 cup (2 sticks) unsalted butter or	(about 2 cups plus 2 tablespoons)
margarine, chilled	2 tablespoons lemon juice, or 1 teaspoon
6 large egg yolks	vanilla extract
	1 teaspoon finely grated lemon zest
	(optional)

1. To make the pastry: Combine the flour, sugar, and salt. Cut in the butter to resemble coarse crumbs. Stir in the egg yolks to make a soft dough. Wrap in plastic wrap and refrigerate overnight.
2. Preheat the oven to 450 degrees.
3. To make the meringue: Beat the egg whites on low until foamy, about 30 seconds. Increase the speed to high and beat until soft peaks form, 1 to 2 minutes. Gradually add the sugar and beat until stiff and glossy, 5 to 8 minutes. Gradually stir in the nuts, lemon juice, and zest if using.
4. Form the pastry into about forty-eight 3/4-inch balls. Place the balls on a lightly floured surface and roll into thin 3-inch rounds. Place the rounds on large ungreased baking sheets and spoon or pipe a little meringue mixture into the center of each round.
5. Bake until golden brown, about 12 minutes. Transfer to a rack and let cool. Store in an airtight container at room temperature for up to 5 days or in the freezer for up to 6 months.

MERINGUE

 Meringue, named for the German town of Mehringen, seems to date back to the sixteenth century, when it was called "imitation snow." By the seventeenth century, Italian, French, and German cookbooks reveal a multitude of diverse meringue recipes. Around this time, Jewish cooks adopted this innovation to make a variety of cookies.

Meringue is a mixture of beaten egg whites and sugar. By adding ingredients or varying the cooking methods, the mixture is transformed into a variety of treats. There are three basic types of meringue: soft meringue, hard meringue (called *meringues ordinaires* or Swiss meringue), and Italian meringue. Swiss meringue contains a larger amount of sugar than the soft variation and is baked at a low temperature until hard and dry. Soft meringue, generally used as a topping for pies and baked Alaska, is baked at a high temperature until lightly browned, or poached as for floating islands. Italian meringue is made by beating a hot sugar syrup into beaten egg whites.

Zimtsterne ❧ *(German Cinnamon Stars)*

These nut meringues are also called *erstesternen* ("first stars"), a reference to the heavenly signs indicating the end of a fast day. They are traditionally served by German Jews at the meal following Yom Kippur.

1¹/2 cups (about 8 ounces) hazelnuts or blanched almonds, finely ground	*Pinch of salt*
1 teaspoon ground cinnamon	*1¹/2 cups confectioners' sugar*
³/4 teaspoon grated lemon zest	*About ¹/2 cup additional confectioners' sugar for rolling*
¹/4 cup egg whites (about 2 large)	

1. Preheat the oven to 350 degrees. Line a large baking sheet with parchment paper or aluminum foil.

2. Combine the nuts, cinnamon, and zest. Beat the egg whites on low speed until foamy, about 30 seconds. Add the salt, increase the speed to medium-high, and beat until soft peaks form, 1 to 2 minutes. Gradually add the confectioners' sugar and beat until stiff and glossy, 5 to 8 minutes. Reserve one-third of the meringue (about ¹/3 cup) and fold the nut mixture into the remaining meringue.

3. Place a large piece of waxed paper on a flat surface and sprinkle with additional confectioners' sugar. Place the nut mixture on the sugar, lightly sprinkle with more confectioners' sugar, top with a second piece of waxed paper, and roll out ¹/4 inch thick. Remove the top piece of waxed paper. Using a cookie cutter dipped in water, cut into 2-inch star shapes or use a sharp knife to cut into diamonds. Reroll and cut any scraps. Place on the prepared baking sheet.

4. Bake until set, 10 to 12 minutes. Spread the reserved meringue over the top of the cookies and bake until the tops are lightly colored, about 5 minutes. Transfer to a rack and let cool. *Zimtsternen* taste best if allowed to stand for 24 hours. Store in an airtight container at room temperature for up to 3 weeks.

CINNAMON

*Take also the chief spices, of flowing myrrh five hundred shekels, and of sweet
cinnamon half so much, even two hundred and fifty, and of sweet calamus
two hundred and fifty, and cassia five hundred . . .*

—EXODUS 30:23–24

 Cinnamon, the bark of a tropical evergreen tree of the laurel family native to Sri Lanka, has long been one of the world's favorite spices, so cherished that its source was once hidden. Twice a year, in May and October, the inner bark is harvested, then rolled into quills. The outer cork layer is removed, and the remaining layer is left to dry.

In the early twentieth century, the price of cinnamon skyrocketed, and Americans began to substitute inexpensive cassia, the bark of a laurel tree native to Burma (but sometimes called Chinese cinnamon). As a result, today most of the cinnamon sold in America and the flavor most Americans associate with this spice is actually the stronger-flavored cassia. Cinnamon has a pale tan color, pleasing fragrance, and sweet-pungent, slightly citrusy flavor with a hint of cloves. Cassia is a less delicate spice with a reddish brown (almost coppery) hue and a spicy-sweet flavor that is best for savory dishes.

Cinnamon has long been a Jewish favorite, serving as one of the ingredients in the anointing oil used to consecrate the priests and Temple vessels, as well as a component of the Temple incense. The Talmud states that "the kindling of Jerusalem were of cinnamon trees" (Shabbat 63a). It is certainly ubiquitous to Jewish desserts across the globe.

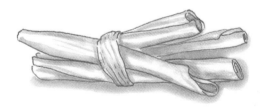

Weisskichlach ❧ *(Hungarian Sugar Cookies)*

ABOUT THIRTY 4-INCH OR SIXTY 2½-INCH COOKIES

This dough contains a lower proportion of fat than butter cookies and also includes a little liquid. The large proportion of sugar and smaller proportion of flour in this dough makes for a tender cookie. Using shortening produces a crisper, chewier cookie. Doughs containing baking soda and no acid brown quicker and more than those with baking powder. The cookies can be sprinkled with colored sugar before baking or spread with icing afterward.

2¼ cups all-purpose flour

2 teaspoons double-acting baking powder, or ½ teaspoon baking soda

½ teaspoon salt

½ cup (1 stick) unsalted butter or margarine, softened, or ¼ cup butter and ¼ cup vegetable shortening

1 cup sugar, preferably superfine

2 large egg yolks, or 1 large egg

3 tablespoons milk, fruity white wine, or water

1½ teaspoons vanilla extract

---

1. Sift together the flour, baking powder, and salt. Beat the butter until smooth, about 1 minute. Gradually add the sugar and beat until light and fluffy, about 4 minutes. Beat in the egg yolks, then the milk and vanilla. Gradually stir in the flour mixture. Form into a ball, wrap in plastic wrap, and refrigerate until firm, at least 1 hour or up to 1 week. Let stand at room temperature until malleable, about 40 minutes.

2. Preheat the oven to 375 degrees.

3. Divide the dough in half. On a piece of waxed paper or plastic wrap or on a floured surface, roll out each half ⅛ to ¼ inch thick. (The thinner the cookie, the crisper it will be.) Cut out rounds, squares, or other desired shapes and place on ungreased baking sheets.

4. Bake until lightly golden, 8 to 11 minutes. Let the cookies stand until firm, about 1 minute, then remove to a rack and let cool completely. Store in an airtight container at room temperature for up to 1 week or in the freezer for up to 6 months.

VARIATIONS

Tahinov Hatz (Armenian Tahini Cookies): Omit the milk and add 1 cup tahini (sesame seed paste) and 1 cup finely chopped walnuts.

Geback (German Sugar Cookies): Add 1 1/2 teaspoons ground cinnamon.

Weisskichlach mit Kummel (Hungarian Caraway Sugar Cookies): Add 1 tablespoon caraway seeds.

Kranzli ❧ *(Hungarian Shortbread Cookies)*

ABOUT FORTY 3-INCH COOKIES

This is a common treat for Sabbath lunch or afternoon in many Hungarian households. The egg yolks make the cookies firmer than Scottish shortbread.

About 2 1/4 cups all-purpose flour, sifted	*4 large egg yolks*
1/2 teaspoon salt	*1 teaspoon vanilla extract or lemon juice*
1 cup (2 sticks) unsalted butter or margarine, chilled	*1 large egg white (optional)*
2 1/2 cups confectioners' sugar	*About 1 cup coarsely broken sugar cubes (optional)*

1. Preheat the oven to 350 degrees.
2. Combine the flour and salt. Cut in the butter to resemble coarse crumbs. Add the sugar. Stir in the yolks and vanilla. Knead briefly until the dough just holds together. Form into a ball, flatten slightly, wrap, and refrigerate overnight. Let stand at room temperature until malleable, about 40 minutes.
3. On a piece of waxed paper or plastic wrap or on a lightly floured surface, roll out the dough 1/2 inch thick. Cut into 2- to 3-inch rounds or squares and place on ungreased baking sheets.
4. If desired, beat the egg white until stiff but not dry. Brush the dough with the beaten egg white, then sprinkle with the sugar crystals.
5. Bake until golden brown, about 12 minutes. Let the cookies stand until firm, about 1 minute, then remove to a rack and let cool completely. Store in an airtight container at room temperature for up to 1 week or in the freezer for up to 6 months.

VARIATIONS

Chocolate Shortbread: Sift the flour with 1/2 cup unsweetened cocoa powder, preferably alkalized (Dutch processed).

Coconut Shortbread: Add 1 1/3 cups (3 1/2 ounces) grated unsweetened desiccated coconut and, if desired, 1/8 teaspoon almond extract.

Lemon Shortbread: Add 1 to 2 tablespoons grated lemon zest.

Nut Shortbread: Add 1 cup coarsely chopped almonds, hazelnuts, pecans, or walnuts.

Poppy Shortbread: Add 3 tablespoons poppy seeds. For Lemon-Poppy Shortbread, also add 1 to 2 tablespoons grated lemon zest.

HUNGARY

 In 800, Charlemagne made the land to the west of the Danube a tributary, and in the process, its Jewish community, which had lived in the area since Roman times, was united with the Ashkenazim. The Ashkenazic influence was further enriched with the arrival of immigrants fleeing the Crusaders and other massacres in the West.

At the end of the ninth century, a nomadic group called the Magyars settled in the area. With the Ottoman domination of the region beginning in 1526, the Jews of Hungary experienced unprecedented opportunities, and the previously demoralized Jewish community began to thrive. The makeup of the Hungarian Jewish community underwent other changes as Sephardic Jews made their way to the area. Following the Ottoman retreat in 1687, Austria filled the power vacuum in Hungary for the following two centuries.

Beginning in the mid-seventeenth century, the size of the Hungarian Jewish community was greatly augmented with the arrival of immigrants escaping from troubles in Poland. Hungary would remain host to one of the largest Jewish communities. However, of the 800,000 Jews living in Hungary in 1941, only about 200,000 survived the Holocaust. The subsequent Communist rule led to emigration, and today the Hungarian Jewish community numbers only about 70,000.

The arrival of the Turks produced, among other important side effects, a major improvement in Hungarian cooking. Austrian domination further transformed the culture and food. As a result of the varied influences, Hungarian-Jewish cuisine evolved into the liveliest form of Ashkenazic cooking. Hungarians have a penchant for creating rich desserts (generally much sweeter than their Austrian counterparts), ranging from *makos metelt* (sweetened noodles with poppy seeds) to elaborate tortes. Unquestionably, the favorite of all is the classic strudel.

Farfel Torten ❧ *(Hungarian "Farfel" Bars)*

ABOUT FIFTY 2-BY-1½-INCH BARS

In this treat, some of the dough is grated into pellets like farfel, the traditional Ashkenazic egg noodle dough; hence its name. My mother makes a version without the top pastry layer that she calls florentines.

Pastry:

4 cups all-purpose flour

1 teaspoon double-acting baking powder

1/8 teaspoon salt

1 cup (2 sticks) vegetable shortening or
    margarine, softened

1 cup sugar

5 large egg yolks

Several drops of lemon juice or water

Meringue:

8 ounces walnuts, finely chopped
    (about 2²/₃ cups)

2 teaspoons unsweetened cocoa powder
    (optional)

1 teaspoon grated lemon zest

1 teaspoon grated orange zest (optional)

5 large egg whites

1/3 cup sugar

1/2 teaspoon vanilla extract

About 1 cup apricot, seedless raspberry,
    or strawberry jam, or 1/2 cup
    strawberry jam mixed with 1/2 cup
    tart plum preserves

---

1. To make the pastry: Sift together the flour, baking powder, and salt. Beat the shortening and sugar until light and creamy, about 5 minutes. Beat in the egg yolks, one at a time. Add the lemon juice. Stir in the flour mixture and knead to make a very firm dough. Divide the dough in half, form into discs, wrap, and refrigerate overnight. Coarsely grate one half of the dough. Let the remaining half stand at room temperature until malleable, about 40 minutes.

2. Preheat the oven to 350 degrees. Grease a 15½-by-10½-inch jelly roll pan.

3. To make the meringue: Combine the walnuts, cocoa powder if using, and zest. Beat the egg whites on low speed until foamy, about 30 seconds. Increase the speed to medium-high and beat until soft peaks form, 1 to 2 minutes. Gradually add the sugar and beat until stiff and glossy, 5 to 8 minutes. Fold in the walnut mixture and vanilla.

4. On a piece of waxed paper or plastic wrap or on a lightly floured surface, roll out the dough to fit the bottom of the pan and transfer to the pan. Spread with the jam, then top with the meringue. Sprinkle the grated dough over the top.

5. Bake until golden brown, about 1 hour. While still warm, cut into squares or bars. Store in an airtight container at room temperature for up to 1 week or in the freezer for up to 6 months.

VARIATIONS

Omit the top layer of grated pastry. Do not fold the walnut mixture into the meringue. Instead, sprinkle half of the walnut mixture over the jam, spread the meringue on top, and sprinkle with the remaining nut mixture.

Florentines: Omit the walnut mixture from the meringue, as well as the top layer of grated pastry.

Vajas Pogácha ❧ *(Hungarian Sour Cream Cookies)*

ABOUT THIRTY 3-INCH COOKIES

These cookies, also called *pogacheles*, are a modern version of a yeast-based treat. Sour cream produces a tender crumb and pleasantly mellow, tart flavor.

2 cups all-purpose flour	1/2 cup (1 stick) unsalted butter, softened
1/2 teaspoon double-acting baking powder	1/2 cup sugar, preferably superfine
	2 large egg yolks, or 1 large egg
1/2 teaspoon baking soda	1/2 cup sour cream
Pinch of salt	1/2 teaspoon vanilla extract

1. Preheat the oven to 350 degrees.
2. Sift together the flour, baking powder, baking soda, and salt. Beat the butter until smooth, about 1 minute. Gradually add the sugar and beat until light and creamy, about 4 minutes. Beat in the egg yolks, one at a time. Add the sour cream and vanilla. Stir in the flour mixture.
3. On a piece of waxed paper or plastic wrap or on a lightly floured surface, roll out the dough 1/4 inch thick. Cut into 3-inch rounds and place on 2 large ungreased baking sheets.
4. Bake until lightly browned, about 12 minutes. Let the cookies stand until firm, about 1 minute, then remove to a rack and let cool completely. Store in an airtight container at room temperature for up to 1 week or in the freezer for up to 6 months.

Hadgi Badah ❧ *(Iraqi Cardamom-Almond Cookies)*

These cookies, a favorite of Iraqi Jews, are traditionally served during Purim and at the meal following Yom Kippur.

2 cups all-purpose flour	2 cups (10 ounces) ground blanched
1 teaspoon ground cardamom	almonds
1/2 teaspoon salt	Rose water for moistening hands
1/4 teaspoon double-acting baking	(optional)
powder	About 6 dozen whole almonds
1 1/3 cups sugar	(optional)
4 large eggs	

1. Preheat the oven to 350 degrees. Line several large baking sheets with parchment paper or grease.

2. Sift together the flour, cardamom, salt, and baking powder. Beat together the sugar and eggs until light and smooth. Stir in the flour mixture, then the ground almonds.

3. Form the dough into 1-inch balls, moistening your hands with rose water if using. Place on the prepared baking sheets and flatten slightly. If desired, press a whole almond into the center of each cookie.

4. Bake until lightly browned, about 12 minutes. Let the cookies stand until firm, about 1 minute, then remove to a rack and let cool completely. Store in an airtight container at room temperature for up to 1 week or in the freezer for up to 6 months.

Ghribi ❧ *(Moroccan Shortbread Cookies)*

These simple cookies, also spelled *ghouribi,* appear at nearly every Moroccan celebration.

2 cups all-purpose flour, sifted	1/2 cup vegetable oil
1/2 cup sugar	Ground cinnamon for sprinkling
1/4 teaspoon salt	(optional)

1. Preheat the oven to 350 degrees.
2. Combine the flour, sugar, and salt. Stir in the oil.
3. Form into 1 1/2-inch balls and place on 2 large ungreased baking sheets. Or roll the dough balls into thin rounds. If desired, sprinkle lightly with the cinnamon.
4. Bake until firm but not colored, about 30 minutes. Transfer to a rack and let cool. Store in an airtight container at room temperature for up to 1 week or in the freezer for up to 6 months.

VARIATIONS

Kurabie (Moroccan Almond Cookies): Add 1 tablespoon tahini (sesame seed paste), 2 teaspoons almond extract, and 1 teaspoon ground cinnamon. If desired, brush with lightly beaten egg and place a whole almond in the center of each cookie.

Ras Tahini (Moroccan Sesame Paste Cookies): Substitute 1 cup tahini (sesame seed paste) for the oil and add 1/4 cup water, 1 teaspoon ground cinnamon, and if desired, 1/4 teaspoon ground cloves.

Nane Berenji  *(Persian Rice Flour Cookies)*

ABOUT 48 COOKIES

Many modern versions of this cookie call for butter, but earlier recipes used oil because dairy products were once rare in Middle Eastern Jewish baking. These delicate bright white cookies are traditionally served during Purim and Passover. Persians never accepted the Ashkenazic restrictions against eating rice during Passover.

---

1 cup (2 sticks) unsalted butter or margarine, softened, or $3/4$ cup vegetable oil

$2/3$ cup granulated sugar, or 1 cup confectioners' sugar

1 large egg

2 tablespoons rose water and/or $1/2$ to 1 teaspoon ground cardamom

1 teaspoon vanilla extract

$1/4$ teaspoon salt

$1^1/2$ cups rice flour (see page 338) or cream of rice

About 3 tablespoons finely chopped almonds or pistachios (optional)

---

1. Beat the butter until smooth, about 1 minute. Gradually add the sugar and beat until light and fluffy, about 4 minutes. Beat in the egg, rose water, vanilla, and salt. Stir in the rice flour. Wrap in plastic wrap and refrigerate for at least 4 hours or overnight.
2. Preheat the oven to 350 degrees.
3. Shape the dough into 1-inch balls, place 2 inches apart on ungreased baking sheets, and flatten slightly. Sprinkle with the nuts if using.
4. Bake until set but not browned, about 15 minutes. Let the cookies stand until firm, about 4 minutes, then remove to a rack and let cool completely. Store in an airtight container at room temperature for up to 3 days or in the freezer for up to 6 months.

Biscochos de Huevo ❧ *(Sephardic Cookie Rings)*

ABOUT 80 MEDIUM COOKIES

These doughnut-shaped cookies, also called *biscochos dulces* and *kaak*, are one of the most widespread of Sephardic cookies. Proficient home bakers pride themselves on being able to produce batch after batch of uniform shapes.

4¹/2 cups all-purpose flour	*1 cup sugar*
4 teaspoons double-acting baking powder	*¹/2 cup vegetable oil*
	¹/2 teaspoon vanilla extract
Pinch of salt	*Egg wash (1 egg beaten with 1 teaspoon*
3 large eggs	*water and 1 teaspoon sugar)*

1. Preheat the oven to 350 degrees.
2. Sift together the flour, baking powder, and salt. Beat the eggs, sugar, oil, and vanilla until light. Gradually stir in the flour mixture to make a soft dough.
3. Roll the dough into ¹/2-inch-thick ropes. Cut into 4- or 5-inch lengths and bring the ends together to form rings. If desired, cut small incisions on the outer edge of the rings at ¹/2- or 1-inch intervals. Or on a piece of waxed paper or plastic wrap or on a lightly floured surface, roll out the dough ¹/4 inch thick and cut into 2-inch squares. Place on ungreased baking sheets and brush with the egg wash.
4. Bake until golden brown, about 20 minutes. Let the cookies stand until firm, about 1 minute, then remove to a rack and let cool completely. For crisper cookies, turn off the oven and let dry for 10 to 20 minutes. Store in an airtight container for up to 1 week or in the freezer for up to 6 months.

VARIATIONS

Sephardic Orange Cookie Rings: Add 1 tablespoon orange blossom water and 2 to 3 teaspoons grated orange zest.

Reshicas (Greek Pretzel-Shaped Cookies): These are customarily served to break the fast of Yom Kippur. Loop the ends of the dough ropes over the middle to produce a pretzel shape. After brushing the dough rings with the egg wash, sprinkle with about 1 cup sesame seeds.

Biscochos de Susam/Kaak ib Sumsum (Sephardic Sesame Cookie Rings): These cookies, also called *taraleekoos,* are customarily served to break the fast of Yom Kippur. After brushing the dough rings with the egg wash, sprinkle with about 1 cup sesame seeds.

Biscochos de Muez/Kaak ib Loz (Sephardic Nut Cookie Rings): After brushing the dough rings with the egg wash, sprinkle with about 1 cup chopped almonds, pistachios, or walnuts.

Barazeh (Middle Eastern Sesame Seed Cookies): Combine $1/2$ cup sesame seeds, 1 tablespoon honey, and 1 tablespoon warm water. Shape the dough into 1-inch balls and dip half of each ball into the sesame mixture.

SESAME SEEDS

 Upon ripening, the pods of an herbaceous Middle Eastern plant split open to reveal a cache of small oval seeds. There are two basic varieties of sesame—tan and black. The tan seeds are also hulled and sold as white seeds. Tan and white seeds possess a nutty sweet flavor and no aroma. Black seeds are more pungent than the lighter ones. Unless otherwise specified, always use the tan seeds.

Sesame seeds, possibly native to Africa, have been grown in the Middle East since at least 3000 BCE, used whole, ground into a paste, and pressed for the oil. The Talmud (Shev. 2:7) noted sesame's use as a spice in a number of pastries. Among Ashkenazim, sesame seeds play a limited culinary role, primarily sprinkled on baked goods as a garnish.

Sesame oil (the seeds contain about 50 percent oil) is used not only for cooking but also to fuel lamps in Iraq, Syria, Egypt, and India. Middle Eastern sesame oil is made from raw sesame seeds, while Oriental sesame oil, which has a dark brown color and nutty flavor, is made from toasted sesame seeds.

Toasting brings out the sesame's flavor. To toast, spread the seeds over a baking sheet, place in a 350-degree oven, and bake, turning occasionally, until golden, about 10 minutes. Or stir the seeds in a dry heavy skillet over medium-low heat until lightly browned. Be careful—they burn quickly.

Biscochos de Almendra ❧ *(Sephardic Almond Cookies)*

ABOUT THIRTY-SIX 2-INCH OR TWENTY-FOUR 3-INCH COOKIES

This simple cookie remains one of the tastiest.

---

1 cup all-purpose flour, sifted

1/2 cup finely ground blanched almonds or hazelnuts

1/2 teaspoon double-acting baking powder

1/4 teaspoon salt

1/2 cup (1 stick) unsalted butter or margarine, softened

1/2 cup sugar

1 large egg

1/4 teaspoon almond extract, or 1/2 teaspoon vanilla extract

1/4 teaspoon rose water or ground cinnamon

---

1. Preheat the oven to 375 degrees.
2. Combine the flour, almonds, baking powder, and salt. Beat the butter until smooth, about 1 minute. Gradually add the sugar and beat until light and fluffy, about 4 minutes. Beat in the egg. Add the extract and rose water. Stir in the flour mixture.
3. Drop the dough by the tablespoonful (for 2-inch cookies), 2 inches apart, or 2 tablespoonfuls (for 3-inch cookies), 3 inches apart, onto 2 large ungreased baking sheets and flatten slightly.
4. Bake until golden brown, 8 to 12 minutes. Let the cookies stand until firm, about 1 minute, then remove to a rack and let cool completely. Store in an airtight container for up to 1 week or in the freezer for up to 6 months.

VARIATION

Selloo (Moroccan Almond-Sesame Cookies): Add 1/4 cup finely ground sesame seeds, 3/4 teaspoon ground anise, and 1/4 teaspoon ground cinnamon.

Graybeh ❧ *(Syrian Butter Cookie Bracelets)*

ABOUT 50 COOKIES

Versions of *graybeh/ghorayebah* are found in most parts of the former Ottoman Empire. Syrian housewives commonly keep a container filled with these tender cookie rounds on hand for guests.

$2^2/3$ cups all-purpose flour, or $1^1/3$ cups flour and $1^1/3$ cups fine semolina

1 teaspoon double-acting baking powder

$^1/4$ teaspoon salt

1 cup (2 sticks) unsalted butter or margarine, softened, or $^1/2$ cup (1 stick) butter and $^1/2$ cup vegetable shortening

$^3/4$ cup sugar, preferably superfine

2 large egg yolks, or 1 large egg

$1^1/2$ teaspoons vanilla extract

About 50 pistachios, or $^1/2$ cup sesame seeds (optional)

1. Sift together the flour, baking powder, and salt. Beat the butter until smooth, about 1 minute. Gradually add the sugar and beat until light and fluffy, about 4 minutes. Beat in the egg yolks, then the vanilla. Stir in the flour mixture. Wrap in plastic wrap and refrigerate for at least 1 hour.

2. Preheat the oven to 375 degrees.

3. Roll the dough or pipe through a pastry bag into 3- or 4-inch-long ropes. Place 2 inches apart on ungreased baking sheets, bring the ends together, and arrange one end slightly over the other end. If desired, press a pistachio at the conjunction point or dip the tops into sesame seeds.

4. Bake until set but not browned, about 8 minutes. Let the cookies stand until firm, about 2 minutes, then remove to a rack and let cool completely. Store in an airtight container for up to 1 week or in the freezer for up to 6 months.

Biscochos de Raki ❧ *(Turkish Anise Cookies)*

ABOUT 36 COOKIES

The Turks, never as strict as other Muslims in outlawing alcohol, frequently add their favorite liquor to baked goods.

3 cups all-purpose flour	³/₄ cup sugar
1 tablespoon double-acting baking powder	¹/₂ cup vegetable oil
Pinch of salt	Egg wash (1 large egg beaten with 1 teaspoon water) (optional)
1 cup raki *or* ouzo *(anise liqueur)*	About ³/₄ cup sesame seeds (optional)

1. Sift together the flour, baking powder, and salt. Combine the *raki*, sugar, and oil. Stir into the flour mixture, adding more flour if necessary to make a firm dough. Cover and refrigerate overnight.

2. Preheat the oven to 375 degrees. Line 3 large baking sheets with parchment paper or grease and dust with flour.

3. Roll the dough into ¹/₂-inch-thick ropes. Cut into 4- or 5-inch lengths and bring the ends together to form rings. If desired, cut small incisions on the outer edge of the rings at ¹/₂- or 1-inch intervals. If desired, brush with the egg wash and sprinkle with the sesame seeds. Place on the prepared baking sheets.

4. Bake until golden brown, about 15 minutes. Let the cookies stand until firm, about 1 minute, then remove to a rack and let cool completely. Store in an airtight container for up to 1 week or in the freezer for up to 6 months.

Canela ❧ *(Turkish Cinnamon-Walnut Crescents)*

ABOUT THIRTY 4-INCH CRESCENTS

The crescent is the official symbol of Turkey, and Turkish men traditionally sport crescent-shaped mustaches. So it is not surprising that the cookies are commonly formed into curved shapes.

2$^1/_4$ cups all-purpose flour, sifted
1 cup (about 2$^1/_2$ ounces) ground
*   walnuts*
2 teaspoons double-acting baking
*   powder, or $^1/_2$ teaspoon baking soda*
1 teaspoon ground cinnamon
$^1/_2$ teaspoon salt

$^1/_2$ cup (1 stick) unsalted butter or
*   margarine, softened*
1 cup sugar, or $^1/_2$ cup granulated sugar
*   and $^1/_2$ cup brown sugar*
1 large egg
3 tablespoons water
1$^1/_2$ teaspoons vanilla extract

---

1. Combine the flour, nuts, baking powder, cinnamon, and salt. Beat the butter until smooth, about 1 minute. Gradually add the sugar and beat until light and fluffy, about 4 minutes. Beat in the egg, then the water and vanilla. Gradually stir in the flour mixture. Form into a ball, wrap in plastic wrap, and refrigerate for at least 1 hour.
2. Preheat the oven to 375 degrees.
3. Form the dough into 1-inch balls, roll the balls into $^1/_4$-inch-thick ropes, then bend into crescents. Place on ungreased baking sheets.
4. Bake until light golden, 8 to 11 minutes. Let the cookies stand until firm, about 1 minute, then remove to a rack to cool completely. Store in an airtight container for up to 1 week or in the freezer for up to 6 months..

Pastries *and* Filled Cookies

*In the next world a person will have to give an accounting for
the food that he looked at but did not eat.*
—*TALMUD YERUSHALMI,* KIDDUSHIN:
PEREK RIVI, HALACHA 12

FLOUR AND FAT PASTES ARE AMONG MAN'S EARLIEST DISHES, AND FROM PRIMITIVE TIMES, PASTRIES HAVE SERVED AS A WAY TO MARK A SPECIAL OCCASION OR, IN THE MORE MUNDANE, TO ENWRAP AND UPLIFT LEFTOVERS OR SCARCE FOODS TO MAKE A TASTY AND hearty meal. For much of history, delicate pastry, which requires a finely milled flour, was the province of the wealthy or reserved for special occasions. Still, a surprising variety of pastries were concocted using whole-wheat or rye-wheat flour. In Europe, when sugar replaced honey as the primary sweetener, baking began to evolve, and *patissiers* of *la grande cuisine* elevated pastry making to new heights. Nonetheless, old-fashioned home-made treats maintain a special place in our hearts.

Tenderness is an essential quality of a well-made pastry, and the type of flour used is key to the proper outcome. Too much gluten produces a tough pastry; insufficient gluten results in a dough that will not hold together. In addition, the higher the protein, the quicker the pastry browns, so it is preferable to use pastry flour or bleached all-purpose flour. Unbleached flour, which contains more protein than bleached, produces a crisper, tougher pastry with a raw flour undertone. Do not use cake flour or bread flour.

A little acid is sometimes substituted for an equal amount of water to relax the gluten, making the dough easier to handle and the pastry more tender, as well as to slow down browning, reduce shrinkage, and add flavor. Use $1^1/4$ teaspoons cider vinegar or lemon juice or 1 to 2 tablespoons sour cream for every $1^1/4$ cups of flour.

Salt is added to the dough as a flavor enhancer. Sugar may be included for flavor, a delicate texture, and a more golden color. For even distribution, the salt and sugar are combined with the flour or dissolved in the water. A little baking powder tenderizes the pastry and counters shrinkage.

Cold suppresses gluten development and gives fat the proper consistency, so chill the ingredients. Water builds up gluten and is the bane of tender pastry. Still, a little liquid is necessary in order to bind the dough and build up enough gluten so that the crust holds its shape. Ice water relaxes the gluten, producing a flakier pastry (in place of ice, you can pour the water into a metal bowl and place in the freezer for about 15 minutes). Use a fork, rubber spatula (using a folding motion), or food processor to mix in water. The dough should be neither wet nor crumbly. If it is too dry, cut in a few more drops of water or place in a food processor and pulse in a little additional water. Form the dough into discs, wrap, and refrigerate for at least 30 minutes to relax the gluten.

Let the dough stand at room temperature until malleable but not soft, 10 to 40 minutes. Lightly flour a flat surface to prevent sticking. Marble, which is naturally cool, provides the best surface for rolling pastry. Waxed paper and plastic wrap eliminate the need to add any more flour to the dough, which reduces tenderness and turns bitter during baking. A pastry cloth reduces the amount of flour needed to prevent sticking. Using a lightly floured rolling pin, apply a firm, steady pressure to roll the dough from the center outward. If not using waxed paper, move the pastry occasionally and sprinkle the surface lightly with flour. Afterward, brush off any excess flour from the pastry. If the dough sticks to the waxed paper, refrigerate until firm.

Hamantaschen ❧ *(Ashkenazic Filled Triangular Cookies)*

ABOUT SIXTY 3-INCH COOKIES

Cookie dough, thanks to its ease of preparation and longer shelf life, has become the more widespread type of *hamantaschen* by far. The yeast-raised version can be found on pages 72–73.

4 cups pastry or bleached all-purpose flour	1/4 cup orange juice, milk, or water
2 teaspoons double-acting baking powder	2 teaspoons vanilla extract, 1 1/2 teaspoons lemon extract, or 1 teaspoon almond extract
1/2 teaspoon salt	2 teaspoons grated lemon or orange zest (optional)
1 cup (2 sticks) unsalted butter or margarine, softened	About 2 cups hamantaschen filling (pages 73–75), fluden fig filling (page 58), or other favorite filling
1 cup sugar	
3 large eggs	

1. Sift together the flour, baking powder, and salt. Beat the butter until smooth, about 1 minute. Gradually add the sugar and beat until light and fluffy, about 4 minutes. Beat in the eggs, one at a time. Add the juice, vanilla, and zest if using. Stir in the flour mixture to make a soft dough. Wrap in plastic wrap and refrigerate until firm, at least 2 hours or overnight. Let stand at room temperature until malleable but not soft, about 30 minutes.

2. Preheat the oven to 350 degrees.

3. Divide the dough into thirds. On a piece of waxed paper or plastic wrap or on a lightly floured surface, roll out each piece 1/8 inch thick. Cut out 3-inch rounds.

4. Place 1 teaspoon of the filling in the center of each round. Pinch one side tightly covering part of the filling. Pinch the edge of the dough to form a point, then pinch two more points together to form a triangle, folding the sides of the dough over the filling but leaving the center of the filling exposed. (If the ends fail to stick together, moisten with a little cold water.) Place 1 inch apart on ungreased baking sheets.

5. Bake until golden, about 20 minutes. Transfer to a rack and let cool. Store in an airtight container at room temperature for up to 1 week or in the freezer for up to 6 months.

Kaese Knishes ❧ *(Ashkenazic Baked Cheese Pastries)*

ABOUT 24 SMALL KNISHES

Comedians have a theory that words starting with the letter *k* are inherently funny. This probably explains how the knish found its way into Borscht Belt routines and from there into the general American consciousness and culinary repertoire. This eastern European treat, derived from a type of Polish cake called *knysz* and the Franco-German *krepish,* has become the preeminent Ashkenazic filled pastry. The original knishes were stuffed with kasha or meat, but today the most common filling is certainly mashed potato. Soft cheese, rice, fruit, or a combination of these items is used for dessert knishes.

Pastry:

2 cups pastry or bleached all-purpose
   flour

1 teaspoon double-acting baking powder

1/2 teaspoon salt

2 large eggs

2 tablespoons vegetable oil

2 tablespoons water

Zeesih Kaesefullung (Sweet Cheese
   Filling):

1 pound (2 cups) pot or farmer's cheese

2 tablespoons sour cream, or 4 ounces
   cream cheese, softened

1 large egg, lightly beaten

2 to 4 tablespoons sugar

1/2 teaspoon vanilla extract

Pinch of salt

1/2 cup raisins (optional)

Egg wash (1 large egg beaten with
   1 tablespoon water)

1. To make the pastry: Sift together the flour, baking powder, and salt. Combine the eggs, oil, and water. Gradually stir in the flour mixture to make a soft dough. Knead until smooth, about 3 minutes. Wrap in plastic wrap and let stand at room temperature for 1 hour.

2. To make the filling: Beat the pot cheese, sour cream, egg, sugar, vanilla, and salt until smooth. If desired, add the raisins.

3. Preheat the oven to 350 degrees. Line a large baking sheet with parchment paper or lightly grease.

4. On a piece of waxed paper or plastic wrap or on a lightly floured surface, roll out the dough 1/8 inch thick. Cut into 3- or 4-inch rounds or squares. Place a heaping table-

spoon of filling in the center of the dough, draw the edges together to encase the filling, and pinch to seal. Place seam side down on the prepared baking sheet, 1 inch apart, and brush with the egg wash.

5. Bake until lightly browned, about 25 minutes. Serve warm or at room temperature. The knishes can be prepared ahead, cooled, frozen, covered loosely with foil, and reheated at 375 degrees until warmed through, about 15 minutes.

VARIATIONS

Use only 1 egg in the pastry and increase the water to 6 tablespoons. Or omit the eggs and increase the water to 6 tablespoons and the oil to $1/4$ cup.

Fruit and Cheese Knishes: Spoon a little apple, blueberry, or cherry pie filling into the middle of the cheese filling.

Kindli ❧ *(Ashkenazic Cookie Slices)*

ABOUT 42 COOKIES

Originally, these cookies were shaped to look like babies wrapped in blankets; thus the Yiddish name *kindel* ("little children"). Over the course of time, however, inventive cooks found ways to speed up the assembly by rolling up the pastry and cutting it into slices. German and Austrian Jews prefer a poppy seed filling (see page 73), while nuts are favored in Hungary and Poland. Romanians like both types. This honey-laced dough variation is called *piroshkes* in Poland. For a yeast version of *kindli,* see pages 62–63.

Pastry:	Filling:
$4^1/2$ cups pastry or bleached all-purpose flour	$1^1/2$ cups finely chopped almonds, hazelnuts, pecans, or walnuts
1 tablespoon double-acting baking powder	$1/2$ to $3/4$ cup sugar
$1/2$ teaspoon salt	$1/3$ cup dried currants or raisins
4 large egg yolks	1 teaspoon finely grated lemon zest or ground cinnamon
$1/2$ cup orange juice or sweet red wine	$1/2$ cup (6 ounces) apricot or raspberry jam or additional vegetable oil
$1/2$ cup vegetable oil	
$1/4$ cup (3 ounces) honey	

1. To make the pastry: Sift together the flour, baking powder, and salt. Combine the egg yolks, juice, oil, and honey. Stir in the flour mixture and knead briefly until smooth. Divide the dough in half, form into discs, cover, and refrigerate for at least 1 hour or overnight. Let stand at room temperature until malleable, about 40 minutes.

2. Preheat the oven to 350 degrees. Line a large baking sheet with parchment paper or lightly grease.

3. To make the filling: Combine the nuts, sugar, currants, and zest.

4. On a piece of waxed paper or plastic wrap or on a lightly floured surface, roll out each piece of dough into a $1/8$-inch-thick rectangle. Spread with the jam, then sprinkle with the nut mixture.

5. Starting from a long end, roll up the dough jelly roll style. At an angle, cut crosswise into $1/2$-inch-thick slices. Place cut side down on the prepared baking sheet, leaving 1 inch between cookies.

6. Bake until golden brown, 20 to 30 minutes. Remove to a rack and let cool. Store in an airtight container at room temperature for up to 1 week or in the freezer for up 6 months.

VARIATIONS

Original Kindli: Cut the dough into 3-inch rounds, place a teaspoon of the filling in the center, fold over the top and bottom to cover the filling, and tuck in the sides like a baby's blanket.

In the pastry, substitute $1/3$ cup sugar for the honey and increase the oil to $3/4$ cup.

After baking, immediately brush the top of the cookies with honey and sprinkle lightly with poppy seeds (about 1 tablespoon total).

Fluden ❧ *(Ashkenazic Layered Pastry)*

This is the pastry version of the popular Franco-German dessert (see pages 56–57).

---

4 cups bleached all-purpose flour

2 teaspoons double-acting baking powder

³/₄ teaspoon salt

¹/₃ cup sugar

1¹/₂ cups vegetable shortening, or 1 cup shortening and ¹/₂ cup chilled butter or margarine

4 large egg yolks, or 2 large egg yolks and 1 large egg

¹/₂ cup water, or ¹/₄ cup water and ¹/₄ cup milk or sweet white wine

2 tablespoons white wine vinegar or mild cider vinegar

1 recipe fluden *apple, cheese, or fig filling (page 58) or Jam-Nut Filling (page 175)*

---

1. To make the pastry: Sift together the flour, baking powder, and salt. Mix in the sugar. Cut in the shortening to resemble coarse crumbs. Combine the eggs, water, and vinegar. Stir into the flour mixture until the dough just holds together. Form into a ball. To make the pastry in a food processor: In a food processor fitted with a steel blade, combine the flour, sugar, baking powder, and salt. Add the butter and pulse 4 times. Add the shortening and pulse until the consistency of coarse crumbs, about 4 pulses. Combine the eggs, water, and vinegar. Add to the flour mixture and pulse until the dough begins to hold together. If the dough is too dry, pulse in a little additional water, 1 teaspoon at a time. Form into a ball.

2. On a piece of waxed paper or plastic wrap or on a lightly floured surface, roll the dough into a rectangle with the narrow end facing you. Fold the top third of the dough toward you, then fold the bottom third upward. Turn the dough so that a narrow end faces front and roll into a rectangle. Fold in thirds again. Press to hold together. (If the pastry is made without the rolling and folding, it does not turn out as flaky.) Wrap in plastic wrap and refrigerate for at least 4 hours or up to 4 days, or store in the freezer for up to 2 months. Let stand at room temperature until malleable but not soft, about 30 minutes.

3. Preheat the oven to 350 degrees (325 degrees if using a glass pan). Grease a 13-by-9-inch baking pan.

4. Divide the dough into thirds. On a piece of waxed paper or plastic wrap or on a floured surface, roll out each piece of dough into a 13-by-9-inch rectangle. Fit a rectangle into the prepared pan and spread with half of the filling. Repeat the layering with the remaining pastry and filling, ending with pastry.

5. Bake for 20 minutes. Reduce the heat to 325 degrees (300 degrees if using a glass pan) and bake until golden brown, about 40 additional minutes. Place on a rack and let cool for at least 1 hour. Cover and store at room temperature for 1 to 2 days.

VARIATION

Sour Cream Flaky Fluden: Omit the vinegar and egg yolks and add 6 tablespoons sour cream.

Jam-Nut Filling

1 cup (4 ounces) chopped almonds, hazelnuts, pecans, or walnuts	*1 to 1¹/₂ cups (4 to 6 ounces) grated fresh or unsweetened desiccated coconut (optional)*
¹/₂ cup sugar	
2 cups (24 ounces) apricot preserves, strawberry jam, orange marmalade, or Prune Lekvar (page 75)	*1 cup dried currants or raisins (optional)*

Combine the nuts and sugar. Spread the jam over the dough and sprinkle with the nut mixture and, if desired, the coconut and/or currants.

Gebleterter Kugel ❧ *(Ashkenazic Pastry Strudel)*

ABOUT FIFTY-SIX 1-INCH PIECES

In eastern Europe, *fluden* became a version of fruit strudel made from flaky pastry, also called *gebleterter kugel*. A matza meal version is prepared for Passover. Although not as flaky as phyllo, pastry strudels are easier to make, less fragile, and stay fresh longer.

1 recipe fluden *pastry (page 174)*
1 recipe Jam-Nut Filling (page 175)
    or fluden *fig filling (page 58), or*
    4 cups Ashkenazic Poppy Seed Filling
    (page 73)

Sugar for sprinkling (optional)

1. Prepare the pastry through Step 2.
2. Preheat the oven to 375 degrees. Line a large baking sheet with parchment paper or lightly grease.
3. Divide the dough into 4 equal pieces. On pieces of waxed paper or plastic wrap or on a lightly floured surface, roll out each piece of dough into a $1/8$-inch-thick rectangle about 14 inches long.
4. Spread the pastry with the filling, leaving a $1/2$-inch uncovered border on all sides. Starting from a long end, roll up jelly roll style. Place seam side down on the prepared baking sheet. Cut a slash in the top of the rolls at 1-inch intervals. The rolls can be refrigerated overnight or frozen for up to 2 months. If desired, sprinkle the tops of the rolls with a little sugar.
5. Bake until golden brown, about 30 minutes. Slice the warm pastry at the slashes. Serve warm or at room temperature. Store in an airtight container at room temperature for up to 1 week or in the freezer for up to 3 months.

Polster Zipfel ❧ *(Austrian Jam Pockets)*

ABOUT 96 PASTRIES

These cookies are also called Vienna tarts and, in Germany, *blatter teig.*

---

1 recipe rugelach *pastry (page 178)*

About 2¹/₂ cups Apricot Lekvar (page 75), Prune Lekvar (page 75), or fruit jam

---

1. Prepare the pastry through Step 2.
2. On a piece of waxed paper or plastic wrap or on a lightly floured surface, roll out the dough ¹/₈ inch thick. Cut into 2- or 3-inch squares. Spoon 1 teaspoon jam in the center of each square. Bring together 2 diagonal corners over the jam and press to seal. Place on ungreased baking sheets, cover, and refrigerate for at least 1 hour or overnight.
3. Preheat the oven to 350 degrees.
4. Bake until the edges are lightly colored, about 25 minutes. Transfer to a rack and let cool completely. Store in an airtight container at room temperature for up to 1 week or in the freezer for up to 6 months.

VARIATION

Baratfule (Hungarian Jam Pockets): Cut the dough into 3-inch rounds or squares. Spoon about ¹/₂ teaspoon jam in the center of each round. Moisten the edges with water, fold over to form a half moon, and press the curved edge with the tines of a fork. For a nut topping: Brush the tops of the unbaked cookies with 1 lightly beaten egg white (or 1 large egg yolk beaten with 1 tablespoon water) and sprinkle with ¹/₂ cup finely chopped walnuts or 1 cup sliced almonds.

Rugelach ❧ *(Ashkenazic Cookie Crescents)*

64 LARGE, 96 MEDIUM, OR 128 SMALL COOKIES

Recently my mother discussed her plans to bake several batches of *rugelach* for a friend's buffet in Richmond, Virginia, as her contribution to the event. The same day, my sister in Brooklyn informed me that these cookies were among the homemade treats she had amassed in the freezer for her daughter's upcoming bat mitzvah. My sister-in-law in San Diego, California, mentioned that she had them on the menu for Shavuot. Shortly thereafter, I found *rugelach* prominently represented at the Fancy Food Show in New York's Javits Center.

Rugelach ("little rolls"), arguably the best known and most popular of all Ashkenazic pastries in America, originated in Austria. They are relatively easy to make, yet tasty and fancy enough for special occasions. These crescent-shaped cookies consist of a firm, slightly tangy pastry filled with spices or preserves. The dough was originally made with sour cream, but cream cheese has become more popular. Since the pastry contains no water, it is very tender and fragile. *Rugelach* are so popular that I've given a recipe for a large batch; however, it can be halved for smaller lots. For *pareve rugelach,* substitute the cookie dough for *hamantaschen* pastry (page 169).

Pastry:

2 cups (4 sticks) unsalted butter, softened

16 ounces (2 cups) cream cheese, softened, or sour cream

1/4 cup sugar

1 1/2 teaspoons vanilla extract

1 teaspoon salt

4 cups bleached all-purpose flour, sifted

Filling:

1 cup sugar

4 teaspoons ground cinnamon

1/4 cup (1/2 stick) unsalted butter or margarine, melted

1 cup dried currants or dark raisins (optional)

1 1/2 cups finely chopped walnuts or hazelnuts (optional)

Egg wash (1 large egg beaten with 1 teaspoon water)

About 1/4 cup sugar (if desired, mixed with 2 teaspoons ground cinnamon)

---

1. To make the pastry: Beat the butter and cream cheese until smooth, about 1 minute. Gradually add the sugar and beat until light and fluffy, about 4 minutes. Add the vanilla and salt. Gradually beat in the flour. To make the pastry in a food processor: In a food

processor fitted with a steel blade, process the butter and cream cheese until smooth. Blend in the sugar, vanilla, and salt. Add the flour and process until the dough begins to hold together.

2. Divide the dough into 8 equal pieces. Form into 1-inch-thick discs, wrap, and refrigerate for at least 6 hours or overnight. (For quicker use, place in the refrigerator for 30 minutes, then in the freezer for about 1 hour.) Remove the dough from the refrigerator and let stand until malleable, about 40 minutes.

3. Preheat the oven to 375 degrees.

4. To make the filling: Combine the sugar and cinnamon. Between 2 sheets of waxed paper or plastic wrap or on a lightly floured surface, roll each piece of dough into a 1/8-inch-thick round about 9 inches in diameter. Brush the dough rounds with the melted butter and sprinkle with the cinnamon sugar, leaving a 1/2-inch border uncovered at the edges. If desired, sprinkle with the currants and/or nuts.

5. Cut each round into equal wedges—8 for large cookies, 12 for medium cookies, or 16 for small cookies. Starting from the wide end, roll up the wedges toward the point and gently bend to form a crescent. Unbaked crescents can be frozen for up to 2 months. Do not thaw; increase the baking time by about 6 minutes.

6. Place on ungreased baking sheets, pointed edge down, 1 inch apart. Brush with the egg wash and sprinkle lightly with the sugar.

7. Bake until crisp and golden, 20 to 25 minutes. Let the cookies stand until firm, about 1 minute, then remove to a rack and let cool completely. Store in an airtight container at room temperature for up to 1 week or in the freezer for up to 4 months.

VARIATIONS

Cream Cheese and Sour Cream Rugelach: In the pastry, reduce the butter to 1 cup (2 sticks), use 8 ounces cream cheese and 1 cup sour cream, and add 2 large egg yolks.

Chocolate Rugelach: In the filling, reduce the sugar to 1/2 cup and substitute 1/2 cup unsweetened cocoa powder for the cinnamon.

Jam Rugelach: Substitute about 1 1/2 cups melted apricot jam, seedless raspberry jam, strawberry jam, or Prune Lekvar (page 75) for the cinnamon sugar and butter in the filling.

HINT: ❧ To soften cream cheese quickly, microwave 8 ounces at 30 percent power for about 2 minutes.

Pirishkes ❧ *(Ukrainian Turnovers)*

ABOUT THIRTY-SIX 3-INCH TURNOVERS

There is much confusion over a variety of Russian and Polish pastries, all with names that come from the Slavic word *pir* ("feast"). *Pirishkes* in Yiddish or *piroshki* (singular *piroshok*) in Russian are half-moon-shaped Ukrainian and Russian pastry turnovers. *Piroghi* (singular *pirog*) are large filled pastry pies. They are not the same as the Polish poached pasta dumplings called *pierogi*. Russians use numerous types of dough for *piroshki*, but they are especially fond of those made with sour cream, of which there are many variations. On Shavout and Hanukkah, these are traditionally filled with a cheese (see cheese blintzes, pages 285–87). For *pareve pirishkes*, substitute the pastry from knishes (page 170) or standard flaky pie pastry.

Pastry:	2 *large egg yolks*
3 *cups pastry or bleached all-purpose flour*	
3/4 *teaspoon salt*	About 2 1/2 *cups pirishkes filling (recipes follow)*
1/2 *teaspoon double-acting baking powder*	1 *large egg white, lightly beaten*
	Egg wash (1 large egg yolk beaten with 1 teaspoon water or cream)
3/4 *cup (1 1/2 sticks) unsalted butter, chilled*	About 1 *pint honey for brushing (optional)*
2/3 *cup sour cream*	

1. To make the pastry: Sift together the flour, salt, and baking powder. Cut in the butter to resemble coarse crumbs. Combine the sour cream and egg yolks. Stir into the flour mixture to form a soft dough. (Add a little water if it is too dry.) Divide in half, form into discs, cover with plastic wrap, and refrigerate for at least 30 minutes or up to 2 days. Let stand at room temperature until malleable.

2. Preheat the oven to 375 degrees. Line large baking sheets with parchment paper or lightly grease.

3. On a piece of waxed paper or plastic wrap or on a lightly floured surface, roll out the dough 1/8 inch thick. Cut into 3-inch rounds. Place a heaping teaspoon of the filling in the center. Brush the edges with a little egg white, fold over to form a half moon, and pinch the edges or press with the tines of a fork to seal. Reroll and cut out any excess dough. Store the piroshki in the freezer for up to 1 month. Do not thaw; increase the

baking time by about 6 minutes. Place on the prepared baking sheet, 1 inch apart, and brush the tops with the egg wash.

4. Bake until golden brown, about 20 minutes. If desired, brush the tops of the warm pastry with the honey. Transfer to a rack and let cool completely. Store in an airtight container in a cool place for up to 1 week.

PIRISHKES FILLINGS ✎

Apple Pirishkes

2 pounds (6 to 7 medium) cooking apples, such as Golden Delicious, Granny Smith, Gravenstein, Greening, Jonathan, Macoun, Pippin, Starr, Winesap, or any combination, peeled, cored, and chopped	*1/2 cup coarsely chopped almonds, hazelnuts, or walnuts* *1/2 cup raisins* *1/2 cup sugar* *1 tablespoon grated lemon zest*

Combine all the ingredients in a casserole. Bake in a 350-degree oven until the apples are tender, about 20 minutes. Let cool.

Carrot Pirishkes

2¹/2 pounds carrots, grated *3 cups sugar*	*1/4 cup water* *1/2 teaspoon ground ginger*

Boil all the ingredients in a large saucepan, stirring frequently, until the carrots are soft and the mixture thickened. Let cool.

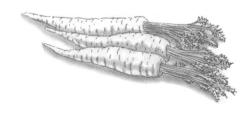

Prune Pirishkes

3/4 cup fresh orange juice

1/4 cup honey

2 tablespoons fresh lemon juice

1 pound (about 4 cups) pitted prunes

1 tablespoon grated orange zest

Stir the orange juice, honey, and lemon juice in a medium saucepan over medium heat until the honey dissolves. Add the prunes, reduce the heat to low, and simmer, stirring occasionally, until soft, about 15 minutes. Drain. Chop the prunes. Stir in the zest and let cool.

PLUMS AND PRUNES

 Plums come in a wide range of flavors (sweet to tart), sizes (1 to 4 inches), and colors (purple, blue, red, green, and yellow). The plum's origin is uncertain, with some experts claiming western Asia and others insisting on China. Whatever its home, the fruit spread very early in history, as plum pits have been found in ancient Egyptian tombs. Since plums not only grew in most parts of northern Europe but could be dried without spoiling for long-term storage, prunes (*gehtrikenthe flohmen*) became the most common fruit of that region used in jams, pastries, *tzimmes*, compotes, and liqueurs. In the Maghreb, prunes are stuffed with nuts or almond paste.

Most American prunes, especially those from California, are made from La Petite d'Agen variety of plum, which yields a very sweet, purplish black prune. Prunes made from Italian (Lombard) plums are tart-sweet, with a winy flavor. Most prunes in central Asia tend to be made from very tart varieties, such as Greengage.

Buricche ❧ *(Italian Turnovers)*

ABOUT TWENTY-FOUR 3-INCH TURNOVERS

*P*asta sfoglia (puff pastry) originated in Florence, Italy, during the Renaissance when ingenious bakers found a way to produce layered pastry like phyllo dough but without the necessity of rolling each piece to paper thinness. The water and tiny pockets of butter in the dough steam and puff up during baking. Around the same time, Sephardic exiles introduced Italian Jews to Iberian turnovers, such as *empanadas. Buricche,* a name probably derived from *burek* (a Turkish turnover), utilizes the Italian Jewish version of puff pastry to make small turnovers. You can substitute store-bought puff pastry, a plain oil pastry, or standard pie pastry. The turnovers are filled with various meat or vegetable concoctions for an appetizer and, for Purim dessert, with various sweet mixtures.

1/2 cup vegetable oil	*Additional flour for sprinkling*
1/2 cup lukewarm water	*1 recipe (about 2 cups)* buricche *filling*
1/2 teaspoon salt	*(recipes follow)*
About 2 1/2 cups pastry or bleached	*Egg wash (1 large egg beaten with*
all-purpose flour, sifted	*1 tablespoon water)*
About 1/2 cup plus 2 tablespoons	
(1 1/4 sticks) unsalted butter or	
margarine, softened	

1. To make the pastry: Combine the oil, water, and salt. Stir in 1 cup of the flour. Gradually stir in enough of the remaining flour to make a soft dough that comes away from the sides of the bowl. Cover and let stand at room temperature for 30 minutes.

2. On a piece of waxed paper or plastic wrap or on a lightly floured surface, roll out the dough into a 1/3-inch-thick rectangle, about 9 by 6 inches. Brush with about 2 tablespoons of the butter and lightly sprinkle with flour. With a narrow end facing you, fold over the top third of the dough, then fold over the uncovered bottom third, forming about a 6-by-3-inch rectangle. Wrap in plastic wrap and refrigerate for about 30 minutes.

3. Roll the dough into a 1/4-inch-thick rectangle. Brush with about 2 tablespoons butter, lightly sprinkle with flour, then fold in thirds as above. Repeat rolling, brushing, and folding 3 more times. Refrigerate the dough for at least 2 hours or overnight. Let stand at room temperature for about 15 minutes before rolling.

continued

4. Preheat the oven to 400 degrees.

5. On a piece of waxed paper or plastic wrap or on a lightly floured surface, roll out the dough 1/8 inch thick. Cut into 3-inch squares or rounds. Spoon 1 tablespoon of the filling in the centers, fold over to form a triangle or half moon, and press the edges to seal. Place on an ungreased baking sheet, 1 inch apart, and brush with the egg wash.

6. Bake until golden brown, 15 to 20 minutes. Transfer to a rack and let cool. Store in an airtight container at room temperature for up to 1 week or in the freezer for up to 6 months.

VARIATION

ABOUT FORTY 3-INCH TURNOVERS

3/4 cup plus 1 tablespoon vegetable oil

1 cup lukewarm water

1 teaspoon salt

About 4 cups pastry or bleached
  all-purpose flour, sifted

About 3/4 cup (1 1/2 sticks) unsalted
  butter or margarine, softened

Additional flour for sprinkling

Proceed as above, but roll the dough into a 12-by-8-inch rectangle.

BURRICHE FILLINGS ✎

Almond Filling

Use about 2 cups Sephardic Almond Paste (page 368).

Cinnamon Filling

1 1/2 cups sugar

2 tablespoons ground cinnamon

About 1/4 cup water, or 2 tablespoons
  brandy and 2 tablespoons water

Combine all the ingredients to make a thick paste.

Winter Squash Filling

2 pounds winter squash, such as butternut, peeled, seeded, and diced
1 large egg, lightly beaten
Pinch of grated nutmeg

Pinch of salt
1/3 cup crushed amaretti (almond macaroons) (optional)

Steam the squash over boiling water until tender, about 10 minutes. Or halve and seed the squash, place on a baking sheet, and bake in a 400-degree oven until tender, about 1 hour. Let cool, then scoop out the squash. Puree (there should be about 2 cups). Add the egg, nutmeg, salt, and, if desired, the amaretti.

VARIATION

Pumpkin Filling: Substitute 2 cups pure-pack canned pumpkin for the squash.

Sfratti ❧ *(Italian Nut-Filled "Sticks")*

S*fratti* means "sticks" in Italian, as well as "evicted," for at one time landlords were allowed to persuade unwanted and delinquent tenants to leave by force of a rod. A similar practice was employed to chase away Jews during all-too-frequent periods of expulsion. This nut-filled cookie, a popular Italian Rosh Hashanah treat, got its name from its resemblance to a stick, the Jewish sense of humor transforming an object of persecution into a sweet symbol.

Pastry:	Filling:
3 cups pastry or bleached all-purpose flour, sifted	*1 cup (12 ounces) honey*
1 cup sugar	*2¹/₂ cups (about 12¹/₂ ounces) walnuts, chopped*
¹/₄ teaspoon salt	*2 teaspoons grated orange zest*
¹/₃ cup unsalted butter or margarine, chilled	*2 teaspoons grated lemon zest (optional)*
About ²/₃ cup sweet or dry white wine	*³/₄ teaspoon ground cinnamon*
	¹/₄ teaspoon ground cloves
	¹/₈ to ¹/₄ teaspoon freshly grated black pepper
	Egg wash (1 large egg beaten with 1 tablespoon water)

1. To make the pastry: Combine the flour, sugar, and salt. Cut in the butter to resemble coarse crumbs. Sprinkle a little wine over a section of the flour, then mix with a fork to moisten. Push the moistened dough aside and continue adding enough wine until the dough just holds together. Divide in half. Using your fingertips, lightly press and knead into balls. Flatten into discs, wrap, and refrigerate for at least 1 hour or up to 3 days. Let stand at room temperature until malleable but not soft.

2. To make the filling: In a medium saucepan over medium heat, bring the honey to a boil and cook for 5 minutes. Be careful; it may foam up. Add the remaining filling ingredients and cook, stirring constantly, for another 5 minutes. Remove from the heat and let

stand, stirring occasionally, until the mixture is cool enough to handle but not set. Pour onto a floured surface, divide into 6 equal portions, and shape the portions into 14-inch-long sticks.

3. Preheat the oven to 375 degrees. Line a large baking sheet with parchment paper or grease.

4. On a piece of waxed paper or plastic wrap or on a lightly floured surface, roll each piece of dough into a 14-by-12-inch rectangle, then cut each rectangle lengthwise into three 14-by-4-inch rectangles. Place a nut strip near a long side of each rectangle and roll up from the filling side. Cut into 2-inch sticks. Place seam side down on the prepared baking sheet, leaving 1 inch between the cookies, and brush with the egg wash.

5. Bake until golden, about 20 minutes. Transfer to a rack and let cool. Wrap in aluminum foil until ready to serve. Store in an airtight container at room temperature for up to 2 weeks.

VARIATION

Oil Pastry: Substitute $1/3$ cup vegetable oil for the butter and combine it with the wine.

Tortelli Dolci ❧ *(Italian Cheese Turnovers)*

Although *tortelli* (meaning "round shaped") generally refers to a boiled filled pasta similar to ravioli, in this recipe it applies to a baked turnover. The ricotta filling, typical of Italian desserts, is a popular Shavuot treat.

Pastry:	3 large eggs, lightly beaten
4 cups pastry or bleached all-purpose	About ½ cup sugar
flour	¼ cup pine nuts
1 teaspoon double-acting baking powder	1 teaspoon vanilla extract, or
½ teaspoon salt	2 teaspoons grated lemon zest
¾ cup water	¼ cup candied citron peel (page 366),
½ cup vegetable oil	or 1 cup raisins (optional)
½ cup sugar	
2 large eggs, lightly beaten	Egg wash (1 large egg beaten with
	1 tablespoon water)
Filling:	About ¼ cup confectioners' sugar for
2 cups (1 pound) ricotta cheese, drained	dusting

1. To make the pastry: Sift together the flour, baking powder, and salt. Blend together the water, oil, sugar, and eggs. Stir into the flour mixture to make a soft dough. Place on a lightly floured surface and knead until smooth. Cover and let stand at room temperature for at least 30 minutes.

2. Preheat the oven to 375 degrees.

3. To make the filling: Combine all the filling ingredients.

4. On a piece of waxed paper or plastic wrap or on a lightly floured surface, roll out the dough ⅛ inch thick and cut into 3-inch rounds.

5. Place 1 teaspoon of the filling in the center of each round. Fold in half over the filling to form a half moon and press the rounded edge with the tines of a fork to seal. The tortelli can be stored in the freezer for up to 2 months. Do not thaw. Place the tortelli on ungreased baking sheets, 1 inch apart, and brush the tops with the egg wash.

6. Bake until golden brown, about 20 minutes for fresh; about 30 minutes for frozen. Transfer to a rack and let cool. Sprinkle with confectioners' sugar. Store in an airtight container at room temperature for 1 day or in the freezer for up to 4 months.

VARIATIONS

Oil-Butter Pastry: Omit the eggs and baking powder and add $^1/_2$ cup (1 stick) softened butter or margarine.

Rocciata (Italian Pastry Roll): Divide the dough in half and roll each half into a 27-by-6-inch rectangle. Spread about 3 cups of the filling lengthwise along the center, leaving a 2-inch border on both sides. Fold the long sides over the filling and pinch the seams and ends to seal. Place seam side down on a greased baking sheet and bake in a 375-degree oven until golden, about 35 minutes. Cut crosswise into slices.

CITRON (ETROG)

 Citron, the earliest cultivated species of citrus, is a large oblong fruit with a fragrant, very thick rind enclosing a sparse sour pulp. It probably originated in southwestern China or Arabia but, early on, spread westward. In ancient Greece and Rome, it was called a Median or Persian apple. A Greek historian wrote of the citron: "Its fruit is not edible but it has an exquisite odor, as also have the leaves which are used as protection from moths in clothing. . . . The citron bears fruit continuously. While some fruit is falling with ripeness other fruit is just starting." The *etrog,* the only citrus mentioned in the Bible, is the biblical *etz peri hadar* ("fruit of the *hadar* tree") and one of the four species used in the Sukkot ritual. According to one legend, the *etrog* was the tree of good and evil in the Garden of Eden. Citron is used primarily in preserves and as candied peel (see page 366).

Ma'amoul ❧ *(Middle Eastern Filled Cookies)*

Ma'amoul, ("filled" in Arabic) rank as one of the most ancient extant pastries. They are made throughout the Middle East, going by a variety of names, including *menenas* in Egypt, *klaitcha* in Iran, *kileicha* in Iraq, and *kasmay* in Kurdistan. There are several variations of these filled cookies. The dough can be made from all flour, all semolina, or part of each. (Semolina makes a crunchier, crumblier pastry.) Sometimes a little yeast is added to the dough. As with most Middle Eastern pastries, the dough is not inherently sweet. Nut is the most common filling, but date is also popular. Syrians make several versions, including *ras-ib-adjway* (with a date and walnut filling) and *krabeej* (dipped into a sugar cream). North Africans like to simmer the cookies in a sugar syrup for a few minutes. Serious cooks use a special wooden press called a *tabi* to form the cookie and impress ornate designs on the surface: floral for a date filling and geometric for nuts. *Ma'amoul* are traditional on many festive occasions, most notably Purim and Hanukkah.

Pastry:	Filling:
3¹/₄ cups bleached all-purpose flour, sifted, or 2 cups flour and 1 cup fine semolina or farina	8 ounces walnuts, almonds, or pistachios, finely chopped (about 2 cups)
2 tablespoons sugar	¹/₂ to ³/₄ cup sugar
Pinch of salt	1 to 2 tablespoons rose water or orange blossom water
1 cup (2 sticks) unsalted butter or margarine, chilled	¹/₂ teaspoon ground cinnamon (optional)
1 tablespoon orange blossom water or rose water	
About 3 tablespoons water	About ¹/₄ cup confectioners' sugar for dusting

1. To make the pastry: Combine the flour, sugar, and salt. Cut in the butter to resemble coarse crumbs. Stir in the orange blossom water and enough water until the mixture holds together. Knead briefly to form a soft dough. Cover and refrigerate for about 30 minutes.
2. Preheat the oven to 350 degrees. Line several baking sheets with parchment paper or aluminum foil.
3. To make the filling: Combine all the filling ingredients.

4. Form the dough into 1¼-inch balls. Hollow out the balls using your thumb and fill with a heaping teaspoon of the filling. Press the sides of the opening together to cover the filling and gently re-form into balls or crescents. If desired, score designs in the dough with a fork or knife. Place the cookies, 1 inch apart, on the prepared baking sheets.

5. Bake until lightly colored but not browned, about 20 minutes. Let the cookies stand until firm, about 5 minutes, then transfer to a rack and let cool completely. They firm more as they cool. Sprinkle with confectioners' sugar. Store in an airtight container at room temperature for up to 1 week.

VARIATIONS

Ghotab (Persian Filled Cookies): Use almonds in the filling and add 1 to 2 teaspoons ground cardamom. Use 2 tablespoons rose water and omit the cinnamon.

Krabeej/Karabij (Syrian Marshmallow-Topped Cookies): In Syria, *krabeej* are coated with a sugar cream called *naatiffe*. In America, the similar and more readily available marshmallow cream is usually substituted for it. Do not sprinkle the cookies with confectioners' sugar. Just before serving, dip the tops into marshmallow cream and lightly sprinkle with ground cinnamon.

Ras-ib-adjway (Syrian Date-and-Walnut-Filled Cookies): Soak 1 pound pitted dates in cold water for several hours. Drain and pat dry. Puree in a food processor. Add ½ to 1 cup chopped walnuts, 1 teaspoon grated orange zest, and 1 teaspoon ground cinnamon. Use as the filling in Step 4.

HINTS: ❧ If you have trouble forming the dough balls into cylinders, here are two alternative methods of preparing *ma'amoul*. Divide the dough into 3 or 4 pieces and roll into thin rectangles (do not flour the surface).

1. Cut out 3-inch rounds, place a heaping teaspoon of the filling in the center of each, and bring the sides of the dough over the filling to form balls. Or place a heaping teaspoon of the filling at the bottom of each round, roll up from the filling end, and form into crescents.

2. Spread the filling over each rectangle, leaving a ½-inch border on all sides. Roll up jelly roll style, flatten the pastry slightly by rolling and pressing, and cut diagonally into ¾-inch-thick slices.

Makrud ❧ *(Northwest African Date-Filled Cookies)*

The name of these cookies, meaning "wound" in Arabic, refers to rolling up the filling in the semolina dough. *Makrud* are popular Hanukkah and Purim treats.

Pastry:

1¼ cups bleached all-purpose flour, sifted

1¼ cups (7½ ounces) semolina flour

½ teaspoon salt

6 tablespoons vegetable oil, heated slightly

About 1 cup water

Date Filling:

½ cup water

4 ounces (about 1 cup) dried dates, pitted and chopped

2 teaspoons grated orange zest

¼ teaspoon ground cinnamon

¼ teaspoon ground cloves

Syrup:

1½ cups water

1 cup sugar

2 to 3 tablespoons lemon juice, or 1 tablespoon orange blossom water

1. To make the pastry: Combine the all-purpose flour, semolina flour, and salt in a large bowl. Make a well in the center, pour in the oil, and mix well. Gradually stir in the water and briefly knead until the dough holds together. Cover and refrigerate for about 30 minutes.

2. To make the filling: Bring the water to a low boil in a small saucepan over medium heat. Add the dates, zest, cinnamon, and cloves and stir until smooth. Remove from the heat and let cool.

3. Preheat the oven to 350 degrees. Line a large baking sheet with parchment paper or lightly grease.

4. Divide the dough into 4 equal parts. On waxed paper or plastic wrap or on a floured surface, roll each piece of dough into a ½-inch-thick rectangle. Spread one-fourth of the filling over each rectangle. Starting from a long end, roll up jelly roll style. At an angle, cut into ½-inch-thick slices. Place cut side up on the prepared baking sheets. Or divide the dough into 24 equal pieces, form into balls, roll into thin rounds, spoon 1 teaspoon filling in the centers, bring the edges together over the filling, and press to seal.

5. Bake until golden brown, 15 to 20 minutes. Transfer to a rack and let cool.

6. To make the syrup: Stir all the syrup ingredients over low heat until the sugar dissolves, about 5 minutes. Stop stirring, increase the heat to medium, and cook until thickened, about 10 minutes.

7. In batches, dip the cookies into the warm syrup and simmer for 2 minutes. Drain well, place on a platter, and let cool. Store at room temperature for up to 1 week.

VARIATIONS

Honey Syrup: Substitute 1 cup honey for the sugar and reduce the water to $1/2$ cup.

Fried Makrud: Heat about 2 inches of vegetable oil to 375 degrees and, in batches, fry the *makrud* until golden brown on all sides.

CLOVES

 Cloves (the word means "nail" in French, referring to its shape) are the unopened buds of an evergreen tree native to the Moluccas in the East Indies. The flavor of this most aromatic and strongest of spices, derived from the chemical compound eugenol, is rather pungent, so it should be used sparingly. The oil in cloves acts as an antiseptic as well as a preservative. Cloves complement both sweet and savory foods. As an essential part of *garam masala,* the spice is indispensable to Indian cuisine. Use whole nails in stews, marinades, pickles, and hot beverages (tea, wine, and mulled cider). Add ground cloves to baked goods and fruits. The intensely aromatic clove is the most common spice used in the *havdallah* ceremony, marking the conclusion of the Sabbath.

Kaab el Gh'zal ❧ *(Moroccan Almond-Filled Crescents)*

These cookies, made with an almond paste filling and a dough flavored with orange blossom water, are a Moroccan dessert variation of the widespread Middle Eastern turnover *sambusak*. The name *kaab el gh'zal*, sometimes shortened to *kabuzel*, means "gazelle horn" in Arabic, and the crescent shape of the cookies is reminiscent of the species, now nearly extinct in Morocco. In Fez, the cookies are dipped into sugar syrup flavored with orange blossom water (see *atar*, page 265).

Filling:	Pastry:
1 cup (5 ounces) blanched almonds, finely ground	*2²/₃ cups bleached all-purpose flour, sifted*
¹/₄ to ¹/₂ cup sugar	*Pinch of salt*
Pinch of salt	*1 cup (2 sticks) unsalted butter or margarine, chilled*
¹/₂ teaspoon ground cinnamon (optional)	*About 6 tablespoons orange blossom water, or 1 tablespoon orange blossom water and 5 tablespoons ice water*
About 1 tablespoon orange blossom water or egg white	

1. To make the filling: In a food processor, finely grind the almonds, sugar, salt, and cinnamon if using. Add enough orange blossom water to make a paste. Cover and refrigerate overnight or up to 2 weeks.
2. To make the pastry: Combine the flour and salt. Cut in the butter to resemble coarse crumbs. Stir in enough orange blossom water until the mixture holds together. Knead briefly to form a soft, pliable dough. Cover and refrigerate for at least 1 hour.
3. Preheat the oven to 375 degrees. Line large baking sheets with parchment paper or lightly grease.
4. Form the dough into 1-inch balls. On waxed paper or plastic wrap or on a lightly floured surface, roll the balls into thin rounds about 3 inches in diameter. Spread a heaping teaspoon of the filling into a 2-inch-long crescent shape near the lower edge of each round. (For large cookies, form into 6-inch rounds and fill with 1 heaping tablespoon of

the filling.) Fold the other half of the dough over the filling and pinch to seal. Using a fluted pastry wheel, trim the curved edge. Bend into a crescent. Place the cookies, 1 inch apart, on the prepared baking sheets.

5. Bake until lightly colored but not browned, 15 to 20 minutes. Let the cookies stand until firm, about 5 minutes, then transfer to a rack and let cool completely. Store in an airtight container at room temperature for up to 1 week.

VARIATION

Oil Pastry: Substitute $^1/_3$ cup vegetable oil for the butter and add 2 large egg yolks. Combine the oil and egg yolks with the orange blossom water. This is richer than the traditional Arabic pastry.

Travados ❧ *(Sephardic Pastry Horns)*

ABOUT 50 COOKIES

These Sephardic crescents, actually a nut-filled *sambusak,* are a common sight on special occasions, notably Purim. The inclusion of wine or orange juice in the dough marks it as a Jewish version. Balkan Jews call these cookies *roscas di alhasu* ("Haman's ears"), an allusion to the curved shape's similarity to an ear. Calcutta Jews prepare an almond paste–filled version called *badam sambusak. Travados* are commonly served with mint tea.

Pastry:

$3^1/2$ cups pastry or bleached all-purpose
    flour

$1/4$ teaspoon baking soda

$1/8$ teaspoon salt

1 cup vegetable oil

$1/2$ cup orange juice or sweet red or
    white wine, or $1/2$ cup water and
    1 tablespoon orange blossom water

$1/2$ cup sugar

Filling:

2 cups ground walnuts or blanched
    almonds, or 1 cup each

$1/4$ cup sugar

1 large egg, or $1/4$ cup orange
    marmalade, or 2 tablespoons orange
    blossom water

$1/4$ to $1/2$ teaspoon ground cinnamon

Syrup:

$3/4$ cup sugar

$3/4$ cup water

$3/4$ cup (9 ounces) honey

1 teaspoon lemon juice

1. To make the pastry: Sift together the flour, baking soda, and salt. Combine the oil, juice, and sugar. Gradually add the flour mixture to form a soft, nonsticky dough. Wrap in plastic wrap and refrigerate for at least 30 minutes.
2. Preheat the oven to 350 degrees. Grease a large baking sheet.
3. To make the filling: Combine all the filling ingredients.
4. On waxed paper or plastic wrap or on a lightly floured surface, roll out the dough $1/8$ inch thick. Cut into 3-inch rounds. Place 1 teaspoon filling in the center of each round, fold over to form a half moon, and pinch the edges to seal. If desired, run a fluted pas-

try wheel around the curved side. Bend slightly to form a crescent. The pastries can be frozen for up to 2 months. Do not thaw. Place on the prepared baking sheet.

5. Bake until lightly colored, about 20 minutes for fresh; about 30 minutes for frozen. Remove to a rack and let cool completely. *Travados* can be frozen for up to 2 months, thawed, then dipped in the syrup.

6. To make the syrup: Stir the sugar and water over low heat until the sugar dissolves, about 5 minutes. Stir in the honey and lemon juice. Increase the heat to medium, bring to a boil, and cook without stirring until slightly syrupy, about 5 minutes (it will register 225 degrees on a candy thermometer).

7. In batches, drop the cooled *travados* into the warm syrup and simmer for 1 minute. Remove, letting the excess syrup drip off, and place on a platter. Let cool. Store in an airtight container at room temperature for up to 1 week.

VARIATION

Omit the syrup and dredge the warm *travados* in confectioners' sugar.

Empanadas Dulces ↝ *(Sephardic Sweet Turnovers)*

ABOUT FORTY 3-INCH TURNOVERS

Empanadas, from the Spanish *empanar* ("to cover with bread"), are found in most Spanish-speaking countries, each with its own variation. Sephardic versions date back to before the Expulsion in 1492. The rabbinic literature of that time, including the preeminent code of Jewish law, the *Shulchan Orech* by Yoseph Caro, made note of these turnovers. As Sephardim in the Ottoman Empire merged their food with the local cuisine, which featured an assortment of pastry turnovers collectively known as *borek* or *burek*, *borekas/empanadas* became the most popular of Sephardic pastries. This is a dessert variation.

Pastry:

1 cup vegetable shortening, or
    10 tablespoons chilled butter
    and 6 tablespoons shortening

3 cups pastry or bleached all-purpose
    flour, sifted

1 teaspoon salt

2 to 4 tablespoons sugar (optional)

About ¼ cup water

2 large egg yolks, lightly beaten

1 tablespoon white wine vinegar, cider
    vinegar, or lemon juice

About 2 cups empanadas filling (recipes
    follow)

¼ cup olive oil or egg wash (1 large egg
    beaten with 1 tablespoon water)

---

1. To make the pastry: Cut the shortening into the flour to resemble coarse crumbs. Stir the salt and the sugar if using into the water. Blend in the egg yolks and vinegar. Add to the flour mixture and stir until the dough holds together. If necessary, sprinkle a few additional drops of water on any dry flour and press into the remainder of the dough. To make the pastry in a food processor: In the work bowl of a food processor fitted with a metal blade, combine the flour, salt, and sugar if using. Add the shortening and pulse briefly until the mixture resembles coarse crumbs. Combine the water, egg yolks, and vinegar. With the machine running, add the egg mixture, 1 tablespoon at a time, until the dough holds together. Cover with plastic wrap, flatten into a disc, and refrigerate for at least 30 minutes or up to 4 days. Let stand at room temperature until malleable but not soft, about 30 minutes.

2. Preheat the oven to 375 degrees. Line several large baking sheets with parchment paper or lightly grease.

3. On a piece of waxed paper or plastic wrap or on a lightly floured surface, roll out the dough $1/8$ inch thick and cut out 4-inch rounds. Or form the dough into $1^{1}/4$-inch balls and roll into $1/8$-inch-thick rounds.

4. Place 1 heaping teaspoon of the filling in the center of each round. Brush the edges with water, fold over to create a half moon, and press to seal the edges and evenly distribute the filling. Crimp the edges with your fingers or the tines of a fork. *Empanadas* can be covered and stored in the refrigerator for up to 1 day. Place on the prepared baking sheets, 1 inch apart, and brush the tops with the oil.

5. Bake until golden brown, about 20 minutes. Serve warm or at room temperature. *Empanadas* can be frozen for up to 4 months and reheated in a 350-degree oven for about 20 minutes.

EMPANADAS FILLINGS ❧

Gomo de Muez *(Nut Filling)*

$1^{1}/2$ *cups (about 6 ounces) finely chopped blanched almonds, pistachios, walnuts, or any combination, or 1 cup chopped almonds and 1 cup cooked rice* About $3/4$ *cup sugar*	*1 to 2 teaspoons ground cinnamon, rose water, or orange blossom water* $1/4$ *teaspoon ground cloves, or* $1/2$ *teaspoon grated lemon or orange zest (optional)*

Combine all the ingredients.

Gomo de Calabaza *(Pumpkin Filling)*

2 cups (16 ounces) pure-pack canned pumpkin or cooked and mashed pumpkin or sweet potatoes *1 large egg, lightly beaten*	*1 tablespoon all-purpose flour* $1/3$ *cup granulated or brown sugar* $1/2$ *to 1 teaspoon ground cinnamon* *Pinch of salt*

Combine all the ingredients.

Kadayif ❧ *(Middle Eastern Shredded Wheat Pastry)*

K*adayif/kadaif* in Turkish or *konafa/kanafe* in Arabic is unprocessed shredded wheat. Although unknown to many Westerners, in the Middle East, this pastry is nearly as popular as the more familiar baklava. The wiry dough is available fresh (it keeps for about two months in the refrigerator) or frozen in Middle Eastern and Greek specialty stores. Nut-filled *kadayif* is a beloved treat for Purim; cheese-filled, for Shavuot and Hanukkah.

Syrup:

3 *cups sugar, or 2 cups sugar and 1 cup*
   honey

1$^1/_2$ *cups water*

1 *tablespoon light corn syrup*

1 to 3 *teaspoons fresh lemon juice*

1 *teaspoon rose water (optional)*

$^3/_4$ *cup (1$^1/_2$ sticks) unsalted butter or*
   margarine, melted and cooled

1 *pound* kadayif *pastry, shredded (pry*
   apart the strands)

1 *recipe* kadayif *filling (recipes follow)*

A few drops water

1. To make the syrup: Stir the sugar, water, corn syrup, and lemon juice in a medium saucepan over low heat until the sugar dissolves, about 5 minutes. Stop stirring, increase the heat to medium, and cook until slightly syrupy, about 5 minutes (it will register 225 degrees on a candy thermometer). Let cool. If desired, add the rose water.

2. Preheat the oven to 350 degrees.

3. Drizzle the butter over the *kadayif* and toss to coat. Spread half of the *kadayif* in an ungreased 13-by-9-inch baking pan or 10-inch round springform pan and press gently to flatten. Spread with the filling, leaving a $^1/_2$-inch border on all sides. Top with the remaining *kadayif* and sprinkle lightly with the water.

4. Bake until golden brown, 30 to 45 minutes. Drizzle the cooled syrup over the hot pastry. If desired, for a smooth surface, invert onto a tray. Let cool for at least 2$^1/_2$ hours. Cut into 1- to 2-inch squares. *Kadayif* tastes best on the day it is made. Store at room temperature; if using the cheese filling, store only up to 8 hours.

VARIATION

Multi-Layered Kadayif: Layer one-third of the *kadayif* in the baking pan, top with half of the filling, half of the remaining *kadayif*, the remaining filling, and then the remaining *kadayif*.

KADAYIF FILLINGS

Kadayif bil Crema   *(Cream Filling)*

ABOUT 3 CUPS

¹/₄ cup cornstarch	*2 cups milk*
2 tablespoons sugar	*1 cup heavy cream*

Combine the cornstarch and sugar. Gradually stir in 1 cup milk. Bring the remaining 1 cup milk to a low boil in a medium saucepan. Gradually stir in the cornstarch mixture. Stir until thickened and bubbly. Remove from the heat and beat in the cream. Let cool.

Kadayif bil Jiben   *(Cheese-Cream Filling)*

ABOUT 5 CUPS

2 tablespoons cornstarch	*1 cup heavy cream*
2 tablespoons sugar	*2 pounds (4 cups) ricotta cheese*
²/₃ cup milk	

Combine the cornstarch and sugar. Gradually stir in the milk. Bring the cream to a low boil in a medium saucepan. Gradually stir in the cornstarch mixture. Reduce the heat to low and stir until thickened. Cover with plastic wrap and let cool. Stir in the ricotta.

Kadayif bil Jiben *(Cheese Filling)*

ABOUT 3 CUPS

$1^1/_3$ *pounds (3 cups) ricotta cheese*	*1 teaspoon rose water, orange blossom*
2 tablespoons sugar	*water, or ground cinnamon*

Combine all the ingredients.

Kadayif bil Joz *(Nut Filling)*

ABOUT 2 CUPS

2 cups (about 8 ounces) finely chopped	$^1/_4$ *cup sugar*
blanched almonds, walnuts,	*1 teaspoon ground cinnamon or rose*
pistachios, or any combination	*water*

Combine all the ingredients.

PISTACHIOS

 Pistachios grow on a small deciduous tree native to Persia, the area in which the best are still grown. These pale green nuts covered with a papery skin have been found in some of the earliest archeological sites in Iran and Iraq. They were one of the few nuts mentioned in the Bible by name and among the choice fruits of Canaan sent by Jacob to the prime minister of Egypt. Pistachios remain favorites in the Middle East.

After harvesting, the nuts are dried, a process that splits most of the shells. The traditional method of processing also stains the shell, and therefore many merchants dye them red. Pistachios have a subtle flavor that most Americans associate with salt, since most pistachios are sold heavily salted, or with almonds, since almond extract is used to flavor pistachio ice cream. In the Middle East, pistachios are used like almonds in pilafs, sauces, and such desserts as cookies, baklava, *ma'amoul* (filled cookies), and puddings.

Tarte Alsacienne ❧ *(Alsatian Fruit Custard Tart)*

ONE 10-INCH TART

Tarts are straight-sided, flat-bottomed, very crisp pastries made from a sweet, rich dough. Although Americans overwhelmingly prefer slope-sided pies, Europeans favor the more versatile tart, which comes in a large variety of shapes and sizes. In this recipe, the custard and fruit are baked together in the shell.

Pastry:

3/4 cup (1 1/2 sticks) unsalted butter or margarine, softened

1/3 cup sugar

1/2 teaspoon salt

1 large egg

2 cups bleached all-purpose flour

Filling:

2 pounds (4 to 5 cups) peeled, cored, and sliced apples; blueberries; pitted fresh sour cherries; seedless grapes; peeled, cored, and sliced pears; halved and pitted Italian plums; or any combination

1/2 cup heavy cream or nondairy creamer

3 large eggs, lightly beaten

1/2 cup granulated sugar, or 1 1/2 cups confectioners' sugar

1 teaspoon vanilla extract

1 tablespoon kirsch or brandy (optional)

1. To make the pastry: Beat the butter until smooth, about 1 minute. Gradually add the sugar and salt and beat until light and fluffy, about 4 minutes. Beat in the egg. Gradually stir in the flour. The consistency should be that of a sugar cookie dough. If too stiff, add a little ice water or heavy cream. Form into a disc, cover with plastic wrap, and refrigerate for at least 30 minutes or up to 1 week. Let stand at room temperature until malleable, about 40 minutes.

2. On a piece of waxed paper or plastic wrap or on a lightly floured surface, roll the pastry into a 1/8-inch-thick round about 14 inches in diameter. Line a 10- or 11-inch flat-bottomed tart or flan pan with the pastry and trim the edges. If it tears, press scraps in the empty spaces. (Use any leftover dough to make cookies or tartlets.) Prick the bottom and sides of the crust at 1/2-inch intervals with the tines of a fork. Cover with plastic wrap and refrigerate for at least 1 hour or up to 2 days. *continued*

3. Preheat the oven to 400 degrees.
4. Arrange the fruit in the tart shell. Combine the cream, eggs, sugar, vanilla, and kirsch if using and pour over the fruit.
5. Bake for 20 minutes. Reduce the heat to 350 degrees and bake until the pastry is golden and the custard is set, about 25 minutes. Let the tart cool for at least 10 minutes before removing the outer rim of the pan. Serve warm, at room temperature, or chilled.

VARIATIONS

In the filling, substitute $1/2$ cup milk for the cream and add 1 tablespoon cornstarch (dissolve it in the milk).

Zwetschenkuchen (Alsatian Plum Tart): Omit the custard mixture. Arrange $2^{1}/2$ to 3 pounds pitted and halved plums (preferably Italian) in the shell and sprinkle with about $1/3$ cup sugar. Bake at 375 degrees until the fruit is tender and the pastry is golden, about 50 minutes.

KIRSCH

 Kirsch, short for *kirschwasser* (German for "cherry water"), is a colorless liqueur distilled from crushed cherries, common to Alsace and Germany. Sip chilled kirsch straight, add to a sugar syrup, sprinkle over fruit salads, or use to plump dried fruit for baking.

Kada ⤸ *(Georgian Cream Tart)*

Most Georgian desserts reflect a Persian and Ottoman heritage in the form of phyllo pastries and nut confections. This pastry, however, shows a Western influence.

Pastry:	Filling:
1¾ cups bleached all-purpose flour	*6 tablespoons (¾ stick) butter, softened*
1 teaspoon baking soda	*1 cup all-purpose flour*
½ teaspoon salt	*1 cup sugar*
½ cup (1 stick) unsalted butter, softened	*1 teaspoon vanilla extract*
½ cup sugar	
2 large eggs	*Confectioners' sugar for dusting*
¾ cup sour cream	*(optional)*
1 teaspoon vanilla extract	

1. To make the pastry: Sift together the flour, baking soda, and salt. Beat the butter until smooth, about 1 minute. Gradually add the sugar and beat until light and fluffy, about 4 minutes. Beat in the eggs, one at a time. Add the sour cream and vanilla. Blend in the flour mixture. Wrap in plastic wrap and refrigerate until firm, at least 30 minutes.

2. Preheat the oven to 400 degrees. Grease a 10-inch springform pan and dust with flour.

3. To make the filling: Beat all the filling ingredients until smooth.

4. Divide the dough in half. Place one half in the pan and press it to cover the bottom and reach 1 inch up the sides. Spread the filling over the dough.

5. Between 2 pieces of waxed paper or plastic wrap or on a lightly floured surface, roll out the remaining piece of dough into a 10-inch round. Place over the filling and press down on the edges.

6. Bake until golden brown and a tester inserted in the center comes out clean, about 40 minutes. Place on a rack and let cool. If desired, sprinkle with confectioners' sugar.

VARIATION

Georgian Cherry Tart: Combine 1 pound (about 3 cups) pitted sweet cherries, 1/4 cup cherry preserves, 1/2 cup toasted slivered almonds, and 1 teaspoon grated lemon zest and substitute for the filling.

APPLES

As an apple tree among the trees of the forest, so is my beloved among
the sons. Under its shadow I delighted to stand,
and its fruit was sweet to my taste.

—SONG OF SONGS 2:3

 Apples are an old and important component of Jewish lore and cooking, forming the basis of many variations of *charoset* (fruit paste) for the Passover Seder and used in numerous desserts. Apples, frequently dipped in honey, are a widespread Rosh Hashanah food, the sweetness serving as a wish for a sweet year to come. The Song of Songs (2:3) attests to the apple's sweetness, Proverbs (25:11) to its beauty, and Joel (1:12) to its stature as an important crop over 2,500 years ago. In mystical literature, an apple orchard is frequently pictured as a symbol of the Divine Presence.

The apple is the world's most widely cultivated temperate-zone fruit. Pliny the Elder (23–79 CE) listed three dozen different apples. Today there are more than 7,000 horticultural forms, although only about a dozen are grown commercially in the United States. Apples have four basic culinary characteristics—sweetness, tartness, fruitiness, and texture—which vary greatly among varieties. Acidity decreases, sweetness increases, and texture turns mealy during storage. Some varieties, such as Braeburn and Crispin, hold up better than Gala, Macoun, and Red Delicious. The best eating apples have a well-balanced ratio of sweetness and acidity and a crisp, juicy texture. Good examples are Braeburn, Cortland, Crispin, Criterian, Fuji, Gala, Golden Delicious, Granny Smith, Macoun, and Northern Spy. Some apples maintain their shape during baking, while others disintegrate. Slightly tart apples with higher levels of calcium (which helps maintain the cell structure) are best for baking and pastries. Good examples are Golden Delicious, Granny Smith, Jonathan, Newton Pippin, Northern Spy, Rome Beauty, Stayman, Winesap, Yellow Transparent, and York Imperial.

Almas Pite ❧ *(Hungarian Apple Tart)*

ABOUT 24 SERVINGS

Although this is commonly referred to as a cake, it is really a fruit tart. Hungarians love topping this dough with various types of fruit, but apple is far and away the most popular.

Pastry:

3 cups bleached all-purpose flour, sifted

1/2 cup sugar

1/2 teaspoon salt

1 cup (2 sticks) unsalted butter or
   vegetable shortening, chilled

4 large egg yolks

3 tablespoons sour cream

2 tablespoons lemon juice

Filling:

2 pounds (about 6 medium) cooking
   apples, such as Golden Delicious,
   Granny Smith, Gravenstein,
   Greening, Jonathan, Macoun, Pippin,
   Starr, Winesap, or any combination,
   peeled, cored, and diced

1 tablespoon lemon juice

3/4 cup (3 ounces) chopped almonds,
   hazelnuts, or walnuts

1/2 cup sugar

1 teaspoon grated lemon zest

1 teaspoon ground cinnamon

3 tablespoons bread crumbs

Egg wash (1 large egg beaten with
   1 tablespoon water)

1. To make the pastry: Combine the flour, sugar, and salt. Cut in the butter to resemble coarse crumbs. Combine the egg yolks, sour cream, and lemon juice. Stir into the flour mixture to make a soft dough. Divide the dough, with one part slightly larger than the other. Cover and refrigerate for at least 1 hour.
2. Preheat the oven to 350 degrees. Grease a 15 1/2-by-10 1/2-inch jelly roll pan.
3. On a piece of waxed paper or plastic wrap or on a lightly floured surface, roll out the larger dough piece to fit the prepared pan and arrange in the pan.

continued

4. To make the filling: Toss the apples with the lemon juice. Stir in the nuts, sugar, zest, and cinnamon. Sprinkle the bread crumbs over the bottom pastry and spread with the apple mixture.

5. Roll out the remaining dough. Cut into strips and arrange in a lattice pattern over the filling. Brush the pastry with the egg wash.

6. Bake for 30 minutes. Reduce the heat to 300 degrees and bake until the crust is golden, about 30 additional minutes. Place the pan on a rack and let cool. Store at room temperature for up to 1 day.

VARIATIONS

Beat 3 large egg whites until soft peaks form, then gradually beat in 6 tablespoons sugar until stiff and glossy. Fold into the apple mixture.

Turos Pite (Hungarian Cheese Tart): For the filling, combine 2 pounds farmer's or pot cheese (or $1^1/_2$ pounds cheese and $1^1/_2$ cups mashed potatoes), 6 large egg yolks, $1^3/_4$ cups sugar, 6 tablespoons ($^3/_4$ stick) melted butter, 3 tablespoons milk, 2 tablespoons all-purpose flour or fine semolina, 1 tablespoon vanilla extract, $^1/_4$ teaspoon salt, and if desired, 2 teaspoons grated lemon zest and/or 1 cup raisins. Beat 6 egg whites on low speed until foamy, about 30 seconds. Increase the speed to medium-high and beat until stiff but not dry. Fold into the cheese mixture. Substitute for the apple filling.

Crostata ❧ *(Italian Two-Crust Tart)*

Pasta frolla ("fragile pastry"), a sweet, rich dough developed during the Renaissance, has been the basic pastry of Italy ever since. Italian tarts, called *crostate* (*crostata* in the singular), are generally made with a thicker crust than the French type and frequently with a top crust. Fruits, nuts, and jams serve as the basis for most of the fillings. Use any leftover dough to make cookies or tartlets.

Pasta frolla:	1 large egg, lightly beaten
2 1/4 cups bleached all-purpose flour, sifted	1 large egg yolk
1/2 cup sugar	1 teaspoon grated lemon zest or vanilla extract
1/2 teaspoon salt	
3/4 cup plus 2 tablespoons (1 3/4 sticks) unsalted butter or margarine, chilled	1 recipe crostata filling (recipes follow)

1. To make the pastry: Combine the flour, sugar, and salt. Cut in the butter to resemble coarse crumbs. Combine the egg, egg yolk, and zest. Add to the flour and stir until the dough holds together. If it is too dry, add a little water. Place on a lightly floured surface and, using the heel of your hand, gently push a little of the dough down (about 2 tablespoons at a time), then push and smear it away from you. Repeat with the remaining dough. Divide the dough in half, making one half slightly larger than the other. Form into discs, cover with plastic wrap, and refrigerate for at least 1 hour or up to 1 week. Let stand at room temperature until malleable but not soft, about 30 minutes.

2. On a piece of waxed paper or plastic wrap or on a lightly floured surface, roll out the larger piece of dough into a 1/4-inch-thick round. Line a 10- or 11-inch flat-bottomed tart or flan pan with the pastry, leaving a 1-inch overhang. If it tears, press scraps into the empty spaces. Prick the bottom and sides at 1/2-inch intervals with the tines of a fork. Cover with plastic wrap and refrigerate for at least 30 minutes or up to 2 days.

3. Preheat the oven to 350 degrees.

4. Spread the filling evenly over the pastry shell. Roll out the remaining dough into a 1/4-inch-thick round. Arrange over the filling and crimp the edges to seal. Cut several slits in the top to vent the steam. Or cut the upper pastry into 1/2-inch-wide strips and arrange lattice style over the filling.

continued

5. Bake until golden brown, about 50 minutes. Let cool on a rack. Store the fruit or nut tarts at room temperature for up to 3 days or in the freezer. Store the cheese tart at room temperature for up to 8 hours or in the refrigerator for up to 3 days; if desired, warm in a 350-degree oven for about 25 minutes.

VARIATION

Free-Form Crostata: Roll the dough into a ¹⁄₁₆-inch-thick round and transfer to a baking sheet lined with parchment paper. Spread the filling in the center of the round, then bring the edges of the pastry together over most or all of the filling.

CROSTATA FILLINGS ❧

Crostata di Mandorle *(Italian Almond Tart)*

3 large eggs	*³⁄₄ cup (9 ounces) apricot jam, sour*
¹⁄₄ cup sugar	*cherry preserves, seedless raspberry*
7 ounces (³⁄₄ cup) Sephardic Almond	*jam, or orange marmalade*
Paste, crumbled (page 368)	*¹⁄₂ to 1 cup sliced almonds, toasted*
¹⁄₂ cup all-purpose flour	*(optional)*

Beat the eggs and sugar until light and fluffy. Add the almond paste and beat until smooth. Stir in the flour. Spread the jam over the bottom pastry and top with the almond mixture. If desired, sprinkle with the almonds.

Crostata di Ricotta *(Italian Cheese Tart)*

2 tablespoons brandy or marsala	*2 large eggs, lightly beaten*
¹⁄₃ cup golden raisins	*¹⁄₂ cup sugar*
2 cups (1 pound) ricotta cheese, well	*1 teaspoon vanilla extract*
drained	*1 teaspoon grated lemon or orange zest*

Sprinkle the brandy over the raisins and let stand for at least 30 minutes. Drain. Beat together the ricotta, eggs, sugar, vanilla, and zest until smooth. Stir in the raisins.

Spongata *(Italian Fruit-and-Nut Tart)*

1¹/₄ cups apricot jam	¹/₂ cup candied orange peel, chopped
1 cup blanched almonds, toasted and coarsely chopped	(see page 366)
²/₃ cup pine nuts, toasted	¹/₂ cup bread crumbs
¹/₂ cup dried currants or raisins	1 teaspoon ground cinnamon
¹/₂ cup candied citron peel, chopped (see page 366)	1 cup honey
	¹/₂ cup water

Combine the jam, nuts, currants, citron peel, orange peel, bread crumbs, and cinnamon. Bring the honey and water to a boil in a medium saucepan over medium heat, stirring occasionally. Drizzle over the fruit mixture and toss to coat.

Crostata di Fichi *(Italian Fig Tart)*

1 pound (about 3 cups) dried Calimyrna figs, stemmed and coarsely chopped	¹/₂ cup red wine or orange juice
	¹/₄ cup sugar or honey
1 cup water	1 (3-inch) stick cinnamon (optional)

Cook all the ingredients in a medium saucepan over medium-low heat, stirring occasionally, until thickened, about 15 minutes. Discard the cinnamon stick. Let cool completely. The original version leaves the filling chunky, but it can be pureed in a blender or food processor for a smoother texture.

Inchusa de Leche ❧ *(Sephardic Custard Tart)*

ONE 10-INCH TART

The original pastry contained a savory filling, but dessert tarts eventually followed. You can also make this with only a bottom crust.

Pastry:	Filling:
1/2 cup (1 stick) unsalted butter or margarine, softened	*1 teaspoon cornstarch*
1/3 cup sugar	*2 cups milk*
1/2 teaspoon salt	*4 large egg yolks, lightly beaten*
1 large egg	*3/4 cup sugar*
1 large egg yolk	*1 teaspoon grated lemon zest (optional)*
1 teaspoon lemon juice or cider vinegar	*1/4 cup (1/2 stick) butter*
2 cups bleached all-purpose flour, sifted	*1 teaspoon vanilla extract*

1. To make the pastry: Beat the butter until smooth, about 1 minute. Gradually add the sugar and salt and beat until light and fluffy, about 4 minutes. Beat in the egg, egg yolk, and lemon juice. Gradually stir in the flour. If the dough is too stiff, add a little ice water. Divide the dough in half, making one half slightly larger than the other. Form into discs, cover with plastic wrap, and refrigerate for at least 1 hour or up to 1 week. Let stand at room temperature until malleable but not soft, about 30 minutes.

2. On a piece of waxed paper or plastic wrap or on a lightly floured surface, roll out the larger piece of dough into a 1/4-inch-thick round. Line a 10- or 11-inch flat-bottomed tart or flan pan with the pastry, leaving a 1-inch overhang (if it tears, press scraps into the empty spaces), or place on a baking sheet lined with parchment paper. Prick the bottom and sides with a fork. Cover with plastic wrap and refrigerate for at least 1 hour or up to 2 days.

3. To make the filling: Dissolve the cornstarch in a little milk, then stir in the remaining milk. Blend in the egg yolks, sugar, and zest if using. Cook over medium-low heat, stirring frequently at first and constantly after a few minutes, until the mixture begins to bubble and thicken. Remove from the heat, add the butter and vanilla, and stir until smooth. Press a piece of plastic wrap against the surface and let cool.

4. Preheat the oven to 350 degrees.
5. Spread the filling evenly over the pastry shell. Roll out the remaining dough into a $1/4$-inch-thick round. Arrange over the filling, crimp the edges to seal, and cut several slits in the top to vent the steam. Or cut the upper pastry into $1/2$-inch-wide strips and arrange lattice style over the filling.
6. Bake until golden brown, about 50 minutes. Let cool on a rack.

VARIATION

Quesadas de Leche (Sephardic Custard Tartlets): With a name derived from *queso*, Spanish for "cheese," this pastry is related to the Spanish cheese turnover *quesadilla*. Cut the pastry into 3-inch rounds and press into greased muffin tins. Spoon in the filling and, if desired, top with another dough round. Bake in a 350-degree oven for about 30 minutes.

Inchusa de Vijna ❧ *(Sephardic Cherry Tart)*

ONE 10-INCH TART

There are two types of domesticated cherries: sweet (such as Bing) and sour (Morello). The former is primarily eaten fresh, while sour cherries, which are smaller and paler, are used in cooking, baking, and liqueurs. The cherry growing season is among the shortest of any fruit, lasting from early June to late July. There are several mechanical pitters available. To pit by hand, gently press down on the stem end to loosen the pit. Using the index finger and thumb of your other hand placed near the bottom of the cherry, press until the pit pops out of the top.

When cherries are cooked whole, the pits impart a slight almond flavor. To duplicate this effect, add almond extract when using pitted cherries.

---

1 recipe inchusa de leche *pastry*
  (page 212)

Filling:
2 pounds sour cherries, pitted (about
  4 cups)

$1/2$ cup sugar

Water

4 teaspoons cornstarch

$1/4$ teaspoon almond extract (optional)

---

1. Prepare the pastry through Step 1.
2. On a piece of waxed paper or plastic wrap or on a lightly floured surface, roll out the larger piece of dough into a $1/4$-inch-thick round. Line a 10- or 11-inch flat-bottomed tart or flan pan with the pastry. If it tears, press scraps into the empty spaces. Prick the bottom and sides at $1/2$-inch intervals with the tines of a fork. Cover with plastic wrap and refrigerate for at least 1 hour or up to 2 days.
3. Preheat the oven to 400 degrees.
4. Line the bottom and sides of the pastry shell with aluminum foil and fill with pie weights or dried beans, pressing them against the sides. Place on a baking sheet and bake until the pastry is set, about 15 minutes. Reduce the heat to 350 degrees, remove the foil and weights, and bake until lightly browned, about 5 minutes. Place on a rack and let cool.
5. To make the filling: Place the cherries in a bowl, sprinkle with the sugar, and let stand for 1 hour. Drain the liquid from the cherries into a measuring cup and add enough

water to measure $3/4$ cup. Stir a little of the cherry liquid into the cornstarch to dissolve, then add the remaining liquid. Cook in a small saucepan over low heat, stirring constantly, until thickened and bubbly. Remove from the heat and, if desired, stir in the almond extract. Stir in the cherries and pour into the shell.

6. Preheat the oven to 375 degrees.
7. Roll out the remaining dough into a $1/4$-inch-thick round. Arrange over the filling and trim the edges. Cut several slits in the top to vent the steam.
8. Bake until golden, about 35 minutes. Let the tart cool for at least 10 minutes before removing the outer rim of the pan. Serve warm or at room temperature.

VARIATION

Inchusa de Fruta (Sephardic Fruit Tart): Use only the bottom crust. Combine 2 tablespoons sugar and 1 tablespoon flour and sprinkle over the bottom of the prebaked tart shell. Arrange 6 to 7 cups sliced fruit (apples, apricots, cherries, peaches, pears, or plums) on top and sprinkle with 3 tablespoons sugar. Bake at 350 degrees until the fruit is tender, about 25 minutes.

Phyllo *and* Strudel

*And their father Israel said unto them: If it be so, do this: take of the
choice fruits of the land in your vessels, and carry down a present
to the man, a little balm, and a little honey, spices
and ladanum, pistachios and almonds.*

—GENESIS 43:11

PHYLLO/FILO (GREEK FOR "LEAF"), CALLED *FILA* IN ARABIC AND *YUFKA* IN TURKISH, IS A SIMPLE DOUGH STRETCHED PAPER THIN. IT ORIGINATED IN PERSIA MORE THAN A THOUSAND YEARS AGO AND WAS INTRODUCED TO EUROPE BY THE TURKS. WHEN THESE DELICATE sheets are layered with fat and baked, they produce crisp, flaky pastry used in a wide variety of desserts.

Making phyllo is a time-consuming and complicated procedure, but it is available frozen in most groceries. (Many markets, however, let the packages thaw and then refreeze them, resulting in dough that sticks and crumbles.) A 1-pound box contains twenty to twenty-five leaves about 17 by 12 inches. Thaw the phyllo in the refrigerator for at least eight hours; thaw completely before using or it will crumble. Do not thaw at room temperature or the sheets will stick together. Unopened, phyllo will keep for almost a month in the refrigerator. Remove it from the refrigerator about two hours before using. Reroll any unused dough, wrap tightly in plastic wrap, and store in the refrigerator for up to two weeks. Do not refreeze.

Phyllo dries out very quickly, so keep it moist but not wet—if dried, it becomes brittle; if too damp, it turns gummy. Unroll the phyllo onto a flat surface and cover completely with plastic wrap, then a damp towel. Work with only one sheet at a time. Assembled phyllo pastry can be refrigerated for up to a day or frozen. Do not thaw before baking or it will be soggy.

Brush phyllo lightly with fat, 1 to 2 teaspoons per sheet. Saturating the leaves with fat results in a clumpy mass. On the other hand, do not skimp or the pastry will be heavy. Use a soft pastry brush or large feather for brushing or apply with a spritzer bottle. Clarified butter produces the crispest pastry. For fewer calories and greater ease, mist the leaves with cooking spray.

Fila/Strudelblatter ❧ *(Phyllo/Strudel Dough)*

ABOUT 1 POUND; ENOUGH FOR A 3- TO 4-FOOT-LONG STRUDEL

Old World strudel makers take their pastry very seriously, ritualistically performing each step. Many incorporate an egg or egg whites into the dough for strength, while others add only a little oil and sometimes acid to produce a more tender pastry. Some bakers insist on *glatt* (smooth) flour, while others demand *griffig* (rough). The flour must contain a large amount of protein in order to stretch and not tear. Do not use bleached flour, which lacks sufficient gluten. The brand of flour, as well as the baker's skill, will affect the extent to which the dough can be stretched. This recipe reaches from 4 to 6 feet. *Strudelblatter* is left as one large piece of dough for easy rolling, while phyllo is cut into pieces to facilitate stacking.

2 cups bread or unbleached all-purpose flour, or 1 cup each	*1 1/2 teaspoons fresh lemon juice or white vinegar*
About 2/3 cup warm water	*1/2 teaspoon salt*
3 tablespoons vegetable oil	*Additional vegetable oil for brushing*

1. Put the flour in a bowl and make a well in the center. Combine the water, oil, lemon juice, and salt and pour into the well. Stir, adding more warm water if necessary to make a sticky dough. On a floured surface, knead until smooth and elastic, about 10 minutes. The dough is traditionally kneaded, using a dough scraper, by lifting it 2 feet above the work surface and letting it drop. To make the dough in a food processor: In the bowl of a food processor fitted with a metal blade, combine the flour and salt. Add the oil and lemon juice (and the egg if using—see Variation) and process until well blended, about 5 seconds. With the machine on, gradually add enough water until the dough holds together. Scrape down the sides and process until smooth and elastic. When kneaded, the dough can be divided in half if desired to make smaller pieces of stretched dough in Step 4.

2. Form into a ball and lightly cover with oil, about 1 teaspoon. Cover with a bowl or plastic wrap and let rest for at least 30 minutes.

3. Cover a table (4-foot square to 6 by 4 feet) with a cloth that drapes over the sides. Sprinkle with flour. Place the dough in the center and, using a rolling pin, roll out as thinly as possible. Brush lightly with oil and let rest for several minutes.

4. Remove any rings and lightly flour your hands. Beginning from the center of the dough, place your hands, palms down, under the dough. Using the back of your hands, gently lift and stretch the dough toward you—do not use your fingers, which tend to tear the dough. Stretching can also be done with two people working across from each other. Continue stretching the dough, paying particular attention to any thick areas, until it covers the table and is uniformly thin and transparent, about 15 minutes. Patch any large tears with a piece of dough trimmed from the sides and stretched. Using scissors, trim off the thick edges. Brush lightly with oil and let dry for 15 minutes.

VARIATIONS

Add 1 lightly beaten large egg and reduce the water to about $1/2$ cup.

Phyllo: Cut the stretched dough into six to ten 17-by-12-inch rectangles, stack the rectangles on top of each other, and wrap well in plastic wrap. Reroll the scraps for additional sheets.

Strudel

*S**trudel** is the German word for "whirlpool," a fitting appellation for this roll of fruit, nuts, and delicate pastry. Originally, this Teutonic dish consisted of fruit preserves rolled up in a thick dough. Then Hungarians learned about phyllo from the Turks, perhaps by way of Jewish merchants who traveled between the two countries or later during the Ottoman occupation of southeastern Europe, and rather promptly began substituting this thin pastry. Austrians, Germans, and Romanians quickly recognized the greatness of this innovation and became equally as fanatic about their "whirlpools." In a region justly renowned for its cakes and pastry, unquestionably the favorite of all is strudel.

Since classic strudel making was such a demanding process, many housewives limited it to special occasions, sometimes preparing it only once or twice a year—most notably for Rosh Hashanah and Sukkot. Apple strudel is the perfect High Holiday food, encompassing many of the traditional culinary symbols—sweet, filled, and fruity. Use Ashkenazic Poppy Seed Filling (page 73) for Purim, and cheese for Shavuot and Hanukkah. Any firm filling can be used for a strudel. Juicy fruits, such as apples, cherries, and plums, are thickened with *brusel* (sautéed bread crumbs) or cake crumbs. Fruit strudels are commonly served with *schlag* (German for "whipped cream").

---

1 recipe strudelblatter (page 218), stretched
About 1 cup melted butter or vegetable oil for brushing
1 cup dry bread crumbs or mandelbrot crumbs, or 1 cup bread crumbs sautéed in 2 tablespoons butter or margarine until golden

1 recipe strudel filling (pages 223–24)
Confectioners' sugar for dusting (optional)

---

1. Preheat the oven to 400 degrees. Grease a large baking sheet.
2. Brush the dough, still on its cloth, with the butter. Sprinkle the crumbs over the lower two-thirds of the pastry, leaving a 4-inch border on 3 sides. Spread the filling, discarding any accumulated liquid, over the crumbs.

3. Lift the cloth under the filling end of the dough and drop the bottom edge of the dough over part of the filling. Use the sides of the cloth to flip over the 4-inch sides of the dough. The roll will now be about 3 feet long. Brush the top and sides of the dough with butter. From the filling end, gradually lift the cloth higher, allowing the dough to roll over itself to the end. Carefully roll or lift, seam side down, onto the prepared baking sheet. If the strudel is too large for the baking sheet, bend it into a horseshoe shape. Brush with butter.

4. Bake for 10 minutes. Reduce the heat to 350 degrees, turn the baking sheet around in the oven, and continue baking until golden brown, about 30 minutes. Place the baking sheet on a rack and let cool slightly. Cut the strudel into 2-inch slices. If desired, dust with confectioners' sugar. Store at room temperature for up to 2 days or freeze; reheat in a 350-degree oven for about 20 minutes.

Phyllo Strudel

ONE 30-INCH-LONG STRUDEL; FIFTEEN 2-INCH-WIDE PIECES

In this version, sheets of phyllo dough are arranged with overlapping sides to imitate *strudelblatter.* You can make smaller strudels by aligning half the phyllo sheets in a single row.

---

16 sheets phyllo dough, each about 18 by 12 inches

About 1 cup (2 sticks) unsalted butter or margarine, melted

1 cup dry bread crumbs or mandelbrot crumbs, or 1 cup bread crumbs sautéed in 2 tablespoons butter or margarine until golden

1 recipe strudel filling (recipes follow)

Confectioners' sugar for dusting (optional)

---

1. Preheat the oven to 375 degrees. Grease a large baking sheet.
2. Cover a flat surface with a cloth at least 4 by 4 feet. Place 1 sheet of phyllo near the edge of the cloth with a long side facing you and lightly brush with butter. Align a second phyllo sheet along the short edge of the first sheet, overlapping by 2 inches, and lightly brush with butter. Align 2 more sheets along the long edges of the first 2 sheets, overlapping by 2 inches, and lightly brush with butter. Align 2 more sheets along the long edges of the second 2 sheets, overlapping by 2 inches, and brush with butter. Align 2 more sheets along the long edges of the third sheets, overlapping by 2 inches, and brush with butter or margarine. Arrange the remaining 8 sheets on top of the bottom layer of phyllo and brush with butter. You should have about a 40-by-34-inch double-layered rectangle.
3. Sprinkle the bread crumbs over the third of the phyllo rectangle closest to you, leaving a 2-inch border along the end and sides. Spread the filling over the crumbs.
4. Fold the 2-inch bottom of the phyllo over the filling, then fold the sides of the pastry over the filling. From the filling end, lift the cloth and roll up the strudel jelly roll style. The strudel can be refrigerated for up to 1 day or frozen. Do not thaw; increase the baking time by about 10 minutes.
5. Place the strudel, seam side down, on the prepared baking sheet and brush with butter. Bake until golden brown, about 40 minutes. Let cool slightly. The strudel may be covered loosely, stored at room temperature for up to 1 day, and reheated at 400 degrees. Cut into serving portions. If desired, sprinkle with the confectioners' sugar.

STRUDEL FILLINGS ❧

Apfel Strudelfulle *(Apple Strudel Filling)*

ABOUT 5 CUPS; ENOUGH FOR A 3- TO 4-FOOT-LONG STRUDEL

1/2 cup raisins

2 tablespoons dark rum, kirsch, or water

2 pounds (about 5 medium) tart cooking apples, such as Golden Delicious, Granny Smith, Gravenstein, Greening, Jonathan, Macoun, Pippin, Rome, Starr, Winesap, Yellow Transparent, or any combination, peeled, cored, and thinly sliced

1 tablespoon fresh lemon juice

About 1/2 cup sugar

1/2 cup finely chopped toasted walnuts, or 1/4 cup fine semolina

3/4 teaspoon ground cinnamon

Pinch of salt

2 teaspoons grated lemon zest (optional)

1/4 teaspoon ground nutmeg (optional)

Soak the raisins in the rum for 30 minutes. Drain. Toss the apples with the lemon juice. Combine the apples, raisins, sugar, walnuts (to help absorb some of the excess liquid), cinnamon, salt, and if desired, the zest and/or nutmeg. Do not let the apples stand long or they will start to exude their liquid.

VARIATION

Apple-Raspberry Strudel: Substitute 1/2 cup fresh or frozen raspberries for the raisins and omit the rum.

Kirschen Strudelfulle *(Cherry Strudel Filling)*

ABOUT 4 CUPS; ENOUGH FOR A 3- TO 4-FOOT-LONG STRUDEL

4 cups (about 2 pounds) sour cherries, pitted

About 1 cup sugar

6 tablespoons ground blanched almonds (optional)

1 teaspoon grated lemon zest, or 1/4 teaspoon ground cinnamon

Combine all the ingredients.

Birn Strudelfulle *(Pear Strudel Filling)*

ABOUT 4½ CUPS; ENOUGH FOR A 3- TO 4-FOOT-LONG STRUDEL

1½ pounds (about 4 large) Bartlett or
  Anjou pears, peeled, cored, and diced
1 tablespoon lemon juice
½ cup coarsely chopped hazelnuts,
  walnuts, or pecans
½ cup raisins, dried sour cherries, or
  chopped dried pears

About ½ cup sugar
1 teaspoon grated lemon zest, or
  ¼ teaspoon ground nutmeg
½ teaspoon ground cinnamon

Toss the pears with the lemon juice. Add the remaining ingredients.

Kaese Strudelfulle *(Cheese Strudel Filling)*

ABOUT 4½ CUPS; ENOUGH FOR A 3- TO 4-FOOT-LONG STRUDEL

This is delicious topped with a half recipe of the Cherry Strudel Filling (page 223).

---

1 pound cream cheese, softened, or
  8 ounces cream cheese and
  8 ounces small-curd cottage
  cheese or pot cheese
About ¾ cup sugar
3 large egg yolks
½ cup sour cream or heavy cream

1 tablespoon cornstarch, or
  2 tablespoons all-purpose flour,
  or ¼ cup fine semolina
1½ teaspoons vanilla extract
¼ teaspoon salt
1 teaspoon grated lemon zest (optional)
¾ cup golden raisins (optional)

Beat the cream cheese until smooth. Gradually beat in the sugar. Beat in the egg yolks. Blend in the sour cream, cornstarch, vanilla, salt, and zest. Add the raisins if using. Or process all the ingredients except the raisins in a food processor or blender until smooth.

VARIATION

Beat 3 large egg whites until stiff and fold into the cheese mixture.

Sansathicos ❧ *(Middle Eastern Nut-Filled Phyllo Triangles)*

ABOUT 48 PASTRIES

S mall, triangular-shaped phyllo pastries are found throughout the Middle East and Mediterranean area. Nut-filled turnovers, also called *trigona,* are a traditional Purim treat.

1 pound (about 24 sheets) phyllo dough	*2 cups hot sugar syrup (see* atar, *page*
About ³/₄ cup vegetable oil, melted	*265) or confectioners' sugar for*
butter, or melted margarine	*dusting*
1 recipe Sephardic Nut Filling	*Toasted sesame seeds (optional)*
(page 227)	

1. Preheat the oven to 350 degrees. Grease a large baking sheet.
2. Cut the phyllo lengthwise into 4-inch-wide strips. Place 1 strip on a flat surface and lightly brush with oil. Place a heaping tablespoon of the filling in the center of the strip about 1 inch from one end. Fold a corner of the dough diagonally over the filling, forming a triangle. Brush the corner flap with oil and continue folding, maintaining the triangular shape, until the end of the strip. The triangles can be refrigerated for up to 24 hours or frozen. Do not thaw; increase the baking time by about 10 minutes.
3. Place the triangles on the prepared baking sheets and brush with oil. Bake until crisp and golden, about 30 minutes. Let cool. Or deep-fry the triangles in hot vegetable oil until crisp and browned, about 5 minutes.
4. In batches, dip the cooled pastries into the warm syrup, remove, and if desired, sprinkle with the sesame seeds. Or sprinkle the triangles with confectioners' sugar.

Briates ❧ *(Middle Eastern Phyllo Rolls)*

48 SMALL ROLLS

During my junior year of college, while studying in Israel, I was introduced to the cuisine of many non-Ashkenazic communities. I was particularly enchanted by the large assortment of Middle Eastern flaky pastries. Among the most popular of these treats are phyllo rolls variously called *briates* ("rolls"), *dedos* ("sticks"), *asabia* ("fingers"), and in Morocco, *cigares/sigares* and *garros* ("cigars"). You can also fill these pastries with non-traditional mixtures such as Ashkenazic Poppy Seed Filling (page 73) and Sweet Cheese Filling (page 170).

---

1 pound (about 24 sheets) phyllo dough
About 1 cup vegetable oil, melted butter,
   or melted margarine

1 recipe Sephardic phyllo filling (recipes
   follow)

---

1. Preheat the oven to 350 degrees. Grease a large baking sheet.
2. Lay the stack of phyllo sheets on a flat surface and cut in half lengthwise. Cover with plastic wrap and a damp towel when not in use.
3. Place 1 phyllo strip on a flat surface and lightly brush with oil. Spoon about 1 tablespoon of the filling in a thin strip about 1 inch from the narrow end closest to you, leaving a 1-inch border on both sides. Fold the bottom 1 inch of the phyllo over the filling, then fold in the uncovered 1 inch on both long sides. Starting from the filling end, roll up jelly roll style. The rolls can be refrigerated at this point for up to 1 day or frozen for up to 3 months. Do not thaw; increase the baking time by about 10 minutes.
4. Place the rolls, seam side down, on the prepared baking sheet and brush with oil. Bake until crisp and golden brown, about 30 minutes. Let cool. Store in an airtight container at room temperature for up to 1 week or in the freezer for up to 3 months.

VARIATIONS

Travados de Fila (Sephardic Nut-Filled Rolls): Use the Sephardic Nut Filling but reduce the sugar in the filling to 1/4 cup. Dip the hot rolls into cooled sugar syrup (see *atar*, page 265) and allow to penetrate, about 2 minutes. Do *not* dip in the syrup before freezing.

Rodanches (Sephardic Phyllo Coils): Moroccans serve almond paste–filled coils called roses at weddings and other special occasions. To make the coils, gently push the rolls from both ends toward the center, causing the dough to crimp. Starting from one end, curl each roll into a coil. Pack the coils together (to prevent uncoiling), seam side down, on the prepared baking sheet.

Floyeres (Greek Semolina Rolls): Use about 4 cups *galacto* (semolina pudding, page 232) for the filling.

SEPHARDIC PHYLLO FILLINGS ❧

Gomo de Muez *(Sephardic Nut Filling)*

ABOUT 5 CUPS

You can also use Sephardic Almond Paste (page 368) as a phyllo filling.

4 cups finely chopped almonds, pistachios, walnuts, or any combination	*3 tablespoons rose water, or 3 tablespoons orange blossom water, or 2 teaspoons grated orange zest (optional)*
About 1¹/₄ cups sugar	
2 teaspoons ground cinnamon and/or ¹/₂ teaspoon ground cardamom	

Combine all the ingredients.

VARIATIONS

Reduce the nuts to 2 cups, increase the sugar to 2 cups, and add ¹/₂ cup sesame seeds and ¹/₂ cup poppy seeds.

Add ¹/₂ cup fresh or grated unsweetened desiccated coconut.

Gomo de Datittle *(Sephardic Date Filling)*

1 pound (about 3 cups) pitted dates	*1 to 2 teaspoons grated orange zest*
1/2 to 1 cup chopped almonds or walnuts	*1/2 teaspoon ground cloves (optional)*
1 teaspoon ground cinnamon	

In a food processor, process the dates until smooth. Stir in the remaining ingredients.

Gomo de Manzana *(Sephardic Apple Filling)*

2 large (about 12 ounces) apples, peeled, cored, and shredded	*About 1/4 cup sugar*
8 ounces (2 cups) walnuts, ground	*1 teaspoon ground cinnamon*
1/2 cup dried currants or raisins	*Pinch of ground allspice or cloves*
	1 tablespoon tapioca (optional)

Combine all the ingredients.

Gomo de Calabaza *(Sephardic Pumpkin Filling)*

Pumpkin has become a traditional Rosh Hashanah food for Sephardim, its many seeds a symbol of fruitfulness. This filling is also very popular among Georgian Jews.

4 cups (about 2 pounds raw) mashed cooked pumpkin, winter squash, or sweet potatoes	*Pinch of salt*
	1 to 2 teaspoons ground cinnamon
3/4 cup sugar	*1/2 teaspoon ground nutmeg or allspice*
1/2 cup honey or brown sugar	*1 large egg, lightly beaten*

Cook the pumpkin, sugar, honey, and salt over medium-low heat, stirring frequently, until dry. Stir in the spices and let cool. Add the egg.

Asabia bi Sutlach ❧ *(Syrian Pudding "Fingers")*

ABOUT 72 ROLLS

Filling:

$^{1}/_{2}$ cup cornstarch or potato starch

4 cups milk

$^{1}/_{2}$ cup sugar

$^{1}/_{2}$ teaspoon rose water or orange
  blossom water, or 1 teaspoon vanilla
  extract

24 sheets (about 1 pound) phyllo dough

About 1 cup butter or margarine, melted

1. To make the filling: Dissolve the cornstarch in about 1 cup milk, then stir in the remaining milk and the sugar. Bring to a low boil, reduce the heat to medium-low, and simmer, stirring constantly, until thickened and bubbly, about 5 minutes. Remove from the heat and stir in the rose water. Spread $^{1}/_{2}$ inch thick over a 15$^{1}/_{2}$-by-10$^{1}/_{2}$-inch jelly roll pan and let cool. Refrigerate until firm. Cut into about 72 bars, 2 inches long and 1 inch wide.

2. Preheat the oven to 350 degrees. Grease a large baking sheet.

3. Lay the stack of phyllo sheets on a flat surface and cut lengthwise into thirds. Place 1 phyllo strip on a flat surface and lightly brush with butter. Arrange a pudding bar about 1 inch from the narrow end of the phyllo strip. Fold the bottom 1 inch of the phyllo over the filling, then fold in the uncovered sides. Starting from the filling end, roll up jelly roll style.

4. Place the rolls, seam side down, on the prepared baking sheet and brush with butter. Bake until crisp and golden brown, about 30 minutes. Serve warm or at room temperature. Store in an airtight container at room temperature for 1 day.

SYRIAN STYLE

 A strong Jewish presence in the land to the north of Israel dates back to biblical days. In Roman times, the Jewish community of Syria was one of the largest and wealthiest in the world. The Turkish conquest in 1516 and the subsequent arrival of a large number of Sephardim led to the emergence of Aleppo as the center of trade between the Ottoman Empire and Europe, while Damascus became a banking hub, with Syrian Jews playing a major role in the activities of both places. The building of the Suez Canal and other changes in international trade, plus a shift in the political climate in Syria in the late nineteenth century, caused the economic and societal situations to deteriorate. Syrian Jews began emigrating, primarily to Israel, Beirut, and America. In the face of the anti-Jewish persecution that erupted in 1948, most of the country's remaining Jews fled. Today less than a few thousand Jews remain.

The cuisine of the Levant—Syria, Lebanon, and Iraq—is a blending of Persian, Arabic, Turkish, and Iberian influences. The Sabbath, holidays, and other special occasions give Syrian Jews opportunities to display their culinary, decorative, and organizational skills, subsumed under the term *suffeh*. Syrian women take pride in their *suffeh*, which requires much planning and preparation. Syrian desserts tend to be extremely sweet and are usually drenched in syrup. *Kaak* (sesame rings) are ubiquitous. A traditional Syrian Rosh Hashanah dessert might include *ras-ib-adjway* (date-filled cookies) and *hellou* (candied fruit or vegetable). Hanukkah features *atayef* (filled pancakes) and *ma'amoul* (nut-filled cookies). Purim feasts generally include *graybeh* (bracelet-shaped cookies), symbolizing Esther's jewelry.

Galactopita ❧ *(Greek Individual Semolina Custard Pies)*

10 SERVINGS

Centuries of Persian control over western Asia, central Asia, and India left its imprint on the cuisine of those areas. In turn, the Turks absorbed Persian fare and spread it to the regions under its control. Therefore, much of the fare enjoyed throughout the Middle East, as well as in Greece and Rome, can be directly traced to the Persians and Turks. This dish, derived from the Turkish *galactoboureko*, is the result of centuries of culinary evolution.

---

10 sheets phyllo

About ¹/₂ cup (1 stick) unsalted butter or
margarine, melted

About 2 cups galacto *(semolina pudding,*
page 232)

Confectioners' sugar or ground
cinnamon for sprinkling (optional)

---

1. Preheat the oven to 350 degrees. Grease 2 large baking sheets.
2. Place 1 sheet of phyllo on a work surface with a narrow end facing you and brush lightly with butter. Spread about 3 tablespoons of the pudding over the bottom 5 inches of the phyllo. Fold the right and left sides of the phyllo over the filling so that the edges meet in the center. Lightly brush with butter. Fold the lower third of the phyllo upward and brush lightly with butter, then fold down the upper third of the phyllo. Place on the prepared baking sheet, seam side down, and brush with butter. Repeat with the remaining phyllo and pudding.
3. Bake until golden brown, about 15 minutes. If desired, dust with confectioners' sugar or ground cinnamon. Serve warm or at room temperature.

Galactoboureko ❧ *(Turkish Semolina Custard Pie)*

Until recently, the bulk of the southern European diet consisted of porridges—what the Greeks called *sitos*, the Romans *puls*, and the Jews *dysah*. These gruels were usually served plain or flavored with onions, garlic, and herbs. For a special treat, they were cooked with milk (*gala* in Greek) and sweetened with a touch of honey. Among the foods that the Turks brought with them from central Asia was a dumpling called *bugra*, which evolved into an assortment of pastries collectively known as *borek*. Over the years, these dishes were combined and refined, giving rise to this popular Turkish and Greek treat. The semolina filling has a smooth, creamy texture similar to that of cheesecake. Versions of this dish are also made with a rice flour pudding.

Galacto (Semolina Pudding):

1/4 cup (1/2 stick) unsalted butter

3/4 cup (41/2 ounces) fine semolina (not semolina flour)

4 cups milk

1 cup sugar

1/4 teaspoon salt

4 large eggs

2 teaspoons vanilla extract

1/2 cup finely chopped dried apricots, golden raisins, or finely chopped blanched almonds (optional)

1 teaspoon grated orange or lemon zest (optional)

16 sheets phyllo

About 1/2 cup (1 stick) unsalted butter or margarine, melted

About 2 cups cooled sugar syrup (see atar, page 265) or confectioners' sugar for dusting

1. To make the pudding: Melt the butter in a large saucepan over medium heat. Stir in the semolina. Gradually stir in the milk. Add the sugar and salt. Reduce the heat to medium-low and simmer, stirring frequently, until the mixture thickens, about 10 minutes. Remove from the heat and beat in the eggs, one at a time. Stir in the vanilla. Add the apricots and/or zest if using. Press a piece of plastic wrap against the surface and let cool. The pudding can be stored in the refrigerator for up to 2 days.

2. Preheat the oven to 350 degrees (325 degrees if using a glass pan). Grease a 13-by-9-inch baking pan.

3. Place a sheet of phyllo in the prepared pan, letting the edges drape over the sides, and lightly brush with butter. Repeat with 7 more sheets.

4. Spread with the cooled pudding and turn the overhanging sides of the pastry over the filling. Cut the remaining 8 phyllo sheets into 13-by-9-inch rectangles and arrange on top of the filling, brushing each with butter. Using a sharp knife, cut crosswise through the top layer of phyllo into 2-inch-wide strips.

5. Bake until the pastry is golden brown, about 35 minutes. Cut into diamond shapes or squares. Drizzle with the cooled syrup or sprinkle with confectioners' sugar. Serve warm or at room temperature.

Bougatsa ❧ *(Greek Cheese-Filled Phyllo Pastries)*

12 MEDIUM OR 24 SMALL PASTRIES

Middle Eastern cooks use phyllo to make large pastries as well as small treats and, over the course of time, have developed numerous intriguing fillings for phyllo pies. It is hardly surprising that the Greeks, who have long enjoyed cheesecakes, adapted cheese as a filling. *Bougatsa*, also called *staka*, was originally made with water buffalo or sheep's milk cream. Most modern versions use cow's milk. Any leftover filling and phyllo are customarily mixed together, rolled into 6-inch-long ropes, formed into rings, and baked to make cookies called *bougarsokouloura*. *Bougatsa* is a traditional Shavuot dessert.

Filling:

24 ounces (3 cups) mitzithra, *ricotta, or
farmer's cheese*

12 ounces cream cheese, softened

1 cup sugar

6 large eggs

2 teaspoons vanilla extract

1/4 teaspoon salt

2 tablespoons orange blossom water, or
1 teaspoon ground cinnamon, or
1/2 teaspoon grated nutmeg (optional)

14 sheets phyllo

About 1/2 cup (1 stick) unsalted butter or
margarine, melted

Confectioners' sugar for dusting, or
1 1/2 cups cooled sugar syrup (see
atar, *page 265*)

1. Preheat the oven to 350 degrees (325 degrees if using a glass pan). Grease a 13-by-9-inch baking pan.
2. To make the filling: In a food processor or blender or with a beater, process all the filling ingredients until smooth.
3. Place a sheet of phyllo in the prepared pan, letting the edges drape over the sides, and lightly brush with butter. Repeat with 7 more sheets.
4. Spread the filling evenly over the pastry and turn the overhanging sides of the pastry over the filling. Cut the remaining 6 phyllo sheets into 13-by-9-inch rectangles and arrange on top of the filling, brushing each with butter. Using a sharp knife, score the top of the phyllo, without reaching the filling, into twelve 3-inch squares or diamond shapes or twenty-four 1 1/2-inch squares.

5. Bake until golden brown, about 40 minutes. Dust with confectioners' sugar or drizzle the cooled syrup over the hot pastry. Let the pastry cool, then cut through the scored marks.

VARIATION

Free-form Bougasta: This makes 2 large pies. Stack 6 phyllo sheets on a flat surface, brushing each with melted butter. Spread half of the filling in a 7-inch square in the center of the stack. One at a time, fold over the edges to enclose the filling. Make a second pie with the remaining phyllo and filling. Place seam side down on a greased baking sheet, brush with butter, and bake at 350 degrees until golden brown, about 20 minutes. Cut into wedges.

SAY CHEESE

 Most American and northern European cheeses are made from cow's milk. In Asia and the Mediterranean, however, goat and sheep cheeses are more prevalent. Although the raw milk of ruminants differs little in taste, aging brings out a wide range of flavors, colors, and aromas. Cheese made from goat's or sheep's milk has a more piquant flavor—varying slightly according to the animal's feed and the amount of salt added—and a whiter color than cow's milk cheese. *Fromage blanc*, a fresh goat cheese (under seven days old), has a very mild flavor and, because it is so young, a very soft texture. Feta (*ricotta salata*), generally made from sheep's milk and preserved in brine, has a slightly nutty flavor and a texture that ranges from creamy to dry. *Mitzithra* (pronounced "me-ZITH-rah"), made from feta and *kefalotyri* by-products, comes both fresh and aged. Until recently, many Middle Eastern families made their own soft cheese (called *queso blanco* or *queso fresco* in Ladino and *jiben beida* in Arabic) by adding rennet to unpasteurized milk. These soft cheeses serve as an appetizer or a side dish for breakfast and dinner, usually accompanied by olives, and are also used to fill pastries.

For centuries, European farmers have used the milk remaining after skimming the cream to make a homemade cheese aptly called "cottage." Today this unripe cow's milk cheese with a slightly acidic flavor is usually made by adding a bacterial culture to produce lactic acid, which coagulates the protein, separating the curds and whey. Pot cheese, also called baker's cheese and hoop cheese, is plain curd with most of the whey drained off. Farmer's cheese is drained (pressed) cottage cheese mixed with a little cream. Ricotta is a soft Italian cottage cheese. *Anthotyro* is a Greek cheese similar to ricotta but saltier.

Baklava ❧ *(Middle Eastern Nut-Filled Multilayered Pastry)*

ABOUT 36 SMALL DIAMOND-SHAPED PASTRIES

Baklava (from the Farsi for "many leaves"), a pastry perfected by royal bakers in the sultan's palace in Istanbul, consists of layers of phyllo filled with nuts and spices and drenched in a syrup. It has become a traditional Middle Eastern Rosh Hashanah and Purim treat but is enjoyed at celebrations throughout the year. There are numerous variations of baklava, many a closely guarded secret passed down within families. A walnut filling is more prevalent in the Levant, while pistachios and pistachio-almond fillings are preferred in Iran. Blanched almonds are traditional on Rosh Hashanah to produce a light color so that the year should be *dulce y aclarada* ("sweet and bright"). Sephardim refrain from serving dark-colored pastries such as those made from walnuts on Rosh Hashanah, which would portend a dark year. Although purists disdain anything except the classic nut filling, some cooks innovate by adding such items as dates and chocolate chips. Hungarians make an apricot version. This very rich treat is usually served in small portions.

Syrup:

3 cups sugar, or 2 cups sugar and 1 cup honey

1½ cups water

2 tablespoons lemon juice

2 tablespoons light corn syrup (optional)

2 (3-inch) sticks cinnamon, or 1 teaspoon ground cinnamon (optional)

4 to 6 whole cloves, or ½ teaspoon ground cardamom (optional)

Filling:

1 pound blanched almonds, pistachios, walnuts, or any combination, finely chopped or coarsely ground (about 4 cups)

¼ cup sugar

1 to 2 teaspoons ground cinnamon

¼ teaspoon ground cloves or cardamom (optional)

1 pound (about 24 sheets) phyllo dough

About 1 cup (2 sticks) melted butter or vegetable oil

1. To make the syrup: Stir the sugar, water, lemon juice, and if using, the corn syrup, cinnamon sticks, and/or cloves over low heat until the sugar dissolves, about 5 minutes. Stop stirring, increase the heat to medium, and cook until the mixture is slightly syrupy, about 5 minutes (it will register 225 degrees on a candy thermometer). Discard the cinnamon sticks and whole cloves. Let cool.

2. To make the filling: Combine all the filling ingredients.
3. Preheat the oven to 350 degrees. Grease a 12-by-9-inch or 13-by-9-inch baking pan or 15-by-10-inch jelly roll pan.
4. Place a sheet of phyllo in the prepared pan and lightly brush with butter. Repeat with 7 more sheets. Spread with half of the filling. Top with 8 more sheets, brushing each with butter. Use any torn sheets in the middle layer. Spread with the remaining nut mixture and end with a top layer of 8 sheets, continuing to brush each with butter. Trim any overhanging edges.
5. Using a sharp knife, cut 6 equal lengthwise strips (about $1^3/4$ inches wide) through the top layer of pastry. Make $1^1/2$-inch-wide diagonal cuts across the strips to form diamond shapes.
6. Just before baking, lightly sprinkle the top of the pastry with cold water. This inhibits the pastry from curling. Bake for 20 minutes. Reduce the heat to 300 degrees and bake until golden brown, about 15 additional minutes.
7. Cut through the scored lines. Drizzle the cooled syrup slowly over the hot baklava and let cool for at least 4 hours. Cover and store at room temperature for up to 1 week. If the baklava dries out while being stored, drizzle with a little additional hot syrup.

VARIATIONS

Instead of brushing each layer of phyllo with butter, cut the unbaked baklava into diamonds all the way through, drizzle with 1 cup vegetable oil, and let stand for 10 minutes before baking.

Persian Baklava: Use the almonds and cardamom in the filling. Omit the lemon juice and cinnamon from the syrup and add $1/4$ cup rose water or 1 tablespoon orange blossom water after it has cooled.

Paklava (Azerbaijani Baklava): For the filling, use 2 cups blanched almonds, 2 cups unsalted pistachios, $1/4$ cup sugar, 1 teaspoon ground cardamom, and 1 teaspoon ground cinnamon. Crush $1/4$ teaspoon saffron threads and let steep in 3 tablespoons of the melted butter for 15 minutes and use to brush the top sheet of phyllo.

Malfuf ❧ *(Persian Phyllo Tubes)*

These tubes, also called *bourma/boorma*, are popular Persian, Iraqi, and Armenian Purim treats.

Gomo de Muez (Nut Filling):

4 cups finely chopped almonds, pistachios, walnuts, or any combination

1/2 cup sugar

1 to 2 tablespoons rose water or orange blossom water, or 1 teaspoon grated orange zest

1 teaspoon ground cinnamon (optional)

1 pound (about 24 sheets) phyllo dough

About 1 cup vegetable oil, melted butter, or melted margarine

2 cups sugar syrup (see atar, page 265) or confectioners' sugar for dusting

1. To make the filling: Combine all the filling ingredients.
2. Grease a large baking sheet or two 13-by-9-inch baking pans. Cut the phyllo sheets in half crosswise to make 9-by-6-inch to 12-by-8-inch rectangles. Cover the sheets with plastic wrap and a damp towel when not in use. Place 1 strip on a flat surface and lightly brush with oil. Spread about 2 teaspoons of the filling along a narrow end of the phyllo strip, leaving a 1/2-inch border on both sides and a 1 1/2-inch border on the bottom.
3. Fold the bottom border over the filling. Place the handle of a wooden spoon, a 1/2-inch-thick wooden dowel, or a pencil along the filling end and loosely roll the phyllo around the handle to the end of the sheet to form a cylinder. Gently push the ends toward the center to crimp, then slide out the spoon.
4. Place the rolls on the prepared baking sheets and brush with oil. Refrigerate for at least 10 minutes or up to 1 day. The tubes can be stored in the freezer for up to 3 months. Do not thaw; increase the baking time by about 10 minutes.
5. Preheat the oven to 350 degrees.
6. Bake until crisp and golden brown, about 20 minutes. Dip the warm tubes into the cooled syrup or dust with confectioners' sugar.

VARIATION

Farareer (Middle Eastern "Bird's Nests"): These coils of pastry, called *bulbul yuvasi* in Turkey, resemble tiny bird's nests, hence the whimsical name. Unroll the tubes about $1/2$ inch, then bring the ends together, the unrolled portion inward, to form a ring. If desired, spoon about 1 tablespoon of the nut filling into the center of the baked nests before drizzling with the syrup.

ALMONDS

 The almond, the kernel of a peach-like fruit native to the Middle East, was one of the earliest cultivated trees. There are two kinds of almonds: sweet and bitter. The former is edible. The bitter almond, however, contains poisonous prussic acid. When the bitter almond's harmful acid is removed, the remaining pulp is fermented and distilled to produce almond extract.

Almonds are the most frequently mentioned nut in the Bible. They are one of the "fruits of the land" sent by Jacob to Pharaoh. An almond branch served as the rod of Aaron (Numbers 17:8). Ecclesiastes uses the almond as a symbol of human life (12:5). These nuts are nearly omnipresent in Sephardic desserts and celebrations, used in numerous confections, pastries, cookies, and cakes. Almonds—either plain, mixed with raisins, or candied—were once ubiquitous at Ashkenazic life-cycle events.

Fried Pastries

. . . if your offering be fried in a pot . . .
—LEVITICUS 2:5–7

DEEP-FRIED FOOD IS IMMERSED COMPLETELY IN HOT FAT, WHICH GIVES IT A CRUNCHY TEXTURE ON THE OUTSIDE AND A MOIST INTERIOR. DURING FRYING, THE WATER INSIDE THE FOOD FORMS STEAM, WHICH ACTS AS A SHIELD TO LIMIT THE ABSORPTION OF fat. After the steam evaporates, however, the fat will enter the food. Most deep-fried items consist of either a dough or a food with a coating of batter or breading, which forms a protective layer that keeps out the fat, while the interior steams. The higher the fat content of the dough or coating, the more fat it will absorb. However, the presence of egg yolks in the dough restricts the absorption of oil, making for a less greasy treat. A little sugar in the dough helps it to brown, but too much sugar results in overbrowning.

If the temperature is too low, the oil will reach the interior before the batter can form a protective barrier. If the oil is too hot, the coating will burn before the inside has fully cooked. The best temperature for frying batter-coated or breaded foods is 350 to 370 degrees for large pieces and 375 to 380 degrees for small or thin pieces. To test the temperature without a thermometer, drop a cube of soft white bread in the oil; if it is 375 degrees, the bread should brown in 35 seconds.

For deep-frying, use an oil with a high smoke point, the temperature at which it begins to decompose and produce fatty acids that ruin the flavor of the food. Recommended oils include safflower, soybean, corn, canola, cottonseed, and untoasted sesame. To impart a nutty flavor, use peanut or sunflower oil. The oil must be clean or it will not create the agitation necessary to seal the food.

At the flash point, about 600 degrees, tiny flames will appear on the surface of the oil. Do not attempt to extinguish a fat fire by using water, as it will only cause the oil to spatter, further spreading the flames. Smother the fire with baking soda, salt, or the lid of a pot.

Fill the pot no more than halfway with oil to allow room for bubbling. Do not add more food than can be fried in a single layer or too many items, or the temperature of the oil will drop below the proper level. A golden brown exterior is generally a sign of doneness. After frying each batch, skim out any crumbs and let the oil return to the required temperature before adding the next lot. After cooking, let the oil cool before moving the pot.

Frying and Hanukkah

The festival of Hanukkah commemorates the rededication of the Temple following the successful revolt of the Maccabees, a family of freedom fighters, and their small band of followers, against Emperor Antiochus and the Syrian-Greek forces in 165 BCE. As the priests began the task of purifying the Temple, they found only one small vial of untainted olive oil fit for use in the menorah. Although there was only enough oil to last for one day, the lamp continued to burn for eight days until undefiled oil became available. To commemorate the events, fried pastries became the preeminent Hanukkah food, symbolizing the miracle of the oil. Middle Eastern Jews traditionally serve similar items on Purim "to connect miracle with miracle," the physical salvation of the Jews by Mordechai and Esther and the spiritual salvation by the Maccabees. In many Sephardic communities during Hanukkah and Purim, members of wealthier families bring trays of these sweets to less fortunate ones.

Loukoumades ❧ *(Greek Anise Fritters)*

ABOUT 24 FRITTERS

This relatively modern and easy-to-prepare version of an ancient yeast dough treat has an anise flavor due to the presence of *ouzo*.

3 cups all-purpose flour	*1 tablespoon olive or vegetable oil*
1 teaspoon baking soda	*1/2 teaspoon vanilla extract*
1/4 teaspoon salt	*Vegetable oil for deep-frying*
1 cup water	*Confectioners' sugar for dusting or*
1/4 cup ouzo or raki (anise liqueur)	*warm sugar syrup (see atar,*
1 large egg, lightly beaten	*page 265) for dipping*
2 tablespoons sugar	

1. Sift together the flour, baking soda, and salt. Combine the water, *ouzo*, egg, sugar, oil, and vanilla. Stir into the flour mixture to make a loose batter. Cover and let stand at room temperature for 30 minutes.

2. Heat at least 1 inch of oil over medium heat to 375 degrees.

3. Dip a tablespoon into cold water and use the spoon to drop the batter into the hot oil. (Moisten your fingers to prevent sticking when pushing the batter off the spoon.) In batches, fry the fritters, turning occasionally, until golden brown on all sides, about 3 minutes. Remove with a wire mesh skimmer or tongs and drain on a wire rack. Sprinkle with confectioners' sugar or dip the cooled fritters into warm sugar syrup.

Frucht Fritlach ❧ *(Ashkenazic Fruit Fritters)*

12 TO 18 FRITTERS

This loose batter is perfect for coating pieces of fruit. The consistency must be thick enough to adhere to the food. A thin batter will disintegrate in the oil, while one that is too thick will have a spongy texture. A proper batter will drop (or perhaps "blop") off the spoon, not run off in a steady stream. If necessary, adjust the consistency by adding a little flour or liquid. Beer produces a harder, crunchy coating.

1¼ cups all-purpose flour	1½ tablespoons sugar
1 tablespoon potato starch or cornstarch	1 tablespoon rum or brandy (optional)
¼ teaspoon salt	Vegetable, sunflower, or peanut oil for
1 large egg, separated	deep-frying
1 tablespoon vegetable oil	Sliced fresh fruit
½ cup milk, flat beer, sweet wine, or	½ cup confectioners' or superfine sugar
water	for sprinkling

1. Sift together the flour, potato starch, and salt. Blend together the egg yolk and oil. Stir in the milk, sugar, and rum if using. Add to the flour mixture and stir until smooth. Let stand at room temperature for at least 1 hour.
2. Beat the egg white on low speed until foamy, about 30 seconds. Increase the speed to medium-high and beat until soft peaks form, about 2 minutes. Gently fold into the batter.
3. Heat at least 1 inch of oil over medium heat to 375 degrees.
4. Dip the fruit slices into the batter. Fry in batches of 3 or 4, turning once, until golden brown on all sides, about 1½ minutes per side. Remove with tongs or a wire mesh skimmer and drain on a wire rack. You can keep the fritters warm in a 250-degree oven while preparing the remaining fritters. Sprinkle with the sugar and serve warm.

VARIATIONS

Apfel Fritlach (Ashkenazic Apple Fritters): Peel and core 3 medium apples, then cut into ¼-inch-thick rings. If desired, combine 3 tablespoons sugar and ½ teaspoon ground cinnamon; dredge the apple rings in the cinnamon sugar to coat before dipping in the batter. Or let the apple slices macerate in 3 tablespoons rum, kirsch, or brandy and 2 tablespoons sugar, turning occasionally, for 1 hour.

Meges Bomba (Hungarian Cherry Fritters): Add 1^1/$_2$ cups pitted sour cherries to the batter and drop the batter by spoonfuls into the oil.

Frittelle di Fichi (Italian Fig Fritters): Peel 16 firm fresh figs, soak in 1 cup dark rum or brandy for 1 hour, drain, and dip the figs into the batter.

Frittelle di Pere (Italian Pear Fritters): Peel and core 3 medium pears, then cut lengthwise into ^{1}/$_2$-inch-thick slices.

Pineapple Fritters: Peel, core, and slice 1 pineapple or use 8 well-drained canned pineapple rings.

Fritlach ❧ *(Ashkenazic Sweet Fritters)*

ABOUT 30 SMALL OR 24 MEDIUM FRITTERS

---

2 cups all-purpose flour

4 teaspoons double-acting baking powder

³/4 teaspoon salt

¹/2 teaspoon ground cinnamon (optional)

¹/2 teaspoon grated nutmeg (optional)

2 large eggs

²/3 cup milk, flat beer, or water, or ¹/3 cup milk and ¹/3 cup beer

¹/4 to ¹/2 cup sugar

2 tablespoons vegetable oil or melted butter, margarine, or vegetable shortening

1 teaspoon vanilla extract, or 2 tablespoons brandy

Vegetable, sunflower, or peanut oil for deep-frying

Confectioners' sugar for dusting

---

1. Sift together the flour, baking powder, salt, and spices if using. Combine the eggs, milk, sugar, oil, and vanilla. Stir into the flour mixture to make a loose batter. Cover and let stand for about 1 hour.
2. Heat at least 1 inch of oil over medium heat to 375 degrees.
3. Drop the batter by teaspoonfuls or tablespoonfuls into the oil and fry, turning once, until puffed and golden brown on all sides, about 1¹/2 minutes per side. Remove with a wire mesh skimmer or tongs and drain on a wire rack. You can keep the *fritlach* warm in a 250-degree oven while preparing the remaining fritters. Sprinkle with confectioners' sugar.

VARIATION

Omit the baking powder. Increase the eggs to 4. Separate the eggs and combine the yolks with the milk, sugar, oil, and vanilla. Beat the egg whites until stiff but not dry and fold into the batter.

Malpuah ✌ *(Bombay Banana Fritters)*

ABOUT 24 MEDIUM FRITTERS

When tablespoons of this batter are fried without any fruit, the fritters are called *puah*. Substitute other sliced fruit, such as apples and pineapples, for the bananas.

---

*2 cups all-purpose flour, preferably
    unbleached
1/2 cup sugar
3/4 teaspoon salt
1 cup coconut milk, milk, or water
2 large eggs*

*1 teaspoon vanilla extract
Peanut or vegetable oil for deep-frying
6 medium bananas, cut crosswise into
    1 1/2- to 2-inch-long pieces
Confectioners' sugar for dusting*

---

1. Combine the flour, sugar, and salt. Blend together the milk, eggs, and vanilla. Stir into the flour mixture to make a thick batter. Cover and let stand at room temperature for at least 1 hour.
2. Heat at least 1 inch of oil over medium heat to 375 degrees.
3. Dip the banana pieces into the batter. Fry in batches, turning occasionally, until puffed and golden brown on all sides, about 1 1/2 minutes per side. Remove with tongs or a wire mesh skimmer and drain on a wire rack. Serve warm or cooled. You can keep the fritters warm in a 250-degree oven while preparing the remaining fritters. Store at room temperature for up to 6 hours. Sprinkle with confectioners' sugar.

VARIATION

Banana-Nut Fritters: Finely grind 1 cup toasted almonds or hazelnuts with 2 tablespoons all-purpose flour. Roll the banana pieces in the nut mixture before dipping into the batter.

BENE ISRAEL (BOMBAY)

 The oldest and largest Indian Jewish community is the Bene Israel of Bombay. According to local tradition, its origins date to a group of Jews fleeing Antiochus Epiphanes in 175 BCE. When a storm wrecked their ship in the Indian Ocean off the Konkan coast, seven men and seven women managed to make it ashore. This small group maintained its Jewish identity and continued to adhere to Jewish rituals, including the Sabbath, biblical festivals, dietary laws, and circumcision. The Hindus always treated the Jewish minority benignly, considering them literally to be "outcaste." Members of the Bene Israel earned their livelihood primarily in the preparation and selling of sesame oil; thus the name Shanwar Teli (Saturday oilmen) among their Hindu neighbors—Saturday referring to their refusal to work on the Sabbath.

In the mid-1700s, a Cochini Jew arranged for the release of a Jewish prisoner of war who turned out to be a Bene Israel, and other Indian Jews and the rest of the world learned of this lost group. Having had no contact with world Jewry for nearly 2,000 years, the Bene Israel were unaware of the Talmud, rabbis, synagogues, and other ritual developments that originated after their separation.

Mohandas Gandhi's liberalization of the caste system spurred a Zionist spirit among many Bene Israel as the removal of India's strict social barriers unleashed the threat of a previously unthinkable assimilation. Subsequently, Nehru's anti-Zionism further stirred their pro-Israel sentiments. In response, more than 12,000 of the Bene Israel immigrated to Israel during the 1950s and 1960s. Today their community in Israel and the United States numbers about 50,000, while only about 4,500 remain in India.

The cuisine of the Bene Israel, relatively simple fare, is drawn from their Hindu neighbors. Maharashta lies between the rice-eating region to the south and the wheat-eating area to the north, and therefore the inhabitants liberally use both grains. The dishes are redolent with spices. Coconuts and mangoes are cooking staples. *Malida* (a sweetened rice, coconut, and fruit dish) is served at all festive occasions.

Koeksisters ❦ *(Dutch Pastry Twists)*

ABOUT 18 PASTRIES

W hile most Dutch Jewish cooking reflects an Ashkenazic heritage, these braided pastries (the name is pronounced "KO-uk-sis-ters") reveal a lingering Sephardic influence.

Syrup:

1/2 cup sugar

1/4 cup water

1/2 cup honey

1 tablespoon lemon juice

1/4 teaspoon ground cardamom or cinnamon

Pastry:

2 cups all-purpose flour

2 teaspoons double-acting baking powder

1/8 teaspoon salt

1 tablespoon sugar

2 tablespoons vegetable shortening, butter, or margarine, chilled

About 1 cup milk or water, or 2/3 cup milk or water and 1 large egg yolk

Vegetable, sunflower, or peanut oil for deep-frying

1. To make the syrup: Stir the sugar, water, honey, and lemon juice in a small saucepan over low heat until the sugar dissolves, about 5 minutes. Stop stirring, increase the heat to medium, and cook until the mixture is slightly syrupy, about 5 minutes (it will register 225 degrees on a candy thermometer). Add the cardamom and simmer until the flavors meld, about 2 minutes. Let cool, then chill.

2. To make the pastry: Sift together the flour, baking powder, and salt. Add the sugar. Cut in the shortening to resemble small crumbs. Stir in enough milk to make a soft dough. Knead briefly to combine, about 1 minute, then form into a ball. Cover and let stand at room temperature for about 30 minutes.

3. On a piece of waxed paper or plastic wrap or on a lightly floured surface, roll the pastry into a 1/4-inch-thick rectangle. Cut into strips 3 inches long and 1/3 inch wide. Braid 3 dough strips together, pinching the ends to seal.

continued

4. Heat about 2 inches of oil over medium heat to 375 degrees.

5. Fry the braids in batches of 3 to 4, turning once, until golden and crisp, about 1 minute per side. Remove with tongs or a wire mesh skimmer and drain on a wire rack.

6. Dip the hot *koeksisters* into the chilled syrup, letting the excess drip off. Place on a serving platter.

VARIATION

Increase the sugar in the syrup to $3/4$ cup and reduce the honey to 1 tablespoon.

GOING DUTCH

After Charles of Burgundy, whose holdings included the northwestern part of Europe called the Netherlands (Low Countries), ascended to the Spanish throne in 1516, the area's small Jewish community was expelled and the Inquisition instituted. Charles and his son Phillip II, the latter best known for sending the ill-fated Spanish Armada against England, also persecuted the region's Protestants, who proceeded to revolt. In 1581, the Netherlands, unofficially called Holland after the country's largest province, declared its independence, although Spain did not officially recognize this move until 1648. The century and a half following the revolt was the Golden Age of the Dutch Republic, with the Netherlands emerging as a major economic and colonizing power.

Beginning in the early sixteenth century, a steady stream of Conversos from Spain and Portugal made their way to the freer conditions in the Netherlands, although the Dutch did not officially allow Conversos to practice Judaism openly until 1615. The area also became a haven for persecuted Ashkenazic and Italian Jews. Amsterdam, which in the early seventeenth century became a center of world trade, also emerged as a great Jewish center.

In 1630, the Dutch occupied the northwestern Brazilian state of Pernambuco, a center of the sugar industry. Soon a number of enterprising Dutch Jews, mostly Sephardim, migrated to its capital, Recife. When Portugal reclaimed the area in 1654, the Jews fled. In September of that year, a band of twenty-three of these outcasts accidentally landed in another Dutch colony, New Amsterdam. The group decided to put down roots in the growing settlement, and the population generally accepted the newcomers. Governor Peter Stuyvesant, however, sought to have them expelled. The parent Dutch West India Company, which counted many Jews among its stockholders, insisted that the Recife refugees be allowed to remain. This first Jewish settlement in North America was the genesis of the American Jewish community.

Dutch cooking is a synthesis of plain and hearty German-influenced fare and exotic ingredients and dishes imported from the country's former colonies. The Netherlands is noted for its appetite for dairy products, which are amply represented in butter- and cream-laden desserts. Local liqueurs or hot cocoa commonly accompany Dutch desserts.

Ozeni Haman ❧ *(Haman's Ears)*

The underlying theme of most Purim pastries is shape, whereby a person symbolically erases Haman's name by eating a pastry formed to represent part of the villainous prime minister's clothing or anatomy, most notably his pocket, hat, foot, or ear. The most widespread of these Purim pastries are deep-fried strips of dough known under an assortment of local names, most meaning "Haman's ears," including *ozeni Haman* in Hebrew, *orejas de Haman* in Ladino, *orecchi de Aman* in Italy, *aftia tou Amman* in Greece, *haman-muetzen* in Germany, *hamansooren* in Holland, *hojuelos de Haman* ("Haman's leaves") in Morocco, *burbushella* in Georgia, and *roscas di alhashu* in the Balkans. Ear-shaped pastries are derived from the medieval custom of cutting off a criminal's ear before execution, as well as the legend that Haman's ears were triangular in shape, like a donkey's. When not served during Purim, these pastry strips are called *shamlias* (Ladino for "frills") by Sephardim and *gushfil* by Persians.

This dough is worked enough to create pockets of air, which puff up in the pastry rolls during frying.

---

3 large eggs, lightly beaten

2 tablespoons vegetable oil

2 tablespoons granulated or
  confectioners' sugar

2 tablespoons brandy, rum, orange juice,
  or water

1/4 teaspoon salt

1 teaspoon finely grated lemon zest, or
  1/4 cup finely chopped blanched
  almonds, or 1 teaspoon ground
  cinnamon (optional)

About 2 cups all-purpose flour, sifted

Vegetable, sunflower, or peanut oil for
  deep-frying

About 1 cup confectioners' sugar, or
  2 cups warm sugar syrup (see atar,
  page 265)

---

1. Blend together the eggs, oil, sugar, brandy, salt, and zest if using. Gradually stir in enough of the flour to make a soft dough. On a lightly floured surface, knead until smooth, 5 to 10 minutes. Cover and let stand at room temperature for at least 30 minutes.

2. Divide the dough in half. On a piece of waxed paper or plastic wrap or on a lightly floured surface, roll each piece of dough into a 1/8-inch-thick rectangle. With a pastry cutter or sharp knife, cut into 1-inch-wide by 4- to 6-inch-long strips. Pinch each strip in the center and twist the ends.

3. Heat about 2 inches of oil over medium heat to 375 degrees.

4. Deep-fry the strips in batches, turning, until golden brown on both sides, about 1 minute per side. Remove with tongs or a wire mesh skimmer and drain on a wire rack. Sprinkle generously with confectioners' sugar or dip the cooled pastries into the warm syrup. Store in an airtight container at room temperature.

VARIATIONS

Orejas de Haman (Sephardic Haman's Ears): Cut the dough into 3- to 4-inch rounds, cut each round in half, and pinch the center of the straight edge to suggest an ear.

Heizenblauzen (Austrian "Blow-Hots"): These pastries are also called *schunzuchen* in Alsace and Switzerland. Cut the dough into 2-inch squares, cut a slit in the center of each square, and pull one corner through the slit. If desired, add 2 tablespoons ground cinnamon to the confectioners' sugar for dusting.

Diples (Greek Honey Rolls): Add 1/2 teaspoon double-acting baking powder to the dough. Cut into 6-by-4-inch rectangles. Working with 1 rectangle at a time, drop it into a large pot of oil, immediately turn it, and using 2 forks, roll up into a cylinder. Continue frying until golden. Dip into a honey syrup (see *atar,* page 265).

Strufali (Italian Honey Balls): This is similar to and possibly the forebear of the Ashkenazic *teiglach*. Add 1/2 teaspoon double-acting baking powder to the dough. Roll the dough into 1/2-inch-thick ropes, cut the ropes into 1/2-inch pieces, and toss lightly with flour. After frying, drizzle 2 cups of warmed honey over the warm pastry and toss to coat. Line a bowl with plastic wrap, spoon the honey balls into the bowl, cover, and refrigerate. Invert onto a serving plate and remove the plastic wrap. If desired, sprinkle with sesame seeds.

Debla ❧ *(Moroccan Sweetened Rose Pastries)*

This is the Moroccan variation of fried pastry. Using the semolina produces an interesting crunchy texture. There is also a nut-filled version utilizing the traditional triangular shape for Purim.

Syrup:

2 cups sugar, or 1 cup sugar and 1 cup
   honey

1 cup water

1 to 3 tablespoons fresh lemon juice

*$1/2$ teaspoon double-acting baking
   powder*

$1/8$ teaspoon salt

4 large eggs, lightly beaten

*1 teaspoon grated orange or lemon zest
   (optional)*

Pastry:

*About $2^2/3$ cups all-purpose flour, or
   $1^1/2$ cups flour and 1 cup fine
   semolina*

1 teaspoon sugar

*Vegetable, sunflower, or peanut oil for
   deep-frying*

*Ground cinnamon or chopped pistachios
   for sprinkling (optional)*

1. To make the syrup: Stir the sugar, water, and lemon juice over low heat until the sugar dissolves, about 5 minutes. Stop stirring, increase the heat to medium, and cook until syrupy, about 10 minutes.

2. To make the pastry: Sift together the flour, sugar, baking powder, and salt. Beat the eggs until thick and creamy, about 5 minutes. If desired, add the zest. Gradually stir in the flour mixture to make a soft dough. Place on a lightly floured surface and, using oiled hands, knead until smooth and uniform, about 5 minutes.

3. On a piece of waxed paper or plastic wrap or on a lightly floured surface, roll the dough into a $1/8$-inch-thick rectangle. Cut into 3-by-$1/2$-inch strips.

4. Heat at least 3 inches of oil over medium heat to 370 degrees.

5. Dip a metal tablespoon into the hot oil. Wrap a dough strip around the spoon, overlapping the edges to form a rose-like shape. Place in the oil and use another spoon to gradually remove the *debla* so that the dough retains a coiled shape. Fry, turning, until golden on all sides, about 1 minute per side. Remove with a wire mesh skimmer or tongs.

6. Carefully place the pastry in the warm syrup and simmer for 2 minutes. Transfer to a wire rack or piece of waxed paper, and, if desired, sprinkle with the cinnamon. Let cool.

VARIATION

Debla (Moroccan Nut-Filled Turnovers): Combine 1/2 cup ground almonds or walnuts and 2 tablespoons sugar. Cut the dough into 2-inch squares. Place 1/2 teaspoon of the nut mixture in the center of each square, fold in half to form triangles, and press the edges to seal. Fry until golden on both sides. Simmer in the syrup as above.

Samsa ❧ *(Bukharan Fried Dumplings)*

ABOUT 60 SMALL OR 36 MEDIUM DUMPLINGS

The cuisine of Central Asia was greatly affected by that of its two powerful neighbors, Persia and China. These dumplings, reflecting both influences, are served on Purim and other festive occasions. The thin dumpling skins (called *pi* in Chinese and *gyoza* in Japan) differ from wonton skins by the absence of eggs. Commercial dumpling skins are available in Asian food stores and many grocery stores (about 50 wrappers per pound). Frying the dumplings produces a crisp texture, caramelized flavor, and rich color.

Pastry:

1 1/2 cups all-purpose flour

1/2 teaspoon salt

About 2/3 cup lukewarm water

Filling:

6 ounces walnuts, finely ground (about 2 cups)

1/4 cup sugar

1 1/2 tablespoons unsalted butter or margarine, softened

Vegetable, sunflower, or peanut oil for deep-frying

1. To make the pastry: Combine the flour and salt. Stir in enough water to make a soft dough. On a lightly floured surface, knead until smooth, 5 to 10 minutes. Cover and let stand at room temperature for 30 minutes.

2. To make the filling: Combine all the filling ingredients.

3. On a piece of waxed paper or plastic wrap or on a lightly floured surface, roll the dough into a thin rectangle about 18 by 16 inches. Cut into 2- or 3-inch squares. Wrap and store in the refrigerator for up to 3 days or in the freezer for up to 2 months.

4. Place a heaping teaspoon of the filling in the center of each square. Moisten the edges with water, bring the 4 corners of the dough together over the filling to meet in the center, and press the edges to seal.

5. Heat at least 2 inches of oil over medium heat to 375 degrees.

6. Fry the *samsa* in batches, turning, until golden brown on all sides, about 1 1/2 minutes per side. Remove with a wire mesh skimmer or tongs and drain on a wire rack.

UZBEKISTAN/BUKHARA

 In the heart of Central Asia, adjacent to the Aral Sea, lies Uzbekistan, a semiarid, sparsely populated land. The fabled Silk Road, starting in China and ending at the eastern Mediterranean, once passed through this area, carrying the riches of the Orient and engendering great wealth in the legendary trading towns of Samarkand, Tashkent, and Bukhara. Such abundance inevitably resulted in the intrusion of outsiders. Alexander the Great conquered the region in 334 BCE. Persia controlled the area for centuries. Arabs arrived in the ninth century, and the country has remained primarily Muslim ever since. The Golden Age came to an abrupt end in 1220 when the Mongols under Genghis Khan devastated the region, as well as its Jewish community.

According to local tradition, Bukhara is the site of the biblical Habor (II Kings 17:6), one of the places to which the Assyrians exiled the Ten Tribes. Another tradition claims that the first Jews settled in the area soon after the Persians had conquered Babylon in 539 BCE. The earliest mention of Jews in the region was in the early fourth century when Samuel bar Bisna refused to drink wine in Margiana, now located in Turkmenistan (Babylonian Talmud Avodah Zorah 31b). The Jewish community was augmented in the late fifth century with the arrival of refugees fleeing the intensified Zoroastrian persecutions in Persia. Benjamin of Tudela noted that there were 50,000 Jews living in Samarkand at the time of his visit about 1170. After the destruction of Samarkand, the term Bukharan, referring to an inhabitant of another former khanate, was commonly used to include all the Jews of the Uzbeki and Tajikistan regions.

In the mid-1800s, Bukharan Jews began making their way to Israel. Soviet repression following the Russian Revolution of 1917 led to intensified Zionist sentiment. Taking advantage of occasional liberal Soviet immigration policies or sneaking across the Afghani border, many Bukharan Jews reached Israel, where they now number about 66,000. About 20,000 Jews remain in Uzbekistan, with another 12,000 in neighboring Kazakhstan, 3,500 in Kyrgystan, and 2,000 each in Turkmenistan and Tajikistan.

Visitors to an Uzbeki house are given the royal treatment and presented with a *dastarkhan* (offering tray) featuring an array of treats, including confections, pastries, dried fruit, nuts, and preserves. Confections, including *khalva* (halvah) and *lawves/yanchmish* (walnut candies), and pastries reflect a marked Persian influence. The *dastarkhan* is always accompanied by a samovar of green tea.

Singara ✦ *(Cochini Semolina-Filled Turnovers)*

TWELVE 4-INCH PASTRIES

These turnovers, also called *kushli*, are a synthesis of southern Indian and Middle Eastern cuisines. They are commonly served on Hanukkah, as well as at the meal following Yom Kippur. The filling is a form of halvah. Cochinis also use the filling to make fritters called *neyyappam*.

Pastry:
1 cup all-purpose flour
1/8 teaspoon baking soda
Pinch of salt
2 tablespoons unsalted butter or margarine, chilled
About 1/2 cup water

Filling:
8 to 10 cardamom pods, or about 1 teaspoon ground cardamom
1/4 cup (1/2 stick) unsalted butter or margarine
1 cup fine semolina or farina
1/2 cup grated coconut, preferably fresh
2 tablespoons ground blanched almonds
1 cup sugar
2 tablespoons dried currants, raisins, chopped dates, or dried apricots

Vegetable or sunflower oil for deep-frying

1. To make the pastry: Sift together the flour, baking soda, and salt. Cut in the butter to resemble fine crumbs. Stir in enough water to make a firm dough. Form into a ball, cover, and let stand at room temperature for at least 30 minutes.

2. To make the filling: Discard the outer shell of the cardamom pods and crush the seeds. Melt the butter in a medium saucepan over medium heat. Add the semolina, coconut, and almonds and sauté until golden. Add the sugar, currants, and cardamom and cook, stirring frequently, until the sugar melts, about 5 minutes. Let cool.

3. Divide the dough into 12 equal portions and form into balls. On waxed paper or plastic wrap or on a lightly floured surface, roll into 4-inch rounds. Spoon a heaping tablespoon of the filling into the center of each round, fold over to form a half-moon shape, and press the edges to seal. Or form into cones, fill, and fold the top over to seal.

4. Heat at least 1 inch of oil over medium heat to 350 degrees.
5. Fry the pastries in batches, turning once, until golden brown on both sides, about 45 seconds per side. Remove with tongs or a wire mesh skimmer and drain on a wire rack. Or bake the turnovers in a 350-degree oven until golden brown, about 25 minutes.

VARIATION

Coconut-Filled Turnovers: Combine $1^1/2$ cups grated fresh or unsweetened desiccated coconut, $^1/2$ cup sugar, and about 2 tablespoons rose water and use for the filling.

CARDAMOM

 A native of India, cardamom is a brittle pod packed with clusters of intensely flavored tiny black seeds. The pods are usually steeped in liquid or bruised before using to release their flavor. Bruising is traditionally done with a mortar and pestle, but you can also slightly crush them in a plastic bag using a rolling pin or skillet. Four pods yield about $^1/4$ teaspoon ground cardamom. Cardamom follows only saffron among spices in expense, but a little goes a long way. It is the most fragrant of spices (the scent is a combination of citrus, camphor, and eucalyptus) and has a bittersweet flavor somewhat similar to anise. Green pods, preferred in India and the Middle East, have a sweeter flavor and aroma than white pods. The latter are green pods that have been bleached, making them more pungent. Black pods, a staple of African cooking, have a smoky, nut-like flavor. Indians add whole pods to stews, vegetable dishes, and rice dishes such as pudding and pilaf (discard the pods before serving) and use ground cardamom in curries and confections. In Scandinavia, ground white pods are used to flavor baked goods. In the Middle East, cardamom is used to flavor fruit compotes, pilafs, rice puddings, and a coffee drink called *gahwa*. Add several bruised pods to coffee grounds or tea before brewing.

Gulam Jamun 🌰 *(Indian Milk Fritters)*

ABOUT 20 BALLS

Although *gulam* means "rose water" in Hindi, some people omit it from the ingredients in this recipe. Originally, this dish was made by cooking the milk over low heat for an extended period until thickened. The invention of dry milk powder led to this easier version. *Gulam jamun* is a traditional Hannukah treat among the Bene Israel of Bombay, combining the holiday's two primary food symbols—dairy and fried.

Dough:	Syrup:
1 cup nonfat dry milk powder	*2 cups granulated or brown sugar*
1/4 cup unbleached all-purpose flour	*2 cups water*
1/4 teaspoon baking soda	*4 to 5 cardamom pods, or 1/4 to*
3 tablespoons unsalted butter, melted	*1/2 teaspoon ground cardamom*
and cooled	*1 teaspoon rose water (optional)*
3 to 4 tablespoons milk	
Vegetable oil for deep-frying	

1. To make the dough: Combine the milk powder, flour, and baking soda. Drizzle with the butter and rub between your fingers until the mixture resembles fine crumbs. Gradually stir in the milk until the dough just holds together. Knead briefly until smooth. Divide the dough into 20 equal balls, each about 1 1/2 teaspoons.

2. Heat at least 1 inch of oil over medium heat to 350 degrees.

3. Fry the balls in batches, turning frequently, until golden brown on all sides, about 4 minutes. Remove with a wire mesh skimmer and place on a wire rack to drain. Let cool.

4. To make the syrup: Stir the sugar and water over low heat until the sugar dissolves, about 5 minutes. Stop stirring, increase the heat to medium, and cook until the mixture is slightly thickened, about 5 minutes (it will register 225 degrees on a candy thermometer). Meanwhile, discard the outer shell of the cardamom pods and crush the seeds. Stir the cardamom and rose water, if using, into the syrup.

5. Drizzle the warm syrup over the cooled fritters and let stand for at least 3 hours. Serve the fritters, chilled or at room temperature, in a little syrup. The fritters can be covered and stored in the syrup in the refrigerator for up to 1 month.

Bolos de Queso ✤ *(Sephardic Cheese Fritters)*

ABOUT 48 FRITTERS

Sephardim developed a way to use up stale bread by soaking it in milk, mixing it with cheese, and then frying spoonfuls of the batter. Over the centuries, cooks refined these *bolos* (Ladino for "balls") and their derivative, *boyos*, producing a variety of sophisticated pastries and fritters. This is a dessert version.

1¹⁄₄ cups all-purpose flour	3 tablespoons sugar
¹⁄₂ teaspoon ground cinnamon	1 tablespoon unsalted butter, melted
¹⁄₈ teaspoon double-acting baking powder	¹⁄₂ teaspoon brandy
¹⁄₈ teaspoon salt	¹⁄₂ teaspoon grated lemon zest
1 pound (2 cups) mild soft goat cheese, queso fresco, *or farmer's cheese*	Vegetable, sunflower, or peanut oil for deep-frying
4 large eggs, lightly beaten	About 2 cups honey syrup or sugar syrup (see atar, page 265) (optional)

1. Sift together the flour, cinnamon, baking powder, and salt. Combine the cheese, eggs, sugar, butter, brandy, and zest. Stir in the flour mixture.
2. Heat at least 1 inch of oil over medium heat to 360 degrees.
3. Drop the batter by tablespoonfuls into the oil and fry, turning, until golden brown on all sides, about 2 minutes. Remove with a wire mesh skimmer and drain on a wire rack. If desired, dip in the syrup.

Zvingous ❧ *(Sephardic Beignets)*

ABOUT 24 MEDIUM OR 36 SMALL PASTRIES

These deep-fried cream puffs are known as *zvingous* in Turkey and Greece, *zengol* in Syria, *beignets* in the Maghreb, and *bimuelos/burmuelos* in Ladino. The dough, called *pâte à choux* by the French (*choux* is French for "cabbage," a reference to the puffed appearance of the pastry), can be shaped to create a variety of treats. The leavening agent is steam, produced when heat melts the fat. As the steam forms, it pushes the batter upward and outward within the flour-and-egg dough, producing a puffed, hollow shell. Since the flour has to be strong enough to allow for adequate expansion, use a high-gluten flour. The eggs should be fresh and at room temperature. The dough is not inherently sweet, as too much sugar results in overbrowning. Middle Easterners commonly dip the puffs in syrup, while the French serve them with warm jam or filled with pastry cream.

1 cup water	4 large eggs
1/2 cup (1 stick) unsalted butter or margarine	Vegetable, sunflower, or peanut oil for deep-frying
1 tablespoon sugar	Confectioners' sugar, cinnamon sugar
1/2 teaspoon salt	(2/3 cup sugar mixed with
1 cup unbleached all-purpose or bread flour	2 teaspoons ground cinnamon), or cold sugar syrup (see atar, page 265)

1. Bring the water, butter, sugar, and salt to a rapid boil in a medium saucepan over medium heat. Remove from the heat, add the flour all at once, and stir with a wooden spoon until the mixture leaves the sides of the pan and forms a ball, about 1 minute. Return to low heat and cook, stirring, until the dough dries slightly, about 1 minute. Let cool slightly, about 10 minutes. If the temperature of the batter is higher than 140 degrees, it will bake the eggs.

2. Beat in the eggs, one at a time, beating well after each addition. Or transfer the dough to a food processor fitted with a metal blade and process for 15 seconds; then, with the machine on, add the eggs all at once and process for 30 seconds. The dough should be soft yet stiff enough to retain its shape. It is ready when it drops with difficulty from a spoon. Let cool completely.

3. Heat at least 2 inches of oil over medium heat to 375 degrees.

4. Dip a teaspoon or tablespoon into the hot oil. In batches, drop the batter by spoonfuls into the oil and fry, turning, until puffed and golden, 2 to 4 minutes. Remove with tongs or a wire mesh skimmer and drain on a rack. Serve warm. The puffs can be placed on a baking sheet and reheated in a 250-degree oven for about 5 minutes. Sprinkle with confectioners' sugar or cinnamon sugar or dip the hot beignets into cold sugar syrup.

VARIATIONS

Almond Beignets: Before frying, sprinkle the dough rounds with chopped almonds.

Orange Beignets: Add 1 teaspoon grated orange zest before adding the eggs.

Tulumbas (Sephardic Stick Beignets): Press the batter through a funnel or pipe through a pastry bag fitted with a 1/2-inch ridged metal tip into 4-inch lengths.

Lokmas ❧ *(Middle Eastern Yeast Fritters)*

These irregularly shaped deep-fried yeast batter balls, called *lokmas* in Turkish, *lou-koumades* in Greek, *awamee* in Arabic, and *bimuelos* in Ladino, are prepared in much the same way today as they were in the time of the Roman Empire. In the Middle East, the fritters are traditionally dipped into a sugar syrup, while Europeans prefer to roll them in sugar.

Batter:	*2¹/₂ cups all-purpose flour*
1 (¹/₄-ounce) package (2¹/₄ teaspoons) active dry yeast, or 1 (0.6-ounce) cake fresh yeast	*¹/₈ teaspoon salt*
	1 large egg, lightly beaten (optional)
2 cups warm water (105 to 110 degrees for dry yeast; 80 to 85 degrees for fresh yeast)	*Vegetable, sesame, or sunflower oil for deep-frying*
	2 cups cooled syrup (see atar, page 265) or confectioners' sugar for dusting
1 teaspoon sugar or honey	

1. To make the batter: Dissolve the yeast in ¹/₄ cup water. Stir in the sugar and let stand until foamy, 5 to 10 minutes. Combine the flour and salt in a large bowl and make a well in the center. Pour the yeast mixture, remaining water, and egg if using into the well and stir until smooth. The dough will be thin. Cover and let rise at room temperature until double in bulk, about 2 hours.

2. Heat at least 1 inch of oil over medium heat to 365 degrees.

3. Stir down the batter. Dip a teaspoon into cold water and use the spoon to drop the dough into the hot oil. Moisten your fingers to prevent sticking. Fry the dough balls in batches, turning occasionally, until golden brown on all sides, about 3 minutes. Remove with a wire mesh skimmer or tongs and drain on a wire rack.

4. Dip the warm fritters into the cooled syrup or sprinkle with confectioners' sugar. Serve immediately. To serve *lokmas* later, let them cool without the syrup and store in an air-tight container. Just before serving, dip into warm syrup.

VARIATION

Zelebi (Middle Eastern Funnel Cakes): This ancient pastry, popular from the Maghreb to India, is called *zelebi/zalabi* ("multiple coils") in Egypt and Yemen, *zangulas* and *cheb-bakiah* in Morocco, *zinghol* in Syria, *zalabia* in Iraq and Iran, and *jalebi* in India. It makes about 12 cakes. Pour the batter from a funnel, squeeze it from a plastic bottle, or press from a pastry bag fitted with a 1/4- to 1/2-inch tip into the hot oil in a spiral fashion to form a coil about 6 inches in diameter.

Atar ❧ *(Middle Eastern Sugar Syrup)*

ABOUT 2 CUPS

This basic syrup, called *atar* or *shira*, is used liberally in the Middle East to moisten pastries. It is usually composed of two parts sugar to one part water. Adding a little corn syrup and lemon juice inhibits crystallization. It is necessary to dissolve all of the sugar over low heat before the mixture boils, as even a single grain can cause crystallization. Do not stir the syrup after it starts to boil, because agitation will also cause crystallization.

When pouring syrup over pastry, the rule is to use cold syrup and hot pastry or vice versa. The contrast in temperatures allows the cake to absorb the syrup, producing a moist rather than soggy result.

---

2 cups sugar, or 1 cup sugar and 1 cup honey

1 cup water

1 to 3 tablespoons fresh lemon juice

1 tablespoon light corn syrup (optional)

1 to 3 teaspoons rose water or orange blossom water (optional)

Stir the sugar, water, lemon juice, and corn syrup if using over low heat until the sugar dissolves, about 5 minutes. Stop stirring. If using a candy thermometer, insert it into the pan now. Increase the heat to medium, bring to a gentle boil, and cook until the mixture is slightly syrupy and reaches the thread stage (225 degrees on a candy thermometer), about 5 minutes. Let cool. If desired, stir in the rose water. The syrup keeps in the refrigerator for several weeks.

Bimuelos ❧ *(Sephardic Raised Doughnuts)*

The Ladino word *bimuelos*, from the Spanish word for fritter (*bunuelo*), can be a bit confusing, as Sephardim also use it in reference to a variety of small fried foods, including pancakes and fritters. In addition, the word is also pronounced *bilmuelos, birmuelos, bulemas, bumuelos,* and *burmuelos.* However, pancakes usually have a phrase attached, as in *bimuelos de patata* ("potato pancakes"). When used alone, *bimuelos* generally refers to various fritters.

Dough:

1 ($^1/_4$-ounce) package (2$^1/_4$ teaspoons)
    active dry yeast, or 1 (0.6-ounce)
    cake fresh yeast

1$^1/_2$ cups warm water (105 to
    110 degrees for dry yeast;
    80 to 85 degrees for fresh yeast)

1 tablespoon sugar

3$^1/_4$ cups unbleached all-purpose flour

1$^1/_2$ tablespoons anise seeds, or
    2 tablespoons ouzo or raki, or 2 to
    3 teaspoons ground cinnamon

$^1/_2$ teaspoon salt

2 tablespoons vegetable oil

Vegetable, sunflower, or peanut oil for
    deep-frying

2 cups cooled sugar syrup or honey
    syrup (see atar, page 265) or
    confectioners' sugar for dusting

Coarsely chopped pistachios for garnish
    (optional)

1. To make the dough: Dissolve the yeast in $^1/_4$ cup warm water. Stir in 1 teaspoon sugar and let stand until foamy, 5 to 10 minutes. Combine the flour, remaining sugar, anise seeds, and salt in a large bowl and make a well in the center. Add the yeast mixture, remaining water, and oil and stir to make a smooth, soft dough. Cover and let stand until double in bulk, about 1$^1/_2$ hours.
2. Heat at least 2 inches of oil over medium heat to 375 degrees.
3. Form the dough into 1-inch balls. Fry in batches, turning occasionally, until golden on all sides, about 1$^1/_2$ minutes per side. Remove with a wire mesh skimmer or tongs and drain on a wire rack.

4. Dip the warm doughnuts into the cooled syrup and, if desired, sprinkle with the pistachios. Or sprinkle with confectioners' sugar. The doughnuts are best served warm. To serve *bimuelos* later, let them cool without the syrup and store in an airtight container. Just before serving, dip into warm syrup.

VARIATION

Reduce the water to 1¼ cups and add 2 large eggs. Although eggs were not traditional in Middle Eastern dough, they are sometimes added today for their richness and ability to reduce oil absorption.

Yoyos ✒ *(Tunisian Orange Doughnuts)*

ABOUT TWENTY-FOUR 3-INCH DOUGHNUTS

This is one of the most popular of all Tunisian pastries prepared both by home cooks and bakeries. The name of this dish is probably a derivative of the Ladino *boyos*, which in turn is derived from *bolos* ("balls"). The original fried dough balls evolved into a doughnut with a hole. These baking powder–raised doughnuts have a denser texture than the airier yeast-raised versions. The surface will be slightly crunchy.

About 3^1/$_2$ cups all-purpose flour

2 teaspoons double-acting baking powder

^{1}/$_2$ teaspoon salt

4 large eggs

6 tablespoons orange juice, milk, or water

^{1}/$_3$ cup sugar

3 tablespoons vegetable oil

1 teaspoon orange blossom water or vanilla extract

1 teaspoon grated orange zest, or 1^1/$_2$ tablespoons finely chopped fresh or unsweetened desiccated coconut

About 6 cups vegetable shortening, peanut oil, or safflower oil for deep-frying

About 2 cups cooled honey syrup (see atar, page 265) or confectioners' sugar for sprinkling

1. Sift together the flour, baking powder, and salt. Combine the eggs, juice, sugar, oil, orange blossom water, and zest. Gradually blend in the flour mixture to make a soft dough. Cover and refrigerate until the dough is easy to handle, about 2 hours.

2. On a lightly floured surface, roll out the dough ^{1}/$_2$ inch thick. Using a floured doughnut cutter or 3-inch biscuit cutter, cut out rounds. (If using a biscuit cutter, cut out the centers with a bottle cap, 1^1/$_4$-inch round cookie cutter, or knife.) Press together and reroll the scraps. Or roll the dough into 2-inch balls, flatten, and poke a large hole in the centers. Place on a lightly floured surface, cover, and let stand for at least 10 minutes. Store at room temperature for up to 2 hours or in the refrigerator for up to 8 hours.

3. Heat at least 2^1/$_2$ inches of shortening over medium heat to 365 degrees.

4. Fry 3 or 4 doughnuts at a time, turning once, until golden on all sides, about 55 seconds per side. Remove with tongs or a wire mesh skimmer and let drain on a wire rack. Dip the warm doughnuts in the cooled syrup or dust with confectioners' sugar.

Oliebollen ~ *(Dutch Yeast Fritters)*

ABOUT 50 SMALL FRITTERS

A Dutch painting by Juan van der Hamen y Leon from 1627 contains images of dough-nuts, reflecting their early presence and importance in the Netherlands. These fritters are a more modern version of the rudimentary *lokmas* (page 264) but less complex than *nachts/oliekoecken* (page 270). The presence of eggs and milk results in a richer fritter than *lokmas* and one that stays fresh longer.

Dough:

About 3 cups unbleached all-purpose flour

3 tablespoons sugar

1/2 teaspoon salt

1/2 teaspoon ground cinnamon (optional)

1/2 teaspoon grated nutmeg (optional)

1 (1/4-ounce) package (2 1/4 teaspoons) active dry yeast, or 1 (0.6-ounce) cake fresh yeast

1 1/2 cups warm milk (120 to 130 degrees), or 1 1/2 cups warm water and 1/2 cup nonfat dry milk

2 large eggs, lightly beaten

About 4 cups vegetable or peanut oil for deep-frying

About 1/4 cup confectioners' sugar for dusting, or 1/3 cup sugar mixed with 1/2 teaspoon ground cinnamon

1. To make the dough: Combine 2 cups of the flour with the sugar, salt, spices if using, and yeast. Blend in the milk, then the eggs. Gradually stir in enough of the remaining flour to make a soft dough that can be dropped from a spoon. Cover and let rise in a warm place until double in bulk, about 1 1/4 hours.
2. Heat at least 1 inch of oil over medium heat to 375 degrees.
3. Stir down the dough. Drop by teaspoonfuls into the oil and fry, turning, until golden brown on all sides, about 3 minutes. Remove with a wire mesh skimmer or tongs and drain on a wire rack. Roll in the sugar.

VARIATION

Raisin Fritters: After stirring down the dough, add 1/2 cup dried currants or raisins, 1 teaspoon grated orange or lemon zest, and if desired, 1/4 cup chopped candied citron (page 366).

Nachts ❧ *(Dutch and German Dough "Knots")*

The word *doughnut* comes from either the Dutch or the German. In both countries, Jewish cooks deep-fried "nuts" or "knots" of yeast *kuchen* dough, also called *oliekoecken* (fried cakes) in Holland, *pfannkuchen* in Germany, and *krapfen* in Austria and eastern Europe.

Dough:

1 (¼-ounce) package (2½ teaspoons) active dry yeast, or 1 (0.6-ounce) cake fresh yeast

¼ cup warm water (105 to 110 degrees for dry yeast; 80 to 85 degrees for fresh yeast)

3 tablespoons sugar

½ cup milk or nondairy creamer

3 tablespoons vegetable shortening, butter, or margarine, melted

1 large egg

½ teaspoon salt

½ to 1 teaspoon grated nutmeg or mace, or ¼ teaspoon vanilla extract, or ½ teaspoon grated lemon zest, or 1 teaspoon grated orange zest (optional)

About 2½ cups unbleached all-purpose flour

About 5 cups vegetable, sunflower, or peanut oil for deep-frying

Confectioners' sugar or granulated sugar for dusting

---

1. To make the dough: Dissolve the yeast in the water. Stir in 1 teaspoon sugar and let stand until foamy, 5 to 10 minutes. Blend in the milk, remaining sugar, shortening, egg, salt, nutmeg if using, and 2 cups flour. Gradually add enough of the remaining flour to make a soft dough.

2. On a lightly floured surface or in a mixer with a dough hook, knead until smooth and springy, about 5 minutes. Place in an oiled bowl, cover, and let rise until double in bulk, about 1½ hours.

3. Punch down the dough. Fold over and press together several times. Place on a lightly floured surface, cover, and let rest for 10 minutes. Roll 1-inch balls of dough into ¾-inch-thick ropes, then tie them into knots. Cover and let rise until doubled, about 1 hour.

4. Heat at least 2 inches of oil over medium heat to 375 degrees.

5. Using an oiled spatula and working in batches, drop the knots, top side down, into the oil. This allows the side exposed to the air to rise while the side in the oil fries. The temperature of the oil should not drop below 350 degrees. Fry, turning once, until golden brown on both sides, about 1 minute per side. Remove with a wire mesh skimmer or tongs and drain on a wire rack. Roll in the sugar.

VARIATION

Honey-Glazed Doughnuts: Combine $2/3$ cup confectioners' sugar and $1/2$ cup honey and spread over the doughnuts.

Frittelle di Hanukkah ❧ *(Italian Anise Fritters)*

ABOUT 35 MEDIUM DOUGHNUTS

The addition of olive oil and anise mark these doughnuts' Mediterranean origins.

---

1 cup dark raisins
1/4 cup white wine, brandy, or rum

Dough:
1 (1/4-ounce) package (21/4 teaspoons)
    active dry yeast, or 1 (0.6-ounce)
    cake fresh yeast
1 cup warm water (105 to 110 degrees
    for dry yeast; 80 to 85 degrees for
    fresh yeast)

3 tablespoons sugar
2 tablespoons extra virgin olive oil or
    vegetable oil
1 to 2 teaspoons anise seeds
1 teaspoon salt
About 3 cups all-purpose flour

1/2 cup pine nuts (optional)
Olive or vegetable oil for deep-frying
About 11/3 cups (1 pound) honey, warmed

---

1. Soak the raisins in the wine while preparing the dough.
2. To make the dough: Dissolve the yeast in 1/4 cup warm water. Stir in 1 teaspoon sugar and let stand until foamy, 5 to 10 minutes. Blend in the remaining water, remaining sugar, oil, anise seeds, salt, and 2 cups flour. Gradually add enough of the remaining flour to make a soft dough.
3. On a lightly floured surface or in a mixer with a dough hook, knead until smooth and springy, about 5 minutes. Drain the raisins. Knead the raisins and, if desired, the pine nuts into the dough. Place in an oiled bowl, cover, and let rise until double in bulk, about 11/2 hours.
4. Punch down the dough. Fold over and press together several times. Let rest for 10 minutes. On a lightly floured surface, roll into a 1/2-inch-thick rectangle about 15 by 7 inches. Cut into diamonds about 3 inches by 1 inch. Cover and let stand until puffy, about 20 minutes.
5. Heat at least 2 inches of oil over medium heat to 375 degrees.
6. Using an oiled spatula and working in batches, drop the diamonds, top side down, into the oil. Fry, turning once, until golden brown on both sides, about 1 minute per side. Remove with a wire mesh skimmer or tongs and drain on a wire rack. Drizzle with the honey.

Sefeng ❧ *(Algerian Raised Doughnuts)*

efeng, or sfenj, are made in various shapes, often with a hole in the center or filled with plums. Like other Middle Eastern treats, they can be dipped in syrup or coated with confectioners' sugar.

Dough:

1 (¼-ounce) package (2½ teaspoons)
    active dry yeast, or 1 (0.6-ounce)
    cake fresh yeast

¾ cup warm water (105 to 110 degrees
    for dry yeast; 80 to 85 degrees for
    fresh yeast), or ¼ cup warm water
    and ½ cup fresh orange juice

¼ cup sugar

2½ cups unbleached all-purpose flour

Pinch of salt

2 large eggs, lightly beaten

1 teaspoon vanilla extract, or
    2 teaspoons grated orange zest

Vegetable, sunflower, or peanut oil for
    deep-frying

2 cups cooled sugar or honey syrup (see
    atar, *page 265*) or confectioners'
    sugar for dusting

---

1. To make the dough: Dissolve the yeast in ¼ cup warm water. Stir in 1 teaspoon sugar and let stand until foamy, 5 to 10 minutes. Combine the flour, remaining sugar, and salt in a large bowl and make a well in the center. Add the yeast mixture, remaining water, eggs, and vanilla and stir until blended.

2. On a lightly floured surface or in a mixer with a dough hook, knead until smooth, 5 to 10 minutes. Cover with a large bowl or pot and let stand until double in bulk, about 1½ hours.

3. Punch down the dough. Fold over and press together several times. Let stand for 10 minutes. With wet hands, take 1-inch balls of dough, roll into a thick strip, and form into a rough circle with a hole in the center. Place in a single layer on a lightly floured surface, cover, and let rise until puffy, about 30 minutes.

4. Heat at least 2 inches of oil over medium heat to 375 degrees.

5. Fry the doughnuts in batches, turning once, until golden on all sides, about 1½ minutes per side. Remove with a wire mesh skimmer or tongs and drain on a wire rack. Dip the warm doughnuts into the cooled syrup or sprinkle with confectioners' sugar.

VARIATION

Form the dough into 1¹/2-inch balls, place a pitted plum or prune in the centers, and press the edges around the fruit to seal.

Sufganiyot ❧ *(Israeli Jelly Doughnuts)*

ABOUT 16 MEDIUM DOUGHNUTS

Polish Jews adopted a local lekvar (prune preserves) or raspberry jam-filled doughnut, called *ponchiks* (*paczki* in Polish) as their favorite Hanukkah dessert. Australian Jews, many of whom emigrated from Poland, still refer to jelly doughnuts as *ponchiks*. When the jelly doughnut made its way to Israel, however, it took the name *sufganiyot*, after a "spongy dough" mentioned in the Talmud. *Sufganiyot* subsequently emerged as the most popular Israeli Hanukkah food, sold throughout the eight-day festival at almost every bakery and market.

Dough:

1 (¹/4-ounce) package (2¹/4 teaspoons) active dry yeast, or 1 (0.6-ounce) cake fresh yeast

¹/4 cup warm water (105 to 110 degrees for dry yeast; 80 to 85 degrees for fresh yeast)

¹/4 cup sugar

³/4 cup milk or nondairy creamer

6 tablespoons (³/4 cup) unsalted butter or margarine, softened

3 large egg yolks, or 2 large eggs

1 teaspoon table salt, or 2 teaspoons kosher salt

¹/2 teaspoon ground nutmeg or mace (optional)

About 3³/4 cups unbleached all-purpose flour

About 5 cups vegetable oil, safflower oil, peanut oil, or vegetable shortening for deep-frying

About 1 cup jelly

Confectioners' or granulated sugar for dusting

1. To make the dough: Dissolve the yeast in the water. Stir in 1 teaspoon sugar and let stand until foamy, 5 to 10 minutes. Blend in the milk, remaining sugar, butter, egg yolks, salt, nutmeg if using, and 2 cups flour. Beat in enough of the remaining flour to make a smooth, soft dough. Cover and let rise until double in bulk, about $1\frac{1}{2}$ hours.

2. Punch down the dough. Fold over and press together several times. Let stand for 10 minutes. Roll out the dough $\frac{1}{4}$ inch thick. Cut out $2\frac{1}{2}$- to 3 $\frac{1}{2}$-inch rounds. Place in a single layer on a lightly floured surface, cover, and let rise until double in bulk, about 1 hour.

3. Heat at least 2 inches of oil over medium heat to 375 degrees.

4. Using an oiled spatula, carefully lift the doughnuts and drop them, top side down, into the oil. If you drop them bottom side down, the doughnuts are difficult to turn and do not puff up as well. The temperature of the oil should not drop below 350 degrees. Fry 3 or 4 at a time without crowding the pan, turning once, until golden brown on all sides, about $1\frac{1}{2}$ minutes per side. Remove with a wire mesh skimmer or tongs and drain on a wire rack.

5. Pierce one end of each doughnut with a thin knife. Place the jelly in a cookie press or a pastry bag fitted with a $\frac{1}{4}$-inch hole or nozzle tip, and pipe through the slit. Roll the doughnuts in the sugar.

VARIATIONS

To make doughnuts without a cookie press or pastry bag: Place 1 teaspoon of jelly in the center of half of the dough rounds. Brush the edges with egg white (save a white from the eggs used to make the dough). Top with a second dough round and press the edges to seal.

Substitute whipped cream, pastry cream, or pudding for the jelly.

Pancakes

If your offering be fried on a griddle . . .
—LEVITICUS 2:5–7

WHEN ANCIENT COOKS ACCIDENTALLY DROPPED A LITTLE GRUEL ON A HOT ROCK OF A CAMPFIRE, THEY DISCOVERED THAT THE RESULTING FLAT CAKE WAS TASTIER THAN PLAIN MUSH. FROM THESE RUDIMENTARY BEGINNINGS SPRANG NOT ONLY PANCAKES but also a wide range of other grain products, including dumplings, fritters, cookies, and breads. The ancient Romans prepared *placenta* (from the Greek, meaning "flat, circular form") and *pulmentum,* both coarse pancakes made from flour and oil and drizzled with honey to serve as dessert. For millennia, the Slavs made pancakes from buckwheat flour, which took on the name *blini.* At some point, cooks began adding eggs to these batters, lightening the cakes, sometimes to the point of becoming omelets.

Pancakes have been in the Jewish cooking repertoire since biblical times. The Italian rabbi Kalonymous ben Kalonymous (1286–1328) included them among the desserts for a Purim feast. Dutch Jews serve *pannekoeken* at the meal following Yom Kippur. Blintzes are a favorite Ashkenazic Shavuot treat. Although the potato *latke* has become the prototypical Ashkenazic Hanukkah food, various Jewish communities developed other forms of pancakes, including those for dessert.

Pancakes cook quickly. The high heat of the cooking surface sets the outside of the pancake, while the short cooking time keeps the interior soft. If the temperature is too high, the exterior will burn before the interior cooks. If the temperature is too low, the result is a hard exterior and dry insides. To test if a pan is ready, sprinkle a few drops of water on it. If the water spatters, it is ready. If it disappears quickly, the pan is too hot.

Pannekoeken ❧ *(Dutch Griddle Cakes)*

ABOUT TWENTY-FOUR 3-INCH OR SIXTEEN 4-INCH PANCAKES

The Dutch originally made their *pannekoeken* from buckwheat, but by the seventeenth century began substituting white flour to make lighter cakes. Griddle cake batter calls for a relatively small amount of flour and limited mixing to produce a tender cake. Bleached all-purpose flour produces a light, fluffy pancake. Cake flour produces a slightly more tender pancake, but one that is flatter and less fluffy.

Since the cooking time for pancakes is short, single-acting baking powder will produce higher-rising cakes. If it is hard to find, you can make your own by combining 1 teaspoon cream of tartar, $1/2$ teaspoon baking soda, and $1/2$ teaspoon cornstarch or potato starch. If using double-acting baking powder, it is preferable to let the batter rest in the refrigerator for at least 1 hour. In high altitudes, use three-fourths the amount of baking powder.

The batter should be pourable without being runny. If it is too thin, the pancakes will be too flat, but if too thick, it will yield heavy cakes. A little sugar is added for tenderness and flavor. Too much sugar, however, results in flat or burned cakes. Since griddle cakes contain so little sugar, they are best served immediately before they cool and toughen.

The higher the proportion of fat in the batter, the less need there is for greasing the pan. If you use too much fat on the pan, the steam emitted by the batter will form pockets on the bottom of the cakes, resulting in a lumpy, mottled surface. Well-seasoned cast-iron and nonstick pans require very little or no fat for greasing.

2 cups all-purpose flour	*$1/4$ cup vegetable oil or melted butter*
1 tablespoon double-acting baking powder, or 4 teaspoons single-acting baking powder	*2 tablespoons sugar or honey*
	$1/2$ teaspoon vanilla extract
	1 cup dried currants or raisins
$3/4$ teaspoon salt	*Vegetable oil or butter for cooking the pancakes*
2 cups milk	
2 large eggs, lightly beaten	*Confectioners' sugar for dusting*

1. Sift together the flour, baking powder, and salt. Combine the milk, eggs, oil, sugar, and vanilla. Add to the flour mixture and stir just to combine. Add the currants. If using single-acting baking powder, use the batter immediately. If using double-acting powder, let the batter rest in the refrigerator for at least 1 hour or overnight.

2. Heat a griddle or large skillet over medium heat until a few drops of water sprinkled on the surface scatter and evaporate. Lightly grease, then wipe with a paper towel.

3. Drop ¼ cup batter for 4-inch pancakes or 2 tablespoonfuls for 3-inch pancakes onto the skillet, spreading to the desired diameter. Cook until bubbles appear on the top and the bottom is lightly browned, about 2 minutes. Turn and cook until golden brown, about 1 minute. The pancakes can be kept warm by placing them in a single layer on a baking sheet in a 200-degree oven. Sprinkle with the confectioners' sugar.

VARIATION

Add 1 teaspoon ground cardamom or cinnamon to the batter.

Atayef ❧ *(Syrian Filled Pancakes)*

ABOUT 50 FOLDED OR 25 DOUBLED SMALL PANCAKES

Syrian Jews enjoy two forms of Hanukkah pancakes: savory cheese or vegetable pancakes called *edjeh* and sweet ones called *atayef.* The original Arabic dish was made with a yeast batter, but the more recently developed baking powder version has become very popular. Cheese-filled *atayef* are traditional on Shavuot.

Orange Syrup:	1 recipe pannekoeken *batter without the*
1 1/2 *cups sugar*	*currants (page 278), or 1 recipe yeast*
3/4 *cup water*	*batter (recipe follows)*
1/2 *medium orange, cut into 4 slices*	1 recipe atayef *filling (recipes follow)*
1 *tablespoon lemon juice*	*Vegetable oil for frying*
	Chopped almonds, pistachios, or
Vegetable oil for cooking the pancakes	*walnuts for sprinkling (optional)*

1. To make the syrup: Stir the sugar and water in a medium saucepan over low heat until the sugar dissolves, about 5 minutes. Add the orange slices and lemon juice and simmer for 30 minutes. Increase the heat and bring to a boil. Remove from the heat and let cool. Discard the orange slices.

2. Heat a large skillet over medium heat until a few drops of water sprinkled on the surface scatter and evaporate. Lightly grease.

3. Drop the batter by 2 tablespoonfuls onto the skillet to form 3-inch pancakes. Cook until bubbles appear on the surface and the bottom is lightly colored. Do not cook the top.

4. Place about 2 teaspoons of the filling in the center of the uncooked side of each pancake. Do this while the pancakes are still warm and soft so that they stick when folded. Fold in half to enclose the filling and press the edges together to seal. Or top each pancake with a second one. The pancakes can be frozen. Do not thaw before frying; increase the cooking time by about 2 minutes.

5. Heat at least 1 inch of oil to about 375 degrees.

6. Fry the filled pancakes in batches, turning once, until golden brown on all sides, about 1 minute per side. Remove with a wire mesh strainer or tongs and drain on a wire rack. Drizzle a little of the cooled orange syrup over the warm pancakes. If desired, sprinkle with the nuts.

VARIATIONS

Unfilled Atayef: Omit the filling. Turn the pancakes and cook on the second side (do not fry). Dip them into the syrup.

Instead of frying the filled pancakes, arrange them on a greased baking sheet, drizzle with $1/2$ cup melted butter, and bake in a 375-degree oven for 10 to 15 minutes.

Rose Syrup: Omit the orange. Bring the syrup to a boil and add the lemon juice. Boil the syrup for about 5 minutes, then remove from the heat and stir in 1 tablespoon rose water.

Yeast Atayef Batter

$1^1/8$ teaspoons ($1/2$ package) active dry yeast	1 large egg
2 cups lukewarm water, or $1/4$ cup lukewarm water and $1^3/4$ cups lukewarm milk	2 tablespoons unsalted butter or margarine, melted
	Pinch of salt
1 tablespoon sugar	2 cups unbleached all-purpose flour

Dissolve the yeast in $1/4$ cup lukewarm water. Stir in 1 teaspoon sugar and let stand until foamy, 5 to 10 minutes. Add the remaining water, remaining sugar, egg, butter, and salt. Gradually stir in the flour to make a smooth batter. Cover and let rise at room temperature for about $1^1/2$ hours.

ATAYEF FILLINGS ❧

Atayef bil Joz *(Nut Filling)*

2 cups (about 6 ounces) medium-fine chopped walnuts or pistachios	1 teaspoon ground cinnamon
$1/2$ to $3/4$ cup sugar	2 to 3 teaspoons orange blossom water or rose water (optional)

Combine all the ingredients.

Atayef bil Jiben *(Cheese Filling)*

---

2 cups (1 pound) ricotta or small-curd cottage cheese, drained	$1/2$ to $3/4$ cup sugar
	1 teaspoon ground cinnamon (optional)

Combine all the ingredients.

Bimuelos de Calabaza ❧ *(Sephardic Pumpkin Pancakes)*

ABOUT 24 SMALL PANCAKES

The presence of pumpkin in a Mediterranean dish is frequently a sign of Sephardic cuisine. This sweet version, symbolic of fertility and the harvest, is traditional for Rosh Hashanah and Sukkot among Sephardim from Turkey and Greece.

---

2 cups cooked mashed pumpkin or winter squash (about 22 ounces raw)	2 teaspoons ground cinnamon
$3/4$ cup all-purpose flour	$1/4$ teaspoon grated nutmeg
2 large eggs	Pinch of salt
$1/3$ to $1/2$ cup granulated or brown sugar	Vegetable oil for frying

---

1. Combine the pumpkin, flour, eggs, sugar, cinnamon, nutmeg, and salt.
2. Heat a thin layer of oil in a large skillet over medium heat.
3. Drop the batter by tablespoonfuls into the oil to form 2-inch pancakes and fry, turning once, until golden brown on both sides, about 2 minutes per side. Drain on paper towels. Serve warm. The pancakes can be kept warm in a 200-degree oven for up to 1 hour. If desired, serve with yogurt or sour cream.

Tiganites ❧ *(Greek Pancakes)*

The name of these pancakes is derived from a Greek word for skillet, *tigani*. There are numerous variations, including some made with rice flour and others with an anise flavor that comes from a little *ouzo.* Passover versions are made with matza meal.

1 cup all-purpose flour	2 tablespoons sugar or honey
3/4 cup whole-wheat flour or rice flour	Olive or vegetable oil for cooking the
1 teaspoon double-acting baking powder	pancakes
1/2 teaspoon salt	Warm honey or sugar syrup (see atar
3 large eggs, lightly beaten	page 265) for drizzling or cinnamon
1 1/2 cups milk, or 3/4 cup milk and	sugar for sprinkling
3/4 cup plain yogurt	Chopped almonds, pistachios, or
2 tablespoons olive or vegetable oil	walnuts for sprinkling

1. Combine the flours, baking powder, and salt. Blend together the eggs, milk, oil, and sugar. Add to the flour mixture and stir just to combine. If the batter is too thick, add a little milk; if too thin, stir in a little flour. Let stand in the refrigerator for at least 1 hour or overnight.
2. Heat a griddle or large skillet over medium heat until a few drops of water sprinkled on the surface scatter and evaporate. Lightly grease, then wipe with a paper towel.
3. Drop the batter by 1/4 cupfuls onto the skillet to form 4-inch pancakes. Cook until bubbles appear on the top and the bottom is lightly browned, about 2 minutes. Turn and cook until golden brown, about 1 minute. Drizzle with the warm honey and sprinkle with the nuts.

VARIATION

Substitute 1 1/4 cups water and 1/4 cup *ouzo* or *raki* (anise-flavored liqueur) for the milk.

Kaese Latkes ❧ *(Ashkenazic Cheese Pancakes)*

ABOUT THIRTY 3-INCH PANCAKES

Cheese pancakes date back to at least the time of ancient Greece, although those early efforts tended to be rather heavy. This lightly sweetened version has a custard-like consistency. Cheese latkes combine both of the Hanukkah culinary symbols, dairy and fried.

2 cups (16 ounces) ricotta, farmer's, or pot cheese	*2 tablespoons sugar*
4 large eggs	*$^1/_2$ teaspoon vanilla extract*
About $^3/_4$ cup all-purpose flour	*About $^1/_2$ teaspoon salt*
	Vegetable oil or butter for frying

1. Beat together the cheese, eggs, flour, sugar, vanilla, and salt until well combined.
2. Heat a thin layer of oil in a large skillet over medium heat.
3. Drop the batter by heaping tablespoonfuls into the oil and fry until bubbles form on the top and the bottom is lightly browned, 2 to 3 minutes. Turn and fry until golden, 1 to 2 minutes. The pancakes can be kept warm by placing them in a single layer on a baking sheet in a 200-degree oven. If desired, serve with sour cream, yogurt, maple syrup, flavored butter, jam, cinnamon sugar, or fresh fruit.

VARIATION

Cassola (Roman Cheese Pancakes): Increase the sugar to 1 cup and omit the flour. These pancakes are so fragile, instead of turning them after frying the bottoms, place the skillet under a broiler until the tops are browned.

Blintzes ❧ *(Eastern European Thin Pancakes)*

ABOUT TWELVE 6-INCH OR EIGHTEEN 5-INCH PANCAKES

For centuries, the Slavs of eastern Europe consumed various pancakes known as *blini.* In the Ukraine, an area once referred to as the bread basket of the Soviet Union, these pancakes were commonly made with buckwheat. Eventually Ukrainian royal cuisine grew more refined and the pancakes became thinner, and sometimes the batter was made with wheat flour. The result was a very thin pancake known as the diminutive *blinchiki* or *naliesniki* and, in Yiddish, *blintz* or *bletlach* ("leaves"). The cakes soon spread to many other countries, being called *palacsinta* in Hungary, *manicotti* in Italy, *plattar* in Scandinavia, *pantras* in India, and *crêpes* in France, from the Latin *crispus* ("curly" or "wrinkled"). In general, a crepe is a rolled (open at the ends) or folded (halved, triangled, or quartered) pancake, while a blintz is one that is folded into a package so as to enclose the filling, all the better for frying.

The key to good blintzes is using the appropriate amount of batter with the right texture, about the consistency of heavy cream. If the batter is too thick, the pancakes will be heavy; if too thin, they will have holes. If the batter is not allowed to rest for at least 2 hours to allow the gluten to relax, the blintzes will be tough and rubbery. If it thickens too much while standing, stir in a little additional liquid.

Do not use too much batter or the blintz will be too thick. Use 2 tablespoons of batter for a 6-inch pan; 3 tablespoons for an 8-inch pan; and $1/4$ cup for a 9- to 10-inch pan. A coffee measure (2 tablespoons) is a useful tool, or fill a $1/4$-cup measure halfway.

---

1 cup milk, nondairy creamer, seltzer, or water	*2 to 3 tablespoons sugar (optional)*
	$1/2$ teaspoon salt
4 large eggs, lightly beaten	*1 cup all-purpose flour*
2 tablespoons vegetable oil or melted and cooled unsalted butter or margarine	*Butter or vegetable oil for frying*
	1 recipe blintz filling (recipes follow)

---

1. To make the batter: Whisk together the milk, eggs, oil, sugar, and salt. Gradually add the flour to make a smooth, thin batter. Strain if there are any lumps. Or process all the ingredients in a blender or food processor. Cover and refrigerate for at least 2 hours or overnight.

continued

2. Heat a little butter in a 6-inch heavy skillet (nonstick is best) over medium heat. Pour in about 2 tablespoons batter, tilting the pan until the batter coats the bottom. Do not add too much batter. Fry until dry on the top and the bottom edges begin to brown, about 1 minute. Flip the blintz onto a plate (it is fried only on one side). Repeat, stacking the blintzes with waxed paper, foil, or dampened paper towels between them. The blintzes can be stored in the refrigerator for up to 4 days or in the freezer for up to 1 month. Return to room temperature.

3. To shape the blintzes: Place 2 to 3 tablespoons filling on the cooked side of each pancake just below the center. Fold the bottom of the pancake over the filling. Fold the sides over and roll up, enclosing the filling completely. The blintzes can be refrigerated overnight or stored in the freezer for up to 1 month. Do not thaw before cooking.

4. To fry the blintzes: Heat a little butter in a large skillet over medium heat. Add the blintzes, seam side down, and fry, turning once, until browned on both sides, about 5 minutes per side for fresh. For frozen blintzes, cover the pan for the first 5 minutes. To bake the blintzes: Arrange in a single layer, seam side down, in a greased baking pan, cover loosely with foil, and bake in a 350-degree oven until hot, about 15 minutes for fresh or about 40 minutes for frozen.

BLINTZ FILLINGS ❧

Blintz Apple Filling

ENOUGH FOR TWELVE 6-INCH BLINTZES

$1/4$ cup ($1/2$ stick) unsalted butter or margarine	About $1/2$ cup granulated or brown sugar
2 pounds (about 6 medium) cooking apples, peeled, cored, and diced	1 teaspoon ground cinnamon, or $1/2$ teaspoon grated lemon zest (optional)

Melt the butter in a large skillet over medium heat. Add the apples and cook, stirring occasionally, until nearly tender, about 10 minutes. Add the sugar and, if desired, the cinnamon, increase the heat to medium-high, and stir until the apples are golden brown and tender but not mushy, about 5 minutes. Let cool.

Blintz Blueberry Filling

3 to 4 tablespoons sugar
1 tablespoon cornstarch or potato
  starch

1/8 teaspoon grated nutmeg, or
  1 teaspoon grated lemon zest
1 1/2 cups blueberries

Combine the sugar, cornstarch, and nutmeg. Add the blueberries and toss to coat.

Blintz Cheese Filling

2 cups (1 pound) ricotta, farmer's, or pot
  cheese, or 1 cup cottage cheese and
  1 cup softened cream cheese
1 large egg
About 1/4 cup sugar
1 teaspoon vanilla extract

1 teaspoon lemon zest, orange zest, or
  ground cinnamon
1/2 teaspoon salt
1/2 cup raisins or chopped dried apricots
  (optional)

Combine all the ingredients.

Blintz Cherry Filling

2 cups pitted tart cherries (about
  1 pound)
1/3 cup granulated or brown sugar

1/4 cup water
1/4 cup kirsch, or 1/8 teaspoon almond
  extract (optional)

Cook the cherries, sugar, and water in a medium saucepan over medium heat until tender. Remove from the heat and stir in the kirsch. Let cool.

Palacsinta ❧ *(Hungarian Crepes)*

ABOUT SIXTEEN 7- OR 8-INCH PANCAKES

3 *large eggs, lightly beaten*	*¹/₄ teaspoon salt*
³/₄ cup milk or water	*1¹/₄ cups all-purpose flour*
2 *tablespoons sugar*	*³/₄ cup seltzer or club soda*
1 *teaspoon vanilla extract or grated*	*About 2 tablespoons butter or vegetable*
lemon zest	*oil for frying*

1. Whisk together the eggs, milk, sugar, vanilla, and salt. Gradually add the flour. Strain if there are any lumps. Let stand in the refrigerator for at least 1 hour or overnight.
2. Just before frying, stir in the seltzer to make a smooth, thin batter with the consistency of heavy cream.
3. Heat a 7- or 8-inch heavy skillet (nonstick is best) over medium heat and spread with a little butter. Pour in 2¹/₂ to 3 tablespoons batter, tilting the pan until the batter coats the bottom. Do not add too much batter. Fry until the edges begin to brown, about 1 minute. Turn the crepe over and fry until lightly colored, about 30 seconds. Flip the crepe onto a plate. Repeat, stacking the crepes between sheets of waxed paper or foil.

VARIATIONS

Pareve Palacsinta: Omit the milk, add ¹/₂ cup orange juice, and increase the seltzer to 1¹/₃ cups (add the seltzer with the eggs).

Omit the seltzer. Increase the eggs to 8 and the milk to 1 cup.

Palacsinta Teszta (Hungarian Baked Crepes): Spread the crepes with 2 tablespoons apricot jam, sprinkle with sliced almonds, and roll up. Place in a greased 13-by-9-inch baking pan, top with 2 cups sour cream, and bake at 325 degrees until heated through, about 12 minutes.

Langolo Palacsinta Alabardos ❧
(Hungarian Crepes with Chocolate Sauce)

8 SERVINGS

About 2 cups whipped cream, chopped
nuts, or pastry cream
16 (7- to 8-inch) palacsinta *(page 288)*
2 to 3 cups Hungarian Chocolate Sauce
(recipe follows)

Chopped almonds, hazelnuts, pecans, or
walnuts for garnish (optional)

Spread about 2 tablespoons filling over each crepe. Roll up jelly roll style. Or fold in half to form a half-moon shape, then fold in half again to form a triangle. Or fold in half, then roll the ends toward the center to form a triangular cone. Drizzle with the chocolate sauce and, if desired, sprinkle with the nuts.

VARIATIONS

Toltott Palacsinta (Hungarian Whipped Cream–Filled Crepes): Whip 1 cup heavy cream with ³/4 cup confectioners' sugar (or to taste) until stiff. If desired, fold in ¹/2 to 1 cup chopped almonds, hazelnuts, or walnuts. Omit the chocolate sauce and top each rolled or folded crepe with a dollop of whipped cream.

Gyumolcsiz Palacsinta (Hungarian Jam-Filled Crepes): Spread the crepes with Prune Lekvar or Apricot Lekvar (page 75) or your favorite jam. If desired, flambé in a matching flavor of liqueur.

Makos Palacsinta (Hungarian Poppy Seed Crepes): Omit the chocolate sauce. Spread each crepe with about 2 tablespoons Ashkenazic Poppy Seed Filling (page 73).

Hungarian Chocolate Sauce

ABOUT 3 CUPS

1/2 cup unsweetened cocoa powder, preferably alkalized (Dutch processed)

2 tablespoons all-purpose flour

4 large egg yolks

1/2 cup sugar

1 cup milk

1 cup heavy cream

4 ounces semisweet or bittersweet chocolate, chopped

Pinch of salt

1 1/2 teaspoons vanilla extract

---

1. Sift together the cocoa powder and flour. Beat the egg yolks and sugar until thick and creamy. Gradually beat in the cocoa mixture.
2. Bring the milk and cream to a simmer in a medium saucepan over medium-low heat. Gradually whisk into the yolk mixture. Return to the saucepan and cook over medium heat, stirring constantly, until the mixture just boils.
3. Remove from the heat, add the chocolate and salt, and stir until smooth. Add the vanilla. Strain into a bowl, press a piece of plastic wrap against the surface, and refrigerate for at least 1 hour.

VARIATION

Increase the milk to 1 1/2 cups and reduce the cream to 2/3 cup and the egg yolks to 3. Do not cook the cream with the sauce, but pour the boiling sauce into a large bowl and beat at low speed until cool. Beat the cream until stiff, then fold into the chocolate mixture.

Dios Palacsinta ✎ *(Hungarian Walnut-Filled Crepes)*

12 CREPES; 6 SERVINGS

Filling:	About 1 tablespoon rum
1/2 cup heavy cream or milk	*1/3 cup raisins (optional)*
1 1/2 cups (about 4 1/4 ounces) ground	
* walnuts*	*12 (7- to 8-inch) palacsinta (page 288)*
1/2 cup sugar	*About 2 tablespoons unsalted butter or*
1/2 teaspoon ground cinnamon, or	* margarine for frying*
* 2 teaspoons grated orange zest*	*1 recipe Hungarian Chocolate Sauce*
	* (page 290)*

1. To make the filling: Bring the cream to a low boil in a medium saucepan over medium heat. Stir in the nuts, sugar, and cinnamon and cook, stirring constantly, for 1 minute. Remove from the heat and stir in the rum and, if desired, the raisins. Press a piece of plastic wrap against the surface and let cool. Store in the refrigerator.

2. Place the crepes, speckled side up, on a flat surface. Spread 1 tablespoon of the filling down the center of each crepe. Fold in half to form a half-moon shape, then fold in half again to form a triangle.

3. Melt the butter in a large skillet over medium heat. Add the crepes and fry, turning once, until lightly browned on both sides, about 1 minute per side. Or arrange the filled crepes slightly overlapping in a greased shallow baking pan and bake in a 300-degree oven until heated through, about 10 minutes.

4. Transfer 2 crepes to each serving plate and drizzle with the chocolate sauce.

Petar ❧ *(Cochin Crepes)*

ABOUT EIGHTEEN 5-INCH, FIFTEEN 6-INCH, OR TWELVE 8-INCH PANCAKES

This is a synthesis of Indian and European cuisines.

1¼ cups coconut milk (see page 312)

1 large egg, lightly beaten

2 tablespoons unsalted butter or
  margarine, melted

1 tablespoon sugar

1 teaspoon vanilla extract

⅛ teaspoon salt

1 cup unbleached all-purpose flour

Butter or vegetable oil for cooking the
  crepes

Filling:

2½ cups (8 ounces) grated coconut,
  preferably fresh

1¼ cups sugar

Pinch of ground cardamom (optional)

2 tablespoons water

---

1. Whisk together the coconut milk, egg, butter, sugar, vanilla, and salt. Gradually whisk in the flour to make a smooth, thin batter with the consistency of heavy cream. Strain if there are any lumps. Or process all the ingredients in a blender or food processor until smooth. Cover and let stand in the refrigerator for at least 2 hours or up to 2 days.

2. Heat a 5-, 6-, or 8-inch heavy skillet (cast-iron or nonstick is best) over medium heat. Brush lightly with butter.

3. Pour in about 2 tablespoons batter for a 5- to 6-inch pan or 3 tablespoons for an 8-inch pan, tilting the pan until the batter just coats the bottom.

4. Cook until the edges begin to brown, about 45 seconds. Turn the crepe over and cook until golden, about 30 seconds. Flip onto a plate lined with waxed paper. Stack the crepes between pieces of waxed paper, foil, or dampened paper towels.

5. To make the filling: Combine all the filling ingredients.

6. Spread 2 to 3 tablespoons of the filling over each crepe, leaving a ½-inch border on all sides. Roll up jelly roll style. Allow 2 crepes per person. The crepes can be stored in the refrigerator for up to 4 days or frozen for up to 2 months. Return to room temperature.

COCHIN CONNECTIONS

 According to local legend, the Jews of the Malabar coast in southwestern India are descended from Judean exiles who fled from the troops of Nebuchadnezzar. Others claim their origins date back to sailors in King Solomon's fleet who remained in the area. The first verification of a Jewish community existing in the region is a pair of copper plates recording seventy-two special privileges granted to the Jews by the local ruler, dated by some scholars to 379 CE. Benjamin of Tudela recorded about 1,000 black Jews in Cochin in the 1100s. At its height, the Cochini Jewish community never numbered much more than 3,000.

Unlike the Bene Israel of Bombay, the Jews of Cochin remained in contact with other Jewish communities, interacting with Jews across the Arabian Sea. The Jews divided themselves into three distinct groups: Kala (blacks); whites, called Paradesi (foreigners); and descendants of freed slaves, called Meshuharim (emancipated). Cochinis, particularly the Kala, were ardent Zionists and, beginning in the 1950s, sacrificed the security and prosperity of the Malabar coast to move to Israel. Today more than 5,000 Cochini Jews are in Israel, many living on *moshavim* (cooperative settlements). Cochini farmers are credited with introducing to Israel such innovations as hothouse agriculture.

The cuisine of southern India is more pungent than in the rest of the country, containing generous amounts of chilies and the indigenous black pepper. Kerala cooks do not have to worry about the freshness of their spices, as they are grown in the vicinity. The primary flavorings are curry leaves and coconut, the latter found in most Cochini sweets.

Baked Puddings
and Kugels

With what does one sanctify the Sabbath?
With sweet foods, spiced wines, and nice vessels.
—MIDRASH TANAYIM ON DEUTERONOMY

THE PREVALENT AMERICAN PERCEPTION OF PUDDING IS THAT OF A SWEET, SMOOTH, SOFT-TEXTURED DISH. FOR THIS REASON, MOST PEOPLE ARE SURPRISED TO DISCOVER THAT THE SOURCE OF THE WORD *PUDDING* IS THE OLD ENGLISH *PODING*, DERIVED FROM THE French *boudin* and originally from the Italian *budino*, referring to types of sausages. Indeed, for much of history, puddings consisted of savory grain or bread mixtures stuffed into animal casings such as intestines and stomachs, then boiled in water. (The Ashkenazic *kishke* and Scottish *haggis* come to mind.) Other rudimentary puddings were baked, such as the Talmudic *kutach*, a savory mixture of bread, sour milk, salt, and oil. Yemenite Jews still prepare a similar dish called *ghininun* (sometimes substituting cottage cheese for the milk), baking it overnight for Sabbath lunch. Other descendants of those ancient bread or grain puddings still exist in the Middle East, most notably halvah.

An old Ashkenazic way of preparing bread pudding was to substitute a broth for the dairy products and to spread it over the Sabbath stew to seal in the moisture or to drop it in the center of the stew. At first, people called this pudding by the same name as the Sabbath stew, *schalet* (from the Old French word meaning "warm," *chald*), now commonly called *cholent*. By 1100, in order to differentiate between the two, many began referring to the pudding as *koogel*, German for a ball or sphere, referring to its shape. In western Europe, these puddings are still called *schalet*, while in eastern Europe *kugel* is the generic term and *schalet* is occasionally applied to some dessert puddings.

At first, kugels were exclusively savory and made from bread or flour. Eventually people began adding eggs, producing a custard consistency. Housewives started cooking these puddings in a covered small, round dish placed inside the stew pot and served them warm alongside the stew for Sabbath lunch. As home ovens became more prevalent, cooks began baking the pudding outside the stew. Kugels began achieving new gastronomical heights around 800 years ago in Germany when cooks started substituting farfel and noodles and, on Passover, matza for the bread mixtures. Later rice and potatoes were used, creating an even wider range of flavors. On occasion, cottage cheese and milk were added to the kugels, a tasty reversion to the dish's original dairy form. By the seventeenth century, with the increasing affordability of sugar, some cooks began sweetening various puddings. Soon Lithuanian and Polish Jews developed a preference for sweet kugels—customarily seasoned with cinnamon and frequently containing raisins—serving them as both a side dish and a dessert. Conversely, many of those from Galicia (an area in southeastern Poland and southwestern Russia) adamantly prepared only savory puddings, which they pronounced *keegals*. Hungarians took the dessert concept even further, layering the sweetened kugels with various fillings.

Sephardim never developed the same passion for baked puddings as Ashkenazim. Nonetheless, they devised some of their own, including *pastichio* (Greek cheese noodle pudding), *pyota* (Greek semolina pudding), and *babanatza* (Greek semolina and raisin pudding).

Apfelschalet ❧ *(Alsatian Apple Charlotte)*

Puddings have come a long way from grain sausages, developing into a vast array of baked and steamed treats. *The New Larousse Gastronomique* (New York, Crown Publishers, 1977) records one of these developments, *schaleth à la Juive*, an apple pastry similar to a *fluden*. The charlotte is a related dish in which a crisp bread casing contrasts with the soft fruit filling. For Passover, substitute moistened matzas for the bread.

---

3 tablespoons unsalted butter or
  margarine

2 pounds tart cooking apples, such as
  Golden Delicious, Granny Smith,
  Gravenstein, Greening, Jonathan,
  Macoun, Pippin, Starr, Winesap, or
  any combination, peeled, cored, and
  sliced (about 7 cups)

1/4 to 1 teaspoon ground cinnamon

1 teaspoon grated lemon zest or vanilla
  extract (optional)

1/4 to 1/2 cup sugar

1 pound stale challah or other egg bread,
  crusts removed, cut into 1/4-inch-thick
  slices (about 24 slices)

1/2 cup clarified butter or melted
  margarine

About 3 tablespoons confectioners' sugar
  for dusting

---

1. Melt the butter in a large skillet over medium heat. Add the apples, cinnamon, and zest if using and sauté until well coated. Cover and cook until the apples are tender but not mushy, about 15 minutes. Stir in the sugar. Let cool.

2. Preheat the oven to 375 degrees.

3. Cut some of the bread slices into strips to fit the sides of a 2-quart charlotte mold (a metal pan with slightly slopping sides) or deep 2-quart casserole. Cut the rest into triangles. Coat the triangles with the butter (by dipping or brushing) and arrange, slightly overlapping, on the bottom of the mold. Coat the bread strips with the butter and arrange, slightly overlapping, along the sides of the pan. Fill with the apple mixture. Coat the remaining slices with butter and arrange, slightly overlapping, over the top.

4. Bake until golden brown, about 40 minutes. Let cool for at least 15 minutes, then invert onto a serving platter. Dust with the confectioners' sugar. Serve warm or at room temperature.

VARIATIONS

Substitute 8 cups chunky sweetened applesauce for the sautéed apple mixture and flavor with the cinnamon and, if desired, the lemon zest.

Stir 4 large egg yolks into the cooled apple mixture, then beat 4 egg whites until stiff but not dry and fold into the apple mixture.

Individual Charlottes: Fit rounds of bread in the bottom of $1/2$-cup muffin tins, line the sides of the cups with overlapping bread slices, fill with the apple mixture, and top with butter-brushed bread rounds. Bake at 400 degrees until golden, about 25 minutes.

Zwetschenschalet (Alsatian Plum Charlotte): Substitute 2 pounds (about 10 medium) pitted and sliced Italian plums for the apples.

Nudlovy Kakyp ❧ *(Czech Soufflé Noodle Pudding)*

Czech cooking is frequently subsumed under that of Austria or Germany, two countries that long dominated it. Yet it possesses certain unique attributes. *Mehlspeisen* (Czech desserts) commonly feature fruits and are typically served warm. This is a popular Czech version of an old Ashkenazic favorite.

For 9-inch square baking pan:	For 13-by-9-inch baking pan:
4 cups milk	5 1/3 cups milk
6 ounces (about 5 cups) medium or large noodles, slightly broken	8 ounces (about 6 cups) medium or large noodles, slightly broken
1/4 teaspoon salt	1/2 teaspoon salt
1 1/2 teaspoons vanilla extract	2 teaspoons vanilla extract
1/2 cup (1 stick) unsalted butter or margarine, softened	10 tablespoons (1 1/4 sticks) unsalted butter or margarine, softened
About 2/3 cup sugar	About 3/4 cup sugar
5 large eggs, separated	6 large eggs, separated
1 1/2 pounds apples, peeled, cored, and thinly sliced (about 4 cups)	2 pounds apples, peeled, cored, and thinly sliced (about 5 cups)

1. Bring the milk to a low boil, add the noodles and salt, and simmer until tender, about 8 minutes. Let cool. Add the vanilla.
2. Preheat the oven to 350 degrees (325 degrees if using a glass pan). Grease the baking pan.
3. Beat the butter until smooth, about 1 minute. Gradually add the sugar and beat until light and fluffy, about 4 minutes. Beat in the egg yolks, one at a time. Add the noodle mixture.
4. Beat the egg whites on low speed until foamy, about 30 seconds. Increase the speed to medium-high and beat until stiff but not dry. Fold into the noodle mixture.
5. Spoon half of the noodle mixture into the prepared pan, scatter the apples over the top, and cover with the remaining noodle mixture.
6. Bake until golden brown, about 35 minutes. Serve warm.

Zeesih Lukshen Kugel ❧ *(Ashkenazic Sweet Noodle Pudding)*

8 TO 10 SERVINGS

The northern Chinese were already eating boiled strips of wheat dough called *mein* by the second century BCE. Noodles spread westward to Persia by at least the seventh century, as demonstrated by the Babylonian Talmud's mention (in Berachot 37b) of *rihata* (from the Farsi *itriyah*), a dish of boiled dough. The Arabs introduced *macaron* to Spain by the tenth century, and it quickly found a prominent place in the Sephardic kitchen. The first record of pasta (originally the name of a barley gruel sprinkled with salt, derived from the Greek *pastos,* meaning "sprinkled") in Italy appeared in a cookbook about 1260, including recipes for vermicelli (literally "little worms") and *tortelli* (filled pasta). Pasta was certainly eaten in Italy well before Marco Polo, who is erroneously credited with bringing the dish back to Venice from China in 1295. It is uncertain, however, whether pasta developed independently in the West or reached Europe by way of Persia.

The first mention of boiled doughs in a European Jewish source appeared in the writings of the Italian rabbi Kalonymous ben Kalonymous (1286–1328), who included macaroni and *tortelli* in a list of dishes served at a Purim feast. (His recommended desserts included tarts, gingerbread, and pancakes.) Considering the frequent interaction between the Jewish communities of Italy and Franco-Germany, pasta must have reached the Rhineland by at least the thirteenth century. Earlier Franco-German dough dishes, such as *vermesel* (fritters) and *krepish* (meat-filled dough), were fried. By the 1400s, chicken soup with noodles was the standard first course for Friday dinner.

It is uncertain whether eastern Europeans learned of pasta from the Tartars (Mongolian tribes who overran the area beginning in 1240 with the sacking of Kiev) or the Italians. Whatever the case, the earliest forms of eastern European pasta were loose doughs similar to the German *spaetzle,* Hungarian *galuska,* and Ashkenazic *einlauf* and grated dough pellets such as the Hungarian *tarhonya* and the Ashkenazic farfel. By the end of the fifteenth century, flat egg noodles (a word derived from the German *nudel,* an enriched grain mixture that was shaped into long rolls and force-fed to geese) were a mainstay of eastern Europe. Hungarians soon devised simple desserts of sweetened noodles tossed with butter, sugar, and poppy seeds or chopped walnuts.

By the time noodles became commonplace in Europe, *frimsel* supplanted the antiquated *vermesel* as the western Yiddish word, as did *lukshen* in eastern Europe. The Yiddish *lukshen* and the Slavic *lokshyna* derived from a Persian noodle dish called *lakshah,* from *kashk,* a Persian term for "cracked barley and wheat" that also gave rise to such well-known dishes as kasha and *kishke.*

300

By 1500, kugels made from farfel had become commonplace in Poland. Eventually the more versatile noodle replaced the earlier form of pasta. Today there are nearly as many variations of noodle kugel as there are cooks: savory or sweet, dairy or pareve, plain or fancy. Dairy kugels are traditional fare for Shavuot and Hanukkah. Noodle kugels are common at many holiday meals and life-cycle events. This recipe can be halved and baked in an 8-inch square pan.

1 pound fine or medium noodles, cooked and drained

1/2 cup unsalted butter or margarine

4 to 6 large eggs, lightly beaten

1/2 to 3/4 cup granulated sugar, brown sugar, or honey

1 teaspoon vanilla extract, or 3 tablespoons lemon juice

About 1 teaspoon salt

1 cup dried fruit (raisins, chopped dried apricots, or chopped pitted prunes), or 2 cups fresh fruit (pitted sweet cherries, coarsely chopped apples, coarsely chopped pears, or any combination) (optional)

3/4 cup sliced almonds or coarsely chopped walnuts (optional)

Topping (optional):

1 cup plain bread crumbs, or 1/2 cup chopped almonds or walnuts

1/4 cup unsalted butter or margarine, melted

1 teaspoon ground cinnamon

1 to 3 teaspoons brown or granulated sugar

1. Preheat the oven to 350 degrees. Grease a 13-by-9-inch baking pan.
2. Put the hot noodles in a large bowl, add the butter, and toss until melted. Add the eggs, sugar, vanilla, salt, and if desired, the fruit and/or nuts. Pour into the prepared pan.
3. To make the topping if using: Combine all the topping ingredients and sprinkle over the kugel.
4. Bake until golden brown, about 1 hour. Serve warm or at room temperature. The kugel freezes well.

VARIATION

Lukshen un Kaese Kugel (Ashkenazic Baked Noodle-Cheese Pudding): Add 2 cups (1 pound) small-curd cottage cheese, farmer's cheese, or pot cheese and 2 cups sour cream (or 1 cup sour cream and 1 cup cream cheese).

Stiriai Metelt ❧ *(Hungarian Noodle Pudding)*

6 TO 8 SERVINGS

Hungarians enriched noodle kugels with the addition of layers of jam or other flavorings. There are even more elaborate versions with several different layers, including Ashkenazic Poppy Seed Filling (page 73) and Prune Levkar or Apricot Lekvar (page 75).

---

4 large eggs, lightly beaten

1 cup sour cream, or 1 cup milk blended with 4 ounces softened cream cheese

1/2 to 3/4 cup granulated sugar, brown sugar, or honey

1/2 cup (1 stick) unsalted butter or margarine, melted

1 teaspoon vanilla extract

About 1 teaspoon salt

1 pound fine or medium noodles, cooked and drained

3/4 cup apricot jam, melted

1/4 teaspoon ground cinnamon

---

1. Preheat the oven to 350 degrees (325 degrees if using a glass pan). Grease a 13-by-9-inch baking pan.
2. Beat together the eggs, sour cream, sugar, butter, vanilla, and salt until light and smooth. Stir in the noodles.
3. Spoon half of the noodle mixture into the prepared pan, spread with the jam, then top with the remaining noodle mixture. Sprinkle with the cinnamon.
4. Bake until golden brown, about 1 hour. Serve warm or at room temperature

Riz ib Assal ❧ *(Syrian Baked Rice Pudding with Honey)*

Middle Easterners make many types of rice pudding; this version is nondairy. During the lengthy cooking time, the rice grains break down, resulting in a smooth texture. Rice puddings flavored with honey and rose water are traditional on Shavuot.

6 cups water	*1 teaspoon rose water, orange blossom*
1/2 teaspoon salt	*water, or vanilla extract*
1 cup medium- or long-grain rice	*1/2 cup cornstarch dissolved in 1 cup*
1 cup (12 ounces) honey	*water*

1. Preheat the oven to 350 degrees. Grease a 2-quart casserole or ring mold or 6 shallow 1-cup dishes.
2. Bring the water and salt to a boil in a large ovenproof saucepan over medium heat. Add the rice, stir briefly to prevent sticking, and cook for 15 minutes.
3. Place the pan in the oven and bake until the water reaches the level of the rice, about 30 minutes.
4. Stir in the honey and bake 1 additional hour.
5. Add the rose water to the cornstarch mixture, then stir into the rice. Bake, stirring occasionally and adding more water if the pudding threatens to burn, until the mixture has a paste-like consistency, about 30 minutes.
6. Pour into the prepared casserole and let stand until set. Run a sharp knife around the edge of the pudding and invert onto a serving platter. Serve warm, at room temperature, or chilled. If desired, garnish with fresh berries.

VARIATIONS

Reduce the honey to 1/2 cup and add 1 cup chopped pitted dates with the honey.

Dairy Baked Rice Pudding: Reduce the water to 4 cups and add 2 cups milk with the honey.

Riz au Pommes ❧ *(Alsatian Baked Rice and Apple Pudding)*

6 TO 8 SERVINGS

This is an elaborate version of an old favorite.

1/4 cup finely ground blanched almonds

Pudding:
1 cup medium- or long-grain rice
6 cups hot milk
1/2 teaspoon salt
1/2 cup sugar
2 tablespoons unsalted butter
2 teaspoons vanilla extract

Filling:
3 to 4 cups applesauce

Custard:
1 1/2 cups heavy cream or half-and-half
1/4 cup sugar
2 large egg yolks, lightly beaten
1 large egg, lightly beaten
1 teaspoon vanilla extract

Meringue Topping:
2 large egg whites
Pinch of salt
1/4 cup sugar
Confectioners' sugar for sprinkling

---

1. Preheat the oven to 350 degrees (325 degrees if using a glass pan). Grease a 9-inch square baking pan and sprinkle with the almonds.
2. To make the pudding: Place the rice, hot milk, and salt in the top of a double boiler over boiling water and cook, stirring occasionally, until the rice is very tender and the mixture is thickened, about 1 hour. (The rice can be cooked more quickly by putting it in a heavy-bottomed saucepan over direct heat, but stir frequently to prevent burning.) Add the sugar and stir until dissolved. Remove from the heat and stir in the butter and vanilla.
3. Spoon one-third of the rice pudding into the prepared baking dish and cover with 1 1/2 to 2 cups applesauce. Top with half of the remaining rice pudding, then another 1 1/2 to 2 cups applesauce. Cover with the remaining pudding.
4. To make the custard: Combine the cream, sugar, egg yolks, egg, and vanilla. Pour over the pudding and poke with the handle of a wooden spoon in several places to let the custard sink in.
5. Bake until nearly set, about 30 minutes.

6. To make the meringue: Beat the egg whites on low speed until foamy, about 30 seconds. Add the salt, increase the speed to medium-high, and beat until soft peaks form, 1 to 2 minutes. Gradually add the sugar and beat until stiff and glossy, 5 to 8 minutes.

7. Spread the meringue over the pudding and lightly sprinkle with confectioners' sugar. Bake until lightly browned, about 15 minutes. Serve warm or at room temperature.

RICE

 Fields in China and India have produced rice for more than 5,000 years, making it the long-time staple of more than half of the human race's diet. The Persians brought rice westward, introducing *orez* (rice) to Israel during the Second Temple period. Tradition considered its whiteness a symbol of purity. By Roman times, Judean rice had become an important export, of which the Talmud boasts, "There is none like it outside Israel." Suggestions for the blessing over this grain included Simeon ha-Chasid's proposal, ". . . who has created delicacies to delight the soul of every living being."

Although members of Alexander the Great's Indian campaign made note of rice, it did not reach Europe until the Arab invasions at the beginning of the ninth century. Most Westerners treated it with indifference. Only in Italy, Spain, and the Balkans did rice become an important part of the European cuisine.

The more than 7,000 varieties of rice are defined by four basic characteristics: size (long, medium, and short), texture, color, and aroma. Each size category contains varying amounts of two primary starches: amylose and amylopectin. Amylose does not gelatinize during cooking, so the larger the proportion, the drier the kernels. In the reverse, amylopectin does gelatinize, so the larger the proportion, the stickier the kernels. Medium-grain rice, which has a larger amount of amylopectin starch than long-grain, produces a stickier, creamier pudding. Too much amylopectin, however, as in short-grain varieties, results in a gritty texture in puddings. The more readily available long-grain rice makes a suitable substitute for medium-grain.

SHAVUOT

Shavuot (Hebrew for "weeks") is a two-day Pilgrim Festival (one day in Israel) commemorating the giving of the Torah at Mount Sinai seven weeks after the Israelites departed Egypt. Milk and honey are the preeminent foods of Shavuot. The Torah is compared to milk and honey (Song of Songs 4:11), and the Bible refers to Israel as a "land flowing with milk and honey" (Exodus 3:8). In addition, tradition recounts that, after receiving the Torah and the laws of *kashrut,* the Jews could no longer eat the meat foods they had prepared beforehand or use any of their cooking utensils, which were now unkosher. Therefore they ate dairy dishes on the first Shavuot. Shavuot also corresponds to the time of the year when young ruminants are being weaned, an abundance of milk making it an obvious choice for the holiday. In addition, dairy products and other white foods such as rice are considered symbols of purity.

Middle Eastern Jews decorate their synagogues on Shavuot with branches and rose petals in recognition of the legend that plants flourished on Mount Sinai during the giving of the Torah; hence the name "Festival of Roses." Accordingly, Middle Eastern Shavuot fare is frequently flavored with rose water, and rose petal preserves are served with the meal.

Sephardic Shavuot desserts include cheese-filled phyllo pastries, *atayef* (cheese-filled pancakes), cheese-filled *kadayif,* rice puddings, and *biscochos Har Sinai* (mounded cookies representing Mount Sinai). Ashkenazic Shavuot treats include cheese blintzes, noodle kugel, rice kugel, cheese knishes, cheese or fruit *kreplach* (filled pasta), cheese *pirogen,* cheese or apple strudel, *schnecken* (yeast pastries), *rugelach* (cream cheese cookies), *kuchen* (coffee cakes), cheese *fluden* (layered pastry), and cheesecake.

Apam ❧ *(Calcutta Coconut Bread Pudding)*

The English introduced European foods, including bread puddings, to India during their control of the subcontinent. The substitution of coconut for milk makes this version perfect for kosher tables.

4 cups coconut milk (page 312), or	1 teaspoon vanilla extract
8 ounces creamed coconut (see Note)	1 pound stale challah or hearty white
dissolved in 4 cups water	bread, crusts removed, cut into 1-inch
3/4 to 1 cup sugar	cubes (about 8 cups)
2 large eggs, slightly beaten	1/4 cup raisins
2 large egg yolks, slightly beaten	1/4 cup slivered blanched almonds

1. Preheat the oven to 325 degrees. Grease a 13-by-9-inch baking pan.
2. Stir the coconut milk and sugar over medium heat until the sugar dissolves. Remove from the heat and let cool slightly, then blend in the eggs, egg yolks, and vanilla.
3. Scatter the bread, raisins, and almonds in the prepared pan. Slowly pour the coconut mixture on top and let stand for 15 minutes.
4. Bake, uncovered, until set and browned, about 1 hour. Serve warm, at room temperature, or chilled.

VARIATION

Substitute 4 cups half-and-half (or 2 cups milk and 2 cups heavy cream) for the coconut milk.

NOTE: ❧ Creamed coconut, available in hard 7-ounce blocks, needs to be dissolved in hot water.

Brot Kugel ❧ *(Ashkenazic Bread Pudding)*

6 TO 8 SERVINGS

This simple dish, which dates back to medieval Alsace, is a transition between the even more ancient *kutach* (Babylonian bread pudding) and the relatively more recent German noodle kugels. Like many other early Jewish puddings, it was customarily baked overnight in the center of a *cholent* (Sabbath stew) at low heat and served for Sabbath lunch. Eventually it was cooked outside the stew and the cooking time shortened. At times, dairy products were reintroduced, the combination of bread and custard an ingenious way to use up leftovers. Bread puddings using leftover challah were particularly popular at a *melaveh malkah* at the end of the Sabbath.

In modern restaurants, various additions and accompanying sauces turn this old-fashioned dessert into a chic treat. This nondairy Ashkenazic version possesses a different texture from the custard types. An egg bread gives the best flavor, but you can substitute a hearty white loaf. When the bread is several days old, it has a bit of a chewy texture after baking.

1 pound stale challah, crusts removed, cut into 1/2-inch-thick slices (about 12 slices)	*1/2 cup softened margarine or* schmaltz *(rendered chicken fat)*
About 4 cups water or chicken broth for soaking	*1/2 to 1 cup granulated or brown sugar*
2 large tart apples or pears or any combination, peeled, cored, and chopped (about 2 cups)	*2 tablespoons water*
	2 tablespoons fresh lemon juice
	1 teaspoon grated lemon zest
	1 teaspoon ground cinnamon
1/3 cup raisins (optional)	*About 1/2 teaspoon salt*
4 large eggs, lightly beaten	*1/8 teaspoon ground ginger or cloves*
	Pinch of grated nutmeg

1. Preheat the oven to 225 degrees. Grease a 13-by-9-inch baking pan or 10-inch tube or Bundt pan.
2. Soak the bread in the water to moisten. Drain and squeeze out most of the excess moisture. Crumble the bread and mix in the apples and raisins if using. Combine the remaining ingredients and stir into the bread mixture.
3. Pour into the prepared pan. Cover and bake for at least 3 hours or overnight. Serve warm.

VARIATIONS

Quick Bread Pudding: Bake the pudding in a 375-degree oven, uncovered, until golden brown, about 1 hour. If desired, separate the eggs, beat the egg whites until stiff, and fold into the batter.

Brot un Flohmen Kugel (Alsatian Bread and Prune Pudding): Alternate layers of the bread mixture with stewed prunes. If desired, brush the kugel occasionally with prune juice.

COCONUT

 The coconut, which may have originated in Malaysia, was widely used in India and the Middle East by the sixth century CE. Portuguese traders introduced the nut to Europe in 1674, and the Spanish named it after a popular clown of the time, Coco. Perhaps the three "eyes" reminded them of a clown's face.

Choose medium-sized coconuts that have a sloshing sound of liquid when shaken. Avoid those with cracks or any sign of mold or deterioration around the eyes. If the juice inside tastes sour or smells soapy, discard the coconut. Refrigerating whole coconuts facilitates mold. Store in a cool, dry place (around 55 degrees) for up to 2 weeks, but preferably use within a few days (since you don't know how long it's been in the store). Shelled coconut flesh should be used within twelve hours.

To open a coconut, use an ice pick to poke holes through two of the "eyes." Place over a container and drain the liquid. Hit the shell with a hammer at the points where the thin ridges cross until it splits. Crack into several smaller pieces. Use a dull knife to separate the flesh and shell. Southeast Asians have a special grater to scrape the flesh from the shell, which produces a fluffier, moister product. If you don't have such a tool, use a paring knife or vegetable peeler to pare off the brown skin, then run chunks of coconut over the small holes of a hand grater. Or use a food processor fitted with a steel blade: cut the coconut meat into $1/2$-inch pieces and, with the machine running, drop through the feed tube and process, stopping occasionally to scrape down the sides. One medium coconut weighing about $1^1/2$ pounds yields about 3 cups grated coconut.

CALCUTTA CUISINE

 Jewish traders visited the province of Bengal in northeast India for centuries, but it was only after Calcutta became the British capital of India in 1772 and emerged as an important commercial center that the first permanent Jewish settlement was established. Merchants were attracted by the economic potential of this alien location, and within a short time the city boasted a large and vibrant Jewish community, maintaining synagogues, schools, hospitals, and other communal and charitable institutions. Since a large percentage of this growing population came from Iraq, the Jews of Calcutta became known as Baghdadis. At its height in the early twentieth century, the Jewish community of Calcutta numbered about 6,000. Today only about forty Jewish families remain in this city on the Hooghly River, a tributary of the Ganges.

Partly because of the more evolved Sephardic-Arabic cuisine of the Baghdadis and partly because of their rather late arrival in the country, the cuisine of Calcutta's Jews evidences less Indian influence than that of other Indian Jewish communities. Although the Baghdadis continued to prepare a great deal of Middle Eastern fare, they eventually added local dishes to their repertoire and adapted their traditional foods to the local ingredients and spices. Characteristic of this synthesis is the Baghdadis' Sabbath bread, a Middle Eastern flat bread sprinkled with *kala jeera/kelonji* (nigella, a seed mistakenly called black onion seed). Bengali desserts, most notably milk-based sweets, are famous throughout India.

Apam ❧ *(Bombay Semolina and Coconut Pudding)*

10 TO 12 SERVINGS

The Bene Israel of Bombay commonly serve this moist treat on the Sabbath. *Apam* is similar to an ancient Teutonic semolina pudding called *greissflammery,* but the flavors of coconut and cardamom mark its Indian heritage.

5 cups water	1 teaspoon vanilla extract
4 cups coconut milk (see page 312)	1/2 teaspoon salt
3 1/3 cups (about 17 1/2 ounces) coarse semolina	1/4 cup raisins (optional)
	1/4 cup slivered blanched almonds
1 cup jaggery (see Note) or brown sugar	(optional)
3 to 4 teaspoons ground cardamom	

1. Preheat the oven to 350 degrees. Grease a 12-inch round baking pan or casserole or two 9-inch pie plates.
2. Bring the water and coconut milk to a boil. Gradually stir in the semolina and cook, stirring frequently, until thickened, about 10 minutes. Stir in the sugar. Remove from the heat and add the cardamom, vanilla, salt, and raisins if using.
3. Pour into the prepared pan. If desired, sprinkle with the almonds. Bake until a tester inserted in the center comes out clean, about 30 minutes. Cut into diamond shapes.

VARIATIONS

Substitute 14 ounces creamed coconut (see Note, page 307) for the coconut milk, increase the water to 8 cups, and simmer until the coconut cream dissolves.

Passover Apam: Substitute 4 cups matza meal for the semolina, but do not cook after stirring it into the coconut milk. Remove from the heat and beat in 6 large eggs, then proceed as above.

NOTE: ❧ Jaggery, called *gur* in Hindi and *piloncillo* in Central America, is brownish raw sugar crystals made by extracting the liquid from sucrose-rich plants.

MILKING THE COCONUT

 Coconut water is the liquid found inside fresh coconuts. More important to cooking is coconut milk, a thicker liquid made by steeping grated coconut flesh in water. When the mixture is left standing in the refrigerator, a thick, sweet coconut cream (with a strong coconut flavor) separates and rises to the top. The thinner liquid left on the bottom is coconut milk. Coconut cream and milk can be substituted for dairy cream and milk in many recipes. If fresh coconuts are unavailable, substitute unsweetened desiccated coconut. Canned coconut milk (most contain thickeners, preservatives, and whitening agents) is usually thicker than fresh coconut milk. Do not confuse it with canned sweetened coconut cream (used in cocktails), a very thick, sugary liquid.

COCONUT MILK

ABOUT 2 CUPS

The delicate flavor of coconut milk deteriorates as it ages, so it's best when fresh.

2 cups water

2 cups grated fresh or unsweetened desiccated coconut

Bring the water to a low boil. Stir in the coconut, remove from the heat, and let cool to room temperature, stirring occasionally, about 2 hours. Puree in a food processor or blender. Strain through a fine cheesecloth. Store in the refrigerator.

Pyota ❧ *(Greek Baked Semolina Pudding)*

This pudding is a popular Purim dish and is also served for **shalosh seudot** ("third meal" of the Sabbath) or a **melava malcha** (post-Sabbath meal). Double the recipe and bake in a 13-by-9-inch baking pan.

$^2/_3$ *cup (4 ounces) fine semolina (not semolina flour)*	$^1/_2$ *cup sugar*
$2^1/_2$ *cups milk*	$^1/_3$ *cup (4 ounces) honey*
$1^1/_2$ *cups water*	$^1/_2$ *teaspoon vanilla extract*
2 tablespoons unsalted butter	$^3/_4$ *to 1 cup coarsely chopped almonds or walnuts (optional)*
5 large eggs	$^1/_2$ *teaspoon ground cinnamon*

1. Place the semolina in a medium saucepan and gradually stir in the milk and water. Bring to a boil, reduce the heat to medium-low, and cook, stirring constantly, until thickened, about 5 minutes. Stir in the butter. Let cool.
2. Preheat the oven to 350 degrees (325 degrees if using a glass pan). Grease a 9- or 10-inch square baking pan.
3. Beat the eggs, sugar, and honey until thick and creamy, about 5 minutes. Blend in the semolina mixture and vanilla. If desired, add the nuts. Pour into the prepared pan and sprinkle with the cinnamon.
4. Bake until set, about 55 minutes. Let cool, then refrigerate for several hours. Serve chilled or at room temperature, accompanied with fresh fruit if desired.

Palacsinta Felfujt ❧ *(Hungarian Blintz Loaf)*

6 TO 8 SERVINGS

Originally this dish consisted of *topfenpalatschinken* (Hungarian cheese crepes) baked in a rich custard. This variation skips the time-consuming process of making blintzes. Double the recipe and bake in a 13-by-9-inch baking pan.

Batter:

1/2 cup all-purpose flour

3 large eggs

3/4 cup sour cream

1/4 cup orange juice

1/4 cup (1/2 stick) unsalted butter or
    margarine, softened

3 tablespoons sugar

1 teaspoon vanilla extract

1 teaspoon double-acting baking powder

1/4 teaspoon salt

Filling:

1 cup (8 ounces) small-curd cottage or
    ricotta cheese

4 ounces cream cheese, softened

1 large egg yolk

2 tablespoons sugar

1/2 teaspoon vanilla extract

1/2 teaspoon fresh lemon juice or ground
    cinnamon (optional)

---

1. Preheat the oven to 350 degrees (325 degrees if using a glass pan). Grease a 9-inch square baking pan.
2. To make the batter: In a blender, food processor, or large bowl, beat together all the batter ingredients until smooth.
3. To make the filling: Combine all the filling ingredients.
4. Pour half of the batter into the prepared pan, drop the filling by heaping tablespoonfuls over the batter, then carefully top with the remaining batter (the layers will mix a bit). The loaf can be covered and refrigerated for up to 24 hours. Return to room temperature before baking.
5. Bake until puffed and lightly browned, 50 to 60 minutes. Serve warm, accompanied with a fruit sauce or fresh fruit if desired.

Budino di Ricotta ❧ *(Roman Cheese Pudding)*

6 TO 8 SERVINGS

Italian Jewish cuisine, some of which ranks among the most ancient in the world, more closely resembles that of Sephardim than the Jewish cooking found in the rest of Europe. This is due in part to its Mediterranean location, as well as to the arrival of a sizable contingent of Iberian exiles following the Expulsion in 1492. Nonetheless, from the ghettos of the Italian cities, especially Rome, came some of the most ancient and authentic of Jewish dishes. Since kosher dietary laws restricted the use of meat sauces and cheese, Italian Jewish dishes tended to be more delicate than those of their non-Jewish neighbors. Although in the twentieth century many Italkim became rather assimilated, most still maintained an abiding affection for the cuisine of their ancestors and zealously preserved it. The origins of this dish date back to the days of the Roman Empire.

1 pound (2 cups) ricotta cheese, at room temperature	*1 teaspoon ground cinnamon or vanilla extract*
3/4 to 1 cup sugar	*2 teaspoons grated orange or lemon zest, or 1 teaspoon each*
4 large eggs, separated	
2 tablespoons brandy, rum, or marsala	*Pinch of salt*
1 1/2 tablespoons all-purpose flour, potato starch, or cornstarch	*1/4 cup golden raisins or chopped candied citron (optional)*

1. Preheat the oven to 300 degrees. Grease a deep 1 1/2- to 2-quart casserole or eight 1-cup ramekins or custard cups.
2. In a food processor or blender, process the ricotta, sugar, egg yolks, brandy, flour, cinnamon, zest, and salt until smooth. If desired, stir in the raisins.
3. Beat the egg whites on low until foamy, about 30 seconds. Increase the speed to medium-high and beat until stiff but not dry. Fold into the cheese mixture.
4. Spoon into the prepared pan. Bake until a wooden tester inserted in the center comes out nearly clean, about 45 minutes for the 2-quart dish or about 30 minutes for the ramekins. Place on a rack and let cool in the pan for at least 15 minutes. Serve warm or at room temperature.

Stovetop Puddings
and Creamy Desserts

Sustain me with dainties . . .
—SONG OF SONGS 2:5

IN THE WARM MEDITERRANEAN CLIMATE, MILK, MOSTLY FROM SHEEP AND GOATS, WAS SELDOM FOUND IN COOKING. INSTEAD, DAIRY WAS PRIMARILY CONSUMED IN THE FERMENTED FORM OF CHEESE AND YOGURT. SIMILARLY, FEW EUROPEANS WOULD DRINK milk except fresh from the animal. Faux milk made from such items as almonds or melon seeds was more common in European dishes than animal milk. Then in the thirteenth century, as cattle raising exploded in much of northern Europe, milk increasingly gained a role in the diet. It was at this time that the Yiddish terms *milchig* (dairy) and *fleishig* (meat) first appeared, words unnecessary among contemporary Jews in the Islamic world, where dairy products were still rarely used in cooking.

During the Middle Ages, puddings began to evolve, including those made without stuffing into animal parts. One early form of medieval pudding was *frumenty* (from *frumentum*, a Latin word for grain), a savory saffron-laced mixture of hulled wheat berries boiled in almond milk and mixed with eggs. As modern cooking superseded that of the medieval kitchen, meat and suet were generally eliminated from most puddings, and semolina or flour was substituted for whole grain. It was the Germans who first began adding honey and sometimes cinnamon, nuts, and dried fruit to these mixtures.

In the seventeenth century, as sugar became more affordable, sweetened puddings proliferated. With the introduction of pasteurization in 1865, milk began to play an increasing role in the kitchen. New thickeners, including tapioca, cornstarch, and potato starch, came into greater use, and the texture of most puddings grew softer and smoother. Various flavorings were added, including the two most popular, chocolate and vanilla, both indigenous to South America. Thus, today pudding generally refers to a sweet, soft-textured, milk-based dessert.

Budino di Cioccolata ❧ *(Italian Chocolate Pudding)*

3 TO 5 SERVINGS; ABOUT 3 CUPS

Serve the pudding plain, spread it in a baked pie shell, spoon over cake slices, or use in parfaits. The addition of eggs is a recent innovation; they impart an added richness.

1/4 cup unsweetened cocoa powder, preferably alkalized (Dutch-processed)

1/3 cup sugar

2 tablespoons cornstarch

1/4 teaspoon ground cinnamon

Pinch of salt

2 to 3 teaspoons instant espresso powder (optional)

2 cups milk or half-and-half

3 large egg yolks, or 2 large eggs, lightly beaten (optional)

3 ounces bittersweet or semisweet chocolate, chopped

1 teaspoon vanilla extract

1 tablespoon chopped candied citron (see page 366) (optional)

1 tablespoon lightly toasted pine nuts (optional)

---

1. Combine the cocoa powder, sugar, cornstarch, cinnamon, salt, and espresso powder if using in a medium nonaluminum saucepan. Gradually stir in the milk. Stir over medium heat until bubbly, about 15 minutes.
2. If desired, gradually stir about 1 cup of the pudding into the egg yolks. Stir the yolk mixture into the saucepan, reduce the heat to low, and cook, stirring, for 2 minutes. Do not boil.
3. Remove from the heat, add the chocolate and vanilla, and stir until smooth. If desired, add the citron and/or pine nuts. Press a piece of plastic wrap or buttered waxed paper against the surface and refrigerate for at least 4 hours.

Masghati Kasehi ❧ *(Persian Cornstarch Pudding)*

6 TO 8 SERVINGS

There are many versions of starch puddings, made with and without milk, in the Middle East. This light pudding, called *al massia/almaziye* by Syrians and *muhalabeeya* by Egyptians, is sometimes served after Rosh Hashanah dinner.

1 cup cornstarch	1/2 cup (1 stick) unsalted butter or
6 cups water	margarine
2 cups sugar	1 to 4 tablespoons rose water
Pinch of salt	1 teaspoon ground cardamom
1/2 cup coarsely chopped blanched	
almonds, pistachios, or walnuts	

1. Dissolve the cornstarch in 2 cups water in a large saucepan. Add the remaining water and the sugar and salt. Bring to a boil, reduce the heat to low, and simmer, stirring constantly, until slightly thickened, about 15 minutes.
2. Stir in the nuts, butter, rose water, and cardamom and simmer until thickened, about 5 minutes. Spoon into serving dishes and chill.

VARIATION

Kheer (Indian Cornstarch Pudding): This is a traditional Rosh Hashanah dessert in Bombay. Substitute 6 cups coconut milk (see page 312) for the water and rose water.

Kissel ❧ *(Slavic Berry Pudding)*

The consistency of this pudding, called *rodgrod* ("red gruel") in Scandinavian countries, runs from that of a thick soup to a molded custard. This is a thicker version. A prune *kissel* is made during the fall and winter. The pudding is traditionally served with whipped cream and slivered almonds.

---

24 ounces (4 cups) fresh or 20 ounces
 frozen raspberries, strawberries,
 blueberries, or any combination
2 cups water, or 1 cup water and 1 cup
 dry red wine
About 1/2 cup sugar

1/8 teaspoon salt
1/4 cup potato starch or cornstarch
 dissolved in 1/2 cup cold water
1 to 2 tablespoons fresh lemon juice or
 berry liqueur

---

1. Puree and strain the berries. If using frozen berries, puree with the juice. There should be about 2 1/3 cups puree. Place over medium-high heat and bring to a boil. Add the water, sugar, and salt and stir until the sugar dissolves, about 3 minutes.
2. Reduce the heat to medium-low, stir in the starch mixture, and simmer, stirring frequently, until the pudding thickens and turns translucent, about 5 minutes. Stir in the lemon juice. Pour into 6 to 8 custard cups. Refrigerate until chilled, at least 2 hours.

VARIATION

For a thinner *kissel*: Increase the water to 4 1/2 cups (plus the 1/2 cup for dissolving the starch) and add the lemon juice with the sugar.

Halvah Gazar ❧ *(Indian Carrot Pudding)*

8 TO 10 SERVINGS

After the Persians introduced halvah to India, cooks there began creating a wide array of variations, such as this one made from carrots.

¹/₃ cup unsalted butter	*1¹/₂ cups heavy cream*
¹/₂ to 1 teaspoon ground cardamom	*1 cup sugar*
1¹/₂ pounds shredded carrots (about 4¹/₂ cups)	*¹/₄ cup golden raisins*
	¹/₄ cup chopped almonds, pecans, pistachios, or walnuts
2¹/₂ cups milk	

1. Melt the butter in a medium saucepan over medium-high heat. Stir in the cardamom. Add the carrots and sauté until softened, about 10 minutes.

2. Add the milk and cream, reduce the heat to medium, and cook, stirring frequently, until thickened, about 25 minutes.

3. Add the sugar, raisins, and nuts. Cook, stirring constantly, until reduced and very thick, 10 to 15 minutes. Serve warm or chilled.

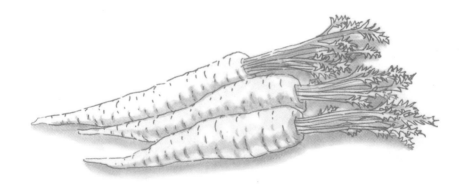

Shrikhand ❧ *(Indian Sweetened Yogurt Cheese)*

6 TO 8 SERVINGS

Yogurt cheese, called *labni* in the Middle East and *dehin* in India, is made by straining the whey from yogurt. This silky dish is prepared for special feasts in the Gujarati section of India. The whey is used to make *panir* (curd cheese) or to cook rice. *Shrikhand* is commonly served in small cups garnished with nuts and accompanied by slices of fresh mango and *poori* (balloon-like bread).

64 ounces (8 cups) plain whole-milk yogurt	1 to 2 cups confectioners' or granulated sugar
4 to 8 cardamom pods, or 1/2 teaspoon ground cardamom	1 to 2 tablespoons rose water (optional)
1/2 teaspoon saffron threads	1/2 cup slivered pistachios or almonds for garnish
1 tablespoon hot milk	

1. Line a colander or large strainer with a coffee filter or double layer of cheesecloth and set over a bowl. Pour in the yogurt, cover with plastic wrap, place in the refrigerator, and let drain until thick, at least 12 hours. The longer the yogurt drips, the thicker the cheese.
2. Open the cardamom pods, scrape out the seeds, discard the pods, and grind the seeds. Dissolve the saffron in the milk.
3. Stir the sugar, cardamom, saffron, and rose water if using into the yogurt cheese and beat until light and smooth. Refrigerate until chilled, at least 1 hour. Garnish each serving with a tablespoon of nuts.

VARIATION

Omit the cardamom, saffron, and rose water and add 1/2 cup chopped raspberries or strawberries.

Indian Coconut Agar-Agar

Alayer of the coconut cream rises to the top as this gel-like dessert sets.

---

^{1}/2 cup agar flakes, 2 tablespoons agar
  powder, or 4 large (0.25-ounce each)
  agar bars, broken into 1-inch pieces
4 cups water
3 cups coconut milk (page 312), or
  7 ounces creamed coconut dissolved
  in 3 cups water

1 cup sugar
About ^{1}/2 teaspoon rose water (optional)

---

1. If using agar bars, soak in the water for at least 1 hour.
2. Bring the agar and water to a boil. Reduce the heat to medium-low and simmer without stirring until the agar dissolves, 3 to 5 minutes for flakes or powder, 10 to 15 minutes for bars.
3. Add the coconut milk and sugar and stir over medium heat until the sugar dissolves. If desired, add the rose water.
4. Pour into a 13-by-9-inch baking pan or individual serving bowls. Let cool, then refrigerate, uncovered, until set, about 2 hours. Cut into diamonds or squares. Serve chilled.

VARIATIONS

Indian Almond Agar-Agar: Substitute 3 cups almond milk for the coconut milk. To make almond milk, pour 3 cups boiling water over 5 ounces ground almonds, cover, and let soak for at least 2 hours. In a blender, puree the almonds and soaking liquid until smooth. Strain through several layers of cheesecloth, squeezing out any liquid.

Indian Rose Water Agar-Agar: Omit the coconut milk and increase the water to 6 cups and the rose water to ^{1}/2 to 1 cup. If desired, add several drops of red food coloring.

Dairy Agar-Agar: Substitute 3 cups half-and-half for the coconut milk and, if desired, 1 tablespoon almond extract for the rose water.

AGAR-AGAR

 Agar-agar, also called *kanten,* is made from several varieties of seaweed. Agar replicates animal gelatin—1 bar agar equals 1^1/$_2$ tablespoons gelatin—with some additional benefits. Agar's setting properties require a smaller proportion to liquid than gelatin. Agar does not liquefy when combined with high-acid fruits. It sets at room temperature. In addition, agar contains a variety of vitamins, as well as fiber.

Available in health food stores, agar comes in bar, flake, and powdered forms. In recipes, these forms are interchangeable. Soak agar bars in cold water until soft, 30 to 60 minutes, break into small pieces, and squeeze out the excess liquid. Agar powder and flakes can be added directly to the liquid without softening. The amount of agar needed varies according to the type of liquid and other ingredients used. As a general rule of thumb, use 2 teaspoons (^{2}/$_3$ ounce) powder, 2 tablespoons flakes, or 1 large (0.25-ounce) bar for every 2 cups of liquid. The secret to ensuring that agar sets properly is to dissolve it completely by cooking in a hot liquid, but not to overcook it.

Leche Frita ❧ *(Sephardic Fried Custard)*

6 TO 8 SERVINGS

The constant stirring that is needed to distribute the heat evenly in a stovetop custard prevents the protein in the eggs from bonding together, so it never sets firmly. For this reason, a little starch is added to produce a custard that is sufficiently thickened to hold its shape. The deep-fried custard squares produce an intriguing contrast of cool, soft interior and warm, crunchy surface.

Custard:	Coating:
2¹/₂ cups milk	1 cup dry bread crumbs
1 (3-inch) cinnamon stick	¹/₄ cup sugar
²/₃ cup sugar	1¹/₂ teaspoons ground cinnamon
6 tablespoons cornstarch or potato starch	1 cup all-purpose flour
	2 large eggs, lightly beaten
¹/₂ teaspoon salt	
3 large eggs, lightly beaten	Vegetable oil for deep-frying
¹/₂ teaspoon vanilla extract	

1. To make the custard: Simmer the milk and cinnamon stick in a medium saucepan over medium-low heat for 15 minutes. Discard the cinnamon stick.

2. Combine the sugar, cornstarch, and salt. Blend into the eggs. In a slow, steady stream, beat in the hot milk. Return to the saucepan and cook over medium-low heat, stirring constantly, until thickened and bubbly, about 5 minutes. Remove from the heat and stir in the vanilla.

3. Pour into a greased 8-inch square baking pan, press a piece of plastic wrap against the surface, and refrigerate until firm, at least 2 hours or overnight. Cut into 2-inch squares.

4. To make the coating: Combine the bread crumbs, sugar, and cinnamon. Dredge the custard squares in the flour, dip in the eggs, then coat on all sides with the bread crumb mixture. Refrigerate, uncovered, for at least 30 minutes.

5. Heat at least 1¹/₂ inches of oil over medium-high heat to 375 degrees.

6. Fry the custard squares in batches, turning once, until golden brown on both sides, about 15 seconds per side. Transfer to a wire rack to drain. Serve warm. To keep warm, place on a wire rack in a 325-degree oven.

HINT: ❧ Egg yolks contain an enzyme (alpha amylase) that feeds on starches. If the yolks are cooked insufficiently to destroy the enzymes, they will consume the starch in the dish as it stands, resulting in a runny mess. If the eggs are cooked too long, however, they lose their thickening ability.

Leche Frita ❧ *(Italian Fried Semolina Pudding)*

ABOUT 24 SQUARES

Semolina gives this dish, whose name means "fried cream," a smooth and creamy texture similar to that of cheesecake. Sephardim prepare a version of this dish, serving it with *vijna* (cherry syrup) and sometimes a dollop of yogurt.

Pudding:	Coating:
4 cups milk	*2 large eggs, lightly beaten*
1 (3-inch) cinnamon stick	*About 2 cups dry bread crumbs or butter*
1 (3-inch) strip lemon zest	*cookie crumbs*
1 (3-inch) strip orange zest	
1 cup sugar	*About 1/4 cup vegetable oil for frying*
Pinch of salt	*Confectioners' sugar for dusting*
2 cups semolina flour, finely ground	*(optional)*
semolina, or farina	
2 large eggs, lightly beaten	
1 teaspoon vanilla extract	

1. To make the pudding: Bring the milk, cinnamon stick, and zest to a simmer over medium-low heat and simmer for 15 minutes. Discard the cinnamon stick and zest. Add the sugar and salt and stir until dissolved, about 3 minutes. Gradually stir in the semolina. Cook, stirring frequently, until thickened, about 10 minutes. Remove from the heat and stir in the eggs and vanilla.

2. Pour into a greased 12-by-8-inch or 13-by-9-inch baking pan, spreading about 1 inch thick. Cover and refrigerate until firm, about 6 hours. Cut into 2-inch squares or 1 1/2-inch diamonds.

3. To coat the pudding: Dip the semolina pieces into the eggs, letting the excess drip off, then coat on all sides with the bread crumbs.

4. Heat a thin layer of oil in a large skillet over medium-high heat.

5. Fry the semolina pieces in batches, turning, until golden brown on both sides, 2 to 3 minutes per side. Drain on paper towels. Serve warm or at room temperature. If desired, sprinkle with confectioners' sugar.

Zerde ❧ *(Azerbaijani Almond Pudding)*

6 TO 8 SERVINGS

The Farsi name of this dish, meaning "yellow," reflects both the bright color of the smooth, saffron-laced pudding and the Persian influence on Azerbaijani cooking.

1/4 teaspoon saffron threads, crushed in a mortar

1 tablespoon warm water

1 1/4 cups ground blanched almonds (about 4 3/4 ounces)

About 1/3 cup sugar

5 cups milk

1 tablespoon unsalted butter

1/4 cup fine semolina (not semolina flour)

2 teaspoons rose water

1/2 teaspoon ground cinnamon

1/4 cup slivered almonds or chopped pistachios (optional)

---

1. Dissolve the saffron in the water. Set aside.
2. Combine the almonds and sugar in a medium saucepan. Gradually stir in the milk. Bring to a boil over medium heat. Remove from the heat and let stand while preparing the semolina.
3. Melt the butter in another medium saucepan over medium heat. Add the semolina and stir until well coated, about 4 minutes. Gradually stir in the almond mixture. Cook, stirring constantly, until thickened, about 15 minutes.
4. Remove from the heat and stir in the saffron water, rose water, cinnamon, and slivered almonds if using. Divide among individual serving dishes and refrigerate until chilled, at least 2 hours.

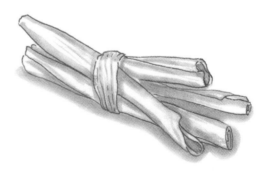

AZERBAIJAN

 Between the Caucasus Mountains and the Caspian Sea lies Persia's former northwestern province. Azerbaijan means the "Land of Flames," referring to its abundant gas and oil reserves, perhaps second only to those of Saudi Arabia. In the eleventh century, the area came under control of the Turks, whose language and customs eventually merged with the existing Persian elements to create a unique society. Following two nineteenth-century wars with Persia, Russia absorbed Azerbaijan into its empire, where it remained until achieving independence in 1991.

Jews have lived in Azerbaijan since shortly after the Persian conquest of Babylon. The medieval traveler Benjamin of Tudela noted a chain of hundreds of congregations in the region. For centuries, Jews lived in mountain towns, where they developed a distinct culture, until marauding bands in the eighteenth century drove them into the cities. The mountain Jews were also known as Tats, the name of their Persian-Hebrew dialect. In the nineteenth century, Ashkenazim arrived in Azerbaijan, supplementing the Jewish population. The elimination of Soviet control and the subsequent struggles following independence led to more than 27,650 Jews emigrating to Israel. About 20,000 Jews remain in Azerbaijan, residing primarily in the capital, Baku, and Kuba.

Azerbaijani cooking reflects strong Persian and Turkish influences, featuring syrup-drenched pastries and rose water–flavored puddings. As in other Muslim countries, alcohol is rare, and instead, the population favors Turkish coffee, tea drunk from tiny glasses, and icy fruit syrup–based drinks called *sharbat.*

Halvah Chosk ❧ *(Persian Flour Pudding)*

6 TO 8 SERVINGS

This traditional Persian Purim and Sabbath lunch treat, also called *halvah ard,* is a version made from flour and has the consistency of bread crumbs.

Syrup:

1 cup water

1½ cups sugar

1 cup (2 sticks) unsalted butter or margarine

2 cups all-purpose flour

¼ teaspoon saffron, or ⅛ teaspoon turmeric

1. To make the syrup: Stir the water and sugar in a medium saucepan over low heat until the sugar dissolves, about 5 minutes. Stop stirring, increase the heat to medium-high, and bring to a boil, about 5 minutes. Reduce the heat to very low, cover, and let stand while you prepare the flour.
2. Melt the butter in a medium saucepan over medium heat. Gradually stir in the flour and cook, stirring constantly, until golden brown, about 15 minutes. Stir in the saffron or turmeric.
3. Remove from the heat and gradually stir in the syrup. Serve warm or at room temperature.

VARIATION

Spiced Flour Halvah: Add ¼ to ½ teaspoon ground cardamom with the saffron. After adding all the syrup, stir in 2 teaspoons ground coriander and 2 tablespoons rose water.

Halvah di Gris ❧ *(Persian Semolina Pudding)*

Although Westerners are most familiar with halvah as a sweetened ground sesame confection, it actually encompasses a variety of sweetened cooked grain puddings popular throughout central Asia and the Middle East. Ironically, although halvah originated in the Middle East and Ashkenazim only recently became familiar with the sesame variation, the word entered the English language by way of Yiddish because the confection was common in twentieth-century Jewish delis.

This firm pudding, also called *halvah aurde sujee,* is made from semolina that is toasted in butter, then steamed to plump the grains. The pudding is popular throughout Central Asia and India, where it is eaten at most celebrations, particularly Purim and Hanukkah. Syrians call this dish *mamounie/ma'mounia,* after the tenth-century caliph Mamoun, and frequently serve it for breakfast or brunch.

Syrup:

3 cups water, or 1 1/2 cups water and
   1 1/2 cups milk

1 1/2 cups sugar

1/4 teaspoon grated nutmeg (optional)

1 1/2 cups (3 sticks) unsalted butter or
   margarine

1 1/2 cups fine or coarse semolina or
   farina

1 cup coarsely chopped blanched
   almonds, pistachios, walnuts, or any
   combination (optional)

1 teaspoon turmeric (optional)

1 teaspoon rose water, or 1 teaspoon
   ground cinnamon, or 1/2 teaspoon
   ground cardamom (optional)

---

1. To make the syrup: Stir the water, sugar, and nutmeg if using in a medium saucepan over low heat until the sugar dissolves, about 5 minutes. Stop stirring, increase the heat to medium-high, and bring to a boil, about 5 minutes. Reduce the heat to very low, cover, and let stand while you prepare the semolina.

2. Melt the butter in a medium saucepan over medium-high heat. Stir in the semolina and, if desired, the nuts and/or turmeric. (Turmeric gives the halvah a bright yellow color.) Reduce the heat to low and cook, stirring constantly, until golden brown, about 20 minutes. For a darker, more intensely flavored halvah, continue cooking until the grains are dark brown, but do not burn.

3. Return the syrup to a boil, then gradually stir into the semolina. Be careful—it spatters. Cook over low heat, stirring constantly, until the liquid evaporates and the mixture comes away easily from the sides of the pan, about 5 minutes. If desired, stir in the rose water.

4. Remove from the heat, cover with a damp cloth, then the pan lid, and let stand for at least 30 minutes. Serve warm or at room temperature.

VARIATION

Indian Raisin-Coconut Semolina Halvah: Add 3 tablespoons raisins, 3 tablespoons grated fresh or unsweetened desiccated coconut, and 1 teaspoon grated orange zest to the syrup.

PERSIA (IRAN)

 The Jewish community of Persia dates back to Cyrus the Great's conquest of Babylon in 538 BCE. Soon thereafter, in Persia's capital of Shushan, the events of the Purim story occurred. Despite long periods of oppression by Zoroastrians and later Shi'ite Muslims, Jews remained in Persia for more than 2,500 years. Beginning in 1502, hostilities between the Shi'ite Persians and Sunnite Ottomans ended the authority of Baghdad's religious leaders over Persian Jewry, leading to its development as a separate cultural community. Although Iran is sometimes considered to be Sephardic, it possesses distinctive customs and its kitchens contain none of the Iberian dishes.

Historically, Jews were scattered throughout Persia, with the largest centers in Teheran and Isfahan. In 1948, of the nearly 95,000 Jews living in Iran, more than 28,000 emigrated to Israel. The revolution of 1979 and the subsequent persecution swelled that number. By 1990, more than 55,000 more fled, primarily to the United States and Israel. Today only about 20,000 of this ancient community remain.

Persia's centuries of control over western and Central Asia, as well as its profound influence on such areas as Greece, Rome, and India, made Persian cuisine one of the world's most influential. The ancient Persians loved elaborate sweets, often to the point of excess. With the recent trend toward lighter desserts such as fresh fruit or fruit compote, the more extravagant fare is generally reserved for special occasions. Persian sweets, called *shirini,* include baklava, *nane shirini* (butter cookies), *nane berenji* (rice flour cookies), *nane nokhochi* (chickpea flour cookies), *toot* (marzipan), halvah (grain confections), *shir berenj* (rice pudding), and *sharbat* (fruit syrup).

Seffa ❧ *(Maghrebi Sweet Couscous)*

Residents of the Maghreb use semolina to make tiny pasta pellets called *kesksu* in Arabic. Unlike pasta made with other types of wheat flour, pasta made from semolina does not become mushy during cooking. The old-fashioned way of making these pellets is to mix semolina flour with water, roll the dough into tiny balls, sift it over a medium-meshed wire sieve to remove any excess flour, then steam the final product over boiling water or a stew. Instant couscous, available at most supermarkets, is prepared by adding boiling water. Although not as fluffy as the classic type, it is more than acceptable for *seffa* and easy to prepare. Israelis make a larger form of couscous, which is lightly toasted; do not substitute for the regular type.

In the Maghreb, couscous is both everyday fare—served in most households, both rich and poor, several times a week—and a food for special occasions. It is most commonly used as the base for flavorful meat, poultry, fish, or vegetable stews. For special occasions, however, it is sweetened and topped with dried fruits and nuts. *Seffa* is also made by mounding couscous on a platter and sprinkling sugar on top instead of stirring it in. *Seffa* with dried fruits is a traditional Moroccan Hanukkah dish. For Rosh Hashanah, it is sprinkled with pomegranate seeds or small grapes. On Tu b'Shevat and other special occasions, it is garnished with *datils rellenos* (stuffed dates, page 350) and dried fruit. Moroccans prefer desserts rich and sugary, and their *seffa* is generally sweeter than Tunisian versions.

---

4 cups boiling water

1 pound (2²/₃ cups) instant couscous

Pinch of salt

About ¹/₂ cup sugar

¹/₂ to 1 teaspoon ground cinnamon, or
 1 tablespoon grated orange zest

¹/₄ cup (¹/₂ stick) melted unsalted butter
 or olive oil

About 1¹/₂ cups milk or almond milk
 (see Variations, page 323), or ³/₄ cup
 orange juice, or ³/₄ cup water and
 1 to 4 tablespoons orange blossom
 water

Additional ground cinnamon for garnish

---

1. Pour the boiling water over the couscous and salt, cover, and let stand for 10 minutes. (If using regular couscous, after soaking, toss with 1 tablespoon vegetable oil, place in a colander, and steam over boiling water, stirring occasionally, for about 20 minutes.) Stir to fluff.

2. Stir the sugar and cinnamon into the butter. Pour over the couscous and toss to coat. Gradually add enough milk to moisten the couscous.

3. Mound the couscous on a large platter and sprinkle with the additional cinnamon. Or for individual servings, pack into custard cups and invert onto serving plates.

VARIATIONS

Couscous Hillo (Moroccan Fruited Couscous): Add $^3/_4$ cup raisins, $^3/_4$ cup chopped pitted dates, $^3/_4$ cup chopped dried apricots, $^3/_4$ cup chopped blanched almonds, and $^3/_4$ cup chopped walnuts or $^1/_3$ cup pine nuts.

Couscous de Cérémonie: Mounded couscous is featured on special occasions, such as weddings and bar mitzvahs. Pack half of the couscous mixture into a large bowl, sprinkle with $^2/_3$ cup ground toasted blanched almonds, top with the remaining couscous, invert onto a serving platter, and sprinkle with ground cinnamon. Garnish with *datils rellenos* (stuffed dates, page 350).

Mesfouf ❧ *(Tunisian Couscous with Pudding)*

6 TO 8 SERVINGS

3 *large egg yolks*	3 *cups milk*
$^3/_4$ *cup sugar*	1 *teaspoon vanilla extract, or*
3 *tablespoons cornstarch*	1$^1/_2$ *teaspoons rose water*
Pinch of salt	4 *cups (*$^1/_2$ *recipe) seffa (page 332)*

1. Beat the egg yolks until light. Gradually add the sugar and beat until thick and creamy. Beat in the cornstarch and salt until smooth.

2. Heat the milk in a medium saucepan. Gradually beat into the egg yolk mixture. Return to the saucepan and cook over medium heat, stirring constantly, until thick and bubbly. Remove from the heat and stir in the vanilla. Press a piece of plastic wrap or buttered waxed paper against the surface and let cool.

3. Spread half of the pudding in the bottom of a 12-inch round or 9-inch square casserole. Cover with 2 cups *seffa*. Spread with the remaining pudding and top with the remaining *seffa*. Refrigerate until chilled.

THE MAGHREB: MOROCCO, ALGERIA, AND TUNISIA

 According to legend, Jews first reached the Maghreb (Arabic for "setting sun," referring to northwestern Africa) during the reign of King Solomon by way of Israel's Phoenician neighbors. (Carthage, a Phoenician colony, was in Tunisia.) The first large Jewish presence in the area appeared after the destruction of the Second Temple. The size of the community was bolstered in 581 CE with the arrival of Spanish Jews fleeing the Visigoth persecution. The Maghreb received another wave of Jewish immigration with the arrival of refugees from Spain in 1492 and Portugal in 1496. In many cities, the Sephardim soon ended up dominating the leadership, culture, and economy.

In 1948, about 300,000 Jews lived in Morocco, and about 130,000 each resided in Algeria and Tunisia. Increasing anti-Jewish sentiment and acts prompted massive immigration, primarily to Israel and France. Almost all Jewish institutions and organizations closed. Today less than 30,000 members of the Jewish community remain in Morocco, 2,000 in Tunisia, and a handful in Algeria.

Over the centuries, a succession of influences—Berber, Phoenician, Roman, Arabic, Moorish, Sephardic, Turkish, and, most recently, French—affected the cooking of the region. To this day, various parts of Morocco have very different styles of cooking: The cuisine of Fez has a strong Arabic flavor, Marrakesh reflects a pronounced Berber heritage, and Tetuan has a strong Spanish influence. Although Maghrebi cooking differs greatly from characteristic Middle Eastern fare, the desserts generally reflect an eastern origin, including nut-filled cookies and syrup-soaked phyllo pastries. Unique to the area, however, are the various forms of sweetened couscous.

Malida ❧ *(Bombay Sweet Rice)*

The *malida* (sweet foods) ceremony accompanies most Bene Israel life-cycle events. After making a blessing to God and giving thanks to the prophet Elijah, rice, dried fruits, and nuts are arranged on a plate, symbolizing the meal offering of the Temple. Afterward, the ingredients, sometimes mixed, are passed for all of the participants to enjoy. The Bene Israel generally like *malida* very sweet, so adjust the amount of sugar according to your preference.

3¹/₃ cups (about 1¹/₄ pounds) medium flaked rice (poha)

1 medium coconut, grated (about 3 cups)

1 cup (6 ounces) jaggery (see Note, page 311), or 2 to 4 cups confectioners' sugar

12 to 16 cardamom pods, crushed, or 1 teaspoon ground cardamom

1 cup raisins

1 cup almonds

1 cup pistachios

1. Soak the rice flakes in cold water to cover for 15 minutes. Drain.
2. Combine the coconut, sugar to taste, and cardamom. Stir in the rice. Add the raisins and nuts.

NOTE: ❧ *Poha/pawa* (flaked rice, also called pounded or pressed rice) consists of husked rice kernels that are cooked, then flattened by rollers until very thin. The resulting grayish white flakes are available in medium and fine. The latter tend to disintegrate in dishes.

Kheer ❧ *(Indian Rice Pudding)*

This cardamom-flavored rice pudding is a favorite treat among the Bene Israel of Bombay. Neither eggs nor additional starch is added. Instead, the pudding is thickened by cooking the rice until it breaks down to a creamy consistency. Basmati (literally "queen of fragrance") is an aromatic and flavorful Asian-grown long-grain variety with a nutty aroma and flavor.

3 *quarts milk*	$^1/_2$ *cup raisins (optional)*
$^1/_2$ *cup basmati rice or other long- or*	*About* $^1/_4$ *teaspoon saffron threads*
medium-grain rice	*(optional)*
$^3/_4$ *cup sugar*	$^1/_2$ *teaspoon vanilla extract*
3 *to* 5 *cardamom pods, bruised, or* $^1/_4$ *to*	$^1/_2$ *cup chopped almonds or pistachios*
$^1/_2$ *teaspoon ground cardamom*	*for garnish (optional)*

1. Bring the milk to a low boil in a large heavy-bottomed saucepan over medium heat. Add the rice, reduce the heat to medium-low, and cook, stirring frequently to prevent sticking, until reduced and thickened, about 2 hours.

2. Add the sugar, cardamom, and the raisins and/or saffron, if using. Cook, stirring constantly, until the sugar dissolves and the flavors meld, about 10 minutes. Remove from the heat and stir in the vanilla. If using cardamom pods, remove them. Serve warm or chilled. If desired, garnish with the nuts.

HINT: ❧ To use a vanilla bean, omit the vanilla extract. Split a vanilla bean in half lengthwise. In a heavy-bottomed medium saucepan, heat the milk and vanilla bean over medium heat until small bubbles appear around the edges. Reduce the heat to very low, cover, and simmer until the vanilla infuses the milk, about 10 minutes. Remove the vanilla bean and, if desired, scrape in the seeds.

Arroz con Leche ❧ *(Sephardic Rice Pudding)*

Rice is the staple of the Sephardic kitchen, except in the Maghreb, where couscous fills that role. In most other areas, rice is served at almost every meal, including Passover meals, plain or mixed with various vegetables, legumes, fruit, and meats. For special occasions, it is colored with saffron (*riz bi saffran* in Arabic). Rice pudding is a standard Sephardic dessert, served both hot and cold and at breakfast, lunch, and dinner. This version has a custard-like consistency.

2 cups water	*1 to 3 tablespoons rose water, or*
1 cup medium- or long-grain rice,	*1 teaspoon vanilla extract, or*
washed and drained	*1 teaspoon vanilla extract*
6 cups milk	*and 1 teaspoon rose water*
$^1/_2$ teaspoon salt	*Ground cinnamon or nutmeg for*
About $^3/_4$ cup sugar	*sprinkling*
2 to 3 large egg yolks	

1. Bring the water to a boil. Add the rice and cook, uncovered, over medium heat, stirring occasionally, until the liquid is absorbed, about 15 minutes.
2. Add the milk and salt. Reduce the heat to low and cook, uncovered, stirring occasionally, until most of the liquid is absorbed, about 45 minutes.
3. Stir in the sugar, then the egg yolks, and cook, stirring, until thickened, about 5 minutes. Remove from the heat and stir in the rose water. Pour into serving bowls and sprinkle with the cinnamon. Serve hot, at room temperature, or chilled.

VARIATIONS

Omit the egg yolks and reduce the milk to 4 cups.

Rizagolon (Greek Lemon Rice Pudding): Add with the sugar $^1/_2$ cup dried currants or raisins and $1^1/_2$ teaspoons grated lemon zest.

Faloudeh ❧ *(Persian Rice Noodle Sharbat)*

This unique dessert is a cross between rice pasta and ices. Rice sticks are very thin off-white rice flour noodles, also called rice vermicelli and, in Chinese, *chow fun* or *mai fun*. When cooked, the noodles turn bright white. Modern versions of *faloudeh* freeze the syrup and noodles in an ice cream maker rather than mixing with crushed ice.

---

4 cups water	8 ounces thin rice noodles or Chinese
1 1/2 cups sugar	rice sticks
2 tablespoons rose water	1/4 cup sharbat albaloo *(recipe follows)*
2 tablespoons fresh lime or lemon juice	*(optional)*

---

1. Stir the water and sugar in a medium saucepan over low heat until the sugar dissolves, about 5 minutes. Increase the heat to medium and bring to a boil. Let cool. Stir in the rose water and lime juice. Pour into ice cube trays and freeze. Crush the ice cubes.

2. Soak the noodles in cold water to cover for 1 hour. Drain. Bring a large pot of water to a boil. Add the noodles and cook until tender, about 5 minutes. Drain. Rinse with cold water and drain.

3. Energetically stir the noodles and the crushed ice together until well mixed. If desired, serve with the *sharbat albaloo*.

RICE FLOUR

 Rice flour (*chaaval ka atta* in India) is ground rice with a slightly grainy texture like fine sand. It is used as a thickening agent and to make batters. It can be found in stores specializing in Indian, Middle Eastern, Spanish, and Chinese fare.

To make rice flour: Soak long-grain white rice in an equal amount of cold water for 30 minutes. Drain, rinse under cold water, drain, spread over a kitchen towel, and pat dry. In a food processor or blender, grind to produce very fine particles. Store in an airtight container at room temperature for up to 3 months.

Sharbat Albaloo ❧ *(Black Cherry Syrup)*

ABOUT 2 CUPS

For more than 2,000 years, Persians have counteracted the effects of hot weather by making a refreshing drink of *sharbat* (a concentrated syrup made from fruit, flower petals, or almonds) mixed with cold water. Eventually they went a step further by stirring *sharbat* into snow and crushed ice to create a frozen treat. Fancier variations, most notably *faloudeh,* contain additions such as noodles. The Arabs, during their occupation of Sicily, introduced *sharbat,* which the Italians renamed *sorbetto,* to Europe. In the dairy-rich northern part of Italy, cream and milk were generally added, resulting in *gelato* (ice cream, from the Italian word *gelare,* "to freeze"). By the time a pamphlet entitled *L'Art de Faire des Glaces* appeared in Paris around 1700, both *sorbet* and *gelato* had become common fare in much of Europe.

Throughout the Middle East, *sharbat* is still commonly served with meals and when entertaining guests. Many Middle Eastern Jews use drinks made with almond or lemon *sharbat* to break the fast of Yom Kippur. To make a drink, remove the cherries and stir 1 to 2 tablespoons *sharbat* into 1 cup cold water. Store the cherries, if desired, in the syrup and serve with vanilla ice cream, sponge or pound cake, or roasted poultry.

---

2 cups sugar	1/4 to 1/2 teaspoon ground cardamom
1 cup water	(optional)
8 ounces (about 1 1/2 cups) tart cherries, pitted	

Stir the sugar and water over low heat until the sugar dissolves. Add the cherries and simmer for 15 minutes. Add the cardamom if using and simmer for 1 minute more. Let cool.

VARIATION

For a more intensely colored syrup, add a slice of raw beet with the cherries. After cooling the syrup, discard the beet.

Sutlach ❧ *(Middle Eastern Rice Flour Pudding)*

6 TO 8 SERVINGS

Sutlach/sutlage ("milk pudding" in Turkish), called *mahallebi/muhalabeeya* in Arabic, is served in many Sephardic households on the Sabbath and at the meal following Yom Kippur. The combination of dairy items and rose water makes it particularly traditional on Shavuot, called the "Festival of Roses." Turkish Jews serve it as the first course of a wedding feast. In Greece *sutlach* is sometimes called *kazan,* after a tin-lined copper pot in which it is commonly made. Nondairy versions are made with *pipitada* (melon seed milk). For *desayano* (Sabbath morning breakfast), some mothers write young children's names with cinnamon on top of individual puddings.

1/2 cup rice flour (see page 338) or cream of rice	*1 to 2 tablespoons rose water or orange blossom water, or 1 teaspoon vanilla extract*
About 1/2 cup sugar	
51/2 cups milk	*Ground cinnamon and/or chopped nuts for garnish (optional)*

1. Combine the rice flour and sugar in a large saucepan. Stir in a little of the milk to make a smooth paste. Gradually stir in the remaining milk.
2. Bring to a boil over medium heat, stirring constantly. Reduce the heat to low and simmer, stirring frequently, until thickened, about 10 minutes.
3. Remove from the heat and stir in the rose water. Pour into serving bowls and, if desired, sprinkle with the cinnamon and/or nuts. Let cool. Serve at room temperature or chilled.

VARIATIONS

Baked Sutlach: Pour the thickened pudding into a greased casserole to a depth of 3 inches and bake at 325 degrees until the top is golden brown, about 50 minutes.

Dodail (Cochin Rice Flour Pudding): Substitute 6 cups coconut milk (page 312) or 12 ounces creamed coconut dissolved in 6 cups water for the milk.

Loz Sutlach (Middle Eastern Almond Rice Flour Pudding): Substitute 1/2 teaspoon almond extract for the rose water. Add 3/4 cup finely ground blanched almonds to the thickened pudding and cook for 1 minute.

Prehito ❧ *(Sephardic Bulgur Pudding)*

Bulgur is whole-wheat kernels that have been steamed or boiled, then dried and cracked. The partial processing removes very little of the kernel's protein, vitamins, and minerals. When rehydrated by soaking in liquid, bulgur nearly triples in volume. The color varies depending on the wheat (red or white) and the preparation method. Bulgur is available in three granulations: fine (also labeled #1), medium (also labeled #2), and coarse. Fine- and medium-grain bulgur, generally prepared by soaking in water, can usually be substituted for each other. The coarse type requires a brief cooking period. Do not substitute cracked wheat or cracked uncooked wheat berries for bulgur.

An important ingredient in Middle Eastern cooking, bulgur is most familiar to Westerners in tabbouleh salad. This grain pudding, called *moustrahana* and *belila* in Turkey, is a traditional Tu b'Shevat and Sukkot dish.

1 cup (6 ounces) fine or medium bulgur	*1/2 cup dried currants or raisins*
3 cups water	*1/4 cup chopped pitted dates (optional)*
1/2 to 3/4 cup sugar or honey	*1 teaspoon ground cinnamon*
1 cup (about 4 ounces) coarsely chopped almonds or walnuts	*Pinch of salt*

Cook the bulgur in the water in a medium saucepan over medium heat until the water is absorbed, about 30 minutes. Add the remaining ingredients and stir until the sugar dissolves. Spoon into a 9-inch square baking pan and place in the refrigerator until chilled. Cut into squares.

VARIATIONS

Baked Prehito: After removing from the heat, stir in 1 lightly beaten large egg. Bake in a 350-degree oven for 40 minutes.

Dairy Prehito: After the liquid is absorbed, add 1 cup milk with the sugar.

Kofyas ❧ *(Middle Eastern Sweetened Wheat Berries)*

ABOUT 9 CUPS

Wheat berries are unprocessed whole wheat with only the outer husk removed. Their nutty flavor and chewy texture are delicious alone or mixed with other grains. Hulled wheat berries (also called shelled or peeled wheat) are white in color, lack whole wheat's flavor, and are stickier and softer when cooked. Since wheat berries resemble teeth, Sephardim customarily serve them at a party to honor a baby's first tooth. Sweetened and mixed with fruits and nuts, it becomes a holiday dish called *kofyas* in Turkey, *assurei* (from an Arabic word for ten) or *koliva* in Greece, and *korkoti* in Georgia, served on Tu b'Shevat, Sukkot, and Rosh Hashanah. Some versions include chickpeas and rice. *Kofyas* is commonly garnished with the similarly shaped pomegranate seeds.

1 pound (about 2 cups) whole wheat berries

8 cups water

About 1¹/₂ cups sugar or honey, or 1 cup sugar and ¹/₂ cup honey

1 to 2 teaspoons ground cinnamon

1 cup raisins or dried currants, or ¹/₂ cup raisins and ¹/₂ cup chopped pitted dates

2 cups (about 8 ounces) coarsely chopped mixed nuts (any combination of almonds, hazelnuts, pine nuts, pistachios, and walnuts)

Pomegranate seeds for garnish (optional)

1. Soak the wheat berries in water to cover overnight. Drain.
2. Bring the wheat berries and 8 cups water to a boil, reduce the heat to medium-low, and simmer until tender but still slightly chewy, about 2 hours. Drain.
3. Add the sugar and cinnamon and stir over medium-low heat until the sugar melts, about 2 minutes. The wheat berries harden a bit when the sugar is added.
4. Remove from the heat and stir in the raisins and nuts. Serve warm, at room temperature, or chilled. If desired, mound the *kofyas* on a platter and garnish with pomegranate seeds.

VARIATIONS

Sleehah (Syrian Anise-Flavored Wheat Berries): Omit the cinnamon. Add $1/4$ cup anise seeds (*shimra* in Arabic) before cooking the wheat berries, or add $1/2$ cup anise liqueur and, if desired, 1 teaspoon rose water with the raisins and nuts.

Creamy Kofyas: Omit the cinnamon. Use honey instead of sugar and combine with 3 cups milk and bring to a low boil. If desired, add 2 tablespoons orange blossom water. Pour over the cooked wheat berries, then stir in the raisins and nuts.

Belila (Middle Eastern Sweetened Barley): Substitute 2 cups pearl barley for the wheat berries. The barley does not require soaking and cooks in about 45 minutes.

Fruit Desserts

*A land of wheat and barley and grapes and figs and
pomegranates; a land of olive oil and date honey.*

—DEUTERONOMY 8:8

THE WORLD ABOUNDS WITH AN INCREDIBLE NUMBER OF PLANTS THAT ARE DISTINGUISHED BY THE SWEETNESS OF THEIR FRUIT. THE TROPICS ALONE ACCOUNT FOR MORE THAN 3,000 SPECIES. ALTHOUGH SOME OF THESE ONCE EXOTIC FRUITS ARE BECOMING A common sight in Western markets, the old standards still retain their mass appeal. Most of these venerable fruits are members of a few families: Rosaceae, which includes apples, pears, quinces, apricots, cherries, peaches, plums, blackberries, raspberries, and strawberries; Rutaceae, which encompasses all citrus fruits; Moraceae, containing figs and mulberries; and Palmae, most notably dates and coconuts.

When the flesh of fruit is exposed to the air, oxidation occurs, resulting in discoloration. Fruits containing an enzyme known as polyphenoloxdase—most notably apples, bananas, pears, and avocados—react even more quickly to oxygen. Heat destroys these enzymes. Immersing the fruit in cold water cuts off access to the air and forestalls browning. Ascorbic acid slows down the process of oxidation. Similarly, sulfur compounds, such as sulfur dioxide, are commonly added to dried fruits to prevent browning.

Many red- or purple-colored fruits, including berries, apples, and grapes, contain anthocyanin, a pigment that reacts chemically with iron, tin, and aluminum, giving food a green or blue tint. Therefore, these fruits should be cooked in a nonreactive utensil.

Cooking fruit with sugar not only sweetens it but also fortifies the cell walls, preventing mushiness, and draws water into the fruit, keeping it moist.

Many of these recipes use dried fruits. To make dried fruit easier to chop, place it in the freezer about 1 hour before chopping. Soaking dried fruit in hot water or alcohol for a few minutes, a step recommended for most cake and pastry recipes, reduces any noticeable chemical odor and produces moister fruit.

Frucht Compote *(Ashkenazic Poached Dried Fruit)*

When I was growing up, this dish of dried fruit poached in sugar syrup was always served at the end of the Passover Seder feast. To be honest, as a child I did not fully appreciate stewed fruit. Today, though, I find it a light, refreshing finish to a meal. Although compote is primarily thought of as a dessert, it also serves as an accompaniment to grilled or roasted meat or poultry.

---

2 pounds (about 7 cups) mixed dried fruit (any combination of apples, apricots, cherries, figs, peaches, pears, pineapple, prunes, and raisins)

8 cups water, or 4 cups dry white wine and 4 cups water

1 cup sugar or honey

6 thin orange slices

6 thin lemon slices

2 (3-inch) cinnamon sticks

1 vanilla bean, split lengthwise, or 3 whole cloves, or 1 (2-inch) piece fresh ginger, thinly sliced (optional)

1/4 to 1/2 cup fruit-flavored brandy, whiskey, or orange liqueur (optional)

---

1. Bring all the ingredients except the brandy to a boil in a large, heavy saucepan over medium heat. Reduce the heat to low and simmer, stirring occasionally, until just tender, about 20 minutes.

2. Remove and reserve the fruit. Increase the heat to high and boil the cooking liquid until reduced to 2 or 3 cups, about 10 minutes. If desired, add the brandy and return to a boil. Remove from the heat and return the fruit. Serve warm or chilled. Store in the refrigerator for up to 4 weeks.

VARIATIONS

Fresh Fruit Compote: Use any combination of sliced and seeded fresh apples, apricots, cantaloupe, cherries, grapes, mangoes, nectarines, papaya, peaches, pears, pineapple, and plums, but reduce the cooking time to about 5 minutes.

Koshkbar (Persian Dried Fruit Compote): Substitute about 2 tablespoons rose water for the brandy.

Kayisi Tatlisi ❧ *(Turkish Poached Dried Apricots)*

Apricots, primarily in dried form, are an important part of Middle Eastern and central European cooking. They are one of the few fruits that do not sweeten after harvesting, so it is rare to find a tasty fresh apricot in areas where they do not grow. Thus, apricots are usually best when dried or canned.

In Turkey, these poached apricots are filled with sweetened *kaymak,* a very thick buffalo cream. Yogurt cheese or whipped cream makes a very suitable substitute.

---

6 ounces (about 1¹/₂ cups) large dried
    apricots
3¹/₂ cups water
¹/₄ cup sugar
1 tablespoon lemon or lime juice

Filling:
¹/₂ cup yogurt cheese (see page 322),
    crème fraîche, or whipped cream
3 to 4 tablespoons sugar

---

1. Soak the apricots in cold water for 1 hour. Drain.
2. Stir the water, sugar, and lemon juice over low heat until the sugar dissolves, about 5 minutes. Add the apricots, cover, and simmer until tender, about 20 minutes. Remove the apricots and let cool. If desired, increase the heat to high and boil the cooking liquid until syrupy, about 5 minutes. Let cool.
3. To make the filling: Combine the yogurt cheese and sugar.
4. Carefully open the apricots and fill each one with about 1 tablespoon of the cheese mixture. If desired, drizzle the syrup over the apricots.

Hellou ❧ *(Middle Eastern Candied Fruits and Vegetables)*

ABOUT 1 QUART

Candied fruits and vegetables, called *hellou/hilu,* are popular throughout the Middle East. Quinces, the most prevalent of these treats, and squash are traditional Rosh Hashanah fare in Turkey, Syria, and Morocco. Some variations, such as fresh walnuts, are rather rare.

2 cups sugar	1 tablespoon light corn syrup (optional)
1 cup water	About 2 pounds fruit (see Variations
2 teaspoons lemon juice, or ¹/₄ teaspoon	below)
cream of tartar	

1. Stir the sugar, water, lemon juice, and corn syrup if using in a large saucepan over low heat until the sugar dissolves, about 5 minutes. Increase the heat to medium and boil without stirring until the syrup reaches the soft-crack stage (290 degrees on a candy thermometer), about 20 minutes.

2. Add the fruit, cover, and return to a boil. Reduce the heat to low and simmer until tender. Let cool.

3. Pour into jars and store in the refrigerator. For long-term storage, pour into sterilized canning jars and process in boiling water according to manufacturer's directions. Serve chilled or at room temperature.

VARIATIONS

Membrillo (Middle Eastern Candied Quince): Use 4 medium (about 3 pounds) quinces, peeled and cut in half from the stem end. You can also thickly slice or grate the quinces. If desired, insert 2 whole cloves into the center of each quince half or add 3 (3-inch) cinnamon sticks to the syrup. The cooking time will be about 45 minutes.

Yatkeen Fijil Hellou (Middle Eastern Candied Pumpkin): Use 2 pounds pumpkin or butternut squash, peeled, seeded, and thinly sliced. If desired, add a few whole cloves, 2 cardamom pods, or 2 grains of mastic (a resin that is pounded into a powder) to the syrup. The cooking time will be about 15 minutes. Store in the syrup or remove the pumpkin from the syrup, place on racks until almost dry, then dredge in superfine sugar.

Teen Hellou (Middle Eastern Candied Figs): Use 2 pounds stemmed dried Calimyrna figs and, if desired, 1 split vanilla bean. The cooking time will be about 20 minutes.

Cheveux d'Ange (Middle Eastern Candied Spaghetti Squash): Cook 1 pound spaghetti squash in boiling water until tender, 20 to 40 minutes. Peel, seed, and let drain in a colander. If desired, add a few drops of rose water or green food coloring to the syrup before adding the squash.

QUINCES

 The quince, a native of western Asia, is a tart-flavored, apple-shaped fruit with an intense aroma when ripe. Early in history, it spread throughout southern Europe and most of Asia, although it is not mentioned in the Bible. Quince dishes are traditional Rosh Hashanah fare in many Sephardic communities.

Quinces have a hard, granular texture and an astringency and therefore cannot be eaten raw. The pale yellow flesh becomes pink and sweet when cooked. The peel and core of quinces have a high pectin content, making them ideal for jams. Indeed, the word for *marmalade* comes from the Portuguese word for *quince, marmelo,* the original fruit in these preserves. Sephardim also poach quinces, cook them to make confections, or add them to meat stews; many of these dishes date back to the time before the Expulsion.

Datils Rellenos ❧ *(Middle Eastern Stuffed Dates)*

ABOUT 3 DOZEN

Stuffed dried fruits, called *tamir mehshi* in Arabic and *forees* in Morocco, are popular Sephardic treats. Although dates are the most common, you can stuff almost any dried fruit, including apricots and prunes. Similar confections are called sugarplums in England.

---

36 *whole almonds (about 2 ounces), or*	36 *medium (about 1 pound) pitted dates*
1 *cup Sephardic Almond Paste (see*	1 *recipe sugar syrup (see* atar, *page 265)*
page 368)	*or sugar for coating (optional)*

Insert an almond into the center of each date. If using almond paste, slit the dates open lengthwise, form the paste into thin rolls, place in the center of each date, and press to close. Serve as is, dip into the sugar syrup, or roll in the sugar.

VARIATIONS

Apricot-Almond-Stuffed Dates: Mince ¹/₂ cup dried apricots and stir into the almond paste.

Coconut-Covered Stuffed Dates: After dipping in the sugar syrup, roll the stuffed dates in about 1¹/₂ cups grated unsweetened desiccated coconut. If desired, combine the coconut with 3 tablespoons anise seeds.

Sesame Dates: Combine ¹/₄ cup tahini (sesame seed paste), ¹/₄ cup honey, ¹/₄ cup water, and 2 teaspoons ground cinnamon. Roll the stuffed dates in the tahini mixture, then in sesame seeds. Place on parchment or waxed paper and let dry.

DATES

The righteous shall flourish like the palm tree.
—PSALM 92:13

 The date, from the Greek *dactylon* ("finger or toe"), a reference to its shape, is a native of the Fertile Crescent. If not the oldest, it is one of the oldest cultivated fruits, dating back more than 5,000 years. The date palm is a temperamental tree and will bear fruit only in select climates and conditions. Nomads spread it throughout the Middle East, then west to Africa. The Moors brought the date to Spain, and later the Spanish transported it to the New World. The date's sweetness has made it a favorite everywhere.

Dates play a prominent role in Jewish tradition. The sages explain that the honey in the phrase "the land flowing with milk and honey" refers to date honey, the primary sweetener of ancient Israel. It was under a date palm that Deborah judged the nation. The branch of the palm is one of the "Four Species" combined during the holiday of Sukkot. The Maccabees used the palm as a symbol of their military success. A number of ancient as well as modern Jewish coins bear a picture of the date palm.

The many varieties of dates vary in size, texture, and color but are generally classified as semisoft or soft. The latter have a higher moisture content, a smaller amount of sugar, and a softer texture. Fresh dates from Israel, with their sweet, winy taste, have recently become available in the West. For fresh dates, look for shiny, smooth skin. Most dates, however, are used in the dried form. Dried dates are about 50 percent sugar; crystallization results with prolonged storage. Dates are delicious in cakes, muffins, cookies, puddings, confections, and fruit salads.

Fijos ❧ *(Sephardic Poached Figs)*

4 SERVINGS

Poached figs are delicious plain or further enhanced by stuffing. Serve in the poaching liquid or use the latter for other dishes, such as a fig sauce or fruit soup.

1¹/₂ cups water

About ¹/₂ cup sugar or honey

1 (4-inch) piece vanilla bean, 1 slice
    lemon rind, or 1 tablespoon grated
    orange zest

8 medium fresh or dried figs

---

1. Stir the water, sugar, and vanilla bean in a medium saucepan over low heat until the sugar dissolves, about 5 minutes. Increase the heat to medium, add the figs in a single layer, cover, and simmer until tender but not mushy, about 5 minutes for fresh figs or 15 to 25 minutes for dried.
2. Remove the figs. Increase the heat to high and boil the cooking liquid until reduced to about 1 cup. Pour over the figs. Serve warm or let the figs cool in the syrup.

VARIATIONS

Baked Figs: Place the ingredients in a greased medium casserole and bake in a 350-degree oven until tender, 25 to 35 minutes.

Stuffed Poached Figs: Cut a slit in each poached fig and, using a melon baller, scoop out the pulp. Let cool. Pipe in sweetened yogurt cheese (see poached apricots, page 347), vanilla ice cream, pastry cream, or ¹/₂ cup heavy cream whipped with 2 to 3 tablespoons confectioners' sugar.

Alsatian Poached Figs: Substitute 1¹/₂ cups Gewürztraminer wine for the water and reduce the sugar to ¹/₄ cup.

Gefulte Feigen (Austrian Chocolate-Stuffed Poached Figs): In the top of a double boiler, melt 3 ounces semisweet or bittersweet chocolate and 6 tablespoons (³/₄ stick) butter or margarine, stirring until smooth. Cool, then place in the refrigerator until firm. Stuff into the poached figs.

Fichi Secci (Italian Stuffed Figs in Wine): Substitute $1^1/2$ cups dry red wine for the water. Stuff the poached figs with ground almonds or walnuts (about $^1/2$ cup total).

Teen Mihshee (Syrian Almond-Stuffed Poached Figs): Stuff each poached fig with a whole almond or a little Sephardic Almond Paste (page 368). If desired, substitute $1^1/2$ cups orange juice for the water.

Incir Tatlisi (Turkish Stuffed Poached Figs): Stuff the poached figs with almond paste or ground almond or walnuts (about $^1/2$ cup total). If desired, serve with whipped cream.

FIGS

"And they gave him a slice of fig cake and two bunches of raisins . . ."
—I SAMUEL 30:12

The fig, a native of Asia Minor, is not a fruit but rather a thick-skinned pod surrounding a pink or reddish flesh containing thousands of tiny fruits. Egyptians were growing figs at least 3,500 years ago, and figs were also an essential part of the diet in ancient Greece and Rome. The fig figures prominently in Jewish tradition; only the grape is mentioned more often in the Bible and Talmud. The phrase "under his fig tree" has become a symbol of peace and prosperity. Some sages claimed that the fig was the Tree of the Knowledge of Good and Evil, since it was the fig tree that initially provided clothing for Adam and Eve. Part of Abigail's special gift to King David consisted of 200 cakes of dried figs (I Samuel 25:18).

There are hundreds of varieties and four main types of figs: green, purple, white, and red. Figs are sold fresh, canned in syrup, and dried. The flavor of dried figs varies according to the variety and the method of processing. Historically, Smyrna figs have been among the most favored in the world. Smyrna figs transplanted to California in 1769 evolved into the medium-size purple-black Mission fig. Calimyrna, a large, many-seeded Smyrna variety, is the most common American-grown dried fig.

Immature figs lack flavor and will not ripen after picking. Mature ones continue to ripen and soften if left at room temperature. Fully developed figs look plump and feel heavy; the "eye" at the bottom of the fruit should be slightly open. Very mature figs tend to exhibit vertical cracks in the skin and bruise easily, but ironically, perfect-looking figs tend to lack flavor. A sour smell is a sign of overmaturation (figs do not rot but ferment). Store fresh figs in a single layer on paper towels in the refrigerator for up to 3 days.

Poires Pochées ❧ *(Alsatian Poached Pears)*

6 SERVINGS

Wild pears and their earliest cultivated descendants possessed stone cells (grit) and sometimes a bitterness. Thus, until the sixteenth century, pears were barely edible without cooking. Although these traits have been bred out of most cultivated varieties, a certain grittiness or bitterness, especially near the core, can still occur. Some beautifully formed pears are dry and tasteless, while plain-looking fruit can be sweet and flavorful.

Alsatians love pears, enjoying them fresh and incorporating them into various desserts. Poaching is a perfect way to utilize underripe pears. When cooked in red wine, the pears take on a delightful crimson hue. Serve these pears in a little of the cooking liquid (the alcohol evaporates during cooking), with a chocolate or raspberry sauce, or with Hungarian Wine Sauce (page 413). Or serve as an accompaniment to sponge cake.

---

6 large firm pears with stems attached, peeled

3 cups red wine, white wine, or water

1/2 to 3/4 cup sugar or honey

2 tablespoons lemon juice

2 or 3 large slices lemon or orange rind, or 4 whole cloves

2 (3-inch) cinnamon sticks, or 1 vanilla bean, split lengthwise

---

1. Cut off a small slice from the bottom of each pear so that it stands upright. Leaving the pears whole, scoop out the core (a melon baller works well) from the bottom.
2. In a large nonreactive saucepan (do not use iron, copper, or brass), combine the wine, sugar (use less sugar if using sweet wine), lemon juice, rind, and cinnamon. Stand the pears in the wine mixture. Bring to a boil over medium-high heat. Cover, reduce the heat to low, and simmer until tender but not mushy, 15 to 30 minutes, depending on the size and variety of the pears. Serve warm, at room temperature, or chilled. Store in the refrigerator.

VARIATIONS

Poires Pochées Farcies (Alsatian Stuffed Poached Pears): Combine 1/3 cup dried currants or raisins, 1/4 cup sugar, 3 tablespoons chopped hazelnuts or walnuts, and 1 tablespoon lemon juice and stuff into the pear cavities before cooking. Or fill the cavities with about 2 tablespoons Sephardic Almond Paste (page 368).

Bahrin Shalet (Alsatian Baked Pear Pie): This was a popular Alsatian Friday night dessert, left to finish cooking in a low oven after the onset of the Sabbath. Slice the poached pears horizontally into quarters. Combine 3^1/4 cups all-purpose flour, 1 cup sugar, ^{1}/4 cup bread crumbs, and ^{1}/8 teaspoon salt. Cut in ^{1}/2 cup (1 stick) margarine. Combine ^{3}/4 cup water and 2 large eggs and stir into the flour mixture to make a soft dough. Roll out ^{1}/2 inch thick, fit into a greased deep casserole, and refrigerate for 30 minutes. Bake in a 375-degree oven until lightly colored, about 20 minutes. Place the pears and a little of the cooking liquid in the shell and bake in a 225-degree oven for about 3 hours. Serve warm.

Tarte au Poires (Alsatian Pear Tarts): Slice the poached pears in half horizontally, arrange on pieces of puff pastry, and lightly sprinkle with confectioners' sugar. Bake in a 400-degree oven until the pastry is puffed and golden, about 40 minutes.

Ayva Tatlisi ❧ *(Turkish Poached Quinces in Pomegranate Syrup)*

6 TO 8 SERVINGS

This Turkish Rosh Hashanah dish, combining two traditional fruits, is served either at the beginning or at the end of the meal. For a special effect, arrange some of the cooked quinces on a baked tart shell or puff pastry.

4 medium slightly unripe quinces (about 8 ounces each)	2 cups pomegranate juice
	1 1/2 to 2 cups sugar
Lemon water (cold water with a squeeze of lemon juice)	1/2 cup fresh lemon juice
	2 (3-inch) cinnamon sticks, or
4 cups water	2 teaspoons ground cinnamon

1. Peel and core the quinces and cut into halves or quarters. Place the quinces in a little lemon water to prevent discoloring. Wrap and tie the quince peels and cores in cheesecloth.
2. Stir the water, pomegranate juice, and sugar in a large saucepan over low heat until the sugar dissolves, about 5 minutes. Increase the heat to medium-high and bring to a boil, about 5 minutes.
3. Add the quinces, cheesecloth, lemon juice, and cinnamon sticks. Reduce the heat to low and simmer without stirring until the quinces are deep pink and tender but not mushy, about 50 minutes.
4. Remove the quinces. Discard the cinnamon sticks and cheesecloth. Boil the cooking liquid until reduced and syrupy, about 20 minutes. Pour over the quinces and let cool.

VARIATIONS

Georgians frequently serve poached quinces, called *kompot iz aivi*, sprinkled with rose water and topped with clotted cream.

Bimbrio/Membrillo (Sephardic Poached Quinces): Omit the pomegranate juice.

Cotognata (Italian Wine-Poached Quinces): Substitute 3 cups red or white wine for the water, pomegranate juice, and lemon juice and add 8 whole cloves.

POMEGRANATES

The pomegranate is not actually a fruit but rather a tough, leathery, reddish brown skin covering a mass of large, shiny, translucent fruits that range in color from deep red to clear. It probably originated in Persia but has been found in 5,000-year-old Canaanite sites, such as Jericho and Gezer.

The pomegranate plays a significant role in Jewish literature and lore. It was one of the fruits brought back from Canaan by the spies sent by Moses. It is spoken of in glowing terms six times in Song of Songs. Its shape was woven onto the robes of the high priest. Brass images of pomegranates were part of the Temple's pillars. Ancient as well as modern Jewish coins pictured them. According to tradition, each pomegranate contains 613 seeds, corresponding to the number of commandments in the Torah.

In the Near East, pomegranate seeds, sometimes mixed with slivered almonds, are tossed with a little honey and orange blossom water for a refreshing dessert. However, the pomegranate's primary role in cooking comes in the form of its juice.

Look for fresh-looking pomegranates with bright, deeply colored skin. The fruit should feel heavy for its size. Avoid any with a broken rind or decay around the calyx (the crown-like top).

To extract pomegranate juice: Cut the fruit in half; do not use an aluminum or carbon knife, which will turn the juice bitter. Squeeze the juice into a strainer, discarding the hard white kernels. Although the seeds can also be processed in a blender and strained, the juice may absorb some of the kernels' bitterness and require the addition of a little sugar to offset it. One large pomegranate (10 ounces or $3^1/_2$ inches) yields about $^2/_3$ cup juice.

Confections

There is always room for sweet things.
—TALMUD MEGILLAH 7B

THE WORD *SUGAR* IS DERIVED FROM THE SANSKRIT WORD *SARKARA* ("GRIT" OR "SAND"), REFLECTING ITS INDIAN ORIGINS. BY 500 BCE, INDIANS WERE ADDING CRUDE *SARKARA* CRYSTALS TO THEIR FOODS. SUGAR, HOWEVER, WAS NOT A COMMON COMMODITY IN ANCIENT times. It is mentioned only twice in the Bible, and then only in references that reflect its rarity and foreignness. "To what purpose is to Me the frankincense that comes from Sheba and the sweet cane from a far country" (Jeremiah 6:20); "You have brought me no sweet cane " (Isaiah 43:24). The first mention of sugar by a Westerner was by Nearchus, a Greek general introduced to the "honey reed" during Alexander the Great's campaign in India. Most ancient Europeans, however, remained unfamiliar with this sweetener.

The Persians were raising sugar cane in their homeland by the fifth century CE. In turn, the Arabs discovered how to refine the cane and subsequently spread it to Africa around 710 and shortly thereafter to Iberia. By the tenth century, the Nile River valley was the home of the world's finest *sukkar*. Documents from the Cairo Genizah (archives) corroborate that Jewish merchants dominated north African sugar planting and production, a role they maintained until modern times.

The introduction of sugar to the Middle East produced a revolution in confections, as sucrose proved far more versatile than other sweeteners in candy making. Indeed, the word *candy* comes from an Arabic word for sugar, *quad*. Soon confectioners in the Middle East were mixing sugar syrups with such items as nuts, seeds, and gum arabic to create a multitude of confections, many of which are still widely enjoyed today, such as marzipan and sesame lozenges.

In the eleventh century, sugar continued its move westward as the Crusaders returned from the Middle East with a taste for the then exotic sweetener. The Venetians quickly gained a monopoly over Europe's sugar trade and developed a method of refining it into uniform crystals. At first, apothecaries possessed exclusive rights to dispense sugar, using it solely as a medicine or to mask the bitter taste of other drugs. In the early thirteenth century, French druggists began coating almonds with sugar, and other confections (from the Latin *conficere*, "to prepare") eventually followed. Thus, it is hardly surprising that the first candy cookbook was written by the famed physician and astrologer Nostradamus (1503–1566), a descendant of Provençal Jews. Because of sugar's high price, however, it remained the sole province of the upper class. While royal chefs experimented with a variety of ingredients, concocting new delicacies to satisfy noble cravings, the masses continued to rely on honey for sweetening.

Sugar arrived in the New World with Columbus on his second trip in 1493, and it soon flourished in the East Indies. By the seventeenth century, the influx of Caribbean sugar cane to Europe meant a marked increase in its availability and, as the price plummeted, its affordability. Sugar suddenly became western Europe's primary sweetener.

In 1747, a German chemist, Andreas Marggraf, discovered the process of producing sucrose from sugar beets. In taste, cooking properties, and nutrition, beet sugar is almost indistinguishable from sugar cane. For Europeans, the sugar beet possesses a major advantage over the more ancient form—sugar cane grows only in tropical and subtropical climates, while beets flourish in a temperate environment. The first sugar beet refining factory was established in Silesia, Germany (now Poland), in 1802. Others, many of them Jewish owned, soon followed in other parts of central and eastern Europe. During Britain's blockade of Napoleonic Europe, the sugar beet gained unprecedented importance as the French, cut off from all Caribbean sources of sugar cane, were forced to turn to the sugar beet to meet Europe's sugar supply. Today one-fourth of America's and almost half of the world's granulated sugar comes from the long white roots of sugar beets.

Considering the Jewish domination of much of Middle Eastern sugar production, it is hardly surprising that sugar early on became a standard ingredient in Sephardic households. In eastern Europe, however, honey remained the primary sweetener until the advent of the sugar beet. Yet even in Europe, differences emerged. Ashkenazim who lived in regions where sugar beets grew, such as Poland, developed a preference for sweeter dishes and added plenty of sugar to their gefilte fish, stuffed cabbage, kugels, and challah. Those from areas such as Galicia and Hungary, where sugar remained an expensive item, generally used much less sugar in their cooking.

The drop in sugar prices made candy accessible to the masses, and soon stores and housewives were developing their skills in producing these sweets. With the onset of the Industrial Revolution, mass-produced candy appeared, the residents of Great Britain being the first to enjoy the benefits of this new technology and still the world's largest consumers of confections. From ancient concoctions of honey mixed with fruits, nuts, and spices to today's more elaborate fluffery, candy has added its own type of enjoyment to life.

Ladu ❧ *(Indian Chickpea Fudge)*

SIX 1-INCH BALLS

*L*adu, "sweet balls" in Hindi, are served during holidays, most notably Purim. They are sometimes coated with white poppy seeds (*khuskhus*).

6 tablespoons ghee *or clarified butter*	1/8 teaspoon ground cardamom or
1 cup chickpea flour, sifted	nutmeg, or 4 to 6 cardamom pods,
2 tablespoons chopped walnuts or	shells discarded and seeds crushed
pistachios (optional)	2/3 cup confectioners' sugar

1. Melt the butter in a large skillet over medium heat. Stir in the chickpea flour and, if desired, the nuts and cook, stirring occasionally, until golden brown, about 15 minutes. Add the cardamom.
2. Remove from the heat, add the sugar, and stir until smooth. Transfer to a platter, spread about 1 inch thick, and let cool.
3. Roll into 1-inch balls or cut into squares or diamonds. Refrigerate until firm. Serve chilled or at room temperature.

HINTS: ❧ Chickpea flour, also called besan and gram flour, is made by grinding toasted chana dal (chickpeas). It is available at Asian and health food stores.

Ghee, an essential element of Indian cuisine, is cooked longer than clarified butter, removing even more impurities. During the extended cooking time, the milk solids brown and the sugar caramelizes, imparting a slightly nutty flavor. Indians use *ghee* for frying and as a spread, and spoon a little over legumes for flavor and smoothness.

Dulce Blanco ❧ *(Sephardic Sugar Paste)*

ABOUT 1¾ CUPS

The Ladino term *dulce* (*glyko* in Greek) includes an array of confections, jellied candies, and preserves. *Dulce blanco* (fondant), also called *sharope*, is a thick, creamy sugar paste. Sephardim prepare a similar paste containing egg whites. These pastes serve as a spread for sweet breads, as well as the base for a variety of candies. *Dulce blanco* can also be melted in the top of a double boiler and used to dip nuts for coating.

On diverse occasions—such as Saturday evening following the Sabbath (starting the new week on a sweet note) or the initial meeting of prospective in-laws—Sephardic hosts customarily offer their guests a *tavla de dulce* (sweet tray) featuring assorted confections and fruit preserves. The *dulce blanco* and preserves are customarily served in small glass or silver bowls arranged on a large silver tray and accompanied by glasses of cold water and small silver spoons. Some people sample a spoonful of the preserves, while others stir them into the water to make a drink. Many insert spoonfuls of *dulce blanco* into the cold water to firm the paste. Once used, the spoons are placed in an extra glass of water. Turkish coffee, often served with pastries, follows the *tavla*.

In the traditional method, the paste is prepared by beating it with a wooden spoon, always moving in the same direction, for at least ten minutes. This version utilizes a food processor for quicker and easier preparation. A little nontraditional corn syrup, which can be omitted for Passover, is added to inhibit crystallization.

2½ *cups sugar*
½ *cup water*

¼ *cup light corn syrup, or* ⅛ *teaspoon*
cream of tartar (optional)

---

1. Stir the sugar, water, and corn syrup in a heavy medium nonaluminum saucepan over low heat until the sugar dissolves, about 5 minutes. Stop stirring, place a candy thermometer in the pan, increase the heat to medium, and bring to a gentle boil. Continue cooking without stirring until the syrup reaches the beginning of the soft-ball stage, or 238 degrees, about 12 minutes. Overcooking evaporates too much liquid, resulting in a dry, crumbly mixture.

2. Pour the syrup into a food processor fitted with a metal blade, insert the thermometer, and let it stand until lukewarm, or 140 degrees, about 30 minutes. Remove the thermometer.

3. Process until the paste is smooth and opaque, about 2 minutes. Pour into a heavy plastic bag or onto plastic wrap, press out any air, seal, and let stand at room temperature to ripen for at least 24 hours. During the ripening stage, the paste becomes softer and smoother. Store at room temperature for up to 1 week or in the refrigerator for up to 6 months. The paste turns grainy when kept for too long.

VARIATIONS

Spread the *dulce* to a 1-inch thickness and cut into about 20 squares or diamonds. If desired, press an almond into each candy or roll them in confectioners' sugar, grated unsweetened desiccated coconut, or ground nuts.

Mustachudos (Sephardic Almond Candy): Sephardim serve this marzipan-like confection at weddings and other special occasions. After the paste is opaque, stir in 1 1/2 cups ground blanched almonds and, if desired, 1 teaspoon rose water or 1/4 teaspoon ground cardamom. Shape into 1-inch balls or roll out 1/2 inch thick and cut into diamonds.

Dulce de Coco (Sephardic Coconut Paste): This popular Passover and holiday sweet, called *joz hind hellou* in Arabic, is often garnished with chopped unsalted pistachios. When the syrup reaches the soft-ball stage, add the grated meat of 1 medium coconut (about 3 cups) and return to a boil. (Do not overcook; it hardens the coconut.) Pour into sterilized jars and let cool. Store in the refrigerator. Serve chilled or at room temperature. You can substitute 1 pound grated unsweetened desiccated coconut for the fresh coconut, toss with 2 tablespoons orange blossom water or rose water, and let soak overnight.

Bonbons: Return the *dulce* to room temperature, shape into 1-inch balls, and roll in ground nuts or grated unsweetened desiccated coconut. For coated bonbons, melt part of the fondant with a few drops of water in the top of a double boiler, tint with food coloring, and dip in the paste balls to coat. Or dip the balls into melted and cooled (about 85 degrees) semisweet or bittersweet chocolate.

Icing: *Dulce blanco* is great for icing cakes and petits fours. Heat it in the top of a double boiler to no more than 105 degrees (*dulce* loses its gloss if heated to a higher temperature), then add enough warm sugar syrup (see *atar*, page 265) to make a pourable mixture, about 1 tablespoon for each cup of paste. For extra effect, tint the paste with food coloring and/or flavor with extracts, cocoa, coffee, peppermint, rum, or citrus zest.

Dulce de Fruta ❧ *(Sephardic Fruit Paste Candies)*

ABOUT TWENTY-FIVE 1-INCH CANDIES

Sephardim enjoy these confections on special occasions, especially **Rosh Hashanah** and **Passover**. Almost any fruit can be used in this process, but hard fruits require cooking and dried ones soaking. Although fruit is naturally sweet, the sugar in this recipe contributes additional sweetness and also intensifies the flavors, contributes body (so that the paste can be cut into shapes), and acts as a preservative.

About 4 cups fruit pulp (see Variations below)

About 4 cups sugar

2 tablespoons fresh lemon juice

Confectioners' or granulated sugar for coating (optional)

---

1. Measure the fruit pulp and place in a heavy medium nonreactive saucepan (do not use iron, copper, or brass). Add 1 cup sugar for each cup of pulp. Bring to a boil, reduce the heat to low, and simmer, stirring frequently, until the mixture thickens and sputters, 30 to 50 minutes. Add the lemon juice and cook, stirring, for 2 minutes.
2. Spread the fruit paste over a greased 13-by-9-inch baking pan or on a baking sheet to a 1-inch thickness. Let cool, then cut into squares or diamonds. Or form the warm fruit paste into 1-inch balls and, if desired, press a walnut half or blanched almond into each ball. Cover with waxed paper and let stand at room temperature overnight. If desired, dredge the candies in confectioners' or granulated sugar to coat. This helps to keep the candies from sticking together. Store between sheets of waxed paper in an airtight container at room temperature.

VARIATIONS

Fruit and Almond Candies: Scatter 1 cup ground blanched almonds in a 13-by-9-inch baking pan or on a baking sheet, spread the fruit paste on top, and sprinkle another 1 cup ground almonds over the fruit paste.

Dulce de Mansana (Sephardic Apple Candies): Cook 3 pounds (10 to 12 medium) coarsely chopped tart apples in 1 1/2 cups apple cider or water over medium heat until tender, 20 to 40 minutes. Drain and let cool. Press through a food mill or strainer. Or use 4 cups unsweetened applesauce.

Dulce de Cayeci (Sephardic Apricot Candies): Soak 1 pound (about 3^1/4 cups) dried apricots in water to cover for at least 2 hours or overnight. Drain, reserving 1 cup of the soaking liquid. In a food processor or food mill, puree the apricots. Add the reserved soaking liquid.

Dulce de Moras (Sephardic Berry Candies): Puree and strain 2 pounds (about 7 cups) stemmed blackberries, mulberries, or raspberries. Add 1 cup water.

Amsath (Indian Mango Candies): This Indian adaptation of the Middle Eastern confection is called *kamrooden* in Calcutta. Use 4 cups strained mango pulp (about 4 pounds or 8 medium mangoes).

Dulce de Shiftili (Sephardic Peach Candies): Halve and pit 2 pounds fresh peaches or apricots. Poach in boiling water for 15 minutes. Drain, peel, and puree. If desired, stir 1 teaspoon almond extract into the thickened paste.

Dulce de Peras (Sephardic Pear Candies): Cook 3 pounds peeled, cored, and chopped pears in 1^1/2 cups water over medium heat until tender, about 30 minutes. Drain and let cool. In a food processor or food mill, puree the pulp.

Dulce de Bimbriyo (Sephardic Quince Candies): Among Greek, Syrian, and Iraqi communities, quince preserves (*kythoni glyko*) and candied quinces are served on Rosh Hashanah and Passover. Peel and slice 3 pounds (about 8 medium) hard and slightly unripe quinces. Cook in 1^1/2 cups water over medium heat until tender, about 30 minutes. Drain and let cool. Mash the pulp and press through a strainer.

Dulce de Bimbriyo y Mansana (Sephardic Quince and Apple Candies): Cook 2 pounds peeled and chopped quinces and 1 pound peeled, cored, and chopped apples in 1^1/2 cups water over medium heat until tender, about 30 minutes. Drain and let cool. In a food processor or food mill, puree the pulp.

Dulce de Portokal y Cidra/Tzukel Frucht ✺
(Candied Citrus Peel)

ABOUT 4 CUPS; 1 ½ POUNDS

When I was about ten years old, I visited a friend's house and witnessed his Polish-born grandmother preparing candied grapefruit peel. Both the process and the final result entranced me. Ever since, I have held a special affection for this ancient treat, a most delicious way of using what otherwise would go to waste. Candied citrus peel can be eaten by itself as a snack or chopped and added to other desserts. Use the peels from citrons (*etrog*), grapefruits, lemons, oranges, tangerines, or any combination.

4 cups (about 1 pound) citrus peels, cut into strips ¼ to ½ inch wide by 2 inches long	Cold water 2 cups sugar ¼ cup light corn syrup (optional)

1. Cover the citrus peels with about 6 cups water, bring to a boil, reduce the heat to low, and simmer for 15 minutes. Drain and repeat the process 2 to 4 times, until the peels are only slightly bitter.

2. Stir the sugar, 2 cups water, and corn syrup if using in a large saucepan over low heat until the sugar dissolves, about 5 minutes. Increase the heat to high and bring to a boil, about 3 minutes.

3. Add the peels, reduce the heat to low, and simmer, stirring occasionally, until the peels are translucent and most of the syrup has been absorbed or the mixture registers 230 degrees on a candy thermometer, about 1 hour.

4. Pour the peels and syrup into a sterilized jar, seal, and refrigerate for at least 2 days. Store in an airtight container at room temperature for up to 2 weeks or in the freezer for several months. Eat as candy, serve as a garnish, or add to cakes, cookies, and puddings.

VARIATIONS

Sugar-Coated Citrus Peel: Drain the peels, place on 1 cup sugar, and toss to coat. Arrange the peels in a single layer on a wire rack and let dry for at least 8 hours.

Chocolate-Covered Citrus Peel: Drain the peels, place on a wire rack, and let dry for at least 8 hours. Dip into melted semisweet or bittersweet chocolate, place on a sheet of waxed paper, and refrigerate until set.

CITRUS FRUIT: INSIDE AND OUT

 Citrus, evergreen plants with shiny leaves and brightly colored fruit, probably originated in India or southwestern China. Over the centuries, through continuous crossing, it developed into one of the largest fruit families. Citrus eventually moved west through Persia into the Middle East and then Greece. Although citrus trees were grown in Italy as early as 50 CE, they disappeared from Europe beginning with the Lombard invasion in 568 and the fall of the Roman Empire. About six centuries later, the Arabs reintroduced them to the Continent by way of Spain and Sicily. Moorish innovations in irrigation led to widespread citrus production in Iberia, as well as several other parts of the Arab world. Most of the medieval Mediterranean citrus production corresponded to centers of Jewish population, probably related to the Jewish practice of growing citron (*etrog*) for Sukkot. In light of the Sephardic affinity for citrus fruit, it is hardly surprising to find it incorporated into many of their dishes.

The epicarp, or *flavedo,* the colored outer part of the citrus rind commonly called zest (from the French word for "peel"), contains sacs of concentrated oils that impart the distinctive citrus flavor to dishes. To grate the zest, it is best to run the whole fruit, rather than one already cut or squeezed, along a grater. For thin slices of zest, use a hand-grating tool, paring knife, or vegetable peeler.

The mesocarp is the white, spongy part of the rind, commonly mislabeled as pith. The latter is actually the thin strip of white membrane in the center of the fruit. The mesocarp contains pectin, which helps to gel jams and marmalades. However, since the mesocarp is extremely bitter, most recipes call for only the zest.

Almendrada ❧ *(Sephardic Almond Paste)*

ABOUT 3 ½ CUPS; 2 POUNDS

For more than a thousand years, nut pastes, both cooked and raw, have been used in the Middle East to make a variety of confections, with almonds serving as the most widely used nut. Almond paste is an uncooked mixture consisting of nearly equal amounts by weight of finely ground blanched almonds and sugar. Marzipan is a cooked almond paste with about twice the amount of sugar as almonds. The two should not be used interchangeably in most recipes. Almond paste, which has a more intense almond flavor than marzipan, is used primarily in baked goods. Marzipan, which is more malleable and less likely to become oily during handling, is generally used to make confections and shapes.

Almendrada is very versatile, forming the basis for a wide variety of Sephardic confections and pastries. It is served at celebrations honoring births, bar mitzvahs, and weddings and on Purim and Passover.

*1 pound blanched almonds, finely
    ground (about 4¼ cups)*
3½ cups confectioners' sugar, or
    2 cup granulated sugar, or
    2 cups confectioners' sugar and
    1⅓ cups superfine sugar

Pinch of salt
1 teaspoon almond extract
About 2 large egg whites

In a food processor fitted with a metal blade, finely grind the almonds, sugar, and salt. Add the almond extract. Gradually add enough of the egg whites to make a cohesive paste. Knead until smooth. Wrap and refrigerate overnight, preferably for 24 hours. Store in the refrigerator for up to 3 weeks or in the freezer for up to a year. If it hardens, microwave on high for several seconds until pliable.

VARIATIONS

Moroccan Almond Paste: Substitute 4 large egg yolks or 2 large eggs for the egg whites.

Persian Almond Paste: Substitute about ½ cup orange blossom water for the egg whites.

Pistachio Paste: Pistachios were once commonly used to make many Middle Eastern confections. However, in areas where they prove too expensive, especially in America, almonds are frequently substituted and a little green food coloring added to retain the traditional look. Substitute 1 pound unsalted pistachios for the almonds.

Almond-Hazelnut Paste: Reduce the almonds to 8 ounces and add 8 ounces peeled hazelnuts.

Kaak Loz ❧ *(Syrian Almond Bracelet)*

ABOUT 40 RINGS

These rings, called *koulourikos* in Greece, are sometimes left to dry at room temperature rather than broiled. They are commonly found at a brit milah.

1 recipe (about 2 pounds) Sephardic Almond Paste (page 368)

1. Roll the almond paste into 3/4-inch-wide ropes and cut into 4-inch-long segments. For an even thickness, roll with your palms, not your fingers. Bring the ends together to form rings. Arrange on baking sheets lined with parchment paper or foil.
2. Place under a preheated broiler until pink, about 2 minutes. Let cool, then invert and place under the broiler for a few seconds to dry. Or bake in a 350-degree oven until pink, about 10 minutes. Let cool. Store in an airtight container at room temperature.

Amandines ✣ *(Sephardic Almond Balls)*

ABOUT 40 SMALL BALLS

---

1 recipe (about 2 pounds) Sephardic
Almond Paste (page 368)

Sugar for coating

Form the almond paste into 1-inch balls and roll in the sugar to coat. Store in an airtight container at room temperature.

VARIATIONS

Cedrini (Italian Filled Almond Balls): Poke a hole in the center of each ball to hollow out, fill with chopped candied citron (page 366), and smooth the almond paste over the hole.

Nuez con Almendrada (Moroccan Walnuts with Almond Paste): If desired, blend a few drops of green food coloring into the almond paste. Press a toasted walnut half onto 2 opposite sides of each almond ball.

Toot (Persian Almond Confection): In Persian, *toot* means mulberry, referring to the confection's shape. When rolling the balls in sugar, lengthen them slightly to form a berry shape. Insert a sliver of pistachio or almond in the wider end to resemble a stem.

Marunchinos (Turkish Almond Mounds): Place the almond balls on a baking sheet lined with parchment paper or dusted with flour. Flatten slightly and press a whole almond in the center of each mound. Bake in a 325-degree oven until lightly browned, about 15 minutes. Let cool on the sheet for about 10 minutes, then transfer to a rack and let cool completely.

Hadgi Badah (Iraqi Almond Mounds): Add $1/2$ teaspoon ground cardamom to the almond paste and prepare as for *Marunchinos* (above).

Mogados de Almendra ❧ *(Sephardic Almond Sticks)*

ABOUT 60 STICKS

1 recipe (about 2 pounds)
  Sephardic Almond Paste (page 368)

Roll the almond paste into ³/4-inch-thick ropes and cut into 1¹/2-inch-long pieces. Store between layers of waxed paper in an airtight container at room temperature.

371

Massapan ❧ *(Marzipan)*

ABOUT 2 POUNDS

Marzipan, whose name is derived from the Arabic *mautaban* (white glazed vessel), became Europe's first popular confection, introduced by the Arabs to Spain around the eleventh century and to Italy about a century later. Italian Jews spread marzipan to their brethren living along the Rhine River valley, and it entered the Ashkenazic culinary repertoire. Although sugar was the sweetener used in this treat in Iberia and the Middle East, early European versions were made with honey. Today marzipan remains a beloved treat, particularly among Sephardim, who serve it at brits, bar mitzvahs, and weddings.

Marzipan is a cooked nut paste containing more sugar, added in the form of a syrup, than raw paste, which gives it a whiter color and smoother, more pliable texture. It is less likely to get oily or crack during handling and is generally formed into decorative shapes and often tinted with food coloring. Miniature fruits are the most common figures. Greeks make foot-shaped marzipan called *folares*, and Italians form Star of Davids for Purim.

2 cups sugar

1 cup water

1/4 cup light corn syrup, or 1 tablespoon
  lemon juice

1 pound finely ground blanched
  almonds (about 4 1/2 cups)

1/2 teaspoon almond extract

2 large egg whites, lightly beaten
  (optional)

Confectioners' sugar for dusting

1. Stir the sugar, water, and corn syrup in a medium saucepan over low heat until the sugar dissolves, about 5 minutes. Stop stirring, increase the heat to medium, and cook until the mixture reaches the soft-ball stage, or 240 degrees on a candy thermometer, about 10 minutes.

2. Remove from the heat and, using a wooden spoon, stir in the almonds, almond extract, and egg whites if using (the whites coagulate, firming the paste). Stir over low heat until the mixture thickens and pulls away from the sides of the pan, about 5 minutes.

3. Dust a flat surface with confectioners' sugar, spoon the marzipan on top, and let cool. Knead until smooth and pliable, about 5 minutes. If you overcooked the marzipan and it's too dry to mold, place in a food processor fitted with a metal blade and blend in a little water. If too moist, knead in a little additional confectioners' sugar. Wrap tightly in plastic wrap. Store in an airtight container in the refrigerator for up to 6 months or in the freezer for up to 1 year. Return to room temperature before using.

HINTS: ❧ To give citrus-shaped marzipan, such as oranges and lemons, a pitted surface, roll on the fine section of a grater. To give berry-shaped marzipan, such as strawberries and raspberries, a bumpy surface, roll them in superfine sugar.

To make almond flowers, roll out the marzipan very thin. Using a 1/2-inch round cutter, cut out rounds. Arrange the rounds in overlapping circles to form flowers. Let stand until dry. If desired, paint with food coloring, using a small brush.

VARIATIONS

Pistachio Marzipan: This version has an attractive light green color. Substitute 1 pound blanched, peeled, and finely ground pistachios for the almonds.

Lawves (Bukharan Walnut Candy): This is served at most life-cycle events and holidays. Substitute 1 1/2 pounds ground walnuts (or 12 ounces walnuts and 12 ounces ground pistachios) for the almonds. Press into a 1-inch-thick rectangle and cut into 2-inch diamonds (about 24).

Jabane (Moroccan Coconut Marzipan): *Jabane* is a traditional Mimouna treat. At the conclusion of Passover, Moroccans celebrate a unique holiday of brotherhood and peace called Mimouna. The name is an Arabic variation of the Hebrew word *emunah* ("faith"), appropriate for the onset of spring. After sunset on the last day of Passover, Moroccan Jews traditionally throw open their doors and hold a community-wide open house. Arab neighbors join in, bringing the Jews their first *chametz* in the form of cakes and milk, which they refrain from drinking during Passover. Crowds of Jews and Arabs then roam from house to house, wishing each other the blessing *terb'hou u'tsa'adu* ("happiness and prosperity") and sampling from the tables laden with goodies. The following day is celebrated with family picnics at which tents, are pitched in recognition of the biblical phrase "How goodly are thy tents, O Jacob." Recently Mimouna festivities have gained increasing popularity in Israel among other Jewish communities.

Add the egg whites and substitute 4 cups grated fresh or unsweetened desiccated coconut for the almonds. Do not cook after adding the coconut (it hardens), but knead until malleable. Divide in half and tint one portion with green food coloring and the other with red food coloring. Form into shapes such as apples, logs, and balls. Roll in sugar to coat. This is also made with half coconut and half almonds.

Martsapades ❧ *(Greek Baked Marzipan)*

ABOUT THIRTY ½-INCH BALLS

These marzipan balls are also served unbaked and may be shaped into various decorative forms.

---

1 recipe (about 2 pounds) Marzipan (page 372)

---

1. Preheat the oven to 250 degrees. Line a large baking sheet with parchment paper or grease.
2. Form the marzipan into ½- or 1-inch balls or roll out ½ inch thick and cut into decorative shapes. Place on the prepared baking sheet.
3. Bake until set and dry but not browned, about 20 minutes. Let cool on the sheets. Store in an airtight container at room temperature.

VARIATIONS

Glazed Marzipan: Dissolve ¼ cup confectioners' sugar in 1 cup water and, if desired, add a few drops of rose water. Dip the cooled balls into the glaze, then roll in confectioners' sugar.

Press a thumb into each ball to make a deep depression and bake as above. After cooling, fill the indentations with *dulce blanco* (Sephardic Sugar Paste, page 362).

Massepain Glacé (Alsatian Iced Marzipan): After cooling the baked marzipan figures, turn them over and spread with a stiff icing made by mixing 2½ cups confectioners' sugar, 1 egg white, and if desired, a few drops of orange blossom water. Arrange, icing side up, on a baking sheet and bake at 250 degrees until dry, about 10 minutes.

Badam Loozena ❧ *(Calcutta Almond Diamonds)*

L*oozena* means "diamond" in Arabic, indicating the shape and Middle Eastern origins of these marzipan-like candies. These confections are a traditional Purim treat in Calcutta.

---

1 cup sugar

1/3 cup water

2 tablespoons rose water

8 ounces ground blanched almonds
  (about 2 1/4 cups)

1 teaspoon ground cinnamon (optional)

1/4 teaspoon ground cardamom
  (optional)

---

1. Stir the sugar and water in a medium saucepan over low heat until the sugar dissolves, about 5 minutes. Stop stirring, increase the heat to medium, and boil until the syrup reaches the thread stage, or about 230 degrees on a candy thermometer, about 6 minutes.

2. Stir in the rose water and cook for 1 minute. Add the almonds and, if desired, the spices and stir until the mixture cleans the sides of the pan, about 10 minutes.

3. Spread the nut mixture over a greased baking sheet or marble slab. Place a piece of parchment or greased waxed paper on top and roll to an even 1/2-inch thickness, about a 12-by-8-inch rectangle. Immediately remove the paper. Using a knife dipped in hot water, cut into diamonds. Store in an airtight container at room temperature.

VARIATIONS

Pista Loozena (Calcutta Pistachio Diamonds): Substitute 8 ounces ground unsalted pistachios for the almonds and omit the spices.

Nariyal Loozena (Calcutta Coconut Diamonds): Substitute 2 2/3 cups (7 ounces) grated fresh coconut (or grated unsweetened desiccated coconut moistened with 2 tablespoons water or rose water) for the almonds and omit the cinnamon.

Tangerine Loozena (Calcutta Tangerine-Almond Diamonds): Substitute 1/2 cup tangerine juice for the water and rose water and add the grated zest of 2 tangerines.

Badam Soukhte ❧ *(Persian Candied Almonds)*

ABOUT 1½ CUPS

This simple form of candied nuts evolved into the more elaborate candy-coated Jordan almonds.

1 cup sugar

1/3 cup water

1¼ cups (6½ ounces) whole
unblanched almonds, raw or lightly
toasted

1/4 teaspoon ground cardamom

1. Stir the sugar and water in a heavy medium saucepan over low heat until the sugar dissolves, about 5 minutes. Stop stirring, increase the heat to medium, and boil until the syrup reaches the thread stage, or 230 degrees on a candy thermometer, about 6 minutes.
2. Add the almonds and cardamom and stir constantly until the syrup becomes bubbly and granular and reaches about 240 degrees.
3. Quickly pour the mixture onto a large greased baking sheet and, using 2 forks, separate the nuts. Let cool. Store in an airtight container at room temperature for up to 2 weeks.

VARIATION

Gebrennte Mandlen (Ashkenazic Burnt Almonds): Substitute 1 teaspoon ground cinnamon for the cardamom.

El Majoun ❧ *(Moroccan Honey Almond Candy)*

ABOUT 36 CANDIES

---

8 ounces (about 1²/₃ cups) blanched whole almonds, toasted, cooled, and finely ground

¹/₂ cup golden raisins, coarsely chopped

¹/₂ cup golden raisins, finely chopped

¹/₃ cup (4 ounces) honey

3 tablespoons unsalted butter or margarine

2 tablespoons minced crystallized ginger

¹/₂ teaspoon ground allspice

¹/₈ teaspoon ground cinnamon

¹/₈ teaspoon ground fennel seeds

¹/₈ teaspoon ground mace

¹/₈ teaspoon grated nutmeg

Pinch of cayenne

Pinch of saffron

About ¹/₂ cup sesame seeds

---

1. Combine all the ingredients except the sesame seeds in a small heavy saucepan. Cook over very low heat, stirring frequently with a wooden spoon, until very thick, about 1 hour.

2. Remove from the heat and let stand until cool enough to handle but still warm. Form into 1-inch balls, then roll in the sesame seeds to coat. Store in an airtight container at room temperature.

NOTE: ❧ Crystallized ginger, also called candied ginger, is made by boiling fresh ginger, cooking it in a sugar syrup, then drying it.

Crocon ❦ *(Sephardic Almond Brittle)*

ABOUT 1¾ POUNDS

When sugar syrup reaches a temperature of more than 300 degrees, the texture of candy made from it changes from chewy to brittle. This confection is harder than American peanut brittle, which contains baking soda.

2 cups sugar	12 ounces (about 2¹/₃ cups) almonds,
²/₃ cup water	raw or lightly toasted, coarsely
¹/₂ teaspoon lemon juice	chopped
1 tablespoon butter, or 1 teaspoon	
vanilla extract (optional)	

1. Stir the sugar, water, and lemon juice in a heavy medium saucepan over low heat until the sugar dissolves, about 5 minutes. Stop stirring, increase the heat to medium-high, and boil, shaking the pan occasionally, until the syrup turns a light brown color and reaches the caramel stage, or 325 degrees on a candy thermometer, about 15 minutes. Dip the base of the pan into a bowl of cold water to stop the cooking.
2. If desired, add the butter. Stir in the nuts. Pour onto a large greased baking sheet and, using an oiled spatula or the back of a spoon, spread to a ¹/₃-inch thickness. Let stand until cool and hard. Break into pieces. Store in an airtight container at room temperature.

VARIATIONS

Coconut-Nut Brittle: Reduce the nuts to 1²/₃ cups (8 ounces) and add 1 cup lightly toasted grated unsweetened desiccated coconut.

Sesame-Nut Brittle: Add 3 tablespoons sesame seeds with the nuts.

Fistokeeyah (Iraqi Pistachio Brittle): Substitute 2 cups unsalted blanched pistachios for the almonds.

Bindookeeyah (Iraqi Hazelnut Brittle): Substitute 2 cups coarsely chopped blanched hazelnuts for the almonds.

Khalva (Bukharan Sesame Paste Candy): This is similar to the type of halvah confection popular in America. Grind 1 pound (3¹/₄ cups) untoasted sesame seeds into a paste and substitute for the nuts.

Susamit ❧ *(Middle Eastern Sesame Seed Candy)*

ABOUT 96 PIECES

Sesame candies, one of the most ancient extant confections, originated in the Middle East, then spread to North Africa, India, and even to parts of eastern Europe, where they became a standard holiday treat. These are also called *simsimeeyah* in Syria, *simsimee* in Calcutta, *pasteli* in the Balkans, *sohan konjidi* in Iran, *koubeta* and, on Purim, *psires tou Amman* ("fleas of Haman") in Greece.

1¹/₂ pounds (about 4¹/₂ cups) sesame seeds	³/₄ cup water
1¹/₂ cups sugar, or ³/₄ cup sugar and 1 cup (12 ounces) honey	1 teaspoon lemon juice

1. Stir the sesame seeds in a large dry skillet over medium heat until golden brown, 5 to 10 minutes. Or spread over a baking sheet and toast in a 350-degree oven, shaking the sheet occasionally, until golden brown, 5 to 10 minutes. Spoon into a bowl and let cool.
2. Stir the sugar, water, and lemon juice in a heavy medium saucepan over low heat until the sugar dissolves, about 5 minutes. Stop stirring, increase the heat to medium, and boil until the syrup reaches the soft-ball stage, or 236 degrees on a candy thermometer, 20 to 30 minutes.
3. Add the sesame seeds and simmer, stirring frequently with a wooden spoon, until thickened, about 10 minutes.
4. Pour onto a greased baking sheet or marble slab. Place a piece of parchment paper or greased waxed paper on top and roll to a ¹/₂-inch thickness. Immediately remove the paper. Dip a sharp knife into hot water and cut into rectangles, squares, or diamonds. Let cool. If desired, wrap individual candies in plastic wrap or waxed paper. Store in an airtight container at room temperature.

Pletzlach ❧ *(Ashkenazic Honey Candy)*

ABOUT 45 PIECES

Long after sugar emerged as the predominant sweetener in confections, honey candies remained popular among eastern European Jews, especially on Passover and Purim. This basic candy, its name derived from *pletzl* (Yiddish for "board") because it is spread into a thin layer, was commonly flavored with inexpensive items, such as nuts, seeds, vegetables, and matza. The candy remains chewy because it is cooked to less than 300 degrees, the point when a syrup becomes brittle. Since honey is more hygroscopic than sucrose and absorbs moisture from the air, candy made from it tends to be sticky. Don't make *pletzlach* on a very humid day.

---

1 pound (1¹/₃ cups) honey   *1 tablespoon lemon juice (optional)*
1 cup sugar

---

1. Stir the honey, sugar, and lemon juice if using in a medium heavy-bottomed saucepan over low heat until the sugar dissolves, about 5 minutes. Stop stirring, increase the heat to medium, and bring to a gentle boil, about 5 minutes. Cook until the syrup turns a light brown and reaches the soft-crack stage, or about 280 degrees on a candy thermometer, about 30 minutes.
2. Pour onto a greased marble slab or baking sheet and spread to a ¹/₂-inch thickness. Let stand until firm but not hard, about 10 minutes.
3. Dip a sharp knife into hot water and cut into 1-inch squares or diamonds. Let cool completely. If desired, wrap individual candies in plastic wrap or waxed paper. Store in an airtight container at room temperature.

VARIATIONS

For a more intense honey flavor, increase the honey to 2 cups and reduce the sugar to ¹/₂ cup.

For a nontraditional variation, drizzle with or dip the candies into melted semisweet or bittersweet chocolate.

Ingberlach (Ashkenazic Ginger Candy): *Ingber* is the Yiddish word for ginger, which is always used in the ground form in Ashkenazic cooking. Add 1 to 2 teaspoons ground ginger.

Farfel Pletzlach (Ashkenazic Matza Candy): After the syrup reaches the soft-crack stage, stir in 2 cups matza farfel, 1 cup coarsely chopped almonds or walnuts, and if desired, 1 to 2 teaspoons ground ginger. Or add 3 cups chopped nuts and 3/4 cup matza farfel.

Noent (Ashkenazic Nut Candy): After the syrup begins to boil, add 1 to 1 1/2 pounds finely chopped almonds, hazelnuts, pecans, or walnuts. Reduce the heat to low and cook, stirring frequently, until thickened and golden, about 30 minutes.

Mohnlach (Ashkenazic Poppy Seed Candy): This was a traditional Ashkenazic Purim treat. After the syrup begins to boil, add 1 pound (about 3 cups) ground poppy seeds, reduce the heat to low, and cook, stirring frequently, until thickened, about 30 minutes. If desired, after it thickens, add 8 ounces (2 cups) coarsely or finely chopped blanched almonds, hazelnuts, pecans, or walnuts.

GEORGIA (GRUZIYA)

 Georgia (Gruziya in Russian) is located at the crossroads of the former spice and silk trade, accounting for the land's once legendary wealth. The area is associated with the biblical Meshech (Genesis 10:2) and a land of metal merchants (Ezekiel 27:13). According to an ancient Georgian legend, the Jews of that area are descended from the Ten Lost Tribes—a contention they support by pointing to the absence of *cohanim* (priests) among their number—who resided in the southern territories. The impact of the Jews was such that many Georgian kings and nobles claimed descent from members of the Judean royal family exiled by Nebuchadnezzar. Historically, most of the Jews were divided among four cities—Kutaisi, Akhaltsikhe, Batum, and Tiflis (now Tbilisi)—and a few farmers were scattered around the countryside.

In 1801, the Russian Empire absorbed the once independent kingdom. The first known national census, held in 1835, revealed 12,234 Jews living in Georgia. Many Gruzinim retained strong Zionistic feelings throughout the Soviet era and, taking advantage of the occasional periods of liberal Soviet emigration policies, emigrated to Israel, leaving about 17,000 Jews in Georgia.

The warm climate and rich soil of Georgia are ideal for agriculture, yielding high-quality produce and vineyards—the area may actually be the original home of the grape. Georgian dessert usually consists of fresh fruit. Noticeably lacking in Georgia are the Middle Eastern–influenced syrup-soaked phyllo treats and halvah common to neighboring Armenia and Azerbaijan. Georgians love sitting around the dinner table after a meal, talking and singing; indeed, it is the favorite Georgian pastime.

Gozinakhi ❧ *(Georgian Honey Walnut Candy)*

Ancient Israelites viewed honey with high regard. Indeed, the Hebrew word for bee, *devorah*, is derived from the root *dvr* ("word"), alluding to the bee's creating honey, which, like the Divine Word, is unique and eternal. Today honey remains an important component in all forms of Jewish cooking, adding a touch of sweetness to everything from stews to desserts.

Almost every Georgian dessert contains walnuts, a favorite food of the country.

---

2 cups (24 ounces) honey
¼ cup sugar

1 pound (about 4 cups) walnuts, finely
chopped

---

1. Stir the honey and sugar in a heavy medium saucepan over low heat until the sugar dissolves, about 5 minutes. Stop stirring, increase the heat to medium, and boil until the syrup reaches the thread stage, or 230 degrees on a candy thermometer, about 8 minutes.
2. Reduce the heat to low, add the walnuts, and stir until the mixture cleans the sides of the pan, about 10 minutes.
3. Pour onto a greased baking sheet, spread to a ½-inch thickness, and smooth the surface. Let stand until firm but not hard, about 10 minutes, then cut into diamond shapes. Let cool completely. Store in an airtight container at room temperature.

Passover Desserts

See how my eyes are brightened
because I tasted a little of this honey.

—I SAMUEL 14:29

NO OTHER HOLIDAY IN THE JEWISH CALENDAR CONTAINS SUCH DIVERSE CULINARY CUSTOMS AMONG THE VARIOUS JEWISH COMMUNITIES AS DOES PASSOVER. THE BIBLE COMMANDS THE CONSUMPTION OF MATZA ON THE FIRST NIGHT OF PASSOVER AND strictly forbids eating or even possessing *chametz* (any type of leavened flour) during the entire holiday. In addition, Ashkenazim eschew *kitniyot* (Hebrew for "legumes") in the context of Passover including grains such as rice, millet, and buckwheat. Many Ashkenazim also abstain from items once grown near or stored with wheat, such as garlic, anise, caraway, coriander, mustard, and sesame seeds. Some Ashkenazim eat derivatives of *kitniyot,* such as oil and syrup, while others do not. In addition, Chasidim do not eat matza mixed with liquid (*gebrochts,* Yiddish for "broken") except on the last day of Passover. Most Sephardim, as a rule, eat only fresh *kitniyot,* such as green peas, fresh fava beans, and green beans, and not dried legumes. Generally, those Sephardim from Arabic-speaking countries eat rice, while those from western Europe do not. Some Middle Eastern Jews abstain from corn and other indigenous American grains. Many Italian and Moroccan Jews refrain from dairy products throughout the entire holiday.

In the past, these dietary restrictions generally resulted in a limited menu among Ashkenazim, based primarily on matza and potatoes. Modern manufacturing combined with an unprecedented boom in products under kosher supervision has led to a wide array of Passover fare. Nonetheless, many time-honored Passover dishes retain their appeal today, and few are as beloved as the various holiday desserts.

Pan de Espagna de Pessah/Pesach Tawrt ❧
(Passover Sponge Cake)

9 TO 12 SERVINGS

This Passover classic is remarkably versatile. By adding various ingredients, you can create a wide range of tasty cakes.

9 large eggs, separated	2 teaspoons grated lemon or orange zest,
1½ cups sugar	or 1 teaspoon each
¼ cup lemon juice, orange juice, or	¾ cup matza cake meal, or ½ cup cake
sweet wine, or 2 tablespoons orange	meal and ¼ cup potato starch
juice and 2 tablespoons lemon juice	

1. Preheat the oven to 325 degrees.
2. Beat the egg whites on low until foamy, about 30 seconds. Increase the speed to high and beat until soft peaks form, 1 to 2 minutes. Gradually add ¾ cup sugar and beat until stiff and glossy, 5 to 8 minutes.
3. Using the same beaters, beat the egg yolks and remaining ¾ cup sugar until pale and creamy, about 10 minutes. Add the lemon juice and zest. Stir in the cake meal. Fold in the egg whites.
4. Pour into an ungreased 10-by-4-inch tube pan, preferably with a removable bottom. Tap the pan to remove any air bubbles. Place on the lowest shelf of the oven and bake until the cake springs back when lightly touched and a tester inserted in the center comes out clean, about 1 hour. Invert the pan onto a bottle and let cool completely. Using a thin knife, loosen the sides of the cake and remove from the pan. Store covered at room temperature for up to 3 days. Use a serrated knife to cut. If desired, serve with fresh fruit and/or Hungarian Wine Sauce (page 413).

VARIATIONS

Passover Banana Cake: Reduce the sugar to 1¼ cups and add 1½ cups mashed very ripe bananas and, if desired, ½ to 1 cup coarsely chopped walnuts or pecans.

Passover Carrot Cake: Add 1⅓ cups grated carrots and, if desired, ½ cup raisins.

Passover Chocolate Cake: Omit the lemon juice and zest and add 3 tablespoons unsweetened cocoa powder dissolved in $^1/4$ cup boiling water and cooled.

Passover Date-Nut Cake: Add 2 cups coarsely chopped dates and $^1/2$ cup coarsely chopped walnuts or pecans.

Passover Mocha Cake: Omit the lemon juice and zest and add 2 tablespoons instant coffee powder and 1 tablespoon unsweetened cocoa powder dissolved in $^1/4$ cup boiling water and cooled.

Passover Pineapple Cake: Omit the lemon juice and add $^1/2$ cup drained crushed pineapple and $^1/2$ teaspoon almond extract.

Passover Spice Cake: Omit the zest. Sift the cake meal with 2 teaspoons ground cinnamon (or 1 teaspoon ground cinnamon and 1 teaspoon ground ginger) and $^1/2$ teaspoon ground cloves.

HINTS: ❧ Superfine sugar produces a softer texture than granulated sugar.

For greater volume, place the uncracked eggs in a bowl of warm water for about 10 minutes.

Since sponge cakes tend to crack in the center, they are baked in a tube pan, preferably one with a removable bottom. The tube sets and dries out the center of the cake, which, if baked in a regular pan, would fall while cooling. Since egg-foam cakes are not very substantial, they are cooled upside down to remain stretched until set.

Use a serrated knife moistened by dipping into water to cut egg-foam cakes. To slice layers, use a long serrated knife to score an even horizontal cut around the outside of the cake. Then, holding the knife level to the scored line, use a sawing motion while rotating the cake to gradually cut through the layer. Lift the delicate layers by sliding a piece of cardboard or the bottom of a springform pan underneath.

Torta de Muez/Nusstorte ❧ *(Flourless Nut Torte)*

Soon after cooks discovered how to leaven cakes with beaten eggs, they began adding nuts and, in the process, greatly reduced the amount of sugar without sacrificing flavor or moistness. Flourless nut cakes prove perfect Passover fare. Sephardim tend to use citrus juice. Ashkenazim historically had only wine available, sometimes only raisin wine. Sephardim generally serve the cake plain, while Hungarians commonly cover it with buttercream or *csokoladé maz* (chocolate glaze).

---

8 large eggs, separated

1/2 cup sugar

1/4 cup orange juice, lemon juice, or sweet wine

1 teaspoon grated lemon or orange zest (optional)

1 cup (about 4 1/2 ounces) finely ground almonds, hazelnuts, pecans, or walnuts, or 3/4 cup ground nuts and 1/4 cup matza cake meal

1 recipe nutty, chocolate, or mocha buttercream (recipes follow) (optional)

---

1. Preheat the oven to 350 degrees. Grease a 9-inch springform pan.
2. Beat the egg yolks and sugar until thick and creamy, about 10 minutes. Stir in the juice and, if desired, the zest. Add the nuts.
3. Beat the egg whites on low speed until foamy, about 30 seconds. Increase the speed to medium-high and beat until stiff but not dry. Fold one-fourth of the whites into the nut mixture to lighten, then gently fold in the remaining whites.
4. Pour into the prepared pan. Bake until the cake springs back when lightly touched and a tester inserted in the center comes out clean, 35 to 45 minutes. Invert and let cool in the pan.
5. To frost: Cut the cake horizontally into 2 or 3 layers and spread with the buttercream. Store in the refrigerator for up to 3 days or in the freezer. Return to room temperature to serve.

Nutty Buttercream

1 cup sugar

1/2 cup water

6 large egg yolks

1 1/2 cups (3 sticks) unsalted butter or margarine, softened

Pinch of salt

1 cup finely chopped toasted almonds, hazelnuts, pecans, or walnuts

1. Stir the sugar and water in a small saucepan over low heat until the sugar dissolves, about 5 minutes. Stop stirring, increase the heat to medium, and boil until the syrup reaches the soft-ball stage, or 240 degrees on a candy thermometer, about 10 minutes.

2. Meanwhile, beat the egg yolks until thick and creamy, about 5 minutes. In a slow, steady stream, beat in the hot syrup. (The syrup should not hit the beaters or it will spatter and solidify.) Continue beating until cool, about 5 minutes.

3. On low speed, gradually beat in the butter, 1 tablespoon at a time. Beat in the salt. Add the nuts. Refrigerate until of spreading consistency or up to 1 week. Return to room temperature before spreading.

VARIATIONS

Chocolate Buttercream: Omit the nuts and gradually add 6 to 8 ounces melted and cooled semisweet or bittersweet chocolate.

Mocha Buttercream: To the Chocolate Buttercream, add 2 tablespoons instant coffee or espresso powder dissolved in 2 teaspoons hot water and cooled.

Pesach Apfelkuchen ✤ *(Ashkenazic Passover Apple Cake)*

9 TO 12 SERVINGS

Since apple cakes have long been among the most popular Ashkenazic baked goods, it is hardly surprising that enterprising cooks adapted them to the dictates of Passover.

4 large (about 2 pounds) cooking apples, such as Golden Delicious, Granny Smith, Gravenstein, Greening, Jonathan, Macoun, Pippin, Starr, Winesap, Yellow Transparent, or any combination, peeled, cored, and coarsely chopped

1 tablespoon orange or lemon juice

1 cup matza cake meal, or ³/4 cup cake meal and ¹/4 cup potato starch

¹/4 cup ground almonds, hazelnuts, pecans, or walnuts

1 teaspoon ground cinnamon, grated orange zest, or grated lemon zest

¹/2 teaspoon salt

8 large eggs, separated

1 cup sugar

Topping (optional):

³/4 cup matza cake meal

¹/2 cup sugar

6 tablespoons (³/4 stick) unsalted butter or margarine, chilled

1. Preheat the oven to 350 degrees (325 degrees if using a glass pan). Grease a 13-by-9-inch baking pan, line with waxed paper, and grease again.
2. Toss the apples with the juice. Combine the cake meal, nuts, cinnamon, and salt. Beat the egg yolks and sugar until thick and creamy, about 10 minutes. Stir in the cake meal mixture and apples.
3. Beat the egg whites on low until foamy, about 30 seconds. Increase the speed to high and beat until stiff but not dry. Fold one-fourth of the egg whites into the apple mixture to lighten, then fold in the remaining whites. Spoon into the prepared pan.
4. To make the topping if using: Combine the cake meal and sugar. Cut in the butter until the mixture resembles coarse crumbs. Sprinkle on top of the cake.
5. Bake until golden, about 45 minutes. Serve warm or at room temperature. Serve plain or with Hungarian Wine Sauce (page 413).

Gâteau à l'Orange ❧ *(Sephardic Orange-Almond Cake)*

9 TO 12 SERVINGS

The uniqueness of this dense, moist, tart cake lies in the inclusion of cooked and mashed whole oranges. It is arguably the most emblematic of Sephardic cakes, featuring two favorite foods—oranges and almonds.

2 large navel oranges, washed (do not peel)	1 1/2 cups (about 6 ounces) finely ground blanched almonds
2 tablespoons orange blossom water, or 1/4 cup orange liqueur, or 1 teaspoon orange extract	1 1/4 cups sugar
	4 large eggs
	2 large eggs, separated

1. Place the oranges in a saucepan, add cold water to cover, and bring to a boil. Cover the pan, reduce the heat to low, and simmer until the oranges are very soft, about 1 hour. Remove the oranges, place in a bowl of cold water, and let stand for 10 minutes. Drain the oranges and pat dry. (Store in the refrigerator for up to 1 day if desired.) Cut the oranges into pieces and discard any seeds. Using a food grinder or food processor, finely grind or puree. Add the orange blossom water.

2. Preheat the oven to 375 degrees. Grease and dust with potato starch or matza cake meal a 9-inch springform pan or two 8-inch round cake pans.

3. Combine the almonds and 1/4 cup sugar. Beat the whole eggs and egg yolks with 3/4 cup sugar until thick and creamy, about 10 minutes. Stir in the oranges and almonds.

4. Beat the egg whites on low speed until foamy, about 30 seconds. Increase the speed to medium-high and beat until soft peaks form, 1 to 2 minutes. Gradually add the remaining 1/4 cup sugar and beat until stiff and glossy, 5 to 8 minutes. Fold into the orange mixture.

5. Pour into the prepared pan. Bake until golden brown, about 1 hour for the springform pan or 40 minutes for the 8-inch pans. Set on a rack and let cool completely. After removing from the pan, wrap in plastic wrap and store at room temperature for up to 1 day or in the refrigerator for up to 3 days.

VARIATION

Do not separate the 2 eggs, but beat them with the whole eggs and 1 cup sugar until thickened. Stir 1 teaspoon Passover baking powder into the ground almonds.

Tishpishti ❧ *(Middle Eastern Honey-Nut Cake)*

24 TO 48 SERVINGS

Tishpishti, also called *revani* (after a sixteenth-century Turkish poet), refers to a variety of syrup-soaked cakes common to the domain of the former Ottoman Empire. Sephardim adapted this sweet, heavy cake by using oil instead of butter and adding a touch of orange. Semolina cakes are common during most of the year, while matza and all-nut versions are popular during Passover. Since it is so sweet, *tishpishti* is always cut into small pieces.

Honey Syrup:

1 cup (12 ounces) honey

2/3 cup water

1/3 cup sugar

1/4 cup fresh lemon juice

Cake:

2 cups (about 6 ounces) finely ground almonds, hazelnuts, pistachios, or walnuts

1 cup matza cake meal

1 cup matza meal

1 teaspoon ground cinnamon

1/2 teaspoon ground cloves

6 large eggs

2 cups sugar

1/2 cup vegetable oil

1 tablespoon grated orange or lemon zest, or 1 1/2 teaspoons each

1. To make the syrup: Stir all the syrup ingredients in a medium saucepan over low heat until the sugar dissolves, about 5 minutes. Stop stirring, increase the heat to medium, bring to a boil, and boil for 1 minute. Let cool.
2. Preheat the oven to 350 degrees (325 degrees if using a glass pan). Grease a 13-by-9-inch baking pan.
3. To make the cake: Combine the nuts, cake meal, matza meal, cinnamon, and cloves. Beat the eggs and sugar until pale and thick, about 10 minutes. Add the oil and zest. Stir in the nut mixture.
4. Pour into the prepared pan. Bake until a tester inserted in the center comes out clean, about 45 minutes.
5. Cut the cake into 1- to 2-inch squares or diamonds. Drizzle the cooled syrup over the warm cake. Serve warm or at room temperature.

VARIATIONS

Omit the matza meal (but not the cake meal). Add 2 tablespoons orange juice or orange blossom water. Reduce the sugar to 1 cup. Separate the eggs and beat the egg yolks with the sugar. Beat the egg whites until stiff but not dry and fold into the batter.

Sugar Syrup: Omit the honey, increase the sugar to 2 cups and the water to 1 cup, and simmer the syrup until slightly thickened, about 10 minutes (it will register 225 degrees on a candy thermometer).

MATZA

 It was in ancient Egypt that many bread-making techniques, most still in use today, were first developed. The Egyptians took their breads very seriously. Indeed, Pharaoh had his chief baker executed when a pebble was found in a loaf (Genesis 40:22). Yeast bread was the pride of the Egyptian upper class, and court bakers strove to create elaborately shaped loaves. So when the Bible wanted to make a stark distinction between Egyptian society and the newly emerged Israelite nation, it chose "poor man's bread," matza, as the symbol.

During the entire holiday of Passover, matza is the only permitted form of bread. The flour for making matza is safeguarded to prevent contact with moisture and therefore fermentation. *Shmurah* (guarded) matza has been watched from the moment of harvest. "Passover flour" is supervised from the time of milling. The water for making matza must stand for at least 24 hours. To eliminate any possibility of *chametz* (any type of leavened flour), both Ashkenazim and Sephardim roll out the dough very thin, perforate it to prevent the formation of air bubbles, then bake it until very crisp. The entire matza-making process, from exposure to moisture until baking, must take place in less than 18 minutes.

Handmade *shmurah* matza generally comes in large, thin rounds and has a nutty taste, more flavorful than the square-shaped machine-made matza. To increase its utility, matza is also ground to make matza meal or finely ground to make matza cake meal. Crumbled and ground matza is used to create an imaginative array of Passover desserts, including pancakes, fritters, dumplings, puddings, pastries, and cakes.

Pesach Mandelbrot ❧ *(Ashkenazic Passover Almond Bread)*

ABOUT TWENTY-FOUR ½-INCH SLICES

Housewives commonly found ways of preparing many of their favorite desserts for Passover, including *mandelbrot*. These cookies keep for a long time, so they are perfect for having on hand for unexpected guests.

1½ cups matza cake meal

2 tablespoons potato starch

¼ teaspoon salt

4 large eggs

1 cup sugar

1 cup vegetable oil

½ teaspoon almond extract, or
    1 teaspoon grated lemon zest and
    1 teaspoon grated orange zest

¾ to 1 cup finely chopped almonds,
    toasted hazelnuts, pistachios, raisins,
    chopped dates, chocolate chips, or
    any combination (optional)

¼ cup sugar mixed with 1 teaspoon
    ground cinnamon (optional)

---

1. Preheat the oven to 350 degrees. Line a large baking sheet with parchment paper or grease.
2. Sift together the cake meal, potato starch, and salt. Beat the eggs and sugar until light and fluffy, 5 to 10 minutes. Add the oil and almond extract. Stir in the cake meal mixture. The dough will be loose. If desired, add the almonds.
3. Divide the dough in half and place on the prepared baking sheet; the dough will be sticky and loose. Each loaf should be 3 inches wide and 1 inch thick. Pat to level the surface. If desired, sprinkle with the cinnamon sugar.
4. Bake until golden brown, about 45 minutes.
5. Using a serrated knife, cut the warm loaves crosswise into ½-inch-thick slices. Place the slices, cut side down, on the baking sheet and bake until golden brown, about 15 minutes. Transfer to a rack and let cool. The cookies will harden further as they stand. Store in an airtight container at room temperature for up to 1 week or in the freezer for up to 1 month.

VARIATION

Butter Mandelbrot: Substitute ½ cup (1 stick) softened butter or margarine for the oil. Beat the butter until smooth. Gradually add the sugar and beat until light and fluffy. Beat in the eggs, one at a time. Add the extract and salt. Stir in the cake meal mixture.

Mustachudos  *(Turkish Nut Crescents)*

ABOUT 24 COOKIES

These chewy Passover cookies get their name, meaning "mustaches," from their crescent shape.

2 cups (about 6 ounces) finely ground walnuts, or 1¹/₄ cups ground almonds and ³/₄ cup ground walnuts	2 teaspoons grated orange zest, or 1 tablespoon rose water, or ¹/₄ teaspoon ground cloves
¹/₂ cup sugar	1 large egg, lightly beaten
1 teaspoon ground cinnamon	Confectioners' sugar for dusting (optional)

1. Preheat the oven to 350 degrees. Line 2 large baking sheets with parchment paper or grease.
2. Combine the nuts, sugar, cinnamon, and zest. Stir in the egg to form a paste. Or process the ingredients in a food processor until the mixture forms a paste.
3. Form the dough into 1-inch balls, then roll between your palms into 2-inch-long by ¹/₂-inch-thick crescents. Place on the prepared baking sheets and flatten slightly.
4. Bake until golden, 10 to 12 minutes. Let cool on the sheets for 10 minutes. If desired, sprinkle with the confectioners' sugar. Transfer to a rack and let cool completely. Store in an airtight container at room temperature for up to 1 week or in the freezer for several months.

VARIATION

Add ¹/₄ cup matza meal and increase the eggs to 3.

Makarondelach ❧ *(Ashkenazic Macaroons)*

Macaroons are a simple mixture of ground nuts, sugar, and egg whites. The name comes from the Italian *maccarone* (paste), reflecting its point of origin as well as its main ingredient, almond paste. (The word *macaroni* comes from the same source, referring to flour paste.) Italian Jews transmitted this flourless cookie to Ashkenazim, who added it to both their Passover and everyday pantry. Macaroons followed only *mandelbrot* and *kichlach* in cookie popularity among eastern Europeans. In America, Passover macaroons became associated with the insipid, leathery canned variety. The real thing, however, is a soft and chewy treat.

---

2 large egg whites

Pinch of salt

2/3 cup sugar

1 teaspoon almond extract or almond liqueur

8 ounces finely ground blanched almonds or hazelnuts (about 2 cups)

About 30 whole almonds or hazelnuts (optional)

---

1. Preheat the oven to 350 degrees. Line large baking sheets with parchment paper or greased aluminum foil.
2. Beat the egg whites on low speed until foamy, about 30 seconds. Add the salt, increase the speed to high, and beat until soft peaks form, 1 to 2 minutes. Gradually add the sugar, 1 tablespoon at a time, and beat until stiff and glossy, 5 to 8 minutes. Add the almond extract. Fold in the ground nuts. Drop by tablespoonfuls, 1 1/2 inches apart, onto the prepared baking sheets. If desired, press an almond into the center of each mound.
3. Bake, switching the baking sheets halfway through, until firm and golden, about 20 minutes. Let cool on the sheets for 2 minutes, then transfer to a rack and let cool completely. Store in an airtight container at room temperature for up to 1 week or in the freezer for up to 1 month.

VARIATIONS

Ricciarelli (Italian Orange Macaroons): Add 1 tablespoon grated orange or tangerine zest.

Chocolate Macaroons: Increase the sugar to $3/4$ cup and add $1^1/2$ ounces melted unsweetened chocolate or $2^1/2$ tablespoons unsweetened cocoa powder.

Coconut Macaroons: Substitute $1^1/3$ cups ($3^1/2$ ounces) grated fresh or dried coconut for the nuts.

Honey Macaroons: Reduce the sugar to $1/2$ cup and add 2 tablespoons honey.

HINTS: ❧ Make sure the nuts are very fresh.

When grinding nuts in a food processor, add a little sugar to keep them from turning greasy.

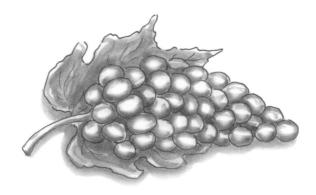

FRUIT OF THE VINE

No celebration can be considered joyous unless there is wine.
—TALMUD

 In the mid-1970s, archeologists digging at Hajji Firuz Tepe near Lake Urmia in the northwest region of Iran excavated a potsherd dating back to 5400–5000 BCE. When researchers chemically analyzed a yellowish residue clinging to this Neolithic piece of pottery, it revealed a calcium salt created when tartaric acid interacts with elements in the soil. Since tartaric acid occurs naturally in any significant amount only in grapes, the residue turned out to be the discovery of the earliest evidence of wine. This date in the late Stone Age, coinciding with mankind's first permanent settlements, demonstrates that wine is at least as old as civilization itself.

Tests also revealed that the wine contained terebinth resin, which probably served as a preservative, giving the wine a piney flavor and bouquet. Thus, these ancient oenologists knew not only how to make wine but how to flavor and preserve it. Indeed, the pottery in which the wine was stored had a narrow neck, a design that made it easy to stopper the vessel and thus keep out airborne bacteria.

Grain, olive oil, and wine formed the basis of the diet and the economy of ancient Israel. Wine, symbolizing joy and fruitfulness, ushers in and out the Sabbath and holidays and also serves as an essential component at the Passover Seder, weddings, and numerous life-cycle events. Various naturally sweet wines, such as late-harvest Riesling or gewürztraminer, botrytised sauvignon blanc, muscat, sauterne, and Asti Spumante, make a fitting complement to desserts.

Masas de Vino ❧ *(Turkish Wine Cookies)*

ABOUT 60 COOKIES

---

1 cup vegetable oil

1 cup sweet wine, or $3/4$ cup sweet wine
   and 1 large egg

1 cup sugar

$1/2$ teaspoon ground cinnamon, or
   1 tablespoon grated orange zest

$1^1/2$ cups ground blanched almonds or
   walnuts (about $4^1/4$ ounces)

3 cups matza cake meal

About 60 whole blanched almonds or
   walnut halves (optional)

---

1. Preheat the oven to 350 degrees.
2. Combine the oil, wine, sugar, and cinnamon. Add the nuts, then gradually stir in the cake meal to make a workable dough.
3. Shape the dough into 1-inch balls, place on ungreased baking sheets, and flatten slightly. Or roll out $1/2$ inch thick and cut into squares or rounds. With the tines of a fork, make a criss-cross pattern on top of each cookie or, if desired, press a whole almond into the center.
4. Bake until lightly colored, 20 to 25 minutes. Let cool on the sheets for 10 minutes, then transfer to a rack and let cool completely. Store in an airtight container at room temperature for up to 5 days.

VARIATIONS

Wine Butter Cookies: Substitute 2 cups (4 sticks) softened butter for the oil. Beat the butter and sugar until light and fluffy, then add the remaining ingredients.

Passover Shortbread: Divide the dough in half, press each half into a 9-inch square baking pan, and prick with the tines of a fork every $1/2$ inch. After baking, cut the warm shortbread into 2-by-1-inch bars.

Pesach Courabie ❧ *(Sephardic Passover Butter Cookies)*

ABOUT 48 COOKIES

---

1 cup (2 sticks) unsalted butter or
    margarine, softened
$3/4$ cup sugar
2 large egg yolks, or 1 large egg yolk and
    1 tablespoon orange juice or brandy

1 teaspoon vanilla extract or grated
    orange zest
$1/4$ teaspoon salt
2 cups matza cake meal

---

1. Beat the butter until smooth, about 1 minute. Gradually add the sugar and beat until light and fluffy, about 4 minutes. Add the egg yolks, vanilla, and salt. Stir in the cake meal. Wrap in plastic wrap and refrigerate for at least 1 hour or up to 3 days.
2. Preheat the oven to 375 degrees.
3. Shape the dough into 1-inch balls, place 2 inches apart on ungreased baking sheets, and flatten. Or roll out the dough on a surface sprinkled with confectioners' sugar until $1/4$ inch thick, cut into 2-inch squares or 3-inch rounds, and transfer to the baking sheets.
4. Bake until set but not browned, 8 to 10 minutes. Let stand until firm, about 1 minute, then transfer to a rack and let cool completely. Store in an airtight container for up to 5 days or in the freezer for several months.

VARIATIONS

Substitute $1/2$ cup vegetable oil for the butter.

Sephardic Passover Nut Cookies: Reduce the cake meal to 1 cup and add $1^1/2$ cups chopped almonds, hazelnuts, pistachios, or walnuts.

Pesach Loukoumades ❧ *(Sephardic Passover Fritters)*

ABOUT 24 FRITTERS

1 cup water
1/2 cup vegetable or olive oil
2 tablespoons sugar
1/4 teaspoon salt
1 cup matza cake meal
1 teaspoon grated lemon or orange zest
  (optional)

4 large eggs
Vegetable oil for deep-frying
1 recipe cooled sugar syrup (see atar,
  page 265) or confectioners' sugar

1. Bring the water, oil, sugar, and salt to a boil in a medium saucepan over medium heat. Add the cake meal all at once and stir with a wooden spoon over medium heat until the mixture leaves the sides of the pan and forms a ball, about 1 minute.
2. Remove from the heat and stir until the mixture is lukewarm, about 5 minutes. (If the batter is hotter than 140 degrees, it will bake the eggs.) If desired, add the zest.
3. Beat in the eggs, one at a time, beating well after each addition. The dough is ready when it drops with difficulty from a spoon. It should be soft yet stiff enough to retain its shape. Let cool completely.
4. Preheat at least 1 inch of oil to 375 degrees.
5. Drop the batter by teaspoonfuls into the hot oil and fry, turning occasionally, until golden brown on all sides. Drain on paper towels. Dip the warm fritters into the cooled syrup or sprinkle with confectioners' sugar.

Zeesih Chremslach ❧ *(Ashkenazic Sweet Matza Meal Pancakes)*

ABOUT SIXTEEN 3-INCH OR THIRTY-SIX 1-INCH PANCAKES

In his cookbook *De re conquinaria libri decem* (Cuisine in Ten Books), the Roman epicure Apicius (fl. 14–37 CE) included a recipe for preparing the popular Roman dish *vermiculos* (Latin for "little worms"): "Cook the finest flour in milk to make a stiff paste. Spread it on a dish, cut it into pieces, that, when fried in fine oil, cover with pepper and honey." During the Middle Ages, however, the original dish disappeared from the Italian culinary repertoire, and the name *vermicelli* was applied to long, thin threads of dough boiled in water.

In the twelfth century, numerous Franco-German rabbis mentioned the custom of eating fried strips of dough in honey called *vermesel* or *verimslish* at the start of the Friday evening meal. At some point, the name for these fritters in honey changed to *gremsel* and eventually *frimsel*, the western Yiddish word for noodles. When the dish reached eastern Europe, the name mutated into *chremsel*. By the late fifteenth century, chicken soup with noodles replaced fried dough strips in honey as the first course for Friday evening dinner, and Ashkenazim ceased to make the original *vermesel*. However, they continued to prepare various descendants of *vermesel*, most notably these popular Passover pancakes.

Yiddish contains numerous words for pancakes, including *chremslach*, *latkes*, *bubeleh*, *pontshkes*, *fasputshes*, and *pfannkuchen*. Among eastern Europeans, pancakes are generally called *chremsel* during Passover and latkes (from the Greek word for "olive oil," *elaion*) during Hanukkah. Some Ashkenazim call plain matza pancakes *bubeleh*, reserving the term *chremslach* for the sweet version. However, all of these terms can be used interchangeably. To further complicate matters, Sephardim prepare a nearly identical dish, *bimuelos de massa*.

Whatever they are called, these pancakes consist primarily of matza meal and eggs. Nonetheless, there are numerous variations: filled with jam or fruit; incorporating leftover *charoset* from the Seder; omitting the nuts; adding mashed potatoes; and even deep-fried. Ashkenazim traditionally coat *chremslach* with honey or top them with jam or dollops of sour cream.

1 cup matza meal	4 large eggs, lightly beaten
1/4 to 1/2 cup finely chopped almonds, hazelnuts, or walnuts	1 cup sweet wine, or 1 cup water and 2 tablespoons sugar
1 teaspoon ground cinnamon	Vegetable oil for frying
About 1/2 teaspoon salt	1 pound (1 1/3 cups) honey

1. Combine the matza meal, nuts, cinnamon, and salt. Combine the eggs and wine. Stir into the matza meal mixture and let stand for at least 30 minutes.

2. Heat about 1/8 inch of oil in a large skillet over medium heat. Drop the batter by teaspoonfuls or tablespoonfuls and fry until lightly browned on the bottom, about 1 minute. Turn and fry until browned, about 30 seconds. Drain on paper towels.

3. Pour off the oil and add the honey to the skillet. Bring to a boil, stirring frequently (the honey may boil up). Add the pancakes and toss to coat. Store in the honey syrup.

NOTE: ❧ One Passover we ran out of vegetable oil, and I was forced to fry the *chremslach* in olive oil. Everyone noted that they tasted the same but turned out softer that year. I don't know if it was the result of the olive oil or other factors.

VARIATIONS

Orange Matza Pancakes: Omit the honey, substitute 1 cup orange juice for the wine, and add 2 tablespoons sugar and 1 teaspoon grated orange zest.

Bimuelos de Minudo de Massa (Sephardic Matza Meal Pancakes): Omit the honey, substitute 1 cup water for the wine, and add 1/4 cup sugar, and, if desired, 1/2 cup dried currants or raisins. Sephardim serve these pancakes with *arrope* (raisin syrup), jam, sugar, or yogurt. To make *arrope*, place 1 pound (3 cups) dark raisins and 6 cups water in a large saucepan and let stand until plump, about 20 minutes. Cover and simmer over low heat until very soft, about 2 hours. Press through a sieve. Add 1 tablespoon fresh lemon juice. Simmer, uncovered, over low heat, stirring occasionally, until thickened, about 30 minutes.

Gefulte Chremslach ❧ *(Ashkenazic Stuffed Matza Pancakes)*

ABOUT 12 PANCAKES

This batter is a little thicker than for standard *chremslach.*

1¹/4 *cups matza meal*	¹/2 *cup warm water*
1 *tablespoon potato starch*	1 *tablespoon vegetable oil or* schmaltz
1 *teaspoon salt*	*(rendered chicken fat)*
¹/4 *teaspoon ground cinnamon or pinch*	1 *recipe (about* 1¹/2 *cups) chremslach*
of ground ginger	*filling (recipes follow)*
3 *large eggs, lightly beaten*	*Vegetable oil or* schmaltz *for frying*

1. Combine the matza meal, potato starch, salt, and cinnamon. Combine the eggs, water, and oil. Stir into the matza meal mixture. Refrigerate until firm, at least 30 minutes.
2. Form the batter by tablespoonfuls into flat 2-inch patties. Spoon a little of the filling into the center of a patty, top with a second patty, and press the edges to seal.
3. Heat ¹/8 inch of oil in a large skillet over medium heat. Fry the chremslach in batches until golden brown on the bottom, about 1 minute. Turn and fry until browned, about 30 seconds. Serve warm.

VARIATION

Baked Stuffed Chremslach: Place the uncooked *chremslach* in a single layer in a greased baking dish, drizzle with a little oil, and bake in a 375-degree oven, turning once, until browned on both sides, about 30 minutes.

CHREMSLACH FILLINGS

Apple Filling

1¹/₂ cups grated tart apple (about 6 ounces)
¹/₂ cup ground almonds, hazelnuts, or walnuts

¹/₄ cup sugar
3 tablespoons matza cake meal
¹/₂ teaspoon ground cinnamon

Combine all the ingredients and let stand for at least 20 minutes.

Jam Filling

1¹/₄ cups cherry preserves or orange marmalade

¹/₂ cup finely chopped almonds or hazelnuts
2 tablespoons matza meal

Combine all the ingredients.

Flaumen (Prune Filling)

1 cup chopped pitted prunes
¹/₃ cup chopped raisins
¹/₄ cup finely chopped almonds, hazelnuts, or walnuts

¹/₄ cup sugar or honey
2 tablespoons fresh lemon juice

Combine all the ingredients.

Bimuelos de Massa/Matza Crimsel ❧
(Matza Farfel Fritters)

ABOUT TWENTY-FOUR 2½-INCH FRITTERS

Although poached matza balls, *knaidlach,* are far and away the most well known Ashkenazic matza dish, deep-fried dumplings are an ancient and still very popular treat. *Crimsel,* called *gremsel/gremselish* in western Europe, are familiar Passover breakfast and dessert fare. For the latter, Ashkenazim commonly sprinkle the fritters with sugar, while Sephardim dip them in a sugar syrup.

---

4 matzas, crumbled

2 cups boiling water

4 large eggs, lightly beaten

1/3 to 3/4 cup sugar

1/2 to 3/4 cup ground almonds

3 tablespoons vegetable oil

1/4 teaspoon salt

1 teaspoon grated lemon zest (optional)

About 1/4 cup matza meal

Vegetable oil for frying

1/4 cup sugar mixed with 1 teaspoon
    ground cinnamon, or 1 recipe cooled
    sugar syrup (see atar, page 265)

---

1. Soak the matzas in the water until softened but not mushy, about 2 minutes. Drain well and squeeze out the excess moisture. Add the eggs, sugar, almonds, oil, salt, zest if using, and enough matza meal to make a soft dough. Cover and refrigerate for at least 30 minutes.
2. Heat at least 1 inch of oil to 375 degrees for fritters or about 1/8 inch oil in a skillet for pancakes.
3. Drop the batter by heaping tablespoons into the oil and fry, turning, until golden brown on all sides. Drain on paper towels.
4. Sprinkle the fritters with the cinnamon sugar or dip the hot fritters into the cooled syrup. Serve warm or at room temperature.

VARIATIONS

Lighter Fritters: Reduce the eggs to 3. Separate the eggs, beat the egg whites until stiff but not dry, and fold into the batter.

Bimuelos de Massa con Muez (Sephardic Matza Farfel Fritters with Nuts): After dipping the fritters into the syrup, sprinkle with chopped almonds, hazelnuts, pistachios, or walnuts.

Matza-Kaese Chremslach (Ashkenazic Cheese Farfel Pancakes): Add 3 tablespoons farmer's, pot, or cottage cheese to the dough.

Raisin Matza Fritters: Add $1/2$ to 1 cup dried currants or raisins and $1/2$ teaspoon ground cinnamon to the dough.

Hungarian Prune-Filled Matza Fritters: Place a pitted prune in the center of each fritter before frying. If desired, stuff a sugar cube or a little cinnamon sugar in the center of the prunes. (The sugar melts.)

Hungarian Strawberry-Filled Matza Fritters: Place a hulled strawberry in the center of each fritter before frying.

Pizzarelle (Italian Matza Farfel Pancakes): Omit the sugar and add $1/2$ cup raisins, $1/4$ to $1/2$ cup leftover *charoset*, and 1 tablespoon grated orange or lemon zest to the dough.

Beolas ❧ *(Tunisian Passover Beignets)*

ABOUT 48 FRITTERS

The soaking syrup reveals the Middle Eastern origin of these Tunisian Passover treats.

Syrup:

1 cup water

1 cup sugar

3 whole cloves, or 1 (2-inch stick)
  cinnamon

Batter:

¹/₂ cup plus 2 tablespoons matza cake
  meal, or ¹/₄ cup cake meal and
  6 tablespoons finely ground almonds

¹/₄ teaspoon salt

6 large eggs

Vegetable oil for deep-frying

1. To make the syrup: Stir all the syrup ingredients in a medium saucepan over low heat until the sugar dissolves, about 5 minutes. Stop stirring, increase the heat to medium, bring to a gentle boil, and cook until the mixture is slightly syrupy, about 5 minutes (it will register 225 degrees on a candy thermometer). Let cool.
2. To make the batter: Combine the cake meal and salt. Beat the eggs until thick and creamy, about 5 minutes. Stir in the matza mixture.
3. Heat at least 1 inch of oil to 375 degrees.
4. Drop the batter by teaspoonfuls into the hot oil and fry, turning occasionally, until golden brown on all sides. Drain on paper towels.
5. Drizzle the cooled syrup over the warm *beolas* and let cool.

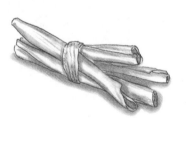

Passover Blintzes

ABOUT TWELVE 6-INCH OR SIXTEEN 5-INCH PANCAKES

As with many classic Jewish dishes, inventive cooks created Passover versions of blintzes. The result in this case is surprisingly light and tender. Unlike pancakes made from flour, the batter does not have to stand before frying.

Potato Starch Batter:	Cake Meal Batter:
4 large eggs	*3 large eggs*
³/₄ cup potato starch	*³/₄ cup matza cake meal*
1 cup water or milk	*1¹/₂ cups water or milk*
1 tablespoon vegetable oil	*1 teaspoon vegetable oil*
¹/₂ teaspoon salt	*¹/₂ teaspoon salt*
1 tablespoon sugar (optional)	*1 tablespoon sugar (optional)*

Vegetable oil or butter for frying
1 recipe blintz filling (page 286–87)

1. Beat the eggs until well blended. Combine the potato starch or cake meal, water, oil, salt, and sugar if using. Gradually beat into the eggs until smooth. Or process all the ingredients in a food processor or blender until smooth.
2. Spread a very thin layer of oil in a heated 5- or 6-inch skillet over medium heat. (The starch has a tendency to sink to the bottom, so stir the batter occasionally.) Pour about 3 tablespoons of the batter into the pan and tilt to coat the bottom. Cook until dry, about 40 seconds. Turn out onto a plate or stack between pieces of waxed paper or damp paper towels. Repeat with the remaining batter, oiling the pan each time.
3. Place the blintzes brown side up, spoon 1 to 2 tablespoons filling near one end of each blintz, fold over the sides, and roll up jelly roll style. The blintzes can be frozen. Do not thaw; heat in a 350-degree oven for about 20 minutes.
4. Arrange the blintzes, seam side down, in a serving dish and warm in a 350-degree oven or fry over medium-high heat, turning, until golden brown on both sides. Serve with sour cream, preserves, or cinnamon sugar.

Peete de Lecha ❧ *(Sephardic Baked Matza Custard)*

Eggs gained a prominent role in cooking relatively late in history. In biblical times, birds and their eggs were generally caught wild. The most common fowl in ancient Israel were doves and their close relative, pigeons, which numbered among the few domesticated species. In ancient Greece, eggs, primarily from geese and ducks, were very rarely found in recipes, while in Rome, even among the wealthy, they were used rather sparingly. It would take the popularization of the prolific chicken during the late Middle Ages to make eggs a common food.

Chickens, descended from a red jungle fowl of Southeast Asia, were domesticated more than 4,500 years ago. Their move westward was rather slow, although a rooster was pictured in the tomb of Tutankaman, dating about 1350 BCE, and a Hebrew seal from the time of the Judean monarchy contained the image of a rooster. However, the chicken's initial popularity and the reason for its spread throughout the Persian, Greek, and Roman empires had nothing to do with its eggs but with the aggressive rooster's ability to fight, one of man's earliest sports. Since this form of entertainment never found favor among Jews, chickens remained a minor figure in Jewish circles until rather late. The fowl of choice for early Ashkenazim was the goose.

The Roman epicure Apicius recorded several recipes incorporating eggs, including one in which they were mixed with milk and honey and cooked over a low fire to make an early form of custard. Other early custards consisted primarily of bread puddings. When an inspired cook decided to omit the bread, modern custard was born. By the fourteenth century, recipes for baked custard were common in cookbooks throughout much of western Europe.

Custard is a luscious dish composed of three basic ingredients: eggs, milk, and sugar. When eggs are heated, the bonds that hold its protein together unfasten. Upon coming in contact with other proteins, these denatured proteins bind together into a network, thickening the liquid. At medium temperatures, these bonds are slack and pliant and the custard is smooth. However, if eggs reach too high a temperature (slightly below 180 degrees; other types of protein have lower solidifying points), the proteins bond together in clumps that squeeze out the liquid, resulting in curdling and weeping. To ensure a smooth and creamy texture, custards are cooked at a moderate temperature, usually in a water bath (which keeps the walls of the dish below 212 degrees). Placing a towel on the bottom of the baking pan insulates the dishes and eliminates bubbles on the bottom.

In this recipe, the milk is scalded (heated) before it is added to the eggs as a way to extract the flavor from the vanilla bean and to dissolve the sugar for more even distribution. Heating the milk also causes its protein to unfasten, so this step promotes the thickening. In addition, the warm custard mixture shortens the cooking time. You can double the recipe and bake it in a 2-quart dish.

2 cups milk, or 1½ cups milk and ½ cup heavy cream	4 large egg yolks, lightly beaten
½ cup plus 2 tablespoons sugar	2 large eggs, lightly beaten
1 vanilla bean, split lengthwise, or 1 teaspoon vanilla extract (see Note)	1 matza, crushed
⅛ teaspoon salt	½ teaspoon ground cinnamon (optional)

1. Preheat the oven to 325 degrees.
2. Stir the milk, sugar, vanilla bean (but not the extract), and salt in a medium saucepan over medium-low heat until the sugar dissolves, about 5 minutes. Do not boil. Remove from the heat, cover, and let stand for 15 minutes.
3. Gradually stir the warm milk mixture into the egg yolks and eggs. Scrape the seeds from the vanilla bean into the custard and discard the pod (if using vanilla extract, add it now). Pour into a 1½-quart baking dish, four 1-cup custard cups, or five ¾-cup custard cups. Sprinkle with the matza and, if desired, the cinnamon.
4. Place a dish towel in the bottom of a large baking pan and set the dish on top. Place in the oven, add hot water to reach halfway up the sides of the dish, and cover loosely with aluminum foil. Bake until the custard is set and registers 170 degrees on an instant-read thermometer, about 1 hour for the baking dish or 40 minutes for the cups. Remove from the water bath and refrigerate until chilled, at least 4 hours or up to 2 days.

N O T E : ❧ Vanilla extract is made by steeping vanilla beans in alcohol, which extracts the flavor and holds it in suspension. Although vanilla extract is handy, its flavor is much less intense than that of vanilla beans, and it also varies more than the flavor of beans. The aroma and essence of vanilla extract dissipate when it is subjected to heat, so add it after cooking.

Asashoo ❧ *(Turkish Matza-Nut Candy)*

ABOUT SEVENTY-FIVE 1½-INCH PIECES

The flavor of this candy varies depending on the floral source of the honey. There are several hundred types of honey derived from various types of nectar. Lighter-colored honeys, such as clover, acacia, and orange blossom, are milder in flavor than darker-colored ones, such as buckwheat, blueberry, and heather.

2 cups sugar	3 cups chopped almonds, hazelnuts,
1 pound (1⅓ cups) honey	pecans, or walnuts (about 12 ounces)
1 cup water	½ teaspoon ground cinnamon
3 cups crumbled matzas	½ teaspoon ground ginger

1. Stir the sugar, honey, and water in a heavy medium saucepan over low heat until the sugar dissolves, about 5 minutes. Stop stirring, increase the heat to medium, and bring to a boil. Cover and cook for about 30 seconds. This dissolves any sugar crystals on the sides of the pan.

2. Uncover and boil gently without stirring until the syrup reaches the soft-crack stage, or 270 degrees on a candy thermometer, about 10 minutes.

3. Remove from the heat and stir in the matzas, nuts, cinnamon, and ginger. Pour onto a greased 15½-by-10½-inch baking sheet and spread evenly. Let cool, then break into pieces. Store in an airtight container at room temperature.

Weinschaum ❧ *(Hungarian Wine Sauce)*

ABOUT 2½ CUPS

This sauce, similar to Italian *zabaglione* and French *sabayon,* is commonly served over sponge cake or fresh fruit. The sauce will separate, so make it shortly before you plan to serve it.

1 cup sugar	*2 cups dry white wine*
1 teaspoon potato starch	*1 cup water*
5 large eggs	*1 teaspoon vanilla or almond extract*
1 teaspoon grated lemon zest (optional)	

1. Combine the sugar and starch. In the top of a large double boiler over barely simmering water (the water should not touch the top pan), beat the eggs, sugar mixture, and lemon zest if using until the mixture is light and the sugar dissolves, about 5 minutes.
2. Gradually add the wine and water and continue beating until the mixture is fluffy and thick enough to coat a spoon, about 10 minutes.
3. Remove the top of the double boiler, place in a larger bowl of ice, and whisk until the custard is cool. Add the vanilla.

Index